Their Finest Hour

Their Finest Hour

Their Finest Hour

Stories of the Men who
Won the Battle of Britain

Nick Thomas

Pen & Sword
AVIATION

First published in Great Britain in 2016 by
Pen & Sword Aviation
an imprint of
Pen & Sword Books Ltd
47 Church Street
Barnsley
South Yorkshire
S70 2AS

Copyright © Nick Thomas 2016

ISBN 978 1 78159 315 8

Typeset in Ehrhardt by
Mac Style Ltd, Bridlington, East Yorkshire
Printed and bound in the UK by CPI Group (UK) Ltd,
Croydon, CRO 4YY

Pen & Sword Books Ltd incorporates the imprints of Pen & Sword
Archaeology, Atlas, Aviation, Battleground, Discovery, Family History,
History, Maritime, Military, Naval, Politics, Railways, Select, Transport,
True Crime, and Fiction, Frontline Books, Leo Cooper, Praetorian Press,
Seaforth Publishing and Wharncliffe.

For a complete list of Pen & Sword titles please contact
PEN & SWORD BOOKS LIMITED
47 Church Street, Barnsley, South Yorkshire, S70 2AS, England
E-mail: enquiries@pen-and-sword.co.uk
Website: www.pen-and-sword.co.uk

Contents

Introduction

Squadron Leader Reginald 'Pissy' Peacock, DFC, No. 235 Squadron (Blenheim)

Flight Lieutenant Jan Kowalski, VM, KW**, DFC, No. 303 Squadron (Hurricane)

Sergeant Leonard 'Joey' Jowitt, MiD, No. 85 Squadron (Hurricane)

Squadron Leader Ernest George 'Gil' Gilbert, No. 64 Squadron (Spitfire)

Squadron Leader Robert 'Robbie' Reid, AEA, No. 46 Squadron (Hurricane)

Pilot Officer Douglas Cyril 'Snowy' Winter, No. 72 Squadron (Spitfire)

Their Finest Hour tells the fascinating stories of six of Churchill's 'Few', each of whom played an important part in the Battle of Britain. Celebrated and much respected on their own squadrons, all have since been largely forgotten. Their achievements and the fortunes of their comrades-in-arms, many of whom died during the battle, are related in detail, some for the first time.

Squadron Leader Reginald 'Pissy' Peacock, DFC, No. 235 Squadron, was the only Blenheim pilot of the Second World War to become a fighter ace. He was awarded the Distinguished Flying Cross; the first to his squadron. Peacock achieved his combat victories – most of them against the enemy's top fighter, the Messerschmitt Bf 109 – as a flying officer during the spring and summer of 1940. Peacock and his navigator formed a formidable fighting force, the latter leaning out of the cockpit window and signaling with a touch on the shoulder when to out-turn the deadly enemy fighters. Peacock's skill in stalking Bf 109s and his close teamwork with his navigator and air-gunner, led to the almost unique triple gallantry award for the Blenheim crew.

Flight Lieutenant Jan Kowalski, VM, KW, DFC,** No. 303 Squadron, was a pre-war flying instructor in Poland. Jan refused to surrender when his homeland was overrun and escaped to Britain, where he became a member of the Polish Air Force in exile. As a sergeant pilot, Jan flew operationally with No. 303 Squadron, which, in the space of seven weeks, destroyed 126 enemy aircraft for the loss of eight of its brave pilots. Flying alongside such aces as František, Feric, Urbanowicz, and their British CO, Kellett, Jan Kowalski took part in many of the squadron's combats, earning the Polish War Cross for gallantry. Jan was later awarded the British Distinguished Flying Cross, and the Polish Virturi Militari (5th Class), along with two Bars to the Polish War Cross.

Sergeant Leonard 'Joey' Jowitt, MiD, No. 85 Squadron, was a pre-war airmen who re-mustered as a sergeant pilot. Jowitt's squadron was posted to France in September 1939, bearing the brunt of the combat during the Battle of France, destroying sixty-four enemy aircraft, for the loss of seven pilots killed-in-action. Jowitt was able to claim at least one He 111 destroyed and was Mentioned-in-Despatches for gallantry for his part in the campaign (one of less than a handful of gallantry awards made to his squadron during the summer of 1940). As the squadron's original records were destroyed due to enemy action, we will never know the full extent of Jowitt's role in the Battle of France, and so No. 85 Squadron's battle is told in full.

Back in the UK and under a new CO, Squadron Leader Peter Townsend, the squadron regrouped ready to defend our shores. Jowitt, as one of the few surviving members of the squadron, was instrumental in training the new pilots, ready for the fight to come. Sadly, he was to be one of the first casualties, dying in the defence of a coastal convoy off Felixstowe on 12 July, the battle only two days old.

Squadron Leader Ernest George 'Gil' Gilbert, No. 64 Squadron. Gil Gilbert's unit was one of the last Battle of Britain squadrons to receive the Vickers Supermarine Spitfire. He only began his initial training on type in April 1940, while still flying operational patrols on Blenheims. Woefully unprepared for combat, the squadron lost three pilots, including their CO, during a single patrol over Dunkirk. Helping to rebuild the squadron, Gil, then a flight sergeant, flew operationally from May to October, damaging or destroying five enemy aircraft and earning a commission. He was greatly respected by his fellow pilots and frequently led patrols, as the most experienced, if not the most senior ranking, pilot. On one occasion, Gil shot down a Bf 109 which was lining-up on another member of the squadron, only to be hit by the enemy's wingman. Somehow, Gil shook off the Bf 109s and nursed his damaged Spitfire back across the Channel, standing in the cockpit to see over the oil-spattered windscreen. Remarkably, he landed without further damage to his aircraft.

Squadron Leader Robert 'Robbie' Reid, AEA, No. 46 Squadron, flew as a pilot officer throughout the Battle of Britain, having a hand in the destruction of three Bf 109s, damaging two more. As a squadron leader, Reid flew rocket-firing Mosquitoes on anti-shipping strikes in the Norwegian fjords during 1944/5. It was while leading one of these mast-height raids during the final weeks of the war that Reid was killed-in-action. Reid's story highlights the otherwise largely forgotten role played by No. 46 Squadron, whose battle cost the lives of so many of its eyewitnesses, their combat reports surviving to give testimony to their exploits.

Pilot Officer Douglas Cyril 'Snowy' Winter, No. 72 Squadron, flew Spitfires during the defence of the Dunkirk beaches, before taking on the Luftwaffe in the skies over Southern England. Winter's squadron suffered heavy losses during the middle phases of the battle and was pulled out of the line in mid–September, but not before the young fighter ace had become yet another casualty. Had he lived, Winter would undoubtedly have been awarded the Distinguished Flying Cross and been rightly acclaimed as one of the heroes of 1940.

Each pilot's story is told through personal accounts, where possible, but also through the pages of their squadron's Operational Record Books (ORB) and combat reports. Occasionally, the extended battle to defend against each raid is narrated through the records of the other squadrons involved, in order to relate the magnitude of the struggle. These provide much background information and help to bring the heroism of these forgotten heroes into sharp focus.

Acknowledgements

Firstly, I should like to acknowledge the work that has been done by innumerable aviation historians before me. Their labours, complimented by the work of squadron diarists, squadron intelligence officers, and the memoirs and recollections of Fighter Command veterans, have provided much of the research material which is vital in any book of this nature.

Of the veterans themselves, I was most fortunate enough to correspond with Jan Kowalski over many years. Jan was generous in his support of my educational displays, particularly as, from the outset, they fully acknowledged the huge contribution of his fellow pilots of No. 303 Squadron. I was fortunate enough to meet Jan at his Nottingham home; enjoying his company and listening to him recall details of his flying career. Jan's letters proved an invaluable aid when compiling the chapter on his story and that of No. 303 Squadron.

Gil Gilbert, like Jan and all of the veterans I have had the great fortune to know, was a quiet and unassuming hero. Gil was initially very reluctant to give anything away about his RAF days and did not consider what he had done to be particularly noteworthy. Gil was, however, full of praise for the men he flew alongside and was kind enough to assist me with exhibitions promoting their stories – through these I was gradually able to piece together Gil's battle.

Both Gil and his daughter, Patricia 'Trish' Gilbert, were generous in allowing me access to photographs and Gil's logbooks.

During research into the story of Squadron Leader Robert 'Robbie' Reid, I was fortunate to come across the website dedicated to the Banff Wing run by his grandson. Simon Reid very generously supplied a number of family photographs, also assisting with information regarding Robert's early family life, for which I am most grateful.

I was also fortunate enough to have access to a small archive of material relating to the remaining pilots; Peacock, Winter and Jowitt. With Jowitt's story I was supported via correspondence with Leonard's nephew, Doug Bray, who provided anecdotal evidence. Doug was also generous in supplying precious images of his uncle during training, as a fully fledged pilot, and while with No. 85 Squadron.

Finally, I should like to acknowledge the many Battle of Britain pilots and aircrew who over the years supported me with my displays and subsequent books and articles – they did so not for their own glorification, but to ensure that their fellow pilots, many of whom paid for the victory with their lives, should be honoured. These chapters represent a continuation of their laudable efforts to ensure that the deeds of Churchill's, or rather Dowding's 'Few', are never forgotten.

Chapter 1

Squadron Leader Reginald John 'Pissy' Peacock, DFC

Reginald John 'Pissy' Peacock flew Bristol Blenheim fighters with No. 235 Squadron and is one of the forgotten heroes of the Battle of Britain. No. 235 Squadron's duel role, being called upon to fly offensive patrols over the Channel, protecting the Channel convoys and flying defensive fighter patrols, meant its pilots were nearly always in action.

On more than one occasion Peacock and his fellow Blenheim pilots found themselves taking on formations of Bf 109s, often coming off victorious. Peacock's personal tally of five enemy aircraft destroyed, or shared, made him the top scoring Blenheim ace of the war.

Reginald John Peacock was born on 3 October 1917, the son of Charles Thomas and Eliza Munro Peacock, of Earls Court, London.

Gaining a good School's Certificate through the grammar school system, Peacock decided, at length, to enlist into the RAF and to follow his long held dream of becoming a pilot. Reginald Peacock was granted a Short Service Commission as acting pilot officer, on probation, in the General Duties branch of the RAF on 24 October 1937 (with effect from 23 August). He was sent to No. 1 RAF Depot, before being posted to No. 7 Flying Training School, Peterborough, on 6 November 1937.

These were the halcyon days of more leisurely pilot training and, having gone through *ab initio* training and Elementary Flying Training School, eight months later Peacock moved on to No. 1 Flying Training School, Leuchars (4 July 1938).

Having completed his pilot training, Pilot Officer Peacock's first posting came on 23 August 1938, when he was sent to No. 801 (FAA) Squadron, then flying the Hawker Osprey III. Two months later (17 October) Peacock was transferred to Fleet Air Arm, Gosport, then flying the Blackburn Shark, Avro Tutor, Miles Magister, Hawker Osprey and Avro 504 aircraft.

A further posting came on 14 March 1939, when Peacock transferred to No. 2 Anti-Aircraft Co-operation Unit, confirmation of his appointment as pilot officer being announced in the *London Gazette* nine days later (23 March).

The political scene on the Continent meant that the RAF was preparing for the real possibility of another European war. As a part of the RAF's expansion programme, No. 235 Squadron was reformed on 30 October 1939. Operating out of RAF Manston, the fighter squadron was under the command of Squadron Leader Ralph I.G. McDougall, with Flying Officer Tony Ridler acting as 'A' Flight Commander. The majority of the squadron's pilots, some ninety per cent, were inexperienced on an operational squadron, having come straight to RAF Manston on completion of their flying training course at No. 2 Flying Training School, Brize Norton, Oxfordshire. There, the pilots had flown the sedate Air Speed Oxford. Squadron Leader McDougall was able to arrange for a small number of Fairey Battles to be assigned to the squadron for training purposes; these arrived in December and were used to give the pilots experience on service types ahead of the arrival of their operational aircraft.

Peacock was posted to No. 235 Squadron on 22 January 1940. On arrival he was assigned to 'B' Flight, under the command of Flight Lieutenant Richard P.Y. 'Dick' Cross.

In February 1940, the first dual-control Blenheim Mk Is arrived and Flight Lieutenant Cross began the process of converting the squadron's pilots. Meanwhile, on 15 February, a Blenheim Mk IV F (a fighter version of the Mark IV, serial No. P4833) arrived from No. 29 Squadron. This was supplemented by further aircraft from No. 23 Squadron, while the squadron's Fairey Battles were ferried away to No. 10 MU, Hullavington.

On a less positive note, the squadron was transferred from Fighter to Coastal Command on 27 February 1940, taking on long-range reconnaissance, escort, and fighter protection duties, along with anti-shipping sorties. These would be the squadron's main roles during the Battle of Britain, although, while seconded to Fighter Command, they also flew on a number of defensive base and sector patrols, fully justifying the coveted clasp. However, unlike the day-fighter units in their former command, the squadron remained on twin-engine aircraft.

Having been granted an extension of his Short Service Commission to six years in 1939, Peacock was promoted to flying officer on 23 March 1940.

With training continuing apace, the Squadron Operational Record Book (ORB) noted that on 4 April, Flying Officer Peacock and Sergeant Allison were despatched to No. 5 MU, Kemble, to collect Blenheim Mk Is (Nos. 1278 and 1279). The squadron remained, however, understrength and flying time was rationed, the less experienced pilots getting preference.

In early April the squadron was transferred away from RAF Manston, the closest RAF airfield to Continental Europe (which made it highly susceptible to bombing as there was little time to react to enemy raids), to RAF North Coates, Norfolk. This proved a stop-gap, and, on 24 April, No. 235 Squadron received orders to transfer to RAF Bircham Newton, thirty miles north of Norwich, which it did the following day. The move meant that they would play a part in escorting east coast convoys as well as continuing its operations further afield. The squadron diarist expressing the thoughts of all concerned when he said they; 'feel very pleased about it all.'

A further boost came with the arrival of five additional Blenheim IV Fs, which were flown from No. 5 MU Kemble, Gloucestershire. The aircraft were allocated to Peacock's 'B' Flight and the young flying officer was amongst the pilots who ferried the new aircraft in.

No. 235 Squadron (which flew as a part of No. 16 Group), was declared operational on 2 May 1940. Flight Lieutenants R.P.Y. Cross, G.A.P. Manwaring (flying L9261), and Pilot Officer A. Booth (flying P4845), individually flew armed reconnaissance missions along the Dutch coast early the same evening. In the squadron's first taste of action, an enemy convoy was attacked by Manwaring and Booth, ten miles off Borkum, Lower Saxony. The Squadron ORB noted: 'A few glorious moments of low strafing.'

That evening parties were held in the various messes. Reginald Peacock, always the 'life and soul', led the celebrations in style, earning the nickname 'Pissy' Peacock, as a result of lying under a barrel of Cameron's bitter and drinking straight from the tap!

Flying Officer Peacock (flying P4844) and Pilot Officer Robinson, were led by Flight Lieutenant Cross on the squadron's next operation, which was flown on 3 May, a reconnaissance off Norway made at 0600 hours. The operation, which resulted in the squadron's second strafing opportunity, focused on a search for E-boats reported in the area off Lista on the southern coast. The patrol experienced machine-gun fire at 0925 hours, but none of the aircraft sustained damage, while getting off a few rounds themselves.

On 5 May, the squadron flew a further reconnaissance operation, this time to the highly defended Wilhelmshaven area, sighting three enemy destroyers near Borkum. The Blenheims of Flight Lieutenant Manwaring (flying P9261 LA-M) and Pilot Officer A. Wales (flying P4844) were bounced by Bf 109s at 1550 hours. Manwaring, who was already flying on one engine, later reported a beam attack by a Bf 109, but skillfully escaped by using boost and shutting down the grills of the dead engine, thereby reducing drag. Meanwhile, Wales received a quarter attack. Oberfeldwebel Reinhold Schmetzer and Unteroffizier Herbert Kaiser both reported their victims as destroyed.

At 0255 hours on 6 May, Flight Lieutenant Cross, Flying Officer Peacock and Pilot Officer Robinson took off to provide escort to Beauforts and Swordfish of Nos. 22 and 815 Squadrons. The aircraft were ordered to fly to the East Frisian Islands, targeting a Nuremberg-class cruiser thought to be in that area. Bad weather and a faulty wireless meant that the formation became split-up and only Cross got anywhere near their target; all the Blenheims landed safely.

Meanwhile, between 1700 and 2015 hours, Flight Lieutenant Manwaring (flying L9261 LA-M) and Pilot Officer Wales (flying K4644), made a reconnaissance of Wilhelmshaven before photographing the Borkum airbase. Scrambled to defend their home base, three Bf 109s engaged the Blenheims, which put up a strong fight, successfully fending off the fighters. While unable to make any claims against the Bf 109s, the pair demonstrated that the Blenheim Fighter could match the Messerschmitt in the air.

During an evening training flight made on 8 May, one of the squadron's Blenheims (P4844, LA-A), which had taken off from RAF Bircham Newton, was lost just after midnight. The aircraft dived into the ground at Bircham Common, about two miles from the airfield, with the loss of all three crew members. Sergeant

Allison's inexperience in night-flying and poor weather conditions were deemed as contributory factors.[1]

The squadron suffered further fatalities during training on the following day, 9 May, when Bristol Blenheim I, K7136, took off at 2310 hours for solo flying practice and suffered an engine failure, stalled while banking and crashed. The Air Accident Investigation found that Pilot Officer Smith had only one hour night flying on Blenheims. Only later did it become common practice to send less experienced pilots up closer to dusk and allow them to become gradually acclimatised with short flights in growing hours of darkness. Meanwhile, young airmen continued to die needlessly, while the penny dropped almost squadron by squadron.[2]

The war entered a new phase when, on 10 May, Hitler unleashed his Blitzkrieg against France and the Low Countries, bringing the direct threat to our shores one step closer. Early that morning Flying Officer Peacock (flying L9404) led Pilot Officers N.A.L. Smith and N.A. Savill on an uneventful patrol of Borkum, extending as far as Texel and the Friesian Islands – the Luftwaffe was apparently too heavily engaged in offensive air operations to send up fighters against a brace of fighter-bombers.

Later that day, during an armed night reconnaissance to the coast of the Netherlands, from Texel to the German Isle of Borkum, flown at 1930 hours, the squadron lost Blenheim IV, N6193 LA-N. The aircraft was crewed by (Pilot) Pilot Officer (77529) R.L. Patterson, (Observer) Lieutenant Ogilvie (RN), and (Wop/AG) Leading Aircraftsman (552170) A.G. Smith. The aircraft had fuel issues and belly landed at 2230 hours, catching fire; the crew were unhurt. Later, an investigation revealed that the accident had been partly due to the pilot's inability to operate the fuel stopcock. This was due to his lack of height, while his 'Mae West' also hindered movement. Believing that the aircraft was under-fuelled, he made an emergency landing. Pilot Officer R.L. Patterson had been forced to deploy the undercarriage manually, but it had not locked correctly and it collapsed on landing, resulting in a fire. The incident was a further example of the inexperience of many of the squadron's pilots.

The squadron's luck turned when it recorded its first combat victory during the early hours of 11 May, when Flight Lieutenant G.A.P. Manwaring (flying L9324) made a convoy escort off Texel. While flying on a circling pattern, and just south of The Hague, an He 111 was sighted. Manwaring positioned himself before firing a burst from astern. Despite the long range, his rounds apparently hit their target and the enemy reconnaissance aircraft erupted in a ball of flames, only Obergefreiter S. Klug escaping by parachute (Unteroffizier E. Steussloff, Unteroffizier R. Wunderlich and Unteroffizier H. von Hoff were killed). It was later discovered that the 'kill' was also claimed by a Dutch anti-aircraft crew who opened fire on the Heinkel at the same moment in time.

While Flying Officer Peacock had missed the action on the previous day, he was in the thick of it on 12 May when he led a section on an early morning patrol off Texel. Peacock (flying L9401 LA-L) was airborne from RAF Manston at 0510 hours, his mission to provide cover for Royal Marines evacuating Queen Wilhelmina

– and what was to become her government in exile – from The Hague. Operating alongside Flying Officer Peacock were Pilot Officers N.A.L. Smith (flying L9324 LA-P) and N.A. Savill (flying L9198 LA-O).

At 0600 hours the Blenheims made a rendezvous with the same number of Hurricanes from No. 151 Squadron over Whistle Light Buoy, just off the Hook of Holland, before heading for their objective.

Reaching the limit of their range, the Hurricanes were forced to turn back at 0630 hours, leaving the Blenheims to stand guard over the Royal Navy vessels.

Suddenly, a number of Bf 110s raked the Blenheims with fire, Peacock seeing yellow tracer streak past his starboard wing. All three pilots immediately took evasive action, their air-gunners firing off rounds as and when the enemy presented a target.

Pilot Officer N.A.L. Smith's Blenheim had a Bf 110 on its tail which proved difficult to shake off. His air-gunner, LAC Thomas Lowry, managed to get the Messerschmitt in his sights, giving it a couple of well-aimed bursts at about 200 yards. The Bf 110 pulled away before lining up another shot. Pilot Officer Savill, however, intervened with a sharp burst from his under-belly machine guns and the enemy fighter fell away into the sea. Savill was awarded one unconfirmed destroyed.

At 0755 hours, just as it looked as though the Blenheims had the upper hand, two groups of four Bf 109s of II./JG 27 launched line astern attacks. The Blenheims turned to meet the enemy, entering into a ten minute spiralling dogfight.

Peacock latched onto a Bf 109 flying off to starboard. Pulling the Blenheim around, he got a clean shot at the Messerschmitt. A five-second burst left the enemy fighter smoking heavily and going down in a spiral. The unconfirmed Bf 109 is thought to have crashed somewhere between the Hook of Holland and The Hague.

Meanwhile, two Bf 109s were targeting Smith's Blenheim from the port and starboard quarters. His air-gunner's turret and cockpit were struck by an accurate volley and L.A.C. Lowry was mortally wounded, as was the observer, Sergeant J. Robertson. Somehow, Smith wrestled with the controls of the stricken Blenheim as it trailed smoke from its starboard engine, crashing in a field in the Nieuwlander Polder, near Hoek van Holland. Smith lay seriously injured in the wreckage till a rescue could be effected, but died later that day in hospital.[3]

During the same engagement the aircraft flown by Pilot Officer Norman A. 'Norm' Savill was bounced by a Bf 109, which followed him down in a steep dive before making a head-on attack. Firing its longer-range cannon, the Bf 109 had the advantage and shells exploded all around, one killing the air-gunner, while the Blenheim caught on fire. Savill fought back and fired a telling burst which hit the Bf 109 in the engine, sending the aircraft into a spiraling dive, Savill being credited with an unconfirmed. With his aircraft damaged by cannon and machine-gun fire, Savill bailed out at low altitude, but was fortunate as his parachute fully deployed. He landed on farmland along the Kloosterweg, between Brielle and Oostvoorne, and was rushed to Vlaardingen hospital, suffering wounds and severe burns. He later became a PoW when the country was overrun.[4]

In their debriefing, Peacock and his crew confirmed seeing their Bf 109 crash (52.02 degrees North, 4.27 degrees East), while a second Messerschmitt was seen burning on the ground (51.52 degrees North, 4.27 degrees East), presumably destroyed by Savill. Smith's Blenheim was last seen with his starboard engine on fire.

The squadron diarist wrote a summary of the operation:

'The formation was attacked over The Hague by eight Me 109s [of IV./JG 27] in two sections of four. These aircraft employed head-on attacks, and Pilot Officer Smith and Pilot Officer Savill were shot down. Flying Officer Peacock shot down one Me 109 and another was seen in flames on the ground, presumably shot down by Savill or Smith.'

Referring to the squadron's own losses, the Squadron ORB added:

'Nothing was seen of one of these [Blenheim] aircraft five minutes after the combat had started, but one was seen with [its] starboard engine on fire; assumed to be 'P', as 'O' was later seen in a field having carried out a landing with the wheels retracted.'

Despite their heavy losses, the squadron had shown it's worth, it's pilots and aircrew had put up a determined fight against the odds and destroyed as many as it had lost. Sadly, Peacock's crew was the only one to make base, but they would continue to wreak havoc among the enemy fighters over the months to come.

Three Blenheims made a patrol of the Flushing area between 0925 and 1410 hours on 12 May. While over the target they sighted a formation of seventeen He 111s and Ju 88s attacking ammunition ships in the estuary. Flying Officer Bain (flying R3623), Pilot Officer Randall (flying L9409), and Sergeant Tubbs (flying N3629), attacked and scattered the enemy.

Meanwhile, Flight Lieutenant R.E.G. Morewood (flying L9467) and Pilot Officer McHardy (flying L9450) were scrambled at 0906 hours to make an offensive patrol covering warships under attack from five Bf 110s. Following the engagement, one bomber was seen to crash in flames, the remaining enemy aircraft heading for home.

The operations continued, as did the losses. During a shipping protection patrol to Ostende, flown on 18 May, Blenheim IV L9395[5] was misidentified and shot down by Sub-Lieutenant Jacquemet, Adjutant Marchais, and Sergeant Dietrich of GC II./8, French Air Force, and crashed in the sea off Nieuport at 1910 hours.

Adjutant Henri Mir of GC II./8, who recognised the aircraft as a Blenheim, tried to alert the attacking pilots, who took it for an He 111. Some accounts suggest that the stricken Blenheim was also attacked by an RAF Hurricane, but no corresponding claim has been traced. This was not the first time that a Bristol Blenheim was shot down by 'friendly' fire, and it would not be the last.

Meanwhile, on 20 May, Blenheim L9256 was lost when it took off from RAF Bircham Newton at 1725 hours on escort duties. The aircraft almost immediately experienced engine failure and collided with Anson N9897 from No. 206 Squadron, which was parked on the ground being refuelled. AC1 L.G. Curry[6] was struck in the head by one of the propellers and died instantly. The crew (Sergeant Bessey, Sergeant H.H.J. Westcott and LAC (552170) A.G. Smith, RAF) escaped without injury, although their aircraft was destroyed by fire.

The remainder of the Blenheims, including Peacock's P6958 LA-O, continued on their convoy patrol over *Impulsive, Intrepid, Esk, Express* and *Ivanhoe*, all prime targets for the Luftwaffe.

More patrols and convoy escorts followed, while between 24 and 30 July, Flying Officer Peacock and his crew (observer Pilot Officer H.K. Wakefield and air-gunner Sergeant W. Wilson) acted as escort for minesweeping operations. The work was fairly mundane, but important nonetheless.

The squadron sustained further casualties during a patrol flown from RAF Bircham Newton at 0415 hours on 24 May, with the loss of two of the crew of L9259. The operation was mounted as an escort to Hudsons of No. 206 Squadron operating between Borkum and the mouth of the Ems. Pilot Officer M.E. Ryan lagged behind the leader and was attacked by two Bf 109s, and shot down by Unteroffizier Otto Rückett of IV.(T)/186 at 0730 hours. The demise of the Blenheim was witnessed by the air-gunner of a Hudson, who watched in horror as it disappeared into the sea off Schiermonnikoog Island.[7]

The squadron also lost Blenheim L6956 while on a reconnaissance of the Zeebrugge area. Taking off from RAF Bircham Newton at 1710 hours, the aircraft spun into the ground near Docking, Norfolk, at 1715 hours. At the controls was Pilot Officer C.D. Warde; who was able to abandon the aircraft by parachute, but the other two crew members were lost.[8]

During the day (24 May), Squadron Leader R.I.G. MacDougall transferred to command No. 17 Squadron, RAF Debden, before becoming a Fighter Controller on 18 July 1940, being replaced by Squadron Leader 'Ronnie' Clarke. Two days later, on 26 May, the squadron transferred to RAF Detling, from where they would play their part in the support of the withdrawal of the BEF from Dunkirk.

At 1805 hours on 27 May, Flight Lieutenant R.P.Y. Cross (flying QY-A), and Pilot Officer D. N. Woodger (flying QY-H), engaged a formation of three He 111s off Nieuport. The enemy aircraft were spotted flying at 10,000ft. Closing to 1,000ft and approaching from the beam, it was then possible to identify the aircraft as hostile.

The Squadron Intelligence Officer's report takes up the narrative:

'Blenheim 'H' was instructed by R/T to break formation and to attack this section from a quarter ahead from port, while "A" was making a similar attack from starboard. This attack was made simultaneously by "A" and "H". The latter opened fire at 400 yards and closed to 300 yards before breaking away, having seen bursts going into the port wing of the third E/A. "H" was unable to continue the engagement as [his] port engine cut and enemy fire through the cockpit had rendered the instruments U/S.

'Blenheim "A" made [its] attack by overtaking on the starboard side and turning in 400 yards ahead, making a quarter-ahead attack on the leader. Sweeping fire made by skidding the aircraft entered No. 1 and followed into No. 2 of the enemy formation. A long burst of nearly fifteen seconds was fired and the leader of the formation was disorganised; the leading aircraft almost went out of control. Blenheim "A" broke away steeply down to starboard and came round to get into position in order to make another similar attack. During this short interval the E/A were able to resume their tight formation.

'After "A" had repeated an exactly similar attack from port, the E/A altered course and proceeded inland at high speed. A trail of blue smoke was seen coming from the starboard engine of No. 1 E/A. The E/A was not pursued as an intense barrage of AA fire was put up from the shore batteries. Throughout the action the fire of the E/A was controlled i.e. the rear-gunners either held their fire or fired in unison.

'The Heinkels did not fire from front guns as they were not brought to bear throughout the action. The rear-gunner of Blenheim "A" put in bursts in each attack on the break away and observed hits made. The enemy aircraft were flying in a tight formation of one span or less.

'All three aircraft were damaged; hits were observed in port wing of No. 3 of enemy formation and in wings and fuselage of Nos. 1 and 2. It is thought that hits were also obtained on the starboard engine of E/A No. 1.

'Blenheim "A" received no hits at all and Blenheim 'H' a few hits through the cockpit, rendering instruments U/S.'

Elsewhere, Flying Officer Peacock led Pilot Officer J. Cronan on a reconnaissance of the Ems estuary, near Krummhörn, Germany. The mission passed off without incident, despite the close proximity of Luftwaffe airfields along its flight path.

Meanwhile, the Dunkirk evacuation was still in full progress and Flying Officer Peacock flew a patrol over the beaches during 29 May, but without encountering the enemy.

The squadron had suffered further losses on 29 May. Blenheim P6909 took off from RAF Detling at 0705 hours in bad weather and circled to return to base. It struck a tree while flying low over a thickly wooded hillock near Sittingbourne, killing Peacock's flight commander, Flight Lieutenant R.P.Y. Cross, along with Sergeant Slocombe. Leading Aircraftman North died in hospital a few days later (1 June).[9]

Three more aircraft were lost in what was a dark day for the squadron. Pilot Officer Cronan took off from RAF Detling in L9260 LA-E at 1131 hours with orders to patrol off the Calais area. His Blenheim was shot down into the Channel off Calais by six Me 109s, after destroying one. The crew, including Sergeant A.O. Lancaster and LAC Peebles, were rescued from their dinghy. During the same patrol, Blenheim L9397 was shot down in flames into the sea off France. There was no opportunity for the crew to escape.[10] Also shot down was Blenheim L9401, piloted by Flight Lieutenant G.A.P. 'Wigs' Manwaring, one of the mainstays of the squadron; his death was felt at all levels.[11]

Later that day Flight Lieutenant A.W. Fletcher arrived as a flight commander.

Peacock flew a defensive patrol over Dunkirk on 30 May, making a dusk patrol the following day, while during the afternoon of 1 June he once again flew over the beaches. Following the fall of Dunkirk, Peacock made a number of patrols in support of the troops holding St Valeria and Cherbourg, before their position became untenable and they had to be evacuated.

Following one of the squadron's patrols over Cherbourg, flown on 12 June, the Squadron ORB reported: 'attack carried out on dive-bomber near Le Havre.' The outcome of the combat was not noted, and must be assumed to have been inconclusive.

A series of Channel and convoy escorts, along with sorties over the now threatened Channel Islands, kept Peacock and the rest of No. 235 Squadron busy until 27 June, when Peacock flew consecutive escorts to minelayers up until the end of the month.

Meanwhile, during the night of 26/27 June, Wing Commander Norman D. Crockett commanded an element of No. 50 Squadron on a mission to bomb Langenhagen airfield near Hanover. At the controls of his Hampden bomber, Crockett led the formation off from RAF Waddington at 2215 hours. They successfully bombed their target before turning for home. Wing Commander Crockett's aircraft was hit by a flak battery of 3./614. Crockett struggled to keep the Hampden in the air on one engine, but encountered difficulties and radioed base at 0359 hours to say he was; 'Going down fifteen miles from Dutch coast'.

Crockett's Hampden (P1239) was lost along with its crew, which consisted of Flight Sergeant William Southey and Sergeants Allan Ingram and Eric Turner. Wing Commander Norman D. Crockett's name is not recorded on the Commonwealth War Graves' site as he may have survived to become a PoW.[12] In response to the Mayday, No. 235 Squadron's 'B' Flight made two section strength searches along the Dutch coast, but without locating the missing aircrew.

Later that day, 'A' Flight's Blenheims took off from RAF Bircham Newton at 1255 hours, tasked with a reconnaissance patrol searching for the invasion barges. The Blenheims made landfall near Noordwijk and turned towards Amsterdam. No. 235 Squadron had flown a similar sortie on the previous day when during their debriefing commented on the enemy's fighter presence. Consequently, the pilots were warned to head south if they encountered fighters, the enemy's main concentrations being to the north.

At 1500 hours, while just south of Schiphol airfield, the Blenheims were attacked by a large number of Bf 109s of II./JG 54, which had just been scrambled off from Soesterberg and Schiphol to intercept.

During the ensuing combat, Flying Officer Peacock (flying N3542 LA-O) destroyed a Bf 109 in the Zuider Zee area, sharing in damaging a second. Peacock's observer, Pilot Officer H.K. Wakefield, later explained how they operated during the combat, which lasted between two to three minutes:

'We found ourselves breaking formation and milling around the sky with 109s as our dancing partners! We knew the Blenheim fighter could turn inside the

109E if we knew precisely when to do it. To this end, we had devised a system for when we were under attack. I moved up from the observer's position, opened the portside window behind the pilot, stuck my head out, looking back along the fuselage, and signalled to Peacock with my thumb exactly when and which direction to turn.

'The Bf 109 made an unsuccessful head-on attack, before approaching from the upper rear port side, closing to less than 400 yards.'

The Messerschmitt had been spotted by Wakefield who signalled hard to starboard. The tight turn left the Bf 109 out of position and it overshot. Peacock pulled the Blenheim around to the right and had the enemy in his sights, firing off a short burst. It was sufficient to force the pilot to abandon the attack.

The air battle was not one-sided and the squadron suffered heavy losses, with four aircraft shot down. Nine crew members were killed, while two died of their wounds and another member of the squadron was made a PoW.

Despite their twists and turns, the enemy managed to hit N3542, shooting away the Perspex cockpit canopy and part of the front window, but neither Peacock nor Wakefield were injured. In the meantime, Peacock had got in a telling burst on one Bf 109 and damaged another, which he shared with a second Blenheim pilot.

Pilot Officer A. Wales (flying L3543 LA-U) was shot down at 1530 hours by Leutnant J. Schypek and Hauptmann Von Bonin of II./JG 76. Wales tried to make a forced landing, but his Blenheim ploughed through a meadow and broke up, part of the wreckage coming to rest against the embankment at the edge of a potato field along the Valkenburgerweg at Oegstgeest.[13]

Another casualty was Blenheim L9447, LA-Y, which was hit by either Unteroffizier W. Schilling of III./JG 21 or Oberleutnant R. von Aspern, Staffelkapitän of II./JG 76, the burst of machine-gun fire mortally wounding Sergeant P.L. Lloyd, and hitting Pilot Officer J.R. Cronan in the shoulder. Sergeant A.O. Lancaster was wounded in the left leg and saw that Cronan was unconscious and slumped over the controls. Just as he tried to extricate Cronan, he recovered and tried to take control of the aircraft again, but there was no response and Cronan gave the order to bail out.

The forward lower hatch refused to open, and so Pilot Officer Cronan and Sergeant Lancaster were forced to use the top hatch. Cronan hit the tail of the aircraft with the side of his face and was knocked unconscious and plummeted to his death without deploying his parachute. Sergeant Lancaster nearly suffered the same fate, only pulling his ripcord at 100ft, but survived to become a PoW. Sergeant Lloyd was found with severe burns and died shortly afterwards. News of the fates of the crewmen only reached the squadron via a Postagram from the International Red Cross on 16 August 1940. The crippled Blenheim had crashed at the Hoogen Dijk, Waverveen, near Vinkeveen.[14]

The Bristol Blenheim IV piloted by Pilot Officer P. Weil (P6957, LA-R) was also lost. He was seen engaging a Bf 109, firing his belly-pack guns. Pulling out of formation, Weil made a tight turn inside his attacker who was joined by a second and then a third assailant. It is believed that Weil and his crew fought back for a full thirteen minutes before Oberleutnant Roloff von Aspern, Oberleutnant Franz Eckerle and Oberfeldwebel Max Stotz could finally claim their victory.[15]

Oberleutnants Roloff von Aspern, Franz Eckerle and Oberfeldwebel Max Stotz then teamed up to take on the Blenheim (P6958, LA-D) piloted by Pilot Officer H.S. Pardoe-Williams, which by then had reached the suburbs of Ouderkerk on Amstel. The Bf 109s closed in and bursts of fire hit the gun turret and cockpit, mortally wounding the crew, while more rounds put the starboard engine out of action. Pardoe-Williams fought with the controls and tried to make a forced-landing, but the aircraft disintegrated in a polder. His crew were killed on impact, while Pardoe-Williams, praised by the enemy for his bravery and skill in trying to make a safe landing, died of his injuries.[16]

Meanwhile, Peacock, having shaken off the remainder of the Bf 109s, headed south and took reconnaissance photographs of the harbour at Amsterdam before following the coast of the Zuider Zee. While flying in the vicinity of Texel, Peacock spotted a lone Heinkel He 115 seaplane, which he engaged, firing off his last rounds, but without causing sufficient damage to make a claim.

Only the Blenheims flown by Peacock and his CO, Ronnie Clarke, made it back to base. It must have been a very sombre debriefing as they and their crews went over the events.

The Squadron's diarist wrote of their losses:

'These four pilots and "Gunner" Saunders, all old members of their squadron, are a great loss as they represent practically all that is left of the original 235 Squadron. "Johnnie" Cronan, a New Zealander, with Sergeant Aubrey Lancaster, put up a splendid show a month ago when shot down into the sea. Weil, Wales and Williams have just recently developed into useful, resourceful fighter pilots, and "Gunner" Saunders, a friendly and amiable fellow, will be universally missed, as will plucky "Phil" Lloyd. As this action took place over the Zuider Zee it is hoped that some of them escaped.'

Peacock flew a patrol near the German coast on 29 June, making a reconnaissance of Terschelling and Texel in the Netherlands. On his return, Peacock learned that he was to be briefly rested, having taken a leading role in the squadron's campaign thus far. He was granted a fortnight's leave, during which he no doubt travelled to spend time with his family in Earls Court, and enjoyed some of the capital's bars and clubs.

Back on operations, Peacock settled into a series of convoy, and latterly minesweeper escorts, which ran from 13 July to the end of the month.

During one of these sorties, a convoy patrol on 18 July, the squadron lost Blenheim N3541 and its crew.[17] Peacock flew the next standing patrol, which passed off without incident.

On the night of the 18/19 July, Flying Officer Peacock flew with what had by then become his regular crew of Pilot Officer H.K. Wakefield and Sergeant W. Wilson, as escort to several Lockheed Hudsons of No. 206 Squadron. The Hudsons' target was Emden, Germany, while the Blenheims also carried four 250lb bombs on a rack under the belly. Despite the difficulties of navigating by night, the two formations successfully bombed the railway yard and invasion barges. Wakefield later recalled that their particular target had been the railway station, which they hit. Fuel consumption had been high, however, and they landed at RAF Docking with, 'less than nine gallons in the tanks.'

The operation was repeated the following night, but without Peacock, whose next operational flight came on 26 July, when he was assigned to the role of escorting minelayers, making two similar escorts on 2 August.

While flying on a reconnaissance during 3 August, Peacock (flying N3542 LA-O) shared in the destruction of an He 115 Seaplane of III./KG 506, piloted by Oberleutnant See Ballier, who was lost with the rest of his crew. Taking off at about 1330 hours, Flight Lieutenant A.W. Fletcher (flying L9446), Flying Officer Peacock (flying N3542) and Pilot Officer R.D. Westlake (flying N3524) flew to their target area off the Danish coast. During the return leg they sighted the German seaplane flying at 1,000ft, 77 miles off Terschelling and made a line astern attack. The aft-gunner fell silent during the first pass, while their second attack saw tracer rounds strike the enemy aircraft. The combat took place at 1620 hours in the Zuider Zee area.

The squadron diarist wrote of the attack against the seaplane:

'It was seen and attacked at 1,000ft by machines in line astern. It dived to sea level and after a second run the rear-gunner of enemy aircraft ceased to fire. Direct hitting [sic] was confirmed by our crews. Three more of a similar type came up, accompanied by a large white seaplane. With ammunition running short our machines re-formed and headed for base. [The] enemy machine [was] reported by air-gunners to have had to land while the others circled round. It is quite unlikely that this machine got home.'

The arrival of a number of new pilots, including the Belgians, Pilot Officers J. Kirkpatrick and H. Gonay, along with Sergeants O.G. Lejeune and R.J.G. Demoulin, led to the squadron requesting an additional eight Blenheims (bringing their complement to twenty-four). This also allowed for the formation of 'C' Flight, which remained non-operational for the time being.

On 7 August, Pilot Officers D.N. Woodger, N.H. Jackson-Smith, and Sergeant K.E. Naish, were on a sweep of the Danish coast when they sighted a number of small ships which they duly attacked with 250lb bombs, raking them with machine-gun fire.

Meanwhile, between 1535 and 1740 hours on the following day, 8 August, 'B' Flight's Flight Lieutenant Fletcher (flying L9446 LA-N), Pilot Officer Wordsworth (flying T1305 LA-M) and Sergeant S.J. Hobbs (flying N3526 LA-K), carried out an escort to aircraft of No. 59 Squadron flying to Le Havre and Trouville. The formation sighted fifteen Bf 110s, eleven of which came down to attack, but were successfully headed off by the Blenheim fighter escort. The Squadron ORB noted that the air-gunners of Blenheims 'M' (Sergeant Mackonochie) and 'K' (Sergeant Marslen) engaged the Bf 110s in a, 'running fight', during which one enemy fighter was, 'shot down in flames'.

On 11 August, during the first day of his flight's detachment to RAF Thorney Island, Peacock (flying N3540 LA-X) led a section strength reconnaissance escort to the French coast. While on their return leg, the Blenheims were attacked by two Bf 109s from JG 2 and JG 27 at 1,200ft near Le Havre. During the ensuing combat one Messerschmitt was destroyed (unconfirmed) and a second damaged; they fell to the concerted fire of Flying Officer Peacock's air-gunner (Sergeant W. Wilson in N3540 LA-X); along with Sergeant H.R. Sutton's air-gunner (Sergeant D.V. Newport in N3533 LA-Q) and Sergeant H.T. Naughtin's air-gunner (Sergeant N.D. Copeland in L9252 LA-U). Return fire left one aircraft slightly damaged. Meanwhile, a Blenheim bomber flying with the formation dropped four 250lb bombs on oil storage facilities at Le Havre.

During his debriefing, Peacock reported: 'Escorted Blenheim to boundary of enemy territory at 15,000ft. On return the patrol attacked at 12,000ft by two Me 109s. One was driven off and the other shot down by the concentrated fire of the rear-gunners.'

Peacock was scrambled twice on 11 & 12 August, flying defensive patrols over RAF Thorney Island. The enemy raids, however, focused their attentions elsewhere and the Blenheims were recalled to conserve fuel.

'*Adler Tag*,' or 'Eagle Day', on 13 August, saw raiders once again approaching overhead. Flight Lieutenant A.W. Fletcher, Flying Officers Peacock and D.K.A. Wordsworth, and Flight Sergeant R. Nelson, along with Sergeants Sutton and S.J. Hobbs, were scrambled to make an airfield defence patrol over Thorney Island. The scramble was repeated on the following day; again the raids did not materialize

The squadron flew a flight strength shipping strike over the North Sea on 15 August. At 1315 hours part of a formation of forty He 111s was intercepted while on their return flight from a mission over Northern England. Flying in T1803, Pilot Officer N.H. Jackson-Smith's air-gunner, Sergeant R.D. Kent, destroyed one bomber, while the remaining five Blenheims drove another He 111 down with one engine out of action and its rear-gunner silenced.

Peacock's 'B' Flight was in the air again on 16 August, making a protection patrol over minelaying vessels. Three He 111s were seen making an approach, but were successfully chased away. Later that day Peacock and the rest of the flight were scrambled to provide fighter cover over the airfield during an air raid alert.

During the following day, Peacock led Flight Sergeant R. Nelson and Sergeants Sutton and Hobbs on further base patrols, that night joining a squadron strength escort to the Battles of Nos. 12 and 142 Squadrons targeting Boulogne.

Meanwhile, Sergeants S.J. Hobbs (flying N3540) later flew a night patrol from Thorney Island, but overshot on landing and wrote the aircraft off; the crew of Sergeant H.W. Ficketts and T.A. Maslen were unhurt.

Early on 18 August, Flying Officer Peacock led Flight Sergeant R. Nelson and Sergeant Sutton into the air on an airfield protection patrol. After about twenty minutes the danger had passed and the order was given to pancake.

The air raid siren sounded at RAF Thorney Island once again at about 1420 hours, and Flying Officer Peacock led Pilot Officer D.K.A. Wordsworth (flying N3533) and Flight Sergeant Nelson (flying N3540) on a scramble.

Flying Officer Peacock (flying L9446 LA-N) and Pilot Officer Wordsworth put their aircraft into a battle-climb and quickly reached the enemy's altitude. Peacock placed himself in a good position and headed straight for the leader of a formation of Ju 87s. He closed to 200 yards before firing a well-aimed burst into the bomber's engine, which was set on fire and the enemy aircraft plunged into the sea off Thorney Island. Pilot Officer Wordsworth (flying N3533 LA-P) destroyed a second, dropping a dinghy for two of the surviving crew. Meanwhile, Flight Sergeant Nelson (flying N3540 LA-Q) claimed a Ju 87 damaged (firing 2,000 rounds).

The official intelligence report read:

'A formation of about twenty-eight Ju 87s and Me 109s started a diving attack on aerodrome. Peacock flew straight for the leader of the lot, who broke away, followed by Peacock, who closed to 200 yards and opened fire. The enemy aircraft's engine burst into flames and crashed into the sea.

'Meanwhile, Wordsworth picked on an '87 and followed him up in a running fight, shooting him down into the sea. Wordsworth jettisoned his dinghy for two German airmen swimming about in the sea off the south coast – "Just for luck", he said.

'Flight Sergeant Nelson fired 2,000 rounds into another '87 but failed to bring him down.'

While some of the enemy did get through and bombed the squadron's home airfield, the damage was light and there were no casualties. The Blenheims were able to land without further incident.

The squadron's work over the previous few days had come to the notice of the Air Ministry. The 'Order of the Day No. 1035', issued by the Secretary of State read: 'Congratulations to your Blenheims on their exploits yesterday'. Group Captain Primrose, DFC, station commander of RAF Bircham Newton, added to the praise, congratulating the squadron on their 'destruction of six enemy aircraft in the past ten days'.

On 19 August, following a busy few days, Peacock's B' Flight was rotated back from RAF Thorney Island to RAF Bircham Newton, being replaced by 'A' Flight, led by Flight Lieutenant F. Flood, but not before Peacock had made a base patrol in response to a potential raid. While these scrambles largely proved false alerts, they placed the Blenheim crews in the front line against the Luftwaffe's raids on the Channel Ports, aviation factories and Fighter Command's airfields – there can be no question that Peacock earned his Battle of Britain clasp.

The Squadron ORB noted that on 21 August, Flying Officer Peacock and Pilot Officer D.K.A. Wordsworth were joined by Sergeant H.R. Sutton on a section strength escort to Hudsons on a bombing mission. The raid passed off without incident. Meanwhile, during a fighter patrol over Thorney Island, Flight Lieutenant Flood pursued and shot down an He 111 which he finally overhauled off Le Havre

'A' Flight was in action again on 23 and 24 August, flying sorties over their temporary base. One of these operations led to the loss of a Blenheim crew, but not to enemy action. At 1645 hours on 24 August, the Blenheim IV of Pilot Officer D.N. Woodger (T1804) was shot down by a Hurricane of No. 1 (RCAF) Squadron while on a scramble to patrol the base against an air raid. The aircraft crashed at Bracklesham, killing both Pilot Officer Woodger and his air-gunner, Sergeant D.L. Wright.[18] The Squadron ORB noted: 'Sergeant Wright's body (the air-gunner) was recovered from the sea riddled with bullets.' Sergeant K.E. Naish's Blenheim also came under attack and had his undercarriage damaged and crash-landed back at base. Another Blenheim successfully evaded the Hurricane's fire.

Meanwhile, the routine patrols continued and Peacock flew an escort on 25 August, while on 27 August there was additional excitement when 'A' Flight's Blenheims were scrambled and vectored onto an He 111 of KG 55 approaching Portsmouth. But on this occasion the raider got away.

Peacock was airborne again on 28 August, when he flew an uneventful minelayer escort between 1830 and 2040 hours.

Further tragedy came when Flying Officer J.S. Priestley (flying L9262) was lost at 1115 hours on 30 August, while flying practice dogfighting.[19] His aircraft went into a spin from which it did not recover. The Blenheim crashed at Barwich Farm, Bagthorpe. Priestly had only recently arrived on the squadron and had less than twenty-four hours on Blenheims. Peacock attended his funeral, which was held on 2 September, before he and the remainder of 'B' Flight flew over to RAF Thorney Island to relieve 'A' Flight.

The same day, while on a section strength convoy escort, Sergeant B.H. Quelch (flying P4835) and his crew, J. Merrett and C. Chrystall, sighted a formation of nine or ten enemy aircraft. Despite having the numerical advantage, the enemy melted away and left the convoy alone. The enemy's unwillingness to engage the twin-engine aircraft was a testament to the fighting credentials of the Blenheim crews. Later, a lone Do 18G seaplane of III./KG 406 was located some 15 miles off Texel. Closing in, Quelch fired a short burst from his belly pack and sent the enemy aircraft straight down into the sea. During debriefing Merrett reported seeing the pilot standing on the wreckage, while his rear-gunner lay motionless. Luftwaffe records reveal that Feldwebel Dietrich Christensen and Leutnant zur See Dietrich Logier were lost.

Quelch was commissioned in December the following year, while still serving with the squadron. He was awarded the DFC, *London Gazette*, 6 February 1945, when back serving with 235 Squadron, one of a number of pilots and aircrew to fly two tours with the unit.

Meanwhile, on 31 August, the Squadron ORB noted some of their aircraft gaining additional firepower: 'Modifications to aircraft: six machines now fitted with double Vickers G.O. guns in rear turret. Five machines free gun for observers use in front. This additional armament had proved most valuable in action.'

During the following day, 1 September, an incident occurred at RAF Bircham Newton which cost the lives of Flying Officer J. Davis and the crew of No. 206 Squadron's Hudson, T9276. The bombed-up Hudson was over-flying the airfield when a Hurricane flew straight across its flight path. Davis pulled back on the controls and avoided a certain collision, but put the Hudson into a stall from which there was insufficient height to recover and the aircraft crashed at No. 235 Squadron's dispersals, in amongst four Blenheims. Flight Lieutenant F.W. Flood, Flying Officer J.H. Laughlin and Pilot Officer J. Coggins, DFM and Bar, raced to the scene. Unable to help the Hudson crew, they immediately set about taxiing the Blenheims out of the danger area. Two of the Hudson's four 250lb bombs detonated in the inferno, but despite the dangers they continued their work, Flood returning to successfully move the fourth aircraft which was already burning fiercely.

Flight Lieutenant Flood was recommended for the George Medal, which several sources give as having being promulgated in the *London Gazette*, 21 January 1941.

The recommendation for the George Medal read:

'Recommended by the Secretary of State for War.
'Flight Lieutenant Frederick William Flood (37582).
'On 7 September 1940, a Hudson aircraft, carrying a full load of bombs, crashed among four Blenheim aircraft and burst into flames. Flight Lieutenant Flood, accompanied by Flying Officer Laughlin and Pilot Officer Coggins, immediately ran to the Blenheims, started the engines of three and taxied them to safety. During this time two bombs on the burning Hudson exploded. Knowing that the remaining bombs were likely to explode any second, Flight Lieutenant Flood ran back, started up the engine of the fourth Blenheim, which had its rudder in the fire and taxied it to safety.

'Throughout, these officers showed complete disregard for their own personal safety in the face of the greatest danger, and it was due to their prompt action, especially Flight Lieutenant Flood, that three of the Blenheims were taken to safety without damage and the fourth with only minor damage.

'Flight Lieutenant Flood was reported "missing" on 11 September 1940. (Flying Officer Laughlin and Pilot Officer Coggins are recommended for appointment as Members of the British Empire Order).'

Flying Officer J.H. Laughlin and Pilot Officer Coggins, DFM and Bar, both received the MBE, *London Gazette*, 21 January 1941. The announcement largely repeats Flood's citation, omitting his name, and skirts around the saving of the fourth aircraft.

The official notification of Flood's Mention-in-Despatches (announced in the *London Gazette* of 17 March 1941, with a note stating 'since missing'), however, does not indicate the award, which is also omitted from his CWGC entry.

Defensive patrols were flown over RAF Thorney Island on 4 September, while at 1700 hours three Blenheims were scrambled, but too late to overhaul a Do 17, which got away when they were forced to abandon the pursuit.

Peacock flew three destroyer protection patrols during early September, making an escort to bombers targeting a French port on 9 September, later making a reconnaissance to photograph the bombing results.

A pre-dawn escort to a photo reconnaissance mission was made on the following day, Peacock flying with his usual crew of Pilot Officer H.K. Wakefield and Sergeant W. Wilson.

Reconnaissance missions, escorts and aerodrome protection patrols were flown throughout 10 September. During an escort to bomber aircraft, flown by the squadron between 1610 and 1810 hours, four Bf 109s and one Bf 110 were sighted, with Flight Lieutenant Fletcher (flying LA-N) sending a Bf 109 into the sea following an astern attack, while Pilot Officer Wordsworth (flying LA-H) and Sergeant Hobbs (flying LA-K) damaged the remaining enemy aircraft.

During the day (10 September) the squadron lost Sergeant C.S.F. Beer, who died in captivity following an earlier mission, although his name has not been noted in the Squadron ORB.[20]

'A' Flight took off from RAF Thorney Island at 1555 hours on 11 September, flying as escort to six Fairey Albacore I torpedo-bombers from No. 826 Naval Air Squadron targeting a convoy of invasion barges located off Calais. Intelligence reported that the vessels were laden with munitions bound for the invasion fleet. Included in the convoy were vessels carrying *Tauchpanzer III* amphibious tanks, vital for the success of Operation Sealion. Accurate flak was encountered, while the Luftwaffe scrambled over a dozen Bf 109s from Pas de Calais to defend this prime target. The air battle began at about 1740 hours when one of the Albacore biplanes 'P' destroyed a Bf 109 as it made an attacking pass. Immediately, Flight Lieutenant F. Flood (flying Z5725 LA-G) dived down onto another which was threatening the bombers, with Pilot Officer P.C. Wickings-Smith and Flying Officer D.K.A. Wordsworth following their section leader. A Messerschmitt singled out the Albacore piloted by Sub-Lieutenant A. Tuke and fired a telling burst, wounding Sub-Lieutenant E.G. Brown in the head. Tuke's air-gunner, sat in the rear of the aircraft, could only get off a passing shot with his 0.303 Vickers. During the general melee, Flight Lieutenant F. Flood's Blenheim was hit by a Bf 109 which attacked as he came to the bomber's aid. The Blenheim went down with Flood and his crew.[21]

Meanwhile, Pilot Officer C.P. Wickings-Smith (flying L9396 LA-E) had a Messerschmitt in his sights as it tried to pick off Albacore L7114 'M', but his own aircraft was hit by Bf 109s of I./JG 52 and III./JG 53. Sergeant R.D.H. Watts was seen to fire his guns right up to the moment his Blenheim hit the water and disintegrated, killing the whole crew.[22] Flying Officer D.K.A. Wordsworth went after one of the Bf 109s, firing a burst which damaged the aircraft and put it into a vertical dive, but Oberleutnant Jakob Stoll was able to pull out at low altitude and nurse his damaged aircraft back to base.

Another Albacore, that piloted by Sub-Lieutenant A.H. Barlow, was also hit, and Barlow mortally wounded. Overall, four of the naval aircraft were badly damaged and a fifth (L7117 'K') was forced to ditch with the loss of their air-gunner (Naval Airman ic, P/JX 154295) James A.M. Stevens. Lieutenant A. Downes and Sub-Lieutenant C. Mallett survived. In reply, No. 826 Squadron had claimed one Bf 109 destroyed.

As previously mentioned, the Albacore (L7114 'M') piloted by Sub-Lieutenant Anthony Montague 'Steady' Tuke, had been hit and caught fire; the crew survived. Tuke went on to be awarded the DSC, *London Gazette*, 13 November 1940. He was later awarded a Bar to the DSC, *London Gazette*, 13 February 1945.

During their debriefing Pilot Officer J. Coggins was able to claim two Bf 109s and a third unconfirmed, while Flying Officer D.K.A. Wordsworth got a probable – two of No. 235 Squadron's Blenheims were lost.

The squadron diary recorded:

'Flight Lieutenant Freddie Flood, known to all on the squadron as "The Negus", had a very successful career in the Australian Air Force to which he proudly belonged. He was a first-class flight commander and popular with us all. His attention to detail and gallant conscientious leadership inspired his flight in a grand way. Shorrocks was a most useful officer and though labouring under the handicap of visual impairment, nevertheless became a reliable observer and navigator. Air-gunner Sergeant Sharp, a resourceful fighting sort, is also a considerable loss to 235; he'd been with us since July. Peter Wickings-Smith recently joined the unit. He was a good amateur crooner and an all-round athlete, following two generations of his family to play rugby for Blackheath. Pilot Officer Alexander 'Bill' Green, a young Ulsterman, was the first observer to join the squadron. He had a shy and retiring disposition, yet Bill had developed into a cool, fearless and impeccable observer. He flapped continuously on the ground, but this subsided immediately he was airborne. He was remarkably keen and was pursuing his ambition to become a pilot. "Little" Watts, the air-gunner, thirty-five years young, behaved with the greatest gallantry. He continued firing for some considerable time after his machine had burst into flames.'

The day's work made the headlines in *The Daily Express* and *The Guardian*, while a congratulatory signal was sent by the Secretary of State for Air, Sir Archibald Sinclair:

'To the C-in-C Coastal Command. Please convey to the squadrons concerned in yesterday's fighting in the Channel my congratulations on their exploits. I deeply regret the losses sustained, but to have carried out their tasks in spite of being attacked by three times their number of fighter aircraft, of which they destroyed three, was a splendid achievement.'
(signed) Archibald Sinclair.

Lieutenant-Commander William Saunders added his personal thanks for the fighter support provided by No. 235 Squadron:

'Had it not been for the magnificent support given to the Albacores by 235 Squadron it is extremely doubtful whether any of our aircraft would have returned as the enemy were in greatly superior numbers, and there was little cloud cover to take advantage of.'
(signed) Lieutenant Commander William Saunders, DSC.

Meanwhile, attacks on German convoys continued and, on 12 September, No. 235 Squadron again provided fighter support to No. 59 Squadron's bombers, before peeling off to make strafing attacks on an enemy oil tanker located off Le Havre. The patrol was made by Pilot Officer D.K.A. Wordsworth (flying LA-H) and Sergeants H.R. Sutton (flying LA-Q), S.J. Hobbs (flying LA-R) and Nelson (flying LA-D). The bombers were attacked by Bf 109s, with No. 59 Squadron's Sergeant West (flying TR-B) successfully fending one off. No. 235 Squadron's Blenheims also took on the Messerschmitts, making a head-on attack, before catching the enemy in their air-gunner's crossfire. So fierce was the Blenheim's defence of their charge that the Bf 109s were forced to take flight and head for cloud cover.

Sergeant D.V. Newport's combat report noted: 'The 109s attacked from above and were met with a wall of crossfire.'

In return the Bf 109 pilots claimed to have damaged a number of Blenheims before being forced to retire, only one of which was allowed as a 'kill'.

The squadron lost another Blenheim on the morning of 13 September, and with it her crew; Sergeants W. Garfield, B. Mesner and A. Kay. Blenheim L9451 LA-V had taken off at 0535 hours with orders to patrol off the Norwegian coast. The lone Blenheim was picked up by German radar and met by Bf 109s, which shot it down between Fedje and Rongevaer at 0800 hours; there were no survivors.[23]

That evening (13 September) Peacock was informed that he had been awarded the DFC, the squadron's first award of the war. Not unnaturally, there was a party held in the mess that evening in Peacock's honour.

Peacock's Distinguished Flying Cross, which it should be noted, did not include his combat victories after 27 June, was promulgated in the *London Gazette*, 13 September 1940:

'Flying Officer Reginald John PEACOCK (40257), No 235 Squadron.
'This officer has carried out approximately 100 hours operational flying as the leader of a section during the last three months. He has on all occasions displayed great coolness and determination. On two occasions his section has been attacked by superior enemy forces and, although on both occasions his two following aircraft have been shot down, he has carried on and completed the patrol on his own. On 12 May, when attacked by eight Me 109s, this officer succeeded in shooting down one and seriously damaging a second. On 27 June, whilst one of six carrying out a reconnaissance of the Zuider

Zee, the formation was attacked by Me 109s. Flying Officer Peacock did all in his power to keep the offensive on our side and, having beaten off the 109s, carried out the reconnaissance of the Zuider Zee on his own. At the end of this patrol he encountered a Heinkel seaplane which he attacked and only broke off the engagement when all his ammunition was expended.'

In the scheme of things, a non-immediate gallantry award normally heralded the end of a tour of operations. Peacock, however, was badly needed on the squadron and so there could be no respite.

Peacock was in action again on 14 September, when he made two base patrols. The following day, he was involved in a scramble at 1110 hours. The Blenheims of Wordsworth and Nelson, led by Peacock, were quickly in the air, providing fighter cover over Thorney Island between 1550 and 1825 hours. Despite a hectic day of raids, nothing approached their sector and they were eventually ordered to pancake. It was at about this time that the squadron's recently formed 'C' Squadron became operational

Further airfield protection patrols were flown on 16 September, when Peacock was scrambled twice, but the threat did not materialise. The squadron was in action again on the eighteenth, the same day that they lost Sergeant J.L. Feather, possibly as a result of wounds received in an earlier operation, having been made a PoW.[24]

The operations continued, with Peacock flying on a minesweeper escort on 21 September and making an uneventful escort patrol on 25 September.

It was time for the next flight rotation, and Flying Officer Peacock's 'B' Flight flew down to RAF Thorney Island on 1 October, resuming their regular defensive patrols. There were, however, no reports of action involving the enemy.

Meanwhile, at 0610 hours on 8 October, Pilot Officers J.O. Fenton (flying LA-U), H.A.C. Goney (flying LA-S) and L. Prevot (flying LA-V), took off on a search for a missing pilot, during which enemy aircraft were engaged. The Squadron ORB recording: 'Two Bf 60s were located and shot down into the sea through the combined efforts of the section.'

Three of No. 235 Squadron's Blenheims took off at 1630 hours on the following day (9 October), making a Hach Patrol (anti-invasion reconnaissance). Pilot Officer J.C. Kirkpatrick (flying N3530 LA-S) is thought to have been shot down by Hauptmann Otto Bertram of Stab III./JG 2 an hour into the patrol, and was last seen at 3,000ft descending into cloud at 1730 hours, before crashing into the Channel.[25]

Peacock and his regular crew had become a tightly knit unit and no one was more delighted than Reginald when it was announced that both his observer and air-gunner were to be awarded gallantry medals for air operations. Pilot Officer H.K. Wakefield was awarded the DFC, *London Gazette*, 22 October:

'The KING has been graciously pleased to approve the undermentioned appointment and awards:-
'The Distinguished Flying Cross.
'Pilot Officer Herbert Kenneth WAKEFIELD (78267), Royal Air Force Volunteer Reserve.'

The same edition carried the announcement of the award of the DFM to their air-gunner, Sergeant William Wilson (553328).

Also honoured was 'B' Flight's commander, Squadron Leader A.W. Fletcher:

'The Distinguished Flying Cross.
'Flight Lieutenant Andrew William FLETCHER (37280).'

At 0800 hours on 14 October, Peacock took off on a search operation for the crew of a lost Hudson of No. 206 Squadron, but nothing was seen. Peacock flew a scramble on 25 October and made three airfield protection patrols on 27 October, with two airfield protection patrols on 2 November.

Despite the Battle of Britain having been won and the threat of invasion averted, there could be no let-up for the squadron, still attached to Fighter Command, although flying in multiple roles.

Meanwhile, Peacock's last operation with the squadron came on 15 November when his crew made a successful reconnaissance, confirming reports of barges seen between Texel and Terschelling. Peacock was not taken off operations, however, as he was one of the squadron's pilots who were transferred to No. 15 Group to help form No. 272 Squadron on 19 November, taking with him his regular crew.

Based at Aldergrove, Northern Ireland, the former No. 235 Squadron pilots and aircrew made up the new unit's 'B' Flight. Meanwhile, No. 236 Squadron supplied 'A' Flight, led by Flying Officer W.S. Moore, with Squadron Leader A.W. Fletcher, DFC, posted to command.

The No. 235 Squadron diarist recorded the departures:

'They were producing a new child – "272" – fathered by Squadron Leader Fletcher. The complexion of 235 is left paler from the loss of so much good blood. Peacock we will all miss, as he was a "foundation member" and shot down the first Me 109 to fall to the squadron on 11 May. His cheerful good-natured temperament and confident mastery of his job as a fighter pilot made him universally respected by all.'

It wasn't long before No. 272 Squadron was declared operational and Peacock flew convoy escorts on 28 November and again on 7 & 17 December, having by then been appointed flight commander. His last sortie of the year came on 29 December, when Peacock made an aborted fighter patrol. A further escort operation followed on 11 January.[26]

With his operational tour officially completed, Peacock was posted to No. 3 OTU, RAF Chivenor, for instructor duties on 22 February 1941. Transferring to No. 2 OTU, RAF Catfoss, on 3 March 1941, Peacock was promoted to the rank of flight lieutenant in September 1941 and advanced to acting squadron leader on 1 August 1941.

On 26 May 1942, Squadron Leader Peacock returned to No. 235 Squadron, then equipped with Beaufighters and operating out of RAF Docking, flying operationally until 5 August 1942, then he transferred back to No. 2 OTU as supernumerary squadron leader.

During his second spell with No. 235 Squadron, Peacock made only eight operational sorties, one at the end of May, five the following month, and two in late July. Most of his operations were reconnaissance, or Rover patrols flown over familiar target areas including Terschelling, Ijmunden and Texel.

Only on one sortie, on 29 June, did Peacock and his navigator, Pilot Officer Gallimore, encounter enemy aircraft. Taking off at 1810 hours, Squadron Leader Peacock was ordered to make a sweep for enemy shipping between Heligoland and Borkum. During the patrol their Beaufighter was attacked by two Bf 109s, resulting in damage to the hydraulic tank – while Gallimore sustained superficial hand wounds. Peacock managed to shake off the enemy and made a normal landing back at base.

Peacock's next posting came on 25 August 1942, when he joined No. 75 OTU, in Aden.

On 20 August 1942, Peacock's former No. 235 Squadron flew out to Malta where it was re-designated No. 227 Squadron, based at Luqa. Reginald Peacock joined the squadron on the 25 January 1943, but was killed-in-action on 5 February 1943, when taking off from El Adem as a passenger in a Hudson of No. 117 Squadron heading for the fortress island. The aircraft lost power and crashed with the loss of all ten on board:[27]

(Nav)	Flight Sergeant L.J. Corfield, No. 117 Squadron
(WoP)	Flight Sergeant G.W. Dixon
(Pilot)	Sergeant W.H. Gladwell, No. 117 Squadron
(WoP/AG)	Flight Sergeant B.G. Hancorn, No. 117 Squadron
(Pilot)	Flight Lieutenant Howard O. Knowles, No. 117 Squadron
	Sergeant Jack H. Manning, No. 117 Squadron
	Flight Lieutenant D.J. Passadora
(Passenger)	Squadron Leader Reginald J. Peacock, DFC
(Nav)	Sergeant Thomas C. Toy, No. 117 Squadron
(Passenger)	Major-General Harry Willans

Squadron Leader Reginald John Peacock, DFC, RAF, was buried at Tobruk Commonwealth War Cemetery, Libya, Plot 10, Row B, Grave 5. Peacock was 25-years-old.

A provisional list of No. 235 Squadron personnel during the Battle of Britain:

Squadron Leader Ronald Neville Clarke	DFC 17.1.41 *(A)*
Squadron Leader Andrew William Fletcher, DFC	Bar to DFC 31.10.41 *(B)*
Squadron Leader Ralph Ian MacDougall	
Flight Lieutenant William Joseph Carr	AFC 1.7.41, KIA 26.8.42
Flight Lieutenant Frederick William Flood, RAAF	GM 21.1.41 *(C)*, MiD 17.3.41 *(D)*, KIA 11.9.40
Flight Lieutenant William Bernard Goddard, DFC *(E)*	KIA 15.6.41
Flight Lieutenant Phillip Ambrose Meynell Stickney	
Flying Officer John Hamilton Laughlin	MBE 21.1.41 *(F)*, DSO 23.3.45 *(G)*
Flying Officer Reginald John Peacock, DFC	
Flying Officer Norman Henry Jackson Smith	DFC 27.5.41 *(H)*
Flying Officer Douglas Kenneth Alfred Wordsworth	DFC 28.7.42 *(I)*, KIA 30.10.41
Pilot Officer Joseph Thomas Ronald Chamberlain	
Pilot Officer John Coggins, DFM *(J)* and Bar *(K)*	MBE 21.1.41 *(L)*, KIA 16.12.40
Pilot Officer Hector Hugh Crawford	KIA 6.2.42 with No. 272 Squadron
Pilot Officer John Tregonwell Davison, RNZAF	GM 11.3.41 *(M)*, OBE 1.1.48
Pilot Officer John Ollis Fenton	KIA 28.5.42
Pilot Officer Henri Alphonse Clement 'Moustique' Gonay	Croix de Guerre (Belgian) 21.7.41, KIA 14.6.44
Pilot Officer Alexander William Valentine Green	KIA 11.9.40
Pilot Officer George Stephen Hebron, RAFVR	
Pilot Officer Donald Charles Howe	
Pilot Officer Lucien Leon Gustav Javaux	KIA 18.10.43 with No. 681 Squadron
Pilot Officer John Alexander Keard	KIA 4.5.44 with No. 101 Squadron

Pilot Officer Raymond Dugdale Kent

Pilot Officer James Charles Kirkpatrick   KIA 9.10.40

Pilot Officer Arthur Guthrie Little

Pilot Officer Allan William Martin   DFC 7.12.43 *(N)*

Pilot Officer Frederick George Paisley   DFC 17.7.45 *(O)*

Pilot Officer Robert Lawson Patterson   KIA 18.7.40

Pilot Officer Ernest Russell Phillips   KIA 14.2.41

Pilot Officer Leon Prevot   DFC 30.10.42 *(P)*, MiD, Knight Order of the Crown, Knight Order of Leopold, Officer in the Order of Leopold, Officer's Cross in the Order of Leopold with Palm, Commander of the Order of Leopold II, Belgian Military Cross 2nd Class, Croix de Guerre 1940 with four Palms (Belgium), Croix de Guerre with Palm (France), La Legion d'Honnuer

Pilot Officer John Sinclair Priestley   KIA 30.8.40

Pilot Officer Norman Alfred Sadler   KIA 16.12.40

Pilot Officer Norman Basil Shorrocks   KIA 11.9.40

Pilot Officer Reginald Taylor

Pilot Officer Richard Ceredig Thomas   KIA 16.8.40

Pilot Officer Herbert Kenneth 'Ollie' Wakefield, DFM

Pilot Officer Richard Douglas Westlake

Pilot Officer Peter Claude Wickings-Smith   KIA 11.9.40

Pilot Officer David Noel Woodger   KIA 24.8.40

Flight Sergeant Richard 'Dick' Nelson

Sergeant Arthur Thomas Rayner Aslett, RAFVR

Sergeant Cyril Sydney Frank Beer   KIA 10.9.49 with No. 22 Squadron

Sergeant Kenneth Leslie Owen Blow   DFC 15.6.43 *(Q)*, KIA 10.12.43 with No. 487 Squadron

Sergeant Richard Waller Brookman   KIA 22.2.41

Sergeant Owen Valentine Burns

Sergeant Anthony Richard Cain   KIA 15.6.41

Sergeant Colin Chrystall   PoW June 1944, DFC 15.1.45 *(R)*

Sergeant Douglas Clifford Cooper

Sergeant Norman Downey Copeland

Sergeant Alfred Stewart Davis

Sergeant Thomas Dawson

Sergeant Orlando John Dee — KIA 13.9.40

Sergeant Rene Jean Ghislain Demoulin — KIA as CO of No. 272 Squadron, Order of Leopold and Croix de Guerre (Belgium)

Sergeant Allan Sydney Dredge — DFC 27.7.43 (*S*), DSO 5.12.44 (*T*), KIA 18.5.45 as WC

Sergeant William Howard Dulwich — KIA 2.8.41 with No. 22 Squadron

Sergeant Ian Love Dunn

Sergeant Cecil Roy Evans — KIA 23.3.41

Sergeant Alfred Douglas Everitt, RAFVR — AEA

Sergeant John Farthing — MBE 1.1.46

Sergeant John Leslie Feather — KIA 18.9.40

Sergeant H.W. Ficketts

Sergeant Stanley Gordon — KIA 28.5.41

Sergeant Gordon Leslie Gould

Sergeant Edward Arthur Graves — KIA 30.8.40

Sergeant Robert Victor Gridley — KIA 13.1.42

Sergeant Hall

Sergeant Leopold Heimes

Sergeant Ralph Walter Hillman — KIA 6.4.41

Sergeant Sydney John Hobbs — KIA 14.8.41 with No. 143 Squadron

Sergeant Howard

Sergeant Brian Frederick Robert Hubbard — KIA 9.11.40

Sergeant Norman Henry Jackson-Smith — DFC 27.5.41

Sergeant Richard Kenneth Howard Johnson — KIA 31.1.45 as WC with No. 272 Squadron

Sergeant George Ernest Keel — KIA 9.10.40

Sergeant John Thornett Lawrence — AFC 14.6.45

Sergeant O.G. Lejeune

Sergeant Alfred Rippon Duke MacConochie

Sergeant James Patrick McCarthy

Sergeant Thomas Francis McCarthy — KIA 6.10.42 with No. 404 Squadron

Sergeant John Reginald McMahon

Sergeant George Sutherland Murray   KIA 23.3.41
MacLeod

Sergeant Thomas Brian Marshall   DFC 20.4.45 *(U)*

Sergeant Thomas Arthur Maslen   KIA 25.10.41

Sergeant William Mason   KIA 14.2.41

Sergeant John Charles Merrett

Sergeant Albert Charles Antoine Michiels   Died 16.7.44

Sergeant William Middlemiss   AFC 1.1.46

Sergeant Kenneth Edward Naish   DFC 19.5.44 *(V)*

Sergeant Harold Thomas Naughton   KIA 28.5.41

Sergeant Edward Arnold Newham

Sergeant Douglas Victor Newport

Sergeant Trevor Walter Oaks

Sergeant William Gethin Owen   DFC 20.7.45 *(W)*

Sergeant John Graham Parsons, RAFVR

Sergeant Harold John Pavitt

Sergeant William Peebles   KIA 7.5.41 with No. 240 Squadron

Sergeant Stanley George Preater

Sergeant Percy Rollo Prosser   KIA 16.12.40

Sergeant Basil Herbert Quelch   DFC 6.2.45 *(X)*

Sergeant John Strachan Ramsay   KIA 27.4.41

Sergeant Charles Alfred Ream

Sergeant Lawrence Hugh Murrell Reece   KIA 18.7.40

Sergeant William Charles Richards   KIA 11.8.41

Sergeant Herbert Wain Rickett   KIA 31.3.45 with No. 229 Squadron

Sergeant Leo Patrick Vincent John Ricks

Sergeant Bruce Robertson Sharp   KIA 11.9.40

Sergeant Philip Alfred Sobey   KIA 9.11.40

Sergeant George Albert Southorn

Sergeant John Henry Spires   DFM 17.6.41 *(Y)*

Sergeant Rodney Murrey Steele

Sergeant N.M. Stranger

Sergeant Reginald Robert Stretch

Sergeant Harold Robert Sutton

Sergeant Reginald Frederick Tatnell	KIA 18.5.41 with No. 272 Squadron
Sergeant Donald Frank Touch	AFC 3.4.45
Sergeant Ronald Yeaman Tucker	KIA 18.6.40
Sergeant John Windsor Unett	KIA 27.12.40 with No. 22 Squadron
Sergeant Francois August Venesoen	DFC 15.12.43 *(Z)*, KIA 6.6.44
Sergeant Donald Sylvester Wallis	KIA 22.2.41
Sergeant Reginald Douglas Haig Watts, RAFVR	KIA 11.9.40
Sergeant Gordon Victor Wedlock	DFM 17.1.41 *(AA)*
Sergeant William Henry James Westcott	
Sergeant Robert White	
Sergeant William Wilson, DFM	
Sergeant Daniel Leslie Wright	KIA 24.8.40

Many of the pilots and aircrew earned gallantry awards for combat which are not mentioned in the main text. Details, where traced, are included below:

(A) Squadron Leader R.N. Clarke was awarded the DFC, *London Gazette*, 17 January 1941:

> 'Distinguished Flying Cross.
> 'Squadron Leader Ronald Neville CLARKE (29063).'

(B) Squadron Leader Fletcher later served as Commanding Officer with No. 272 Squadron and was Mentioned-in-Despatches, *London Gazette*, 1 January 1941, and awarded a Bar to the DFC, *London Gazette*, 31 October 1941, for service in Malta:

> 'Bar to the Distinguished Flying Cross.
> 'Squadron Leader Andrew William FLETCHER, DFC (37280), Reserve of
> Air Force Officers, No. 272 Squadron.'

(C) Flight Lieutenant Frederick William Flood was awarded the GM, *London Gazette*, 21 January 1941. The *London Gazette* entry cannot be traced, while his subsequent MiD does not indicate the award, raising doubt as to whether the award was actually promulgated.

(D) Flight Lieutenant F.W. Flood was Mentioned-in-Despatches, *London Gazette*, 17 March 1941:

> 'Mentioned-in-Despatches.
> 'Flight Lieutenant F.W. FLOOD (37582). Since reported missing.'

(E) Flight Lieutenant Goddard's bravery was recognized by the award of the DFC, announced in the *London Gazette,* of 6 December 1940:

'Distinguished Flying Cross.
'Flight Lieutenant William Bernard GODDARD (36126), No. 235 Squadron.
'In November 1940, this officer was engaged in an attack against two Heinkel 115s. Although severely wounded in the foot, resulting in the loss of three toes, Flight Lieutenant Goddard pressed home his attack to within close-range and succeeded in delivering a long burst after which the enemy aircraft disappeared. Despite suffering from loss of blood, he succeeded in bringing his aircraft and crew back to base. He displayed gallantry and fortitude throughout.'

It is believed that the King pinned Goddard's DFC on his chest while he was still recovering in hospital.

(F) Flying Officer J.H. Laughlin was awarded the MBE, *London Gazette*, 21 January 1941:

'To be Additional Members of the Military Division of the said Most Excellent Order.
'Flying Officer John Hamilton LAUGHLIN (39995).
'In September 1940, an aircraft carrying a full load of bombs crashed among other aircraft and burst into flames. Flying Officer Laughlin, Pilot Officer Coggins and another officer immediately ran to these aircraft, started the engines and taxied them away. During this time two bombs on the burning plane had exploded. The action showed complete disregard for personal safety in the face of the greatest danger and, owing to the officers' promptness, three aircraft were taken to safety without damage and a fourth with only minor damage.'

(G) Squadron Leader J.H. Laughlin, MBE was awarded the DSO, *London Gazette*, 23 March 1945:

'Distinguished Service Order.
'Squadron Leader John Hamilton LAUGHLIN, MBE (39995), RAFO, No. 149 Squadron.'

(H) Flying Officer N.H.J. Smith was awarded the DFC, *London Gazette*, 27 May 1941:

'Distinguished Flying Cross.
'Flying Officer Norman Henry Jackson SMITH (42270), No. 235 Squadron.'

(I) Flight Lieutenant D.K.A. Wordsworth was awarded the DFC, *London Gazette*, 28 July 1943:

'Distinguished Flying Cross.
'Flight Lieutenant Douglas Kenneth Alfred WORDSWORTH (41517) (deceased), No. 212 Squadron, awarded with effect from 22 October 1941.'

(J) Sergeant John Coggins was awarded the DFM, *London Gazette*, 22 November 1938:

'The KING has been graciously pleased to approve of the undermentioned rewards for gallant and distinguished services rendered in Palestine:
'Distinguished Flying Medal.
'563631 Sergeant John COGGINS.'

(K) Coggins was awarded a Bar to the DFM, *London Gazette*, 14 April 1939:

Air Ministry,
14 April 1939
ROYAL AIR FORCE
'The KING has been graciously pleased to approve of the undermentioned rewards for gallant and distinguished services rendered in Palestine:
'Bar to the Distinguished Flying Medal.
'563631 Sergeant John COGGINS, DFM.'

(L) Coggins was later awarded the MBE, *London Gazette*, 21 January 1941:

'Pilot Officer John COGGINS (44458).'
(see citation for Flying Officer J.H. Laughlin on previous page)

(M) Pilot Officer J.T. Davison was awarded the GM, *London Gazette*, 11 March 1941:

'The KING has been graciously pleased to approve the award of the George Medal to:
'Pilot Officer John Tregonwell DAVISON, Royal New Zealand Air Force.
'Pilot Officer Davison was the pilot and Sergeant Brazier the wireless operator/ air observer of an aircraft which took part in a bombing attack on two heavily armed merchant vessels. Pilot Officer Davison was wounded in the foot and thigh, but succeeded in flying his aircraft back to base. Owing to severe damage sustained to the hydraulic gear, he was compelled to make a crash landing, not knowing that a bomb remained hung up on the rack. The bomb exploded on landing, severely wounding the rear-gunner and setting the aircraft on fire. Pilot Officer Davison and Sergeant Brazier jumped clear, but then discovered that

the rear-gunner was still in the aircraft. Regardless of the fire and the likelihood that the petrol tanks might explode, they succeeded in extricating the wounded rear-gunner from the rear cockpit and dragging him to safety. By their courage and gallantry they undoubtedly saved the life of the rear-gunner.'

(N) Flight Lieutenant A.W. Martin was awarded the DFC, *London Gazette*, 7 December 1943:

'Distinguished Flying Cross.
'Flight Lieutenant Allan William MARTIN (78254), Royal Air Force Volunteer Reserve, No. 502 Squadron.'

(O) Acting Wing Commander F.G. Paisey was awarded the Distinguished Flying Cross, *London Gazette*, 17 July 1945:

'Distinguished Flying Cross.
'Acting Wing Commander Frederick George PAISEY (78753), RAFVR, No. 354 Squadron.
'This officer has displayed great skill and courage in attacks on enemy shipping. He has invariably attacked his targets at low-level and has been responsible for the destruction of two of the six enemy ships which have been sunk by the squadron. His devotion to duty has been unfailing.'

(P) Squadron Leader L. Prevot was awarded the DFC, *London Gazette*, 30 October 1942:

'Squadron Leader Leon PREVOT (84285), RAF.
'Distinguished Flying Cross.
'This officer has completed a large number of operational sorties both as flight and squadron commander, and his skillful leadership has been a source of inspiration to his pilots. He has destroyed at least three and probably destroyed a further two enemy aircraft.'

(Q) Sergeant K.L.O. Blow was awarded the DFC, *London Gazette*, 15 June 1943:

'Distinguished Flying Cross
'Warrant Officer Kenneth Leslie Owen BLOW (751684), Royal Air Force Volunteer Reserve, No. 487 (NZ) Squadron.'

(R) Flight Lieutenant Colin Chrystall was awarded the DFC, *London Gazette*, 15 January 1945:

'Distinguished Flying Cross.
'Flight Lieutenant C. CHRYSTALL (46538), RAF, No. 243 Squadron.'

(S) Flying Officer A.S. Dredge was awarded the DFC, *London Gazette*, 27 July 1943:

'Distinguished Flying Cross.
'Flying Officer Alan Sydney DREDGE (63785), Royal Air Force Volunteer Reserve, No. 183 Squadron.'

(T) Acting Squadron Leader A.S. Dredge was awarded the Distinguished Service Order, *London Gazette*, 5 December 1944:

'Distinguished Service Order.
'Acting Squadron Leader Allan Sydney DREDGE, DFC (63758), RAFVR, No. 3 Squadron.
'This officer has led the squadron on a very large number of sorties, involving attacks on a wide range of enemy targets. Shipping, airfields, locomotives and various other targets have been most effectively attacked. Throughout these operations, Squadron Leader Dredge has displayed inspiring leadership, great courage and determination, qualities which have contributed materially to the successes obtained.'

(U) Acting Squadron Leader T.B. Marshall was awarded the DFC, *London Gazette*, 20 April 1945:

'Distinguished Flying-Cross.
'Acting Squadron Leader Thomas Brian MARSHALL (102085), RAFVR, No. 39 Squadron.'

(V) Flight Lieutenant K.E. Naish was awarded the DFC, *London Gazette*, 19 May 1941:

'Distinguished Flying Cross.
'Flight Lieutenant Kenneth Edward NAISH (45447), Royal Air Force, No. 236 Squadron.
'In April 1944, this officer took part in an attack on a convoy off the Dutch Coast. At the commencement of his attack on an escort vessel, his aircraft was hit by anti-aircraft fire. One engine was set on fire, but despite this, Flight Lieutenant Naish pressed home a determined attack. Whilst putting out the flames from the burning engine, Flight Lieutenant Naish was heavily engaged by the anti-aircraft batteries both from the ships and from the shore. Although his aircraft was badly damaged he flew it safely to base where he effected a successful crash-landing.
'This officer displayed a high degree of skill, courage and resolution.'

(W) Flight Lieutenant W.G. Owen was awarded the DFC, *London Gazette*, 20 July 1945:

'Distinguished Flying Cross.
'Flight Lieutenant William Gethin OWEN (103386), RAFVR, No. 48 Squadron.'

(X) Flight Lieutenant B.H. Quelch was awarded the DFC, *London Gazette*, 6 February 1945:

'Distinguished Flying Cross.
'Basil Herbert QUELCH (115130), RAFVR, No. 235 Squadron.'

(Y) Sergeant J.H. Spires was awarded the DFM, *London Gazette*, 17 June 1941: 'for gallantry and devotion to duty in the execution of air operations.'

'Distinguished Flying Medal.
'751252 Sergeant John Henry SPIRES, Royal Air Force Volunteer Reserve, No. 69 Squadron.'

(Z) Pilot Officer Francois August Venesoen was awarded the DFC, *London Gazette*, 15 December 1943, while serving with No. 350 (Belgian) Squadron.

(AA) Sergeant Wedlock had earlier been a pilot with the RAFVR, but had lost his flying status due to the fact that he needed glasses. He joined No. 235 Squadron in March 1940, flying in the role of observer/navigator. On 18 November, while on a reconnaissance over the Dutch coast (flying in Z5732 LA-Y), his Blenheim was damaged by return fire from a number of He 115s. Wedlock's pilot, Flight Lieutenant Goddard, was wounded in the leg (their air-gunner, Sergeant Dawson, may also have suffered wounds).

Wedlock was able to come to the aid of his pilot and assisted in ensuring that the aircraft and crew made it to RAF North Coates. He was later awarded the DFM, *London Gazette*, 17 January 1941:

'The Distinguished Flying Medal.
'115579 Sergeant Gorgon Wedlock, RAFVR.
'This airman has been with the squadron since 1940, and has acted as navigator on almost every operational flight of his section. On the 18 November 1940, the pilot of his aircraft was severely wounded in the leg during an engagement off the Dutch coast. Sergeant Wedlock managed to put a tourniquet round the pilot's leg, keeping it in place under difficult conditions, and managed to navigate the aircraft back to the nearest aerodrome, a distance of 150 miles. It was chiefly due to Sergeant Wedlock's coolness that the pilot remained conscious during the return flight, and that the aircraft and crew landed safely without further damage'.

Notes

1. (Pilot) Sergeant (519436) Victor Allison, RAF, was the son of Walter and Wilhelmina Allison, of St. Albans, Hertfordshire. Allison was 23-years-old and was buried at Boyndie (St Brandan) Old Churchyard, Grave 15. (Observer) Sergeant (746761) Eric Oliver Ferdinand Schmid, RAFVR, was the son of Charles F. Schmid and Edith A. Schmid, of Wood Green, Middlesex. Schmid was 19-years-old and was buried at Great Bircham (St Mary) Churchyard, Plot 1, Row 1, Grave 3. (Wop/AG) Leading Aircraftman (645692) Victor Charles Edward Neirynck, RAF, was the son of Eugene and Bertha Neirynck, of Westcliff-on-Sea. Neirynck was 19-years-old and was buried at Southend-on-Sea (North Road), Cemetery, Plot B, Row 3, Grave 54.

2. Pilot Officer (41958) Walter Fowler Smith, RAF, was the son of George Fowler Smith and Florence Mary Smith, of Hartlebury. Smith was 20-years-old and was buried at Hartlebury (St Mary) Churchyard, north-east of the church.

3. (Pilot) Pilot Officer (40950) Norman Alistair Lloyd Smith, RAF, was the son of Frederick Charles and Elsie Smith, of Cambridge. B.Sc., Hons. (Lond.). Smith was 25-years-old and was buried at The Hague (Westduin) General Cemetery, Allied Plot, Row 3, Grave 47. (Observer), Sergeant (749443) John Conacher Robertson, RAFVR, was the son of Andrew and Davina Robertson, of Perth. Robertson was 20-years-old and was buried at the Hook of Holland General Cemetery, Row F, Joint Grave 57. (Wop/AG) Leading Aircraftman (553205) Thomas Joseph Lowry, RAF, was the son of Martin Joseph and Anne Josephine Lowry, of Chiswick, Middlesex. Lowry was 17-years-old and was buried at the Hook of Holland General Cemetery, Row F, Joint Grave 57.

4. Pilot Officer Savill's crew were killed: (Observer) Sergeant (755141) Henry Raven Sunderland, RAFVR, was the son of Lilian Sunderland, of Berkhamsted, Hertfordshire. Sunderland was 23-years-old and was buried at Oostvoorne Protestant Cemetery, Joint Grave 216. (Wop/AG) Leading Aircraftman (552475) Roy Harry Tyler, RAF, was the son of Harry P. and Constance Ivy Mary Tyler, of Leicester. Tyler was 19-years-old and was buried at Oostvoorne Protestant Cemetery, Joint Grave 216. In August 1967 parts of Blenheim L9189 were excavated (recovery RNLAF-29(27)) at Rozenburg.

5. The crew were: (Pilot) Pilot Officer (41470) Curran Smiley Robinson, RAF, who is remembered on the Runnymede Memorial, Panel 10. (Observer) Sergeant (755471) Donald Vivian Moseley, RAFVR, who was the son of Hubert Henry and Winifred Ellen Moseley, of Gloucester. Moseley was 22-years-old and is remembered on the Runnymede Memorial, Panel 17. (Wop/AG) Leading Aircraftman (638743) Albert Edward Waddington, RAF, who was the son of Hubert and Mabel Waddington, of Northerden, Lancashire. Waddington was 21-years-old and is remembered on the Runnymede Memorial, Panel 24.

6. (Wop/AG) LAC (749948) Leslie George Curry, RAFVR, was buried at Kingston-upon Thames Cemetery, Class C (General), Grave 1024.

7. (Pilot) Pilot Officer (42154) Michael Erskin Ryan, RAF, was the son of Sir Gerald Ellis, 2nd Bart., MA, and Hylda Winifryde Ryan, of Chattisham, Suffolk. Ryan was 20-years-old and was buried at Schiedermonnikoog (Vredenhof) Cemetery, Grave 15. (Observer) Sergeant (748313) William Martin, RAFVR, was the husband of Doris Pittman, of Streatham, London. Martin was buried at Schiedermonnikoog (Vredenhof) Cemetery, Grave 17. (Wop/AG) Leading Aircraftsman (552170) Albert George Smith, RAF, is remembered on the Runnymede Memorial, Panel 24.

8. (Observer) Pilot Officer (78255) Alfred Hall Murphy, RAF, was buried at Great Bircham (St Mary) Cemetery, Plot 1, Row 1, Grave 5. (Wop/AG) Leading Aircraftsman (573130) Ernest Peareth Armstrong, RAF, was the son of Henry Peareth Armstrong and Margaret

Armstrong, of Norton, Stockton-on-Tees. Armstrong was 18-years-old and was buried at Stockton-on-Tees (Durham Road) Cemetery, Section M.1., Church of England, Row O, Grave 17.

9. (Pilot) Flight Lieutenant (40087) Richard Percy Yeo Cross, RAF, was 25-years-old and was buried at Herne Bay Cemetery, Section UR, Grave 2. (Observer) Sergeant (744906) Alan Victor Slocombe, RAFVR, was 31-years-old and was buried at Detling (St Martin) Churchyard Extension, Grave 48. (Wop/AG) Leading Aircraftman (629429) James North, RAF, was 20–years-old and was buried at Huddersfield (Edgerton) Cemetery, Consecrated Section 4, Grave 48.

10. (Pilot) Pilot Officer (42099) Anthony Foster Booth, RAF, was the son of Alan Foster Booth, and Maude Ida Booth, of Selukwe, Southern Rhodesia. Booth was 26-years-old and is remembered on the Runnymede Memorial, Panel 7. (Observer) Sergeant (749407) Douglas James Elliott, RAFVR, was the son of Edward James Elliott and Blanche Elliott; husband of Hilda Elliott, of Kingscote, Gloucestershire. Elliott was 29-years-old and is remembered on the Runnymede Memorial, Panel 14. (Wop/AG) Sergeant (624256) Eric Robert Scott, RAF, was the son of Frederick William and Kate Scott, of Abbeystead, Lancashire. Scott was 21-years-old and is remembered on the Runnymede Memorial, Panel 19.

11. The crew were: (Pilot) Flight Lieutenant (39156) George Arthur Patrick Manwaring, RAF, the son of William and Mary May Manwaring, of Marden, Kent; husband of Zena Jesselin Manwaring. Flight Lieutenant Manwaring was 25-years-old and was buried at Sage War Cemetery, Section 8, Row E, Grave 4. (Observer) Sergeant (581156) Ian MacPhail, RAF, was the son of Alexander John Macphail and Louise Caroline Macphail, of Ramsgate, husband of Jean Caroline Macphail, of Ramsgate, F.R.H.S. MacPhail was 24-years-old and was buried at Ramsgate (St Lawrence) Cemetery, Div. Section G. Grave 243. (Wop/AG) Sergeant (629645) David Beatty Murphy, RAF, was the son of John and Jane Murphy, of Cliftonville, Belfast, Northern Ireland. Murphy was 20-years-old and was buried at Sage War Cemetery, Section 4, Row F, Grave 4.

12. (Pilot) Flight Sergeant (514566) William Thomas Joseph Southey, RAF, was 27-years-old. Southey is remembered on the Runnymede Memorial, Panel 11. (Observer) Sergeant (580958) Allan John Dennis Ingram, RAF, was buried at Norre Havgvig Churchyard. (Wop/AG) Sergeant (614601) Eric Howard Mckenzie Turner, RAF, was the son of Louisa Turner, and stepson of S.S. Turner, of Gorleston, Norfolk. Turner was 20-years-old and is remembered on the Runnymede Memorial, Panel 20.

13. (Pilot) Pilot Officer (41968) Alan Roger Wales, RAF, was the son of Herbert and Bertha Wales, of London. Wales was 20-years-old and was buried at Oegstgeest Protestant Churchyard, Grave 3. (Observer) Sergeant (742691) John Walter Needham, RAFVR, was the son of Augusta Elizabeth Needham, of Kilburn, Middlesex. Needham was 25-years-old and was buried at Oegstgeest Protestant Churchyard, Grave 1. (Wop/AG) Sergeant (629644) Thomas Charles Jordan, RAF, was the son of William Henry and Jane Ellen Jordan, of Belfast, Northern Ireland. Jordan was 18-years-old and was buried at Oegstgeest Protestant Churchyard, Grave 2.

14. (Pilot) Pilot Officer (42109) John Richard Cronan, RAF, was the son of Cyril Preston Cronan and Phyllis Lawrence Cronan, of Birkenhead, Auckland, New Zealand. Cronan was 21-years-old and was buried at Bergen-op-Zoom Canadian War Cemetery, Section 8, Row H, Grave 8. (Observer) Sergeant (755199) A.O. Lancaster became a PoW. (Wop/AG) Sergeant Philip Laurence Lloyd, RAF, was the son of James and Laura Lloyd, of Conwy, Caernarvonshire, Wales. Lloyd was 19-years-old and was buried at Bergen-op-Zoom Canadian War Cemetery, Section 8, Row H, Grave 9.

15. (Pilot) Pilot Officer (41971) Peter Weil, RAF, was the son of Bernard Weil and of Marion Weil (née Dawson), of Burgh Heath, Tadworth, Surrey. Weil was 20-years-old and was buried at Becklingen War Cemetery, Germany, Section 23, Row A, Grave 1. (Observer) Sergeant (755198) Sidney Kendal Bartlett, RAFVR, was the son of John and Isabella Bartlett; husband of Elizabeth Bartlett, of Darlington, Co. Durham. Bartlett was 28-years-old and was buried at The Hague (Westduin) General Cemetery, Allied Plot, Row 3, Grave 49. (Wop/AG) Sergeant (627208) Alan Kempster, RAFVR, was the son of Ida Nicks, of Bradford, Yorkshire. Kempster was buried at Jonkerbos War Cemetery, Section 19, Row H, Grave 6.

16. (Pilot) Pilot Officer (41974) Hugh Spicer Pardoe-Williams, RAF, was the son of Francis Pardoe-Williams, and of Ethel Mary Pardoe-Williams, of Exeter. Pardoe-Williams was 23-years-old and was buried at Amsterdam New Eastern Cemetery, Plot 69, Row A, Grave 12. (Observer) Sergeant (751531) Clifford William Thorley, RAFVR, was buried at Amsterdam New Eastern Cemetery, Plot 69, Row A, Grave 10. (Wop/AG) Pilot Officer (77342) Edward Arthur Saunders, RAFVR, was buried at Amsterdam New Eastern Cemetery, Plot 69, Row A, Grave 8.

17. (Pilot) Pilot Officer (77529) Robert Lawson Patterson, RAFVR, was the son of John Muirhead Patterson and Helen Smith Patterson, of Wormit, Fife. Patterson was 26-years-old and is remembered on the Runnymede Memorial, Panel 9. (Observer) Sergeant (552711) Ronald Yeaman Tucker, RAF, was the son of Anthony Tucker and Jane Elizabeth Tucker, of Leadgate, Cumberland. Tucker was 18-years-old and is remembered on the Runnymede Memorial, Panel 20. (Wop/AG) Sergeant (747825) Lawrence Hugh Murrell Reece, RAFVR, is remembered on the Runnymede Memorial, Panel 18.

18. (Pilot) Pilot Officer (42666) David Noel Woodger, RAF, was the son of Reginald White Woodger and Edith Muriel Woodger, of Old Coulsdon, Surrey. Woodger was 20-years-old and is remembered on the Runnymede Memorial, Panel 10. (Wop/AG) Sergeant Daniel Leslie Wright, RAF, was the son of William Wright and Mary Ann Wright (née Faulkner), of Chasetown, Burntwood. Wright was buried at Chasetown (St Ann) Churchyard, New Section, Row L, Grave 1593.

19. (Pilot) Flying Officer (39934) John Sinclair Priestley, RNZAF, was the son of Josiah Oswald and Margaret Moore Priestley, of Plimmerton, Wellington, New Zealand. Priestly was buried at Great Bircham (St Mary) Churchyard, Plot 1, Row 1, Grave 9. (Wop/AG) Sergeant (632826) Edward Arthur Graves, RAF, was buried at Eastbourne (Langley) Cemetery, Section D, Grave 875. The young air-gunner had been on attachment from No. 22 Squadron, which shared the same airfield.

20. (Wop/AG) Sergeant (751495) Cyril Sydney Frank Beer, RAFVR, was the son of Thomas and Eva Flora Beer, of Prittlewell, Southend-on-Sea, Essex. Beer was buried at Texel (Den Burg) Cemetery, Plot K, Row 3, Grave 67.

21. (Pilot) Flight Lieutenant (37582) Frederick William Flood, RAF, was 25-years-old and is remembered on the Runnymede Memorial, Panel 4. (Observer) Pilot Officer (78265) Norman Basil Shorrocks, RAFVR, is remembered on the Runnymede Memorial, Panel 10. (Wop/AG) Sergeant (628218) Bruce Robertson Sharp, RAFVR, is remembered on the Runnymede Memorial, Panel 19.

22. (Pilot) Pilot Officer (42929) Peter Claude Wickings-Smith, RAF, was the son of Claude Trebeck and Vera Frances Wickings-Smith, of Bedford. Wickings-Smith was 22-years-old and is remembered on the Runnymede Memorial, Panel 10. (Observer) Pilot Officer (78092) Alexander William Valentine Green, RAFVR, was the son of Alexander and Marjory Green, of Craigavad, Co. Down, Northern Ireland. Green was 21-years-old and is remembered on the

Runnymede Memorial, Panel 8. (Wop/AG) Sergeant (746868) Reginald Douglas Haig Watts, RAFVR, was the son of Charles and Alice Louisa Watts, of Far Cotton, Northamptonshire. Watts was 35-years-old and is remembered on the Runnymede Memorial, Panel 20.

23. (Pilot) Sergeant (740997) Walter James Garfield, RAFVR, was the son of Walter S. and Emma May Garfield, of Sutton-in-Ashfield, Nottinghamshire. Garfield was 25-years-old and was buried at Bergen (Mollendal) Church Cemetery, Grave B.5. (Observer) Sergeant (745987) Bertram William Mesner, RAFVR, was the son of Charles and Adelaide Mesner, of Forest Gale, Essex; husband of Jessie Mesner. Mesner was 29-years-old and is remembered on the Runnymede Memorial, Panel 17. (Wop/AG) Sergeant (647610) Archibald Kay, RAF, is remembered on the Runnymede Memorial, Panel 16.

24. Sergeant (641705) John Leslie Feather, RAF, was the son of Mr and Mrs J. Feather, of Liverpool. Feather was buried at Bayeux War Cemetery, Section XXIX, Row J, Grave 3.

25. (Pilot) Pilot Officer (81630) James Charles Kirkpatrick (Belgian), RAFVR, was the son of Robert Closeburn and Yvonne Kirkpatrick of Brussels. He is remembered on the Runnymede Memorial, Panel 9. (Observer) Pilot Officer (82731) Richard Ceredig Thomas, RAF, was buried at Cardiff (Cathays) Cemetery, Section P, Grave 1094. (Wop/AG) Sergeant (751079) George Ernest Keel, RAF, was the son of Allen George and Gertrude Agnes Keel, of Southsea. Keel was 20-years-old and was buried at Portsmouth (Highland Road) Cemetery, Section M, Row 2, Grave 4.

26. The squadron moved to Chivenor in April 1941, having converted to flying Bristol Beaufighters. May saw the squadron transfer to Egypt flying convoy escort operations and ground intruder missions. The squadron had detachments at Cyprus, Malta, and Palestine, while from November the whole squadron was based on Malta.

27. Flight Sergeant (928686) Leslie John Corfield, RAFVR, was the son of Jack and Ethel May Corfield, of Croxley Green, Hertfordshire. Corfield was 22-years-old and was buried at Tobruk Commonwealth War Cemetery, Libya, Plot 10, Row C, Grave 14. Flight Sergeant (614842) George Wallace Dixon, RAF, was the son of Harry and Harietta Dixon of Botcherby, Carlisle. Dixon was 22-years-old and was buried at Tobruk Commonwealth War Cemetery, Libya, Plot 10, Row B, Grave 6. Sergeant (1292395) Williams Henry Gladwell, RAFVR, was the son of Albert David and Priscilla Gladwell, of St Leonard-on-Sea, Sussex, Gladwell was 22-years-old and was buried at Tobruk Commonwealth War Cemetery, Libya, Plot 10, Row C, Grave 9. Flight Sergeant (642375) Brian Godfrey Hancorn, RAF, was the son of John Davies Hancorn and Alice Gertrude Hancorn, of Hereford. Hancorn was 24-years-old and was buried at Tobruk Commonwealth War Cemetery, Libya, Plot 10, Row C, Grave 11. Flight Lieutenant (63449) Howard Otis Knowles, RAFVR, was the son of St John Knowles and Arta Otis Knowles, of South Ascot, Berkshire. Knowles was 22-years-old and was buried at Tobruk Commonwealth War Cemetery, Libya, Plot 10, Row B, Grave 2. Sergeant (932188) Jack Herbert Manning, RAFVR, was the son of Herbert Chistie and Mary Dolores Manning, of St Philip, Barbados, British West Indies. Manning was 28-years-old and was buried at Tobruk Commonwealth War Cemetery, Libya, Plot 10, Row C, Grave 13. Flight Lieutenant (79476) Denis Joseph Passadora, RAFVR, was buried at Tobruk Commonwealth War Cemetery, Libya, Plot 10, Row B, Grave 4. Sergeant (1541849) Thomas Charton Toy, RAFVR, was the son of Sarah Toy, of Whitefield, Lancashire. Toy was 21-years-old and was buried at Tobruk Commonwealth War Cemetery, Libya, Plot 10, Row B, Grave 7. Major-General Harry Willans, CB, CBE, DSO, MC, TD, MiD (twice), was the son of James Tetly Willans and Henrietta Mary Willans; husband of Dorothy Joan Willans, of Stevenage, Hertfordshire. Willans, of the Artist's Rifles, was a General Staff Officer, who had served with great distinction with the Bedfordshire Regiment during the First World War.

Chapter 2

Flight Lieutenant Jan Kowalski, VM, KW and Two Bars, DFC

Jan Kowalski and his comrades in No. 303 Squadron played an important role in the decisive phase of the Battle of Britain, when the RAF's Fighter Command was arguably close to ceding partial defeat and withdrawing north of the River Thames. In a period of four-and-a-half weeks the squadron destroyed 126 enemy aircraft for the loss of eight brave pilots.

Jan Kowalski was born in Mircze, in Poland, on 19 November 1916. He joined the PAF at the age of sixteen, entering the NCO's training school established at Bydgoszcz, under General Rayski. Having qualified as an air mechanic in 1935, Jan was later selected for a posting to the air force officer's training centre at Sadkow, completing his pilot training course at Grudziadz. Jan's first squadron posting was to No. 112 Fighter Squadron of 1st Air Force Regiment, Warsaw (part of the Pursuit Brigade commanded by Colonel Stefan Pawlikowski).

In 1937, Jan Kowalski became an instructor at the NCO's Training School, and was still acting in this role when Hitler's forces invaded Poland on 1 September 1939:

'It was nearly the end of our course. The top pupils had been sent to another school to convert for flying fighters. With the remaining pupils we only had a few lessons left, mostly cross-country flights and emergency landings. I had to live on the station as all leave had been cancelled.

'On the morning of 1 September I was awake at 6 o'clock as we usually started flying at 8 o'clock. Suddenly I heard the sound of aircraft engines. It was very unusual to hear someone flying so early in the morning and so I went to the window to have a look. And there they were, German bombers flying about fifty feet above the adjoining building and dropping bombs, the air-gunners strafing the buildings also.

'There was a lot of damage, but also unexploded bombs and one of the hangars was on fire. Our aircraft were outside with little damage.

'About lunchtime we received orders to fly to another school aerodrome that was in central Poland, hoping to be safe there, but this aerodrome was also bombed. Most of our aerodromes were bombed, while our fighters were no match for the Me 109.'

In late September, Jan, along with his students, was evacuated to Romania, from where he made his way to Marseilles at the end of October.

Jan then joined the Polish Air Force in Rennes, France, serving as part of L'Armee de l'Air. Although he had voiced his desire to get onto fighters and hit back at the enemy, Jan's abilities as an instructor were considered more important; he was assigned to teach pupil pilots on multi-engine aircraft.

On the fall of France, Jan made his way to England, where he arrived on 22 June, passing through the Polish Aviation Depot at Blackpool. Here, Jan was forceful in his request to be posted onto a single-seater fighter squadron, but initially found himself in a state of limbo; the Air Ministry had a sudden large influx of overseas pilots, all of whom had to pass through a selection process before being found a unit.

The wealth of highly talented fighter and bomber pilots that arrived on these shores following the fall of France had taken the RAF by surprise, and they were still working out what to do with them. Some had come to the attention of the authorities and found their way straight onto operational squadrons. Meanwhile, plans were put into operation for the establishment of new units, which would be composed largely of overseas volunteers: Americans, Belgians, Canadians, Czechs and Poles. One of these squadrons, No 303 Squadron, was to play a pivotal role in the eventual outcome of the battle.

No. 303 (Kościuszko) Squadron was formed at Northolt, Middlesex, on 2 August 1940, from elements of No. 1 (Warsaw) Squadron commanded by Major Zdzislaw Krasnodebski – who had escaped after fighting in Poland and France – and collected at Blackpool. It had been decided that the new squadron would have both British and Polish senior officers. Squadron Leader R.G. Kellet and Flight Lieutenant J.A. Kent, AFC, headed the skeleton British staff which, during the previous fortnight, had been preparing for the Poles' arrival.

Thirteen Polish Officers, eight NCO pilots and 135 Polish other ranks made up the first intake.

The following is the official list of the British and Polish Officers and the Polish NCO pilots at the squadron's formation:

RAF – Squadron Leader Ronald G. Kellet, Officer Commanding; Flight Lieutenant J.A. Kent, AFC, 'A' Flight; Pilot Officer E.H.L. Hadwen, Acting Adjutant; Pilot Officer J. Walters, Interpreter.

Polish – Major Zdzislaw Krasnodebski, Officer Commanding Squadron; Captain J. Giejsztowt, Signals; Captain Opulski, 'B' Flight Commander (see below); Captain W. Zyborski, Adjutant; Flying Officer Wiorkiewicz, Engineer.

Polish – ('A' Flight) Flying Officer Z. Henneburg, Flight Commander; Flying Officer W. Januszewicz, Pilot Officer M. Feric, Pilot Officer J. Zumbach, Sergeant S. Karubin, Sergeant E. Szaposznikow, Sergeant S. Wojtowicz, Sergeant Wunche.

Polish – ('B' Flight) Flying Officer W. Lapkowski, Flight Commander; Flying Officer L.W. Paszkiewicz, Pilot Officer J. Daszewski, Pilot Officer W. Lokuciewski, Sergeant M. Belc, Sergeant J. František, Sergeant P.P. Gallus, Sergeant K. Krawcynski.

Further reinforcements arrived on 4 August, with Flight Lieutenant A.S. Forbes taking up the role of B' Flight Commander (British). Meanwhile, during the day the first of the squadron's Polish pilots had their initial flying experience on the Hawker Hurricane.

Progress was remarkably fast, owing to the high standard of flying ability amongst the Polish pilots, many of whom had been pre-war instructors. Training almost immediately went from the basics to battle-climbs, tight formation flying and to mock combats.

No. 303 Squadron was placed at a state of 'Readiness for Action' on 17 August, attending the Dengie Flats on 19 & 20 August for gunnery practice. Meanwhile, on 19 August, Sergeant J. Rogowski arrived at the squadron, joining 'A' Flight. Earlier, on 13 August, Sergeant M. Wojciechowski and, on 16 August, Sergeant L. Switon, had arrived to augment 'B' Flight's ranks. A further influx of pilots arrived via Blackpool on 21 August, when Flight Lieutenant S. Pietraszkiewicz, Flying Officers M. Pisarek, Zak and M. Brzozwski, and Sergeants T. Andruszkow and J. Kania were all posted to the squadron. As part of this latter posting came Sergeant Jan Kowalski, who, having served his time as an instructor, was eager to get into the air and fight the Luftwaffe. There was new blood amongst the senior officers too, with the arrival of Flying Officer W. Ubanowicz from No. 145 Squadron, who took over as OC 'A' Flight, while Flight Lieutenant S. Pietraszkiewicz was appointed OC 'B' Flight.

Many of the Polish pilots had been in the country only a few weeks or months and had only a rudimentary grip of English. Jan Kowalski recalled that they quickly picked up the key Fighter Command phrases used over the radio in the air, adding: 'Our extended vocabulary largely came from watching American movies at the cinema. And with our Polish insignia being something of a novelty amongst the British, there was never a shortage of female company to encourage us to go to the movies.'

While Jan was a seasoned pilot, with experience on single and multiple engine aircraft, up until this time most of his flying hours were on biplanes. A study of the Hurricane's flying manual, and four short, but incident free flights in the squadron's Miles Master, under the supervision of Squadron Leader Kellett, meant he was able to progress onto the fighter: 'I went off in the Hurricane and enjoyed every minute of it.'

Polish pilots proved 'naturals' in the air, while their shooting abilities had been keenly demonstrated on the Dengie Flats, but they remained unproven as regards the use of Fighter Command's interception system. Ideally, an RAF officer would always lead a flight or section into combat, but this would put a terrible strain on the CO and his two British flight commanders.

Before they were allowed to fly mock interceptions in the air, the Poles were put through their paces on the ground. Jan Kowalski vividly recalled the scene. Equipped with tricycles, headsets and basic cockpit instruments, and with their forward vision impaired, the pilots were 'vectored' onto 'targets' within the confines of the parade ground. The exercise may have looked peculiar to an onlooker, but it had its merits in that the pilots became used to the system and more accustomed to Fighter Command's terminology, using words like 'Vector', 'Angels', 'Tally-ho', 'Pancake', etc. Naturally, the more they practiced, the greater their interception success rate, and the more natural their use of the code words.

The next step towards being allowed onto operations came on 24 August, when the squadron began flying defensive patrols alongside its training programme. Meanwhile, Keith Park, AOC No. 11 Group, requested that this be extended and that the squadron should be deployed in defending the Group's airfields while his squadrons were on operations. Group Captain S.F. Vincent, CO of RAF Northolt, however, was still concerned with the issue of the language barrier and the Pole's tendency to chatter over the intercom, and resisted the request. This stance was, however, soon to change.

No. 303 Squadron's role was revised as a result of an incident which occurred during the afternoon of 30 August. A training interception was in progress, targeting six Blenheims flying over the St Albans area when 'B' Flight ran into a dogfight between British fighters and a formation of sixty enemy bombers, and a similar number of their fighter escort, flying in an easterly direction at 14,000ft.

The Squadron Diary takes up the narrative:

'During this flight the squadron met the enemy in force over St Albans. One of the enemy aircraft, a Do 17, flying at some distance from the enemy formation, was attacked by Flying Officer Paszkiewicz, who, at a distance of 250 yards, opened fire on the enemy aircraft [closing to 100 yards]. The enemy's right engine took fire. The pilot bailed out by parachute.'

Although initially identified as a Dornier Do 17, it is thought that this aircraft was actually the Bf 110 piloted by Oberfeldwebel Georg Anthony, who was killed. His wireless operator/air-gunner, Unteroffizier Heinrich Nordmeyer, bailed out too low and was paralysed due to a heavy landing while his parachute was still deploying. The same aircraft was hit by No. 56 Squadron's Pilot Officer B.J. Wicks, who made his attack after Paszkiewicz's pass.

Flying Officer L.W. Paszkiewicz, whose radio appeared to malfunction, had tried to signal his intentions to the remainder of the Hurricanes by flying ahead of them and waggling his wings, before peeling off to make his attack. The Hurricanes, however, continued on their flight and escorted the Blenheims safely back to Northolt, preventing them from falling victim to the Bf 109s escorting the enemy raid.

Paszkiewicz was later summoned to his CO's office, where he was both reprimanded for breaking formation without permission, and congratulated on bringing down the squadron's first enemy aircraft.

As a result of the combat victory, No. 303 Squadron was made fully operational. This was one of the major turning points in the campaign, as would soon become apparent.

The squadron's second action came on the following day, 31 August. 'A' Flight was airborne at about 1810 hours and patrolling east of Biggin Hill at 14,000ft when they sighted a formation of sixty-plus enemy aircraft composed of Do 17s and their Bf 109 escort, above and to one side. Squadron Leader R.G. Kellet led his men into the attack, line astern and from out of the sun.

As they closed in, Red 1, Squadron Leader R.G. Kellett, led his section against three of the Bf 109 escort, firing several short bursts at one. The Messerschmitt swerved from one side to the other, before trying to climb out of trouble, but was suddenly engulfed in flames, rolled over and went down.

Flying close by his CO, Red 2, Sergeant S. Karubin, followed his Bf 109 in a dive, firing into the enemy aircraft, which leveled off. Karubin pressed the gun-button again, this time at 200 yards, his rounds registering and setting fire to the enemy fighter. The Messerschmitt went down in flames; there was no parachute.

Red 3, Sergeant E.M. Szaposznikow, focused his attention on the third Bf 109 of the formation, which half-rolled and dived for safety, with Szaposznikow in hot pursuit. The Pole got in a burst as the enemy aircraft leveled out and it fell away into cloud trailing smoke.

Meanwhile, Flying Officer Z. Henneberg climbed to attack four Bf 109s, which he chased, selecting a straggler, firing three bursts at 300 yards. The enemy aircraft crashed into the sea off Newhaven. Yellow 2, Pilot Officer M. Feric, joined Yellow 3, Sergeant K. Wunsche, in attacking a formation of Bf 109s, both shooting down an enemy fighter in flames.

Pilot Officer M. Feric fired only 160 rounds in a deadly pass made at close-range, his combat report reading:

'I was Yellow 2. After fifteen minutes flying we saw about 70 E/A to the northeast. On the way towards them Yellow Section met three Me 109s, which did not see us as we had the sun behind us. The surprise was complete. Each of us took one E/A. A higher section of Me 109s began to descend on us. I gave a short burst at my Me 109 from 70 yards at the fuselage and engine. The engine caught fire. The pilot bailed out and [the] E/A crashed in flames.'

The squadron had given a good account of itself in its first real encounter with the enemy, with the Polish pilots already using the tactic of getting as close as possible to the enemy before firing – this showed not only their bravery, but their combat awareness, as most fighter pilots misjudge their distance in their early combats and waste their ammunition outside their effective range. By waiting until the enemy filled their gun-sights, the Poles not only gained a greater success rate, but also conserved ammunition, and were often able to attack and damage, or destroy, multiple targets during the same sortie.

No. 79 Squadron, based at RAF Biggin Hill, was engaged with the same enemy formation. Their claims and losses may be summarized:

Pilot Officer D.W.A. Stones	one Do 215 destroyed, one Do 215 probably destroyed
Pilot Officer O.V. Tracey	one Do 215 destroyed
Pilot Officer W.H. Millington (flying P3050)	one Do 215 damaged

Pilot Officer W.H. Millington crash-landed on fire following combat with a Bf 109 over Romney at 1800 hours.

Pilot Officer E.J. Morris (flying P3877) crashed on landing with combat damage caused by return fire from a Do 17. Morris had already been wounded during the action.

No. 602 Squadron was assigned to patrol from Gravesend to Biggin Hill, making the following claims:

Sergeant D.W. Elcombe (flying L1040)	one Bf 109 destroyed
Flying Officer W.H. Coverly (flying X4162)	one Bf 109 probably destroyed
Pilot Officer H.M. Moody (flying P9446)	one Bf 109 probably destroyed
Sergeant J. Proctor	one Ju 88 destroyed

On 1 September, the enemy made a number of large raids, including one against RAF Biggin Hill and RAF Kenley, flown between 1330 and 1445 hours. No. 303 Squadron was scrambled at 1405 hours to patrol Northolt, but was held back by the controller and did not encounter the enemy.

The squadron was in action again on 2 September when they were scrambled at 1730 hours to intercept Raid No. 6 in the Chatham area (which was intercepted by No. 72 Squadron and later by No. 46 Squadron), before being vectored onto a second raid (Raid No. 17) approaching Dover at 19,000ft, which they engaged twenty minutes later, closely followed by No. 257 Squadron. Nine Bf 109s attempted to bounce No. 303 Squadron from out of the sun, but were spotted by Green 1, Sergeant J. Rogowski (flying R4217), acting as rearguard along with Green 2, Sergeant J. František (flying P3975).

Due to the attack from the Messerschmitts, Red Section was compelled to take avoiding action and lost sight of the bombers. Green 1, Sergeant J. Rogowski, made a head-on attack against the Bf 109s, breaking up their formation, before pursuing a Bf 109, which crashed in the sea ten miles from the French coast. Sergeant J. František chased another Bf 109 over the French coast, hitting the enemy aircraft in the engine and fuselage. The Messerschmitt, which had latched onto the tail of Flying Officer Z. Henneberg (flying V7246) before being warded off by František's fire, nose-dived into the sea, leaving only a trail of black smoke. Meanwhile, Yellow 1, Flying Officer Z. Henneberg, was drawing closer to the Bf 109 he was chasing, which by this time was nearly over the French coast, firing six bursts into the engine from 150 to 25 yards. The enemy aircraft lost height and speed, and was last seen trailing thick black smoke, with its engine clearly on fire. Flying Officer Henneberg and Sergeant J. František only turned back when enemy ack-ack made things too hot, and both were running short of fuel and ammunition.

Also following the enemy home was Sergeant J. Rogowski, who destroyed a Bf 109 ten miles off the French coast, the fighter being seen to plunge into the sea in flames.

Yellow 2, Pilot Officer M. Feric (flying R4178), overhauled his victim over the French coast, firing two bursts at 150 yards. The Messerschmitt turned over and dived vertically. Feric was forced to pull out of the attack due to his windscreen being obscured by oil, either from the Bf 109 or his own engine, which began emitting smoke. Turning the Merlin off, Feric skillfully glided back over the Channel, making a successful forced landing near Dover.

Of the other squadrons which engaged the same enemy formation, the following were reported:

No. 46 Squadron's claims and losses:

Pilot Officer C.F. Ambrose (flying P2965)	one Bf 109 destroyed (shared)
Sergeant E. Bloor (flying P3063)	one Bf 109 destroyed
Unknown pilots	two Bf 109s and two damaged
Flight Sergeant E.E. Williams (flying P3062)	one Do 215 damaged

Flight Lieutenant Rabagliati (flying P3597) forced-landed near Sittingbourne.

Pilot Officer J.C.L.D. Bailey (flying P3067) was killed while attempting a forced-landing at RAF Detling, following combat damage.

No. 72 Squadron's claims and losses:

Pilot Officer E.E. Males (flying K9940)	one Bf 109 destroyed
Sergeant B. Douthwaite	one Bf 109 damaged

Squadron Leader A.R. Collins' Spitfire, R6806, was damaged by a Bf 109 over the Thames estuary.

No. 257 Squadron made the following claim:

Sergeant R.C. Nutter (flying P3706)	one Bf 109 probably destroyed

The following day, 3 September, saw the squadron in action again, with several scrambles to deal with Bf 109s flying diversionary raids, the main thrust of the day's attacks focusing north of the Thames, only Nos. 1 and 303 Squadrons being called upon to operate south of the river.

While on patrol, the Hurricanes of Flying Officer Z. Henneberg (flying V7246) and Sergeant S. Wojtowicz (flying R2688) were bounced by a pair of Bf 109s over Dungeness. Wojtowicz was slightly injured in the combat and made a forced-landing.

No. 1 Squadron lost Pilot Officer R.H. Shaw[1] (flying P3782), shot down by a Bf 109 south of Maidstone at 1130 hours. At about the same time Flight Lieutenant H.B.L. Hillcoat[2] (flying P3044) was killed-in-action over Kent.

The squadron was in combat again when at 1540 hours, Sergeant J. František (flying R4175), flying as rearguard on a patrol between Maidstone and Dover, sighted a lone Bf 109 below the cloud base and went down to investigate. František put himself into an ideal attacking position before firing a two-second burst into the cockpit. The pilot must had been killed or severely wounded, as the Bf 109 was seen to plummet into the sea, mid-Channel.

During the mid-afternoon of 5 September, the Luftwaffe raided RAF Detling and Thameshaven. The controller scrambled Nos. 17, 46, 66, 72, 222, 249 and 501 Squadrons in order to counter the threat. These were reinforced by Nos. 41, 43, 73 and 601 Squadrons.

At 1456 hours the enemy crossed the coast near Dover in three formations. One turned back almost immediately, while another veered off towards Herne Bay. The third element, which was quickly reinforced by a further wave, came in over North Foreland, heading for the capital.

Squadron Leader R.G. Kellett (flying V7284) led the scramble, taking off at 1505 hours. Once airborne, the Hurricanes were vectored onto a formation of thirty-plus Ju 88s and their Bf 109 escort approaching the Thameshaven oil storage facility. Kellett ordered Red Section to tackle the nearest Messerschmitts, while Blue Section flew behind their protective cover and veered off to engage the bombers.

Red 1, Squadron Leader R.G. Kellett, claimed two Bf 109s destroyed. His combat report, timed at 1505 hours, read:

'I was leading the squadron at 22,000ft near Gillingham, and, seeing AA over the Thames, flew north and saw about thirty-five Ju 88s, escorted by Me 109s. About a dozen Me 109s came down and attacked us. I had manoeuvred up sun of the Me 109s, so my section, Red, took on these Me 109s, leaving the others to attack the bombers. I singled out one Me and did a number of short deflection shots, followed by a long burst from below and astern. [The] E/A caught fire and span down, covering me with oil. I was looking about for the rest of my section when I saw another Me 109. I was able to give it several deflection shots and saw the de Wilde ammunition bursting in the engine, which began to smoke, [the] E/A dived straight down.'

As he pursued the Ju 88s, Kellett's aircraft was exposed to the enemy fighters. Red 3, Sergeant K. Wunsche (flying V7289), saw a Bf 109 lining up on his CO's tail and slipped in behind the diving enemy fighter to fire a long and telling burst at 60 to 70 yards. The Bf 109 erupted into a fireball and fell into the Thames estuary.

Wunsche went on to destroy a second Bf 109 during the general melee. Meanwhile, Red 2, Sergeant S. Karubin (flying P3975), had followed his leader into the gaggle of Messerschmitts, firing at close-range and sending two of the enemy fighters down in flames.

The tenacity of Red Section's assault on the Bf 109 escort worked exactly as Kellett had planned and momentarily opened the door for Flight Lieutenant A.S. Forbes to lead Blue Section into an attack on the bombers. Blue 1, Flight Lieutenant Forbes, selected the left-hand Ju 88 from the rear-most vic of three, firing first from astern, before breaking off to make a pass from the starboard quarter; his final attack being from astern and setting the Ju 88's starboard engine on fire and sending the bomber down. Forbes only broke off the attack to defend himself against the attention of a Bf 109. Meanwhile, Flying Officer W. Lapkowski (flying P2985) focused on the lead Ju 88 of the same vic, firing from 150 yards and setting both engines on fire; the bomber dived earthwards. Lapkowski's Hurricane was targeted and set on fire by a Bf 109 and he was forced to bail out as the engine fire entered his cockpit. He landed near RAF Rochford, Southend, and was taken to Rochford Hospital, suffering from burns and a fractured upper arm:

'I went into attack nine to twelve Ju 88s in vics line astern with Flight Lieutenant Forbes. I fired at a Ju 88; No. 1 of the last vic, at 150 yards [and] the engine began to smoke. I broke off and tried unsuccessfully to find Blue 1. I at once made a second attack, firing at 150 yards and closing from above. Both engines were set on fire and [the] E/A began to dive. At this time I saw the aircraft at which Flight Lieutenant Forbes had been firing falling in such a great cloud of smoke that the aircraft became invisible. I am quite certain that this aircraft was destroyed. Then I was shot [at] by a cannon from behind. My engine caught fire. I turned over onto my back, opened the cockpit cover and, on getting out, I broke my left arm near the shoulder. I was also burnt in the face and left leg.'
(signed) Flying Officer W. Lapkowski.

Blue 3, Sergeant J. František (flying R4175), was momentarily diverted from the bombers when he turned his attention to saving the life of a Spitfire pilot who was about to be strafed in his parachute. František put a two-second burst into the cockpit of the Bf 109, which was seen to plummet into the water. He then attacked the right-hand bomber of the same vic formation, which he destroyed, but not without sustaining combat damage, probably from one of the escorting fighters.

Yellow Section, led by Squadron Leader Z. Krasnodebski (flying P3975), was unable to make any claims. Early on in the engagement they were bounced by an overwhelming force of enemy fighters from above and out of the sun. The section took evasive action, but when they recovered from their dive they were unable to rejoin the battle.

The Squadron Intelligence Officer's summary of the air battle concluded:

'There is little comment to be made concerning this action. The tactics employed by Squadron Leader Kellett did allow Blue Section to get in among the bombers, but the six Hurricanes were too small a force to make any sustained attack on the enemy bombers with so many Me 109s all around and above them.

'Squadron Leader Kellett went into action from a very good position, out of the sun, but the numbers of enemy fighters were soon able to reverse the advantage and the squadron was lucky only to lose one machine.'

The following squadrons were also engaged and made claims:

No. 17 Squadron recorded the following victories:

Squadron Leader A.G. Miller (flying P3033)	one He 111 probably destroyed (shared)
Flight Lieutenant A.W.A. Bayne (flying P3894)	one Bf 109 destroyed
Flying Officer M.B. Czernin (flying V7408)	one Bf 109 destroyed, one He 111 destroyed (shared), one He 111 probably destroyed (shared)
Pilot Officer G.E. Pittman (flying V6553)	one He 111 probably destroyed (shared)
Flight Sergeant C.A. Chew (flying P2794)	one He 111 destroyed (shared)
Sergeant L.H. Bartlett (flying P2994)	one He 111 probably destroyed (shared)
Sergeant G. Griffiths (flying P2972)	one He 111 probably destroyed (shared)

No. 46 Squadron recorded the following victory:

Flight Lieutenant A.C. Rabagliati (flying V7360)	one Bf 109 destroyed
Pilot Officer A.E. Johnson (flying P3053)	one Bf 109 destroyed
Sub-Lieutenant J.C. Carpenter (flying P3201)	one Bf 109 destroyed

No. 72 Squadron recorded the following victories:

Pilot Officer D.F. Holland (flying P9460)	one Bf 109 destroyed, one damaged

No. 73 Squadron recorded the following victories:

Squadron Leader M.W.S. Robinson (flying TP-B)	one He 111 probably destroyed
Sergeant G.W. Brimble (flying TP-K)	one He 111 damaged

No. 222 Squadron recorded the following victories and losses:

Sergeant D.J. Chipping (flying X4057)	one Bf 109 probably destroyed
Sergeant E. Scott (flying P9364)	two Bf 109s probably destroyed

Sergeant D.J. Chipping bailed out (wounded) when his Spitfire was damaged by the Dover Barrage while in combat with Bf 109s at 1500 hours.

No. 249 Squadron recorded the following victories and losses:

Pilot Officer H.J.S. Beazley (flying V6635)	one Bf 109 probably destroyed
Sergeant H.J. Davidson (flying P3667)	one Bf 109 probably destroyed
Sergeant W.L. Davis (flying V6614)	one Do 17 damaged
Sergeant R. Smithson (flying P2863)	one Do17 probably destroyed, one Do17 damaged

Flight Lieutenant R.A. Barton (flying V6625) bailed out following combat with a Bf 109 over Shell Haven at 1530 hours.

No. 501 Squadron recorded the following victories:

Sergeant R.J.K. Gent (flying P5194)	one Bf 109 probably destroyed
Sergeant J.H. Lacey (flying P8816)	two Bf 109s destroyed

Nos. 249 and 303 Squadrons were scrambled at about 0840 hours on 6 September, engaging a large formation of Ju 88s of II./KG 76, along with Do 215s, Do 17s, He 111s and their escort of Bf 109s. The enemy was intercepted over Sevenoaks. Squadron Leader R.G. Kellett (flying V7284) put the squadron into a climb to attack, but the Hurricanes were bounced by unseen Bf 109s.

No. 303 Squadron succeeded in destroying one Do 215, an He 111 and five Bf 109s, with two more claimed as probably destroyed. Their poor initial position, due to lack of altitude relative to the bombers and their fighter escort, however, resulted in damage to five Hurricanes.

Squadron Leader R.G. Kellett's combat report read:

'This was the biggest formation I have seen. It covered an area twenty miles by five. There were many big planes, Dorniers, He 111s and some four-engined. There were the usual Me 110s among them, and formations of Me 109s up to 25,000ft. Fully 300 to 400 E/A. I manoeuvred to do a quarter head–on attack on the bombers. I put a long burst into the port engine of a Do 215, and saw it commence to smoke. Then I did a quarter astern attack and the engine caught fire. Just as I was about to break away, a series of explosions took place in my aircraft. After diving, I realized that it was very difficult to control the aircraft as there was a big hole in the starboard wing [where his ammunition

box had exploded], and the aircraft was flying with [its] starboard wing very low. There was no elevator control and not much rudder control. I managed to get the aircraft down to 140mph and keep it under control with the stick hard back and over to port. Finding Biggin Hill close, I made a landing with the undercarriage down, but without flaps. I returned to Northolt in the evening.'
(signed) Squadron Leader R.G. Kellett

Meanwhile, Yellow 2, Flying Officer W. Urbanowicz, shot down the Bf 109 of Hauptmann Schlichting, reporting:

'I was Yellow Two. With Squadron Leader Krasnodebski [at its head] the section went in to attack. I saw Me 109s and Hurricanes flying across from left to right on each other's tail. One Me 109 then attacked me from starboard. We had a short dogfight. I fired three or four 4-second bursts at 200 yards. The engine caught fire and E/A fell vertically to earth. I circled and attacked a bomber. One Me 109 was in the way and two more attacked me. I had a dogfight with the three Me 109s.'

Yellow 3, Flying Officer M. Feric (flying P3700), destroyed the Bf 109 piloted by Oberleutnant Schüller (missing):

'Suddenly, an Me 109 painted white from his nose to the end of the cockpit zoomed up. I caught him head-on and fired three short bursts at 200-250 yards. He burst into flames and fell to the ground.'
(signed) Pilot Officer Ferric.

Blue 1, Flight Lieutenant A.S. Forbes (flying R4179), closed to within 200 yards of a Bf 109, which he hit with an accurate burst and it was seen to go down. Pulling away he latched onto a second enemy fighter, which he damaged, seeing strikes in the cockpit area before he was forced to pull out of the attack when his own aircraft was hit from astern. A cannon shell entered the cockpit, wounding Forbes and spraying him with petrol. Forbes tried to land, but overshot the field and crash-landed.

Blue 3, Sergeant František, got a Bf 109, firing from the rear quarter, sending it careering out of control, streaming flames and smoke from its engine. František was then attacked by two Bf 109s, but was able to evade their attention, only suffering one round through the tail. He landed at RAF Northolt where his aircraft was quickly repaired.

Sergeant J. František's (flying R4175) combat report recorded the destruction of a Bf 109 over Sevenoaks:

'I was Blue 3. While flying in line astern I noticed two E/A, one of which I attacked from a deflected rear position and fired a burst at a distance of about 150 yards. [The] E/A then dived and I again fired across his cockpit. [The] E/A then turned on his back and dived towards the ground, flames issuing

from the right of his engine. In the meantime I was attacked by two other E/A and hit in the tail. I evaded them and returned to Northolt.'
(signed) Sergeant J. František.

Yellow 1, Squadron Leader Z. Krasnodebski (flying P3974), was badly burned and forced to bail out when his aircraft was hit by cannon shells south of Bexley at 0920 hours. He was sent to Farnborough Hospital and replaced as CO (Polish) by Squadron Leader W. Urbanowicz. Meanwhile, Squadron Leader R.G. Kellett also received wounds and two other pilots were injured.

Sergeant S. Karubin (flying V7290) shot down an He 111, before he fell victim to a Bf 109. He crash-landed at 0915 hours near Pembury and was taken to Pembury Hospital, where his injuries were understood to be slight.

Red 3, Sergeant K. Wunsche (flying 7289), fired a four-second burst into a Bf 109 which was attacking another Hurricane, a second Bf 109 made a head-on attack and the two entered a duel vying for position, out-turning each other until Wunsche fired a two-second burst hitting the Bf 109's engine. The enemy aircraft went down and Wunsche turned his attention to the Hurricane pilot, who was by then descending in his parachute. Wunsche circled the parachute until it nearly reached the ground.

The squadron's claims were recorded in their Operational Record Book (ORB):

'Squadron Leader Kellett (force-landed, wounded), one Do 215
Squadron Leader Krasnodebski, (shot down, wounded and burned)
Flight Lieutenant Forbes, (force-landed, wounded) one Bf 109, one Bf 109 damaged
Flying Officer Feric, one Bf 109, one probable Bf 109
Flying Officer Urbanowicz, one Bf 109
Sergeant František (own aircraft damaged), one Bf 109
Sergeant Karubin (shot down, wounded), one He 111'

The squadron's Intelligence Officer, Flying Officer E.M. Hadwin, noted that the squadron's problems had not been limited to their lack of altitude and airspeed when they were bounced by the enemy:

'As soon as the squadron went into the attack, large numbers of Me 109s dived down from many directions and the squadron broke up. Interference on the R/T had been bad and intercommunication in the squadron was impossible.'

Meanwhile, Squadron Leader J. Grandy (flying R4229) led No. 249 Squadron into the attack, sharing a Bf 109 with Pilot Officer J.H.S. Beazley (flying V6628). Pilot Officer J.R.B. Meaker (flying P5206) claimed two Bf 109s. Sergeant J.M. Bentley-Beard (flying V7313) destroyed a Bf 109, with Flight Lieutenant D.G. Parnall (flying V6559) and Pilot Officer Beazley each probably destroying a Bf 109. During the same air battle Flying Officer P.H.V. Wells (flying P3594) and Pilot Officer R.D.S. Fleming (flying P3579) damaged a Bf 109.

No. 249 Squadron's Pilot Officer Barclay wrote of Kellett:

'The CO was in hospital with some torn muscles in his leg and minor cannon shell wounds. Apparently the squadron was told to re-form at 15,000ft over Eastchurch. The CO, on getting the rendezvous, was told to pancake and as they dived down he was shot up by 109s. As is usually the case, he didn't see what got him.'

No. 1 Squadron also engaged the same formation which earlier had been mauled by No. 303 Squadron, with the following claims and losses:

Pilot Officer R.H. Dibnah (flying P3169)	one Bf 109 destroyed
Pilot Officer G.E. Goodman (flying P2686)	one Bf 109 probably destroyed
Pilot Officer C.M. Statvert (flying P3042)	one Ju 88 destroyed
Flight Lieutenant M.H. Brown (flying L1934)	one Ju 88 damaged

Pilot Officer G.E. Goodman bailed out following combat with a Bf 110 south of Penshurst, Kent, at 0930 hours, safe.

Retiring after their encounter, No. 303 Squadron landed and refuelled and rearmed, ready for their next encounter with the enemy, but there only followed an uneventful patrol between 1310 and 1355 hours, the Luftwaffe raiding targets on the east coast of Kent. Their third operation of the day was against a raid on Thameshaven and was made in the company of No. 1 Squadron between 1725 and 1910 hours. During the patrol Flying Officer W. Januszewicz was shot down at Lenham, Kent, when he tried to tackle three Bf 109s.

No. 303 Squadron was in combat again on the following day, 7 September, when the capital was once again the target in a raid which saw the beginning of the London Blitz.

Scrambled at 1620 hours, the squadron went into a battle-climb and rendezvoused with No. 1 Squadron to engage a force of forty Do 17s, with their escort of Bf 109s flying above and behind. Leading the squadron at 17,000ft, Flight Lieutenant A.S. Forbes (flying R4217) was able to position the Hurricanes above and partially up sun of the enemy to attack the bombers quarter head-on and out of the sun.

Flight Lieutenant A.S. Forbes' report read:

'We were ordered into the air to rendezvous with No. 1 Squadron who took off first. We were sent up to 15,000ft and then to 20,000ft, and proceeded north and then east. No. 1 Squadron remained below us to starboard and in front. I led the squadron up to 24,000ft determined, after our experience yesterday, not to be caught napping at too low an altitude. It is easy to get down to the enemy, and impossible to attack climbing, when the slow speed makes one an easy prey to the Me 109s. I sighted a formation of about forty enemy bombers flying northwards. Their rear-guard of Me 109s were engaged with Spitfires at 25,000-30,000ft. No. 1 Squadron went in to attack the enemy's tail and drew off the remaining fighter escort. It was a perfect combination of circumstances. We were in vics line astern. The AA fire had loosened their formation. As soon as No. 1 Squadron attacked, the enemy wheeled eastwards, and we caught them on the turn. We re-formed towards the enemy and launched the attack in vics breast, striking the formation a little to the rear of centre. They were easy meat. We came at them from partially up sun at a great speed as they turned away from us. I led in, and attacked a Do 215, hitting the starboard wing. Great chunks fell off the wing and engine, which stopped. I gave another good burst into the cockpit and more stuff fell off. [The] E/A fell away sideways in a long glide and hit the sea. I broke away and whilst in a steep turn, a shell hit my starboard wing root and exploded. I felt my leg was wounded, and there were three or four glycol and hydraulic system leaks in the cockpit. I decided to try to return to an aerodrome, and get the machine down whole. I succeeded in regaining Northolt, and landing without mishap.'

Flight Lieutenant A.S. Forbes' wounds were not severe enough to take him off operations for long, and he was quickly back in action leading the squadron.
Meanwhile, Flying Officer L.W. Paszkiewicz (flying V7235) reported:

'At a height of 25,000ft I saw a formation of enemy bombers being attacked by our fighters. I joined them and attacked a Do 215, firing at very close-range. He burst into flames and fell to earth. I then attacked another Do 215 [using the remainder of his ammunition] which burst into flames and both his engines stopped.'

Green 2, Pilot Officer W. Lokuciewaki (flying P3972), filed his combat report, which read:

'When at 20,000ft I noticed enemy bombers flying to the right, being attacked by fighters flying about 1,000ft above them. I attacked a Do 215 and fired from a distance of about 300 yards. [The] E/A began to flame and fell to [the] ground. I then attacked another Do 215, and first saw one and then another engine smoking. I was attacked by two Me 109s and had to break off the engagement.'

Sergeant E. Szaposznikow (flying V7244) reported:

'I attacked a formation of Do 215s, firing two bursts [at] one E/A [which] burst into flames and fell to earth. I dived and having satisfied myself that [the] E/A was finished I pulled out of the dive and made a climbing attack on an Me 109 from a forward position. He also burst into flames and fell to earth.'

Flying Officer W. Urbanowicz (flying R2685), in his debriefing, reported:

'I saw an enemy bomber breaking away from his formation and attacked him from about 300 yards. I drew nearer and firing three bursts [and] saw him burst into flames. I then saw him crash to earth and burn on the ground. Next I attacked an Me 109 and, after firing several bursts at close-range, his engine began to smoke furiously.'

Urbanowicz was unable to confirm the 'kill' as he was forced to disengage when his Hurricane was attacked from astern by another Bf 109.

Flying Officer Z. Henneberg (flying V6605) engaged the enemy, before landing at RAF Detling, short of fuel. His combat report read:

'I attacked a formation of Do 215s, firing three bursts at [the] E/A on port side. My engine began to falter and I fell back a little where I was engaged by three Me 109s. My engine now working normally, I attacked the 109s. After a few seconds one began to smoke, but I had to break away as I was being attacked from the rear. I climbed and met another formation of Me 109s. I attacked from the rear and, after firing two bursts, saw [the] E/A burst into flames and fall to earth.'

Sergeant Pilot S. Wojtowicz (flying V7290) fired all of his ammunition into two Do 215s which he destroyed:

'I attacked a group of Do 215s not in any formation and, after firing three bursts, saw both engines of one E/A catch fire and then the whole machine burst into flames and fell to earth. Turning slightly to the left I found another Do 215 in my sight. I fired a few short bursts and saw his right wing burst into flames near the cockpit. He turned on his right side and fell to earth.'

Pilot Officer J.E.L. Zumbach (flying V7242) reported:

'After contacting [the] enemy bombers I attacked one and fired from a distance of 50 yards a burst of about four seconds. [The] E/A's starboard engine burst into flames, [and the] aircraft went into a spin and fell to earth. I climbed and perceived a Do 215. I attacked and fired from about 30 yards. [The] E/A caught fire and dived to earth. I followed to about 10,000ft [and] watched [the] E/A crash.'

Flying Officer A.S. Forbes later wrote how the success of this combat was due to there being Spitfires above, while No. 1 Squadron was to starboard and made the initial attack, thus drawing off the remaining fighters. This allowed No. 303 Squadron to catch the enemy on the turn at great speed from above, and out of the sun.

Once engaged, the squadron fired short bursts at under 300 yards to shake the enemy air-gunners before closing until the enemy's cockpit or engine filled the gun-sight. They then fired short and accurate bursts down to point-blank range. Forbes noted that their fire ripped great pieces out of the bombers and generally disabled them in a single pass.

Following the debriefing, the squadron's intelligence officer noted the following scores:

'Flight Lieutenant Forbes	one Do 215, one Do 215 probable
Flight Lieutenant Paszkiewicz *[sic]*	two Do 17s
Flying Officer Henneberg	one Me 109 and one Me 109 probable
Flying Officer Pisarek [flying R4173]	(bailed out, shot down by Bf 109) – one Me 109
Pilot Officer Daszewski [flying P3890]	(wounded) one Do 215, one Do 17 probable
Pilot Officer Lokuciewski	one Do 215, one Do 215 probable
Pilot Officer Urbanowicz	one Do 215, one Me 109 probable
Pilot Officer Zumbach	two Do 215s
Sergeant Szaposznikow	one Do 215, one Me 109
Sergeant Wojtowicz	two Do 215s'

The skill, courage and determination of every pilot on the squadron, and the devotion to duty of the ground staff, was undisputable, and the units tally was rapidly outstriping the highest scoring RAF squadrons. Their score rate initially concerned Group Captain Vincent. Believing that the Poles might be getting carried away, as their constant 'chatter' over the radio might have suggested, and inadvertently over-claiming, Vincent accompanied them on a scramble. Group Captain Vincent witnessed at first hand how, during a combat, the Polish pilots closed in on their enemy before firing well-aimed bursts at close range. This left him in no doubt of the accuracy of their shooting and their claims.

No. 303 Squadron's success had its downside for a relative latecomer like Jan – it had proved almost impossible to get a spare Hurricane.

Sergeant Jan Kowalski (flying V7289) made his first operational sortie on 9 September, when No. 303 Squadron, in the company of No. 1 (RCAF) Squadron, was scrambled at 1725 hours. Vectored towards the coast, the wing engaged the enemy over Beachy Head at 1800 hours, when about forty Ju 88s and their escort of Bf 110 and Bf 109s were seen retiring from an earlier raid.

The enemy was escaping southwards at speed, while losing height, when they were sighted by Flight Lieutenant J.A. Kent (flying V6665 RF-J), who positioned the Hurricanes for the attack. Kent closed in, firing two bursts at a Ju 88, leaving its starboard engine in flames. During the pursuit, Pilot Officer Z. Henneberg (V6667 RF-K), kept a Bf 109 off Kent's tail, before a second Messerschmitt had his Hurricane in its sights. Meanwhile, Kent then saw a Bf 110, which he also chased and shot down mid-Channel:

'The starboard engine blew to bits. He was obviously badly hit and turned back towards England. I did a fast turn and found a 109 intent on evening the score.'

Kent was able to out-turn the Bf 109 and gave it two bursts, forcing the fighter to turn for home: 'By this time the 110 was getting very low and the smoke from its starboard engine was getting thicker. The Bf 110 was ten miles off Dungeness when it hit the water and exploded.'

Pilot Officer J.E.L. Zumbach (flying P2685), was attacked by Bf 109s, one of which he destroyed. It was last seen to disappear into cloud, while Zumbach caught another as it banked in front of him, firing a burst into the cockpit and engine from above at thirty yards. He saw his tracer hit as the enemy aircraft rolled on its back and fell away:

> 'I saw a bomber being attacked by a Hurricane (Sergeant František). This Hurricane was being attacked by two Me's, and escaped into cloud. I looked and saw one fighter in front of me. I gave it a two-second burst, and from the starboard wing root many pieces fell off and the E/A burst into flames.'

Zumback was then attacked by five Bf 109s, which he fought off, getting a short burst at one which turned onto its back and disappeared into cloud, leaving a trail of smoke.

Sergeant J. František (flying P3975) destroyed a Bf 109, which was targeting another Hurricane, before claiming an He 111. František's Hurricane was shot – by machine gun – in the radiator, fuselage and port wing, and he made a forced landing in a cabbage field beside the Downs Hotel, one-and-a-half miles north-east of Woodingdean, Brighton:

> 'I saw one Me 109 going in to attack a Hurricane in front of me, I attacked it, starboard beam, firing at 150/100 yards at the engine, which began to burn. He tried to escape by climbing, and I saw him open the cockpit preparing to jump. I shot at the cockpit and the pilot collapsed. The E/A fell in flames to the ground (Horsham area). I went for an He 111, and two Me 109s attacked me.'

František disappeared into cloud, re-emerging to attack one of the bombers:

> 'I came out of cloud, and saw in front of me, ten yards away, also coming out of the cloud, an He 111. I very nearly collided with it, and fired at the front of the fuselage at an angle of 45 degrees from above and behind. The front of the E/A fell to pieces, with the cockpit and both engines in flames.'

František was then attacked by a Bf 109 which hit his Hurricane with four cannon shells, in the port wing, left petrol tank, radiator and seat armour. Fortunately, two Spitfires were on hand to shoot the Messerschmitt down.

Meanwhile, Sergeant K. Wunsche (flying P3700 RF-E) was forced to bail out of his burning Hurricane at 1755 hours, following combat with Bf 109s over Beachy Head. He was admitted to Hove Hospital, wounded in the back and arm, and suffering from slight burns.

The squadron suffered further losses. Pilot Officer J. Daszewski (flying P3890) was severely wounded and bailed out following combat with a Bf 109 over the Thames estuary at 1700 hours. His Hurricane crashed near Loughton, Essex. He was taken to Wildersham Hospital, near Dover. Meanwhile, Flying Officer M. Pisarek (flying R4173), bailed out, safe, following combat with a Bf 109 at 1705 hours while over Loughton, Essex.

Not all of the squadron was able to close to within range. Although Nos. 1 and 603 Squadrons were left out of position, and unable to overhaul the enemy en masse, they were nevertheless able to open the way for No. 303 Squadron to attack the bombers by drawing their fighter cover off into a series of dogfights.

No. 1 Squadron made the following claims:

Flight Lieutenant Holderness (flying V7301)	one Do 215 destroyed
Sergeant A.V. Clowes (flying P3395)	one Bf 109 damaged

No. 603 Squadron made the following claim:

Pilot Officer J.S. Morton (flying X4347)	one He 111 damaged

Nos. 46, 73, 234 and 609 Squadron were scrambled against the same formation, but were unable to make any claims.

Also engaging the raid were Nos. 222, 242, 253 and 310 Squadrons:

No. 222 Squadron made the following claims:

Flying Officer T.A. Vigors (flying X4058)	one Bf 109 destroyed
Pilot Officer J.W. Broadhurst (flying P9469)	one Bf 109 damaged
Pilot Officer H.L. Whitbread (flying N3203)	one Bf 109 destroyed
Sergeant E. Scott (flying P9364)	one Bf 109 damaged

No, 242 Squadron made the following claims:

Squadron Leader D.R.S. Bader (flying P3090)	one Do 17 destroyed
Flight Lieutenant G.E. Ball (flying P3048)	one Bf 109 destroyed
Flight Lieutenant G.S.ff. Powell-Sheddon (flying P3213)	one Do 215 destroyed
Pilot Officer C.R. Bush (flying P3054)	one Bf 110 destroyed
Pilot Officer J.B. Latta (flying V3485)	one Bf 109 destroyed
Pilot Officer W.I. McKnight (flying P2961)	two Bf 109s destroyed
Pilot Officer H.N. Tamblyn (flying R4115)	two Bf 110s destroyed
Sergeant R.E.V.H. Lonsdale (flying P2831)	one Do 215 destroyed
Sergeant E. Richardson (flying P2967)	one Do 215 destroyed

No. 253 Squadron made the following claims:

Unknown pilots	four Ju 88s destroyed

No. 310 Squadron made the following claims:

Flight Lieutenant G.L Sinclair	one Do 17 destroyed
Pilot Officer V. Bergman (flying V7405)	one Bf 110 destroyed
Pilot Officer S. Fejfar	one Bf 110 destroyed
Pilot Officer F. Rypl	one Bf 109 probably destroyed
Pilot Officer S. Zimprich	one Bf 110 damaged, one Do 17 destroyed
Sergeant J. Hubacek	one Bf 110 probably destroyed

No. 303 Squadron was scrambled again at 1650 hours, on 10 September. A Ju 88 was sighted during their patrol, but was too far away to be engaged.

Flight Lieutenant A.S. Forbes (flying V7465) led the squadron on a scramble at 1520 hours on 11 September, forming up with No. 229 Squadron, which had relieved No. 1 (RCAF) Squadron two days earlier. The wing's orders were to patrol Biggin Hill. Vectored onto a raid approaching the Tunbridge Wells area, Flying Officer Paskiewicz (flying V7235) was the first to sight the enemy formation, which was by then over Horsham, and was composed of about 150 Do 215s and He 111s, with Bf 110s above, and Bf 109s around and up to 25,000ft. The Hurricanes entered into combat at 1600 hours, as later reported by their intelligence officer:

'The Squadron went on patrol to intercept enemy raiders coming from the south-east towards London, leading No. 229 Squadron.

'When they met the enemy, No. 229 Squadron, which was below and to their right, went straight in to attack the enemy bombers head-on.

'No. 303 Squadron wheeled round and attacked the centre and rear of the enemy formation, which appears to have been about fifty He 111s and thirty to forty Do 215s strong, while Yellow Section of No. 303 Squadron attacked the fighter escort above No. 229 Squadron. It also appears that at least one other squadron was engaged with enemy fighters at a higher altitude.

'It seems clear from the reports that these attacks broke up the enemy formation, and from conversations with pilots, large quantities of the bombs seem to have been jettisoned in wooded country some twenty-five miles south of London.

'Flying Officer Cebrzynski jumped and fell near Pembury – his parachute did not open. It is believed that he was wounded – if not killed – as he was getting out.'

During the combat Blue 1, Flight Lieutenant A.S. Forbes (flying 7465), claimed two Do 215s. His combat report read:

'The Squadron took off with orders to lead No. 229 Squadron. We climbed up to 19,000ft and were eventually vectored on 50 degrees. We were due north of the enemy when sighted, and turned south, attacking from the east – up sun. We were actually being vectored across the enemy's bow, and it was the wonderful eyesight of the Polish that spotted them some six/seven miles on our right.

'Pilot Officer Paszkiewicz [sic] [flying V7235] spoke to me by R/T and wheeled round. Perceiving that No. 229 Squadron were below and going in to attack the bombers, he led his section to engage the escort fighters above them. I brought up the rear of the squadron after we wheeled. I therefore fired onto the middle of the bomber formation, which was now below me. There were sixty to eighty of them flying in vics of three and five line astern, with the Me 110s above and Me 109s around and above them, stepped up to over 25,000ft.

'As I dived into the attack I saw the crew of the bomber in the middle of the formation bail out, and as far as I could see, they were not being attacked (this is not the first time that members of my squadron have noticed a similar phenomenon, and we have also remarked that the German crews open their parachutes immediately, although they may be a great height up). I took on the left-hand bomber of a section and dived right in on the port wing and engine, which came adrift. I had difficulty in avoiding the wing tip and drew out in order to attack the right-hand bomber of the next section. In fact the slipstream of the bomber which I had just destroyed, threw me so far out, that when I turned in again I found myself in the ideal position to attack the third machine up the line. This left the bomber immediately in front of the destroyed one on my tail. I nevertheless pressed home the attack, and got in a very good burst from about 100 yards on the port engine, wing root, and cockpit. Large chunks fell away from all three, and the E/A immediately swung sharply to the left with its nose dropping. At this moment, I received a severe blow in the back of the right arm, and right thigh. My arm was thrown forward, and I went into a steep dive. When I neared ground level I started to return to base, flying with my left hand. On nearing Heston I began to feel faint and effected a landing. After treatment, I was driven back to Northolt. My machine, after small repairs, is being brought back.'
(signed) Flight Lieutenant A.S. Forbes.

Blue 2, Sergeant J. František (flying V7289), destroyed a Bf 109, damaging an He III H-2 (5548: A1 + DS), killing one crew member and wounding two others. Before returning to base he finished off his ammunition on another Messerschmitt Bf 109:

'While being attacked by Me 109s I made a sharp turn and got onto one of their tails. I fired one burst from 150 yards, and E/A burst into flames.

'After the attack I found myself going into cloud and, on emerging from clouds, I was near an He 111. I chased it, and began firing at close-range, and the starboard engine burst into flames, and E/A fell into sea.

'On my return journey I ran into an Me 109 which I attacked. I saw it smoking and flaming, but had to break off the engagement and return to Northolt, as I had no more ammunition.'

Yellow 1, Flying Officer Z. Henneberg (flying P3939 RF-H), destroyed an He 111 and a Bf 109:

'While chasing enemy bombers, I was attacked by four Me 109s. I engaged them with my section, but they retired. Flying further on, I was passed by one Me 109 which I attacked from the side and set on fire. I was then attacked by three Me 109 and in evading them I ran into an He 111 returning to France. After several bursts I stopped both of his engines and he forced-landed not far from the sea in a damaged condition.'

Yellow Section's Pilot Officer J.E.L. Zumbach (flying R2685) reported:

'My section was attacked by Me 109s. I engaged one and, after firing one or two bursts, he dived into the clouds. I flew further along and noticed an Me 109, presumably damaged, making his way home. I easily overtook him and, after my firing about 100 rounds, he burst into flames and crashed to earth. I then joined two Hurricanes, and we attacked five Me 110s. The Hurricanes broke off the engagement through lack of ammunition, I was left alone, and, having run out of ammunition and being short of petrol, I succeeded in evading the E/A and landing at Biggin Hill to refuel, after which I returned to Northolt.'

Yellow 3, Sergeant E. Szaposznikow (flying V7244), claimed two Bf 110s destroyed:

While flying south-east of London our section was broken up by three Me 109s. Seeing that they were being attacked by five Hurricanes, I turned my attention to the enemy bombers. At the end of the bomber formation, I noticed two Me 110s, which I attacked. The right-hand E/A soon went into a spin with both his engines in flames. The rest of my ammunition I emptied into the right engine of the remaining E/A at very close range, and he also fell in flames.'

Red 3, Sergeant M. Brzezowski (flying V6665 RF-J), claimed two He 111s:

'While flying south-east of London we saw and attacked a number of He 111s. I engaged one and fired a burst from about 100 yards. [The] E/A immediately burst into flames and dived to earth.

'At that moment, I noticed bullets flying past my cockpit. I immediately dived, and in pulling out noticed an He 111 which I attacked and fired four bursts from a distance of about 150 yards. It burst into flames and one of the crew jumped. [The] E/A began to dive to earth. At the same time I noticed a Hurricane on fire. The pilot jumped and, as there were a number of E/A in the vicinity, I circled round the pilot in order to protect him. As my engine seemed to be covered with oil and smoking badly, and also labouring, I prepared to jump, but seeing that there was no danger of the plane catching fire immediately, I landed at Croydon.

'There is a small bullet hole in the port wing of my aircraft. I know that Cebrzynski has been killed and Sergeant Wojtowicz [flying V7242] is missing. After the fight began I saw nothing of either of them. From the direction of our attack I do not think that Sergeant Wojtowicz would have fallen in the sea.'

Green 1, Flying Officer L.W. Paszkiewicz (flying V7235), destroyed a Bf 110:

'Our formation was flying easterly towards Tunbridge Wells. On our left, a little lower, No. 229 Squadron was flying. I noticed to the right of our course bursts [of] AA, and after a bit a large formation of E/A flying north-north-west. I told Blue Leader over the radio and went to the front and led the formation towards the enemy.

'Whereas 229 Squadron was lower, I left them the bombers and attacked the fighters protecting them.

'I was drawn into combat with an Me 110 which I set on fire, but as I was firing from quite a considerable distance away – about 300 yards – I used up all of my ammunition and had to withdraw from combat.'

Green 2, Pilot Officer W. Lokuciewski (flying L2099), destroyed a Bf 109 and a Do 215:

'I was attacked from the front by two Me 109s, which I engaged, and after a short while one burst into flames, and fell into the sea. Returning, having climbed to 12,000ft, I noticed a Do 215 returning to France. I attacked three-quarter from the rear, and after the fifth burst E/A was set on fire and one of the crew jumped out.'

Sergeant S. Wojtowicz (flying V7242 RF-B) engaged six Bf 109s, two of which he destroyed before his aircraft was riddled with bullets and set on fire. Wojtowicz was killed when his Hurricane crashed into Hogtrough Hill, near Westerham. He was posthumously awarded the VM 5th Class. Sergeant Stefan Wojtowicz was 24-years-old.

The squadron also lost Flying Officer Arsen Cebrzynski (flying V6665), who bailed out dead from his Hurricane, which was hit by return fire from an He 111 over Billericay at 1620 hours. Flying Officer Arsen Cebrzynski was 28-years-old.

In a Supplementary Intelligence Patrol report, Flying Officer E.M. Hadwin noted:

'Yesterday, 13.9.40, I went to Westerham and saw the body of Sergeant Wojtowicz – he had been shot in the forehead by a cannon shell and crashed in flames two miles east of Westerham village. Several of the local Special Police stated that they had seen his Hurricane fighting with a number of Me 109s and Me 110s over the hills to the west of Westerham at about 1630 hours on 11.9.40.

'During the few minutes of the combat two Me 109s crashed in the neighbourhood of Westerham, and there is reason to believe that they were accounted for by Sergeant S. Wojtowicz, but no claim has been put in.

'Flying Officer A. Cebrzynski was shot in many places, and one leg was blown completely off. It appears most likely that his harness was severed, and that he fell out of the aeroplane when it turned upside down, it is obvious that he could have been in no position to try to open his parachute.'

No. 229 Squadron made the following claims, mainly in the Reigate – Ramsgate area, suffering losses over Maidstone and Biggin Hill:

Flight Lieutenant W.A. Smith	one He 111 destroyed, shared with three Spitfires
Pilot Officer K.M. Carver (flying N2466)	two He 111s damaged
Pilot Officer J.M.F. Dewar	one He 111 probably destroyed, one Ju 88 damaged
Pilot Officer G.L.J. Doutrepont	one He 111 destroyed (shared), one Do 215 destroyed (shared), one Bf 110 damaged (shared)
Pilot Officer J.W. Hyde	one Do 215 destroyed (shared)
Pilot Officer R.F. Rimmer	one He 111 probably destroyed
Pilot Officer E. Smith	one He 111 probably destroyed
Pilot Officer V.B.S. Verity	one Bf 110 damaged (shared), one Bf 110 damaged

Pilot Officer K.M. Carver (flying N2466), hit by return fire from He 111 and bailed out over Maidstone at 1620 hours, burned.

Pilot Officer M. Ravenhill (flying P3038), bailed out over Biggin Hill at 1600 hours.

Sergeant Kowalski made two uneventful patrols on 14 September and was in the air again twice on the following day, 15 September. The first of these sorties was made at 1120 hours, when No. 303 Squadron was scrambled with orders to rendezvous with No. 229 Squadron and patrol Biggin Hill. The wing was vectored towards south London, where they located a large enemy formation at 20,000ft. The enemy turned south and evaded action. A second formation, composed of twenty Do 215s in loose vics of five, and 'swarms' of Bf 109s, came into sight, approaching from the south. No. 303 Squadron turned, with No. 229 Squadron following, allowing the enemy to cross their front before wheeling east and then south. Because of the disposition of the formations, most of No. 303 Squadron's Hurricanes could only attack the enemy's rear guard, with only one section overhauling the bombers as they neared Folkestone.

Flight Lieutenant J.A. Kent and several other pilots had momentary contacts with Bf 109s, firing only short bursts, seeing their ammunition hit, but were unable to make any claims.

Meanwhile, Flying Officer Z. Henneberg (flying P3120), destroyed one Do 215 and a Bf 109, and two other pilots helped Spitfires to destroy another of the bombers. Flying Officer L.W. Paszkiewicz (flying V7235) and Pilot Officers M. Feric (flying R2685), J.E.L. Zumbach (flying P3577) and M. Pisarek (flying V7465) each destroyed a Bf 109, as did Sergeant M. Wojciechowski (flying V6673), who also shared a Do 215 with Sergeant T. Andruszkow (flying P3939). Sergeant J. František (flying R3089) got a Bf 110. The squadron's only casualty was Pilot Officer W. Lokuciewski (flying P2003), who was wounded in the leg while engaging a Bf 109.

Yellow 1, Flying Officer Z. Henneberg, attacked a Do 215 which had dropped back from the main formation, possibly damaged from an earlier combat. His report read:

'After lengthy chase of Me 109s I perceived a formation of about twenty Do 215s flying towards London, protected by a number of Me 109s. I attacked a Do 215, firing a long burst from a distance of 300 yards, decreasing to about 150 yards. Being attacked by three Me 109s I was forced to break off the engagement with the bombers, but looking round I noticed the right engine and petrol tank of the Do 215 was in flames. Flying south I came across three Me 109s making their way towards the Channel. I gave chase, and firing from a distance of about 300 yards saw one E/A dive in smoke and spin in. I again fired a burst. [The] E/A then slackened speed, and approaching to a distance of about 150 yards, I fired a third burst from the rear left side. [The] E/A hit the water at an angle of about 30 degrees and disappeared, ten kilometers from the coast.'

(signed) Flying Officer Z. Henneberg.

Pilot Officer J.E.L. Zumbach saw a Bf 109 on Flying Officer Henneberg's tail and waded in to his defence:

'On engaging the enemy, Flying Officer Henneberg was attacked by an Me 109. I fired a burst and [the] Me began to smoke and drew away. I followed, and firing a long burst from a distance of 50 to 100 yards, set him on fire. I then climbed and saw about twelve He [111] s returning to France without protecting fighters. I signaled another aircraft who joined me, and we attacked, but scarcely had I begun when my ammunition ran out.'

Red 2, Pilot Officer M. Feric, wrote:

'I was attacked by two Me 109s over the coast at Dungeness. These were reinforced by three other Me 109s and in the ensuing fight I shot one down, firing a long burst from a distance of 300 yards. Being myself engaged, I could not follow subsequent flight of damaged E/A, but Flight Lieutenant J.A. Kent, who was in the vicinity, states that he saw [the] E/A burst into flames and fall to earth.'
(signed) Pilot Officer M. Feric.

Green 2, Sergeant J. František, as ever, was in the thick of the action. His combat report read:

'I attacked two Me 110s and leaving one to [a] Hurricane following me, attacked the other. [The] E/A tried to evade me, but I fired a burst and saw his right engine smoke. I fired another burst, and [the] E/A immediately dived, and fell to earth in flames.'
(signed) Sergeant Josef František.

Pilot Officer M. Pisarek pursued a group of Bf 109s, singling out one which he engaged:

'Flying in a southerly direction I noticed several Me 109s and to the right Do 215s. As I approached the Me 109s first, I engaged them and following on the tail of one, I fired several short bursts, but only after falling to about 400ft did [the] E/A burst into flames and fall into the sea. I began to climb but met nothing more.'

Sergeant M. Wojciechowski attacked a Bf 109 before sighting a Do 215 while on his way back to base:

'I noticed an Me 109 returning towards France. I attacked him from the rear and fired at very close-range and [the] Me burst into flames. Climbing to 18,000ft I met another Me 109 who was smoking slightly, and losing height. There was no other machine in the vicinity. I followed him down to earth where he crashed, but the pilot stepped out of the plane and was arrested. I again climbed and another machine (from 'A' Flight) joined me, [and] we attacked a Dornier, and firing two bursts [the] E/A crashed to earth and burst into flames.'

Red 3, Sergeant T. Andruszkow, attacked the same Dornier:

'With Sergeant Wojciechowski we saw a Do 215 lower and to our right. We both attacked, and watched him fall in flames to the ground.'
(signed) Sergeant T. Andruszkow.

Meanwhile, Flying Officer L.W. Paskiewicz engaged some Bf 109s and Bf 110s:

'Flying at 20,000ft in the region of Folkestone we caught up with two formations of Me 109s and Me 110s above us. The leading aircraft of my section attacked the formation, and I followed. Four Me 109s then attacked from the rear. I engaged them and shot down one which fell in flames in the sea, and the other three fled to France.'

Pilot Officer W. Lokuciewski's combat report was timed at 1245 hours:

'At a height of 18,000ft we noticed E/A flying towards London. We approached, but [the] E/A turned and we attacked them from a deflected angle from the rear and above, but at that moment we ourselves were attacked from the rear by Me 109s. At that same time I noticed another formation of E/A flying towards London, protected by Me 109s and 110s. I broke away, and attacked the Me 109s, together with another section of Hurricanes.

'After firing a few bursts an Me 109 began to smoke and eventually burst into flames. I was then hit [in the wing and fuselage] from the rear by a cannon shell and landed wounded.'

No. 229 Squadron also successfully engaged the enemy, with the following claims and losses:

Flight Lieutenant R.F. Rimmer	two Do 215s destroyed
Pilot Officer V.M.M.M. Ortmans	one Do 215 destroyed (shared)
unknown pilot	one Bf 110 destroyed

Pilot Officer G.L.J. Doutrepont, flying N2537, was killed-in-action, shot down over Sevenoaks at 1150 hours.[3]

Pilot Officer R.R. Smith, flying V6616, bailed out following combat over Sevenoaks at 1200 hours.

Nine of the squadron's Hurricanes were scrambled later that day, at 1420 hours, with orders to patrol their base at 20,000ft. While still in a battle-climb and flying at 6,000ft, they were vectored onto the enemy, who were at 18,000ft. A very large raid was in progress, and while Keith Park had held Nos. 303 and 602 Squadrons back in reserve, now every squadron in No. 11 Group was airborne to meet the menace. No. 303 Squadron engaged the Dorniers as they returned from their mission, but still with their Messerschmitt fighter escort in close attention.

A formation of about 400 enemy aircraft was sighted approaching head-on from the east-south-east in, 'formation vics of three, arranged in series of three in line astern stretching [for] several miles. Me 110s in squadron formations were between the formations of nine bombers a little above, with Me 109s at sides and stepped up above the whole to 25,000ft.'

Squadron Leader R.G. Kellett (flying V7465) led Blue Section into quarter frontal attack onto the bombers, which wheeled eastwards. Red and Yellow Sections engaged the enemy, while another squadron simultaneously attacked the formation about five miles to starboard. The Bf 109s were slow to defend the bombers and the lateral guard missed their opportunity. However, the Messerschmitt Bf 109s drew in and were ready for the second attack, which they compelled to break off. As the enemy formation broke up most of the bombers turned eastward, with others heading due south.

During the ensuing combat, Blue 1, Squadron Leader R.G. Kellett, probably destroyed a Do 215 before claiming a Bf 110:

'I fired at a Do 215 from very close-range – I saw pieces fly off both engines and [the] front of the fuselage. I was immediately attacked by four yellow-nosed Me 109s from all sides and had to dive to get out of it. As I climbed I was again attacked, but by a single Me 110. I had no difficulty in evading him, and got onto his tail. I gave him two good bursts into his starboard engine from the quarter. The engine stopped and smoked, and flames burst from the wing. The enemy aircraft fell flaming into the cloud.'

Blue 2, Flying Officer W. Zak (flying L2099), destroyed a Do 215 over Gravesend at about 1500 hours:

'I attacked the first formation which we met south of London, where I was forced into an engagement with Me 109s who attacked us from the rear. After a few minutes I saw another formation of about fifteen Dos without supporting fighters. I attacked the last in the formation several times, firing several bursts. With the last burst [the] E/A began to pour out clouds of smoke and then both engines were in flames.'
(signed) Pilot Officer W. Zak.

Red 1, Pilot Officer M. Feric (flying R2685), claimed a Bf 110, the engagement taking place at 18,000ft over Gravesend at 1500 hours:

'We intercepted about 150-200 E/A. After attacking the bombers I was engaged by Me 109s and Me 110s. Since I had used up half of my ammunition in attacking [the] enemy bombers I approached to about 100 to 80 yards before firing a burst at an Me 110, which immediately burst into flames and fell into clouds out of control.'
(signed) Pilot Officer M. Feric.

Meanwhile, Blue 3, Sergeant M. Wojciechowski (flying V6673), claimed a Bf 109 of I./LG 2:

'Being near a Messerschmitt I fired a burst, after which he turned and made off towards the sea. I chased him for quite a long time before I was able to shoot him down. The pilot jumped, and I saw him arrested as he landed.'

Red 1, Flying Officer W. Urbanowicz (flying V6684), destroyed two Do 215s:

'After a long chase I attacked and fired a burst from a distance of 200 yards. I again attacked from a nearer distance, and in a short while the enemy bomber dived in flames and fell into the sea. I attacked another three-quarters from the rear, and after a long burst, one engine stopped working; [the enemy] aircraft lost speed, and began to lose height. I again attacked the bomber, and firing from a distance of 150 yards, saw him burst into flames and fall into the sea.'

Blue 3, Sergeant S. Wojciechowski, then destroyed a Bf 109 of IX./JG 53, which was in the process of attacking the Hurricane flown by No. 1 Squadron's Flying Officer Briese:

'I saw several Messerschmitts attacking one Hurricane, and the Hurricane diving. I went in to attack and engaged the Mes at 17,000ft. I fired one burst into one of them, which shook and dived towards the earth. I fired again at another Me and after the second burst his right wing caught fire. I also saw flames inside the cockpit as he fell away from me. I had another on my tail.'

The action was not, however, one-sided, and the squadron lost Sergeant M. Brzezowski (flying P3577), who was reported as missing and later confirmed as killed-in-action, shot down off Gravesend at 1505 hours. Meanwhile, Sergeant T. Andruszkow (flying P3939 RF-M) bailed out at Dartford unhurt, following combat with a Bf 109.

During the day the squadron learned of Squadron Leader R.G. Kellett's award of the Distinguished Flying Cross, which was later promulgated in the *London Gazette*, 1 October 1940.

Squadron Leader R.G. Kellett was awarded the DFC, *London Gazette*, 1 October 1940:

'Distinguished Flying Cross.
'Squadron Leader Ronald Gustave KELLETT, (90082), Auxiliary Air Force.
'By his excellent example and personality this officer has been largely responsible for the success of his squadron, which in one week destroyed thirty-three enemy aircraft, of which Squadron Leader Kellett destroyed three. His leadership and determination in attacking superior numbers of enemy aircraft have instilled the greatest confidence in the other pilots of his squadron.'

At Readiness since before dawn on 16 September, Sergeant Jan Kowalski flew on an uneventful scramble at 0725 hours.

Sergeant Kowalski's next sorties came at 1640 hours on the following day, 17 September, when he took part in a squadron scramble. Nos. 1 (RCAF) and 303 Squadrons were ordered north of Biggin Hill, at 20,000ft, where they pursued several sightings, including a formation of Bf 109s at 27,000ft, but on each occasion their vector was just that little bit too late, and they were unable to close on the enemy. Finally, the controller gave the order to 'pancake'. However, Sergeant Wojciechowski (flying P3975) sighted a number of Bf 109s attacking a formation of Hurricanes and peeled off to assist. He fired at two Bf 109s during the general dogfight, one being seen to crash in flames into the sea.

Meanwhile, news reached the squadron of a further gallantry award, with a richly deserved Distinguished Flying Medal for Sergeant J. František, a Czech pilot who had fought in France alongside the Poles and served with them ever since, being readily accepted into their squadron.

The recommendation read:

'This pilot has proved himself exceptional; not only as a pilot, but in fighting. He has taken part in practically every operational flight carried out by this squadron and has accounted for the following aircraft: three Me 109s, one He 113 [sic], one Junkers 88. These victims are the result of only one week's operations. This pilot not only has a fine spirit, but is an excellent NCO, showing a great example to others in his flight.'

Group Captain Vincent, as CO of Northolt, endorsed the recommendation with the words:

'He has at all times showed great gallantry in attacking vastly superior numbers of enemy aircraft.'

František's DFM was officially announced in the *London Gazette* of 27 September, but carried no citation.

Meanwhile, in Hitler's HQ, the events of 15 September were under analysis when it was acknowledged that: 'The enemy air force is still by no means defeated; on the contrary, it shows increasing activity.' A good measure of this 'increasing activity' can be attributed to No. 303 Squadron, which was already taking a heavy toll on enemy raids, its pilots' tenacity leading to a greater percentage of 'kills' than any other unit at the time.

Four scrambles were flown on 18 September, Jan Kowalski taking part in all of them. No contact with the enemy was made during the first scramble, which took place at 0945 hours. On landing, the ground crews descended on the Hurricanes, quickly checking them over for damage and refuelling them ready for the next scramble (with the patches covering the gun-ports intact, they would be aware that no ammunition had been expended). Jan waited at dispersal, the squadron taking off again at 1220 hours, this time in the company of No. 229 Squadron. Once in the air the Hurricanes were vectored 270 degrees, climbing to 25,000ft and patrolling to the south of Biggin Hill.

A reconnaissance Do 215 was engaged over West Malling with 'A' Flight's Red Section, including Squadron Leader R.G. Kellett (flying V6684), Pilot Officer J.E.L. Zumbach (flying V6681) and Pilot Officer Feric (flying V7244), taking a share in the 'kill'. Three crewmen were seen to bail out of the stricken aircraft before it crashed, ten miles south of RAF West Malling. Meanwhile, two of the squadron's Hurricanes were reported damaged by fire from 'friendly' aircraft, possibly occurring during fighter passes on the Dornier.

Meanwhile, Sergeant J. František (flying V7465), who was acting as weaver, sighted a Bf 109 below:

'I dived towards it, and caught it up near the coast. I attacked it from starboard and quarter behind. I gave it a burst into the engine without effect, then I gave it another burst into the engine and cockpit and it fell into the sea in flames.'

Two further scrambles were made at 1610 and 1705 hours, but no contacts were made.

There was great excitement on the station during the day when General Wladyslaw Sikorski paid a visit to the squadron, meeting all of the pilots and key ground staff before presenting the following gallantry awards:

Virtuti Militari 5th Class

Squadron Leader Z. Krasnodebski
Flying Officer Z. Henneberg
Flying Officer W. Januszewicz
Flying Officer W. Lapkowski
Flying Officer W. Lokuciewski
Flying Officer L.W. Paszkiewicz
Flying Officer M. Pisarek
Flying Officer W. Urbanowicz
Pilot Officer J.K.M. Daszewski
Pilot Officer M. Feric
Pilot Officer J.E.L. Zumbach
Sergeant J. František
Sergeant S. Karubin
Sergeant E. Szaposznikow
Sergeant S. Wojtowicz
Sergeant K. Wunsche

Krzyz Walecznych (Cross of Valour), often referred to as the War Cross.

Flying Officer A. Cebrzynski (posthumously)
Flying Officer Wodecki (Medical Officer)
Sergeant M. Brzezowski
Sergeant J. Rogowski

Sergeant Kowalski's name did not appear on the list of gallantry award recipients, as he was yet to record an aerial victory, having only recently been able to get his name onto the flying roster. Jan flew on two scrambles on 20 September, but once again was frustrated when the enemy refused to engage and the Hurricanes landed without firing their guns.

Flying in the company of Nos. 1 (RCAF) and 229 Squadrons at 1000 hours on 23 September, No. 303 Squadron was ordered to patrol south of Biggin Hill before being vectored towards an enemy formation approaching the Thames estuary.

No. 303 Squadron tangled with a dozen high-flying Bf 109s which tried to bounce them from above and astern. Commanding the squadron in the air, Flight Lieutenant J.A. Kent (flying V6681) led Red Section into a counter attack, claiming a Bf 109 which he shot down fifteen miles off the French coast. While on his return flight, Kent damaged a Potez, which in his memoir, *One of the Few*, he described as an Fw 158, only pulling out of the attack when his engine began to run rough,

Meanwhile, Red 2, Sergeant E. Szaposznikow (flying V7244), chased a Bf 109 which he saw shoot down a Hurricane of No. 229 Squadron. Szaposznikow fired at the Bf 109 at 300 yards, sending it seaward in flames off the French coast:

'I saw about eight Me 109s attack an isolated Hurricane of another squadron. This Hurricane shot at the Me 109 which rolled away right. I attacked it from astern and underneath at 300 yards. The Messerschmitt dived down towards the sea. I used up all my ammunition on it, and it crashed into the sea in mid-Channel.'

Sergeant Jan Kowalski took part in four fighter patrols over 24 and 25 September, but again no contacts were made. Jan was beginning to question as to whether he would ever get the opportunity to emulate Urbanowicz, Feric, Henneberg, or František.

During the early afternoon of 26 September, His Majesty King George VI visited RAF Northolt. Sergeant Jan Kowalski was on duty that afternoon and recalled the scene:

'We lined up in front of dispersal and, when the King arrived, our CO, Squadron Leader Kellett, introduced us individually. The King shook hands with those present.'

While His Majesty The King was being introduced to key members of the ground staff, the scramble bell was rung and the pilots at Readiness, including Sergeant Kowalski, raced to their Hurricanes: 'Some people thought that it was because of the King's visit, but it was not so.'

In a matter of minutes, Kowalski and the rest of the squadron were in action over Portsmouth following the scramble which had been given at 1610 hours. Once airborne Nos. 229, 238 and 303 Squadrons were vectored to the Guildford area at 15,000ft, before being redirected to Portsmouth, where they sighted the enemy over the Supermarine factory at Woolston, entering into combat with a formation of fifty He 111s of KG 55, and their escort of Bf 109s, as the bombers pulled away from the target area.

At 1630 hours, Squadron Leader R.G. Kellett (flying V6681) led Red Section against the Bf 109s, but as fighter opposition did not develop, the squadron attacked the bomber sections in echelon from three-quarters astern. The escorting Bf 109s woke up to the danger and attacked the first rush and the squadron broke up – mostly dogfighting, but with some pursuing bombers over France. Sergeant M. Belc (flying V6673) forced-landed at RAF Biggin Hill and Pilot Officer W. Janusziewicz (flying P3544 RF-H) at Wyton Farm near Fareham – both unhurt.

Kellett reported that they arrived too late and had to individually pursue the enemy aircraft, while No. 229 Squadron was below and to the rear. Later, the squadron's pilots reported that just as the squadron was about to attack they all heard a radio message: 'All Appany aircraft pancake' of which no-one took any notice.

Squadron Leader R.G. Kellett, leading the squadron into the attack, wrote:

'I took the leading Me 109. He dived away and I dived after him. His engine caught fire and he crashed into the sea in flames. My throttle stuck open and I had proceeded a long way from the scene of the combat before I was able to control my machine.'

Red Section's Sergeant T. Andruszkow (flying V6665) destroyed an He 111 and a Do 215, firing 1,289 rounds:

'Following my leader I attacked the last He 111 in formation three-quarters from the rear. I then climbed and saw a Do 215 to my left which I attacked. [The] E/A dived, and I followed and fired several bursts from very short distance. [The] E/A continued his dive and crashed into the sea. I was then attacked by [an] Me 109 which zoomed over me. I followed, but as he continued to draw away I was unable to fire and returned.'
(signed) Sergeant T. Andruszkow.

Blue Leader, Flight Lieutenant A.S. Forbes (flying V7465), destroyed an He 111, seeing pieces flying off it as his rounds struck, while the enemy bomber left a thick trail of jet black smoke in its wake:

'Just before making Portsmouth we lost height to 12,000ft and then again climbed. I could see AA bursts in the sky going in a semi-circle from Portsmouth to Southampton at about 8,000ft. We sighted an enemy formation

on our left just too late to intercept before they dropped their bombs. I saw a huge mushroom of flames on the ground near Hamble. The bombers began to turn and we delivered a three-quarter astern attack, which developed into a stern chase. I got in several good bursts on the starboard engine of an He 111 from which pieces came off, and a dense trail of black smoke. I closed in from 250 yards and owing to my speed had to break sharply to avoid hitting the wing. The slipstream therefore, threw me right over [meanwhile, his Hurricane had been hit by an explosive bullet near to the tip of the port wing]. Sergeant František, who was attacking another He 111 behind me, was able to confirm that my He [111] crashed soon afterwards into the sea in flames.'
(signed) Flight Lieutenant A.S. Forbes.

Blue 2, Flying Officer W. Zak, claimed two He 111s destroyed and another damaged, firing 1,962 rounds:

'To the left of Portsmouth I noticed about fifty bombers. I changed course, and, together with the whole squadron, attacked. I fired a burst at one He 111 from the rear. After which I noticed about nine Me 109s at my rear. The bombers wheeled to the right and I approached another He 111, and from a distance of 50 yards fired a long burst. Both engines began to smoke, and E/A twisting, fell towards earth. I did not see him crash, as I attacked another whom I either damaged or destroyed.'
(signed) Flying Officer Zak.

Sergeant J. František (flying R4175) expended all of his ammunition and destroyed two He 111s. He claimed that he only noticed the pursuit had reached France when the second enemy bomber crashed:

'I attacked one He 111 and after a short while he burst into flames. I then attacked another He 111, and did not notice that I was already over France. I shot [the] E/A down and he fell to earth in France.'
(signed) Sergeant J. František.

Green 2, Sergeant M. Belc, fired all of his ammunition, destroying an He 111 and one of the Bf 109 escort, missing out on the opportunity to claim a second when it crossed the French coast – too many of Fighter Command's pilots had been lost pursuing the enemy over the Channel and they had strict orders not to give chase:

'I attacked the last machine [He 111]. I then noticed above me four Me 109s flying in twos. I attacked the lower pair and after two short bursts, one burst into flames and fell to earth, falling in the neighbourhood of Portsmouth. Chasing the second Me 109 I found myself on the coast of France and returned.'
(signed) Sergeant M. Belc.

Yellow 2, Flying Officer J.E.L. Zumbach (flying V6684), destroyed an He 111, along with a Bf 109, both of which he hit in the cockpit, possibly killing the pilots, firing 2,600 rounds:

'I attacked a formation of He 111s and fired a long burst at the last in the formation, which appeared to explode in the region of the cockpit. [The] E/A fell out of control to earth. I flew towards another formation of E/A and met an Me 109. I fired a burst from a deflection angle from the front, and then another from the rear. The pilot must have been killed as [the] E/A dived into the sea without any visible outward sign of damage. I then chased the rest of the formation, but could not catch them up. I noticed, however, more than four E/As smoking fall into the sea; although none of our aircraft were in the vicinity. Having used all of my ammunition I returned to Northolt.'
(signed) Flying Officer J.E.L. Zumbach.

Green 3, Sergeant Jan Kowalski (flying R3089), claimed a Bf 109 destroyed, firing 2,310 rounds; Kowalski's combat was timed at 1630 hours:

'We met a formation of about fifty He 111s protected by about ten Me 109s. I attacked the bomber from a rear deflection angle, and, just on the point of opening fire, I noticed an Me above and to the left of me. I broke away from the bombers and attacked the Me, firing two long bursts, after which [the] E/A dived in smoke to earth. I did not follow aircraft to earth as I wished to catch up with the rest of enemy formation, but as I was unsuccessful in this I returned to Northolt. There was a mist to height of 5,000ft.'
(signed) Sergeant Jan Kowalski.

Jan recalled the events fifty years on:

'We soon took off and were vectored south, gaining height rapidly. After about fifteen minutes "Bandits" were not far away. Soon we noticed puffs of shells indicating where the formations were. A few minutes later we were over dozens of He 111s escorted by fighters. We were instructed to attack, which we did immediately. I attacked one of [the] He 111s, firing a long burst and dived below. When I was gaining height I noticed one of [the] Me 109s flying east. I went after him and began to fire with all my eight guns. I saw some debris coming off his wings and then there was a terrible bang. I was hit. I dived down and after leveling out at 4,000ft I assessed [the] damage. There was a small hole in [the] left side of [my] cabin and my R/T was no longer working, everything else was okay. I could not see anybody, so I had to find my way back.
    'While repairing the damage to my Hurricane, the service crew found a bullet on the floor, which I have still as a memento.'

In addition to these 'kills', Flying Officers L.W. Paszkiewicz (flying V7235) and W. Urbanowicz (flying P3901), and Pilot Officer B. Grzeszczak (flying P3120), each destroyed an He 111.

Also in combat were Nos. 229 and 238 Squadrons, both of which successfully engaged the enemy.

No. 229 Squadron's claims and losses included:

Flight Lieutenant W.A. Smith (flying P3039)	one He 111 probably destroyed
Pilot Officer J.M.F. Dewar (flying P3712)	one Bf 109 destroyed
Sergeant S.W. Merryweather (flying V6745 RE-Y)	one Bf 109 damaged

Sergeant S.W. Merryweather was wounded following combat with a Bf 110. He force-landed at Hambledon, Surrey.

No. 238 Squadron's claims and losses included:

Pilot Officer V.C. Simmonds (flying P3178)	one Bf 110 destroyed
Pilot Officer J.R. Urwin-Mann (flying P4232)	one Bf 110 destroyed
Pilot Officer J.S. Wigglesworth (flying P3767)	one Bf 110 destroyed
Sergeant J.V. Kucera (flying N2546)	one Bf 110 destroyed

Sergeant V. Horsky (flying P3098) was shot down by Bf 110s over the Solent and killed.[4]

Pilot Officer R.A. Kings (flying P3830) was shot down by a Bf 110 over the Isle of Wight and bailed out, safe.

Sergeant Kowalski's second victory of the battle came the following day, on 27 September, when he took part in both of the squadron's scrambles.

At 0845 hours, No. 303 Squadron, led by Flight Lieutenant Forbes, took off, making a rendezvous with No. 1 (RCAF) Squadron before being vectored onto an enemy formation flying at 15,000ft in the Horsham area. The enemy, which consisted of thirty He 111s, flying in vics of three protected by fifty to sixty Me 109s, line astern, stepped up behind, was targeting London. It was noticed that the majority of the He 111s had a vertical white stripe on the tail fin and from a distance they gave the impression of being 'friendly' aircraft. The squadron attacked the He 111s from astern before being bounced by their escort, which then fled in disorder.

During the Bf 109's initial pass, however, Flying Officer L.W. Paszkiewicz (flying LK1696 RF-M) was caught unawares and shot down.[5]

The bombers wheeled, heading south, as the squadron went in to attack from astern, but the vics of bombers maintained formation throughout, closing up when one or more were shot down. Other Hurricanes were more fortunate and came in to attack the bombers. Immediately afterwards the squadron noticed about forty Do 17s approaching head-on in single line astern formation supported by Me 109s above.

As the Hurricanes came in for the attack, the enemy fighters formed a similar circle above. Only one pilot succeeded in closing in on the Heinkel 111s and Do 17s, shooting one down over land. Two other squadrons of Hurricanes came in and attacked the Dorniers, inflicting heavy casualties.

During the air battle Sergeant T. Andruszkow (flying V6665 RF-J) was killed-in-action when he was shot down over the Horsham area, crashing at Holywych Farm, Cowden, at 0935 hours.[6] His Hurricane was seen by Pilot Officer Zumbach as it flew in front of him:

> 'I shouted, "A hell of a lot of 109s above us!" Suddenly I saw a Hurricane in front of me, going down in a shallow dive with [its] starboard wing on fire, followed by an Me 109. I pulled up violently and started to shoot, aiming at the tail. The Messerschmitt went across the burst, broke up, and went down. The same moment I received a burst of fire. Fortunately, it went high. I threw my machine in a starboard turn. Two Me 109s went past me. I started to run towards the Squadron.'

Meanwhile, Flying Officer W. Zak (flying V7289) was shot down and bailed out near Leatherhead at 0935 hours, moments after sending an He 111 down in flames. Zak was taken to Leatherhead Hospital, suffering from burns to his face and hands.

During the same engagement Flying Officer B. Grzeszczak (flying V7244) attacked a number of Bf 109s, one of which he shot down. Flying Officer W. Urbanowicz (flying P6684) attacked a Bf 110, which flew in a zig-zag pattern to avoid his fire:

> 'I was unable to score a hit. Approaching, however, to about fifty yards I fired the last burst. [The] enemy aircraft began to smoke and, falling on its left side, dived, and crashed to earth about thirty-five miles south of London by the side of some railway lines. One of the crew jumped by parachute.'

Closing in on a second Bf 110, Urbanowicz was attacked by a brace of Bf 109s. Quickly out-turning the enemy, he sent one down in flames.

Flight Lieutenant A.S. Forbes[7] (flying L2099) had tried to engage the Bf 109s, but was unable to overhaul them. Instead, he saw a Ju 88 of II./KG 77 which he raked with fire:

> 'I saw an He 111 [sic] leave the combat and start diving towards the coast. As no one followed him I dived onto him, and caught him up at about 10,000ft. I closed, and after two short bursts, three or four of the crew bailed out. As the enemy aircraft continued in an even dive I thought that the pilot might still be in his place. I therefore decided to destroy the E/A and set fire to the port engine. It crashed in flames either on the shore or just in the sea on the east coast of Kent.'

Pilot Officer J.E.L. Zumbach (flying V6684) shared in the destruction of an He 111:[8]

'I attacked a Heinkel 111 that popped out of the formation. With some others I started to pound him in turn. After a moment the gunner bailed. We were joined by three more machines which, hell knows why, decided it was their duty to shoot at this particular machine, while they had a whole lot of others above us. I got it once more. After the burst it wheeled and rammed into a small town, knocking one house down and setting one on fire.'

Sergeant J. František (flying R4175 RFR), meanwhile, shot down a Ju 88 before encountering a Bf 110 which he also destroyed.

'A' Flight's Red 1, Flying Officer Z. Henneberg (flying V7246 RF-B), claimed a Bf 109 over Horsham:

'I noticed on my right two Me 109s. I attacked one, firing from three-quarters from the rear, from a distance of about 200 yards. After the third burst [the] E/A burst into flames and fell to earth. I then heard three explosions one after the other and smoke began to fill my cockpit. I dived and returned to Northolt. On examining my aircraft I found that it had been hit by three cannon shells, one of which had punctured the radiator.'
(signed) Flying Officer Z. Henneberg.

Red 2, Pilot Officer M. Feric (flying V6681), destroyed one of the escorting Bf 109s before closing in on the bombers, destroying an He 111:

'I attacked an Me 109, and after a short burst [the] enemy aircraft exploded into flames and crashed to earth. I then approached the bombers who were already being attacked by some of our aircraft. I attacked a Heinkel and fired three bursts. The pilot was evidently killed as the machine dived without smoke or flames, and crashed between Croydon and Gatwick. As my aircraft had been hit by machine-gun bullets I returned to Northolt.'

Green 2, Sergeant Jan Kowalski (flying R3089), damaged an He 111, part of a formation of seventy E/A which included Do 17s, Bf 109s and He 111s, while flying at 15,000ft over the Horsham area. Kowalski expended all of his ammunition during the combat, which was timed at 0920 hours:

'On contacting the enemy we attacked three-quarters from the rear. I fired two long bursts at [an] enemy bomber in the last section. [The] E/A broke formation and I again fired a burst from about 200 yards, and [the] starboard motor stopped. [The] E/A began to fly south losing height. I returned to Northolt through lack of ammunition. Returning, I noticed a number of E/A circling in a ring, and over them [were] Me 109s.'
(signed) Sergeant Kowalski J.

Many years later Jan recalled the events surrounding this combat:

'It was our second scramble this morning, 27 September, we flew south as instructed and gaining height rapidly.

'Halfway to the Channel we spotted large formations of bombers which had already been attacked by our fighters. By the time we were ready to attack, the formation of bombers formed an unusual defensive formation – flying in a circle. Thus each aircraft was protected by the aircraft in front. We dived immediately, giving a short burst of machine gun [fire] and dived below. We had to climb again to give another attack. When climbing [for the] second time I spotted one of the bombers flying west. I went after him. It might have been damaged already.

'I started firing, approaching quickly, but saw that there was no response from [the] rear-gunner. I continued firing and the He 111 was losing height rapidly as one of the engines was also smoking.'

Only seven Hurricanes landed at Northolt following the combat, some of these badly damaged.

As had occurred on 26 September, just before the squadron went into the attack a radio message was received by all of the pilots, 'Appany Leader pancake'. Despite the message being delivered in good English and with the authority of a controller, once again the deceit was recognized and the order was ignored.

Meanwhile, No. 1 (RCAF) Squadron also engaged the enemy, but without claiming any 'kills'. They lost Flying Officer O.J. Peterson (flying P3647), who was killed-in-action while in combat with Ju 88s and Bf 109s. He was shot down over Hever, Kent.[9]

The same formation was later attacked by No. 92 Squadron, followed by Nos. 501 Squadron and 253 Squadrons; No. 605 Squadron also taking on the bombers. Finally, No. 66 Squadron took its toll on the raid.

No. 92 Squadron recorded the following 'kills' and losses:

Flight Lieutenant C.B.F. Kingcombe (flying X4418)	one Do 17 probably destroyed, one Do17 damaged
Flying Officer J.F. Drummond (flying X4487)	one Bf 109 destroyed (shared)
Pilot Officer J. Mansel-Lewis (flying X4480)	one Do 17 destroyed
Pilot Officer T.S. Wade (flying P9544)	one Do 17 destroyed
Pilot Officer A.R. Wright (flying X4069)	one Do 17 damaged (shared), one He 111 destroyed (shared)
Sergeant H. Bowen-Morris (flying R6760)	one Do 17 damaged
Unknown	one Do 17 damaged (shared)
Unknown pilot	one He 111 destroyed (shared)
Unknown pilot	one Bf 109 destroyed (shared)

Flight Lieutenant J.A. Paterson (flying X4422) was killed when he was shot down by a Bf 109 over Sevenoaks at 0920 hours.

Flight Sergeant C. Sydney (flying R6767) was shot down and killed over Kingstone, Surrey, at 0940 hours.

No. 253 Squadron recorded the single victory:

Pilot Officer A.F. Eckford	one Bf 110 destroyed

No. 501 Squadron recorded the following combat victories and casualties:

Squadron Leader H.A.V. Hogan (flying V6703)	one Bf 110 destroyed (shared)
Unknown pilot of No. 303 Squadron	one Bf 110 destroyed (shared)
Unknown pilot	one Bf 110 destroyed

Pilot Officer F.C. Harrold (flying P3417 SD-W) was killed when he was shot down by a Bf 109 near Deal at 1010 hours.[10]

Pilot Officer E.B. Rogers (flying V7497) bailed out following combat with Bf 109s over Deal at 1010 hours.

No. 605 Squadron recorded the following 'kills':

Pilot Officer C.F. Currant (flying V6783)	one Bf 110 destroyed
Pilot Officer J.A. Milne (flying R4118)	one Bf 110 destroyed
Sergeant J. Budzinski	one Bf 110 destroyed
Sergeant E.W. Wright (flying P3583)	one Bf 110 probably destroyed
Unknown pilot	one Bf 110 damaged

No. 66 Squadron recorded the following victories:

Flying Officer R.W. Oxspring (flying X4322)	one Bf 110 destroyed shared
Pilot Officer S. Baker (probably flying X4326)	one Bf 110 destroyed
Sergeant H. Cook (flying X4421)	one Bf 110 destroyed, one Bf 110 damaged
Sergeant C.A. Parsons (flying P9515)	one Bf 110 damaged
Unknown Hurricane pilot	one Bf 110 destroyed shared

Squadron Leader R.G. Kellett (flying P3901) led a section strength patrol between 1150 and 1310 hours, probably destroying a Bf 109.

The squadron could only muster six Hurricanes at 1515 hours, mounting a flight strength scramble in the company of No. 1 (RCAF) Squadron as the Luftwaffe again targeted the capital. Flight Lieutenant J.A. Kent (flying P3901) sighted fifteen Ju 88s in vics of five in line astern, stepped up behind, along with their escort of thirty Bf 109s, approaching London from the south-east. Kent led his Hurricanes into the attack.

The bombers immediately turned south and headed back towards the coast, and could only be overhauled by three of the squadron's Hurricanes, which drew close enough to attack from astern and below. Flying Officer W. Urbanowicz (flying P3901) fired a short burst at one Ju 88 which started to smoke and lost height, and after firing a second short burst the crew of three bailed out, landing in the sea just off the coast. He then fired at a second Ju 88 and after a medium length burst it fell into the sea in flames.

Flight Lieutenant J.A. Kent[11] (flying V6684) experienced return fire from the rear-gunner of a Ju 88, which stopped after Kent had fired one short burst into the bomber. He then fired again and the starboard engine stopped, while the port engine began emitting smoke. Flying Officer W. Urbanowicz saw the bomber crash into the sea.

Red 3, Sergeant E. Szaposznikow (flying V7244), was about to fire at a Ju 88, when he was bounced by a Bf 109 which he destroyed, firing 526 rounds:

'After approaching [the] E/A the chase began. Only at the coast did we catch up with the enemy formation. I was left behind alone as I could not keep up the speed of the others, and was attacked by an Me 109 who dived onto me and then rolled. I got onto his tail and fired two bursts. [The] E/A continued its dive and fell into the sea off Brighton.'
 (signed) Sergeant E. Szaposznikow.

Nos. 72 and 605 Squadrons were also vectored onto the same raid, destroying a number of enemy aircraft.

No. 72 Squadron claimed:

Flying Officer J.W. Villa (flying X4419)	one He 111 destroyed
Flight Sergeant H. Steere (flying K9935)	one Bf 109 damaged
Sergeant M.A. Lee (flying X4252)	one He 111 destroyed

No. 605 Squadron made the following claims, with one aircraft lost:

unknown pilot	one Ju 88 destroyed
unknown pilot	one Ju 88 destroyed
unknown pilot	one Ju 88 destroyed (shared)
unknown pilot	one Ju 88 destroyed (shared)

Flying Officer R. Hope (flying P3828) bailed out following combat with a Bf 109 over Ticehurst, Sussex, at 1420 hours, safe.

The squadron flew further patrols and scrambles on 28 & 29 September, but no further claims could be made.

Sergeant Kowalski was in the air again at 1315 hours on 30 September, taking part in the squadron's third operation of the day. No. 303 Squadron was scrambled to rendezvous with Nos. 1 (RCAF) and 229 Squadrons. The wing was vectored on Dungeness. While flying at 14,000ft the Poles sighted a formation of thirty Do 215s and their escort of Bf 109s above them. Only No. 303 Squadron was well positioned to attack.

Yellow Section's Flying Officer W. Urbanowicz (flying P3901) destroyed two Bf 109s near the French coast, while Yellow 2, Pilot Officer J. Radomski (flying P3663), claimed a Do 215. Red 2, Sergeant S. Karubin (flying V7505), destroyed the Bf 109 flown by Unteroffizier Karl Vogel of IV./JG 53, which crashed at Beachy Head:

'After climbing to 22,000ft I noticed a formation of enemy bombers in one large formation and Me's in loose formation of two's. I attacked one Me from below, firing two short bursts. [The] enemy aircraft began to smoke, then burst into flames and fell earthward through the clouds. Next I chased the bomber formation towards the coast, but could not get within reach. I saw two enemy bombers break formation and dive to earth.'

Flying Officer W. Urbanowicz reported at his debriefing:

'Our squadron attacked the bombers from behind and above. After the second attack two enemy aircraft broke away from the formation. One fell smoking into the sea. The other was attacked by our fighters and also fell into the sea smoking.'

Engaging the bombers he spotted their Bf 109 escort:

'I discovered that there were two Me 109s protecting the bomber. From a distance of 50 yards I fired a burst at one of them. Next I fired a longer burst at the other Me 109, who did not smoke or burst into flames, but immediately dived headlong into the sea. I again attacked the bomber from a distance of 30 yards to the rear, and fired once more without result. I continued the attack and the enemy aircraft, which was now over France, made as if to land, hit the ground with its right wing and burst into flames. None of the crew came out.'

This is believed to have been a Do 17 of VIII./KG 2 which burned out at Bertincourt. Pilot Officer J. Radomski, meanwhile, attacked the bomber seen by Urbanowicz:

'One enemy aircraft broke formation and I fired a short burst at his cockpit, then another at the left motor, which stopped. I again fired several bursts, and the last machine also stopped. Whilst firing, a Spitfire joined me, but after the left engine had stopped, flew off. [The] enemy aircraft fell into the sea about fifteen miles from Dungeness.'

While making for base, Flying Officer W. Urbanowicz's[12] engine blew up, resulting in a fierce fire:

'I closed the throttle, turned off the petrol, switched off the engine and side-slipped, as smoke was blinding me. I glided and side-slipped as far as the coast, and landed on shingles without my undercarriage. From the moment of switching off my engine, petrol, smoke and flames continued to issue from exhaust.'

A further scramble was flown at 1640 hours, with Nos. 1 (RCAF), 229 and 303 Squadrons patrolling base. Around 150-200 Bf 109s and Bf 110s were reported in the area, with combat taking place over Brooklands. 'B' Flight approached the bombers heading south-east near Croydon. Sergeant M. Belc (flying P3217) broke away to protect a Hurricane pilot who had bailed out and was under attack from a Bf 109. The remaining aircraft in the flight were bounced by Bf 109s. Sergeant J. František (flying L2099) broke off upwards and covered the flight from enemy attack. He caught one Bf 109 on the turn and destroyed it, and, in the subsequent fight with six others, he probably destroyed another. František escaped into cloud with great difficulty. The rest of the flight tried to continue towards the bombers, but was broken up by Bf 109s.

Squadron Leader R.G. Kellett led a squadron scramble at 1315 hours on 1 October, making rendezvous with No. 1 (RCAF) Squadron. While on patrol they sighted a formation of Bf 109s, but were advised by the controller of the close proximity of their real target; the bombers. Kellett sighted what he believed to be the bombers and peeled off; expecting the squadron to follow, while the Canadians kept their escort at bay. However, Kellett was unable to radio his intentions to No. 1 (RCAF) Squadron as the two units were on different frequencies, while the rest of No. 303 Squadron somehow failed to follow. Suddenly, he found himself up against eighteen Bf 109s bristling with cannon. Kellett dodged the attack, twisting and turning to outmanoeuvre the enemy. During the frantic dogfight, Kellett destroyed one Bf 109, probably accounting for a second before disengaging and making for base.

Sergeant Jan Kowalski flew on two uneventful scrambles on the following day, 2 October, and on three of the squadron's four scrambles on 5 October, missing the first operation, flown between 1110 and 1245 hours with No. 1 (RCAF) Squadron leading. The wing engaged the enemy over Rochester. During the rolling air-battle which went on for well over half an hour, No. 303 Squadron first tackled a group of Bf 110s, which formed a tight defensive circle, with Bf 109s coming down to give additional support. Squadron Leader R.G. Kellett (flying V7504) damaged a Bf 109, Flying Officer Z. Henneberg (flying V6684), Pilot Officer M. Feric[13] (flying V6681) and Sergeant M. Belc[14] (flying V7235) each claimed a Bf 110. Meanwhile, Flying

Officer M. Pisarek (flying V7503) destroyed a Bf 109, badly damaging a second. Sergeant S. Karubin[15] (P3901) destroyed one Bf 109, while Sergeant Suidak (flying N2460) claimed two Bf 109s, sharing a Bf 110 with an unknown Spitfire pilot.

Flying Officer W. Janszewicz was killed when his Hurricane (V7465) crashed in flames at RAF Hawkinge following combat with Bf 109s at 1200 hours, over Stowting, Kent. The squadron's combats were timed at 1140 hours.

Squadron Leader R.G. Kellett (flying V7504), flying as Red 1, fired 284 rounds, engaging a Bf 109, one of seven seen emerging from cloud:

'I led the squadron to attack them in line astern. I got in a good burst from in front and on the quarter of one Me 109, and I saw pieces fall off the engine and starboard wing root. [The] E/A turned right and dived under me. I could not follow it owing to the big dogfight which had developed, involving about 100 aircraft. I had another opportunity for a short burst at another Me 109, but I could not say if I hit it. After half an hour's dogfighting, when the E/A were about five miles over the Channel, we were ordered to "Pancake".' (signed) Squadron Leader R.G. Kellett.

Red 2, Pilot Office M. Feric, fired 146 rounds, targeting a Bf 110 between Rochester and the Channel:

'Over Kent we engaged Me 109s. Meanwhile, it was noticed that Me 110s were also in the vicinity flying in a defensive circle. As Me 110s were above us [at 30,000-20,000ft] we began to climb. I then noticed an Me 110 break away from the circle and diving, make towards the sea; smoking slightly, but maintaining a very high speed. I chased [the] E/A and, catching up with him about seven miles from the coast, fired a burst from a distance of about twenty yards into his cockpit. [The] E/A immediately dived into the sea.'

Yellow 1, Flying Officer Z. Henneberg, fired bursts at a number of Bf 110s before setting one on fire, firing 830 rounds:

'I chased one Me 109 to the coast, but could not get within firing distance. I noticed near the coast a defensive circle of Me 110s. Above them were flying several Me 109s. I attacked an Me 110, but after firing two bursts I observed an Me on my tail. Evading [the] E/A I chased an Me 110 making towards the coast and began to fire from a distance of 250 yards. After firing two bursts [at the] E/A, [it] burst into flames and dived straight for the sea. I was then attacked by three Me 109s and, evading them, returned to Northolt.' (signed) Flying Officer Z. Henneberg.

The squadron suffered a casualty on the ground when Sergeant A. Siudale was killed-in-action at 1205 hours, on 6 October. A lone bomber took advantage of thick cloud cover, dropping twelve 500-kilo bombs on Northolt airfield. Siudale had evidently been trying to take off at the controls of P3120 in order to engage the enemy, or at least remove the aircraft from danger, when a bomb detonated between two hangars, destroying his Hurricane as he taxied. He had only recently opened his score and would no doubt have gone on to wreak havoc amongst the enemy in the air.

No. 303 Squadron was in combat twice on 7 October. Contact was made with what was identified as a formation of 'fifty to sixty Me 109s and He 113s' *[sic]* south of London during their second sortie, which was flown in the company of No. 1 (RCAF) Squadron between 1320 and 1450 hours. The Me 109s came down to attack the Canadians, but No. 303 Squadron's Hurricanes intervened, with Flying Officer M. Pisarek (flying V7503) destroying a Bf 109 over the Channel, while Sergeants M. Belc (flying L2099) and E. Szaposznikow[16] (flying V7244) each destroyed a Bf 109, the latter damaging a second:

> 'We met a formation of Me 109s flying below us. There were three Me 109s, followed by two more. I attacked, [an] E/A [which] began to smoke but evaded me. I then met two more Me 109s over the coast. I attacked one and firing a burst [I] saw [the] E/A dive. I fired from a distance of 150 yards, but there was no sign of smoke or flame, although the E/A fell into the sea just off Brighton.' (signed) Sergeant Szaposznikow.

Kowalski flew on the squadron's two patrols on the following day, 8 October, when the squadron suffered the loss of the Czech, Sergeant J. František[17] (flying R4175) who crashed at Ewell, Surrey, at 0940 hours. The cause of the crash remains unknown, although it had occurred within sight of his girlfriend's house and it has been suggested that the ace had died while performing unauthorized aerobatics.

For Sergeant Kowalski the Battle of Britain was drawing to a close. He flew half a dozen further uneventful scrambles and patrols out of RAF Northolt before the squadron transferred north to RAF Leconfield, late on 11 October. Here the squadron was allowed a period of 'rest' while bringing new pilots through. Kowalski, as a former flying instructor, was used to this role.

Meanwhile, in recognition of his combat victories, Sergeant Jan Kowalski was awarded the Polish Cross of Valour (KW) on 1 February 1941, having already qualified for the Polish Airman's Medal on 20 January 1941, receiving a first Bar on 20 January 1942.

Sergeant Kowalski was posted to No. 315 Squadron, at Acklington, on 22 January 1941, on its formation. Jan flew a number of operational patrols, including regular sweeps, Rodeos and Circus operations, as the RAF took the fight to the enemy. Kowalski was commissioned on 1 June 1942, while a well-earned break from operations came on 5 December, when Jan was sent to No. 58 OTU, Grangemouth, as an instructor.

Jan Kowalski's next posting came on 13 February 1943, when he joined the Polish Fighting Team at West Kirby, being sent with them to the Middle East a month later. Attached to No. 145 Squadron, they flew combat operations over North Africa between 17 March and 12 May, claiming thirty enemy aircraft.

Kowalsi was posted back to the UK following this brief but intense tour, during which he had flown thirty-eight operational sorties, including close support to Allied bombers and strafing ground targets. His next posting was to No. 316 Squadron at Northolt, which came on 21 July 1943. Jan remained with the squadron until 20 October, when he joined HQ, No. 181 Wing. Kowalski was awarded a second Bar to the Polish Cross of Valour on 7 November 1943.

Flying with No. 317 Squadron from 28 April 1944, Jan Kowalski flew escorts and ground strikes well into the following year. Meanwhile, on 8 March 1945, Kowalski was awarded the Virtuti Militari 5th Class (Number 10789), also receiving the DFC, *London Gazette*, 10 April 1946, although his actual medal bears the date '1945' on the lower arm.

The recommendation for Jan Kowalski's Distinguished Flying Cross summed up his flying career with the RAF:

'Flight Lieutenant Jan Kowalski (P-1909)

'During the Battle of Britain, on the 26.9.40, enemy bombers, escorted by fighters, raided Southampton. Flight Lieutenant Kowalski attacked the fighter cover and shot down one Me 109.

'On the 27.9.1940, Flight Lieutenant Kowalski attacked a strong formation of enemy bombers in the vicinity of Gatwick. He kept attacking the formation until he exhausted his ammunition. As a result of this attack he damaged an He 111, putting one of its engines out of action.

'From 14.3.43 – 15.6.43, Flight Lieutenant Kowalski flew with the Polish Fighter Team during the campaign in North Africa. He carried out thirty-eight operational sorties on bomber escorts and ground strafing.

'On the 17.9.44, Flight Lieutenant Kowalski led a flight on an armed recce in the vicinity of BERNAY. The flight was attacked by eight Fw 190s. During the ensuing dogfights five Fw 190s were damaged, without any losses being sustained by the flight.

'On the 26.9.44, Flight Lieutenant Kowalski led a section of four aircraft on an armed recce, in the vicinity of BREDA, a group of enemy transport was observed. In spite of the intense flak which was encountered after the first attack, Flight Lieutenant Kowalski continued to attack the column, diving at it several times. Four enemy MET were left burning and two damaged.

'On 1 January 1945, No. 317 Squadron returned from an operational sortie; enemy aircraft were attacking B60, the wing's home base. In spite of the fact that his cannons had jammed, Flight Lieutenant Kowalski attacked several Fw 190s trying to chase them off.

'Flight Lieutenant Kowalski has taken part in 211 sorties of all descriptions.'

Jan Kowalski was released from the service in December 1948 and settled in England, living out his retirement in Nottingham. In his latter years he was a stalwart of the Battle of Britain Fighter Association, promoting the role of his fellow members of the PAF who had fought so gallantly in the RAF.

Pilots who flew with No. 303 Squadron during the Battle of Britain:

Squadron Leader Ronald Gustave Kellett, AAF, DSO *(A)*, DFC, VM 5th Class *(B)*	(British) Officer Commanding
Squadron Leader Zdzislaw Krasnodebski, VM 5th Class	(Polish) Officer Commanding, KW 31.10.47
Flight Lieutenant Athol Stanhope Forbes, DFC, VM 5th Class	(British) 'B' Flight Commander Bar to DFC *(C)*
Flight Lieutenant John Alexander Kent, DFC *(D)*, AFC	(British) 'A' Flight Commander Bar to DFC 21.10.41 *(E)*
Flying Officer Arsen Cebrzynski	KIA 19.9.40, KW and Bar 23.12.40, Second Bar to KW 31.10.47
Flying Officer Bohdan Grzeszczak	KIA 28.8.41
Flying Officer Zdzislaw Karol Henneburg, VM 5th Class	KW and Bar 1.2.41, DFC 30.10.41, Croix de Guerre, Two Bars to KW
Flying Officer Wojciech Januszewicz, VM 5th Class	KIA 5.10.40
Flying Officer Waclaw Lapkowski, VM 5th Class	KW 1.4.41, Bar 10.4.46, Two Bars to KW 31.10.47, KIA 2.7.41
Flying Officer Witold Lokuciewski, VM 5th Class	KW 1.2.41, Bar to KW 10.9.41, DFC 30.10.41
Flying Officer Ludwik Witold Paszkiewicz, DFC, VM 5th Class	KIA 27.9.40, KW 1.2.41
Flying Officer Marian Pisarek, VM 5th Class	Three Bars to KW 30.10.41, DFC 30.10.41, VM 4th Class 31.10.47
Flying Officer Witold Urbanowicz, VM 5th Class	(Polish) 'A' Flight, Commander KW and Three Bars 1.2.41, DFC 30.1.41, Air Medal (US) 25.9.44 Flying Cross (China)
Flying Officer Walerian Zak	KW and Bar 1.2.41, VM 5th Class 15.11.42, Two Bars to KW 15.2.44, DFC 15.5.44
Pilot Officer Jan Kazimierz Michal Daszewski	KW 30.10.41, Bar to KW, VM 5th Class 20.8.42, Two Bars to KW 31.10.47
Pilot Officer Miroslaw Feric, VM 5th Class	KW 1.2.41, Bar to KW 10.9.41, DFC 30.10.41. Two Bars to KW 31.10.47

Pilot Officer Wojciech Januszewicz, VM 5th Class	KIA 5.10.40
Pilot Officer B. Mierzwa	
Pilot Officer Jan Eugienius Ludwik Zumbach	KW 1.2.41, Bar to KW 10.9.41, VM 5th Class, DFC 30.10.41, Second Bar to KW 20.8.42, Third Bar to KW 5.11.42, Bar to DFC 15.11.42
Sergeant Tadeus Andruszkow	KIA 26.9.40, KW 1.2.41
Sergeant Marian Belc	KW 1.2.41, Bar to KW 15.7.41, VM 5th Class 10.9.41, DFC 15.11.42, Two Bars to KW 31.10.47
Sergeant M. Brzezwski, KW	KIA 15.9.40
Sergeant Josef František, DFM and Bar *(F)*	KW and Three Bars 1.2.41, MC (Czech), VM 5th Class, C de G (France) 15.7.41
Sergeant Pawel Piotr Gallus	KW 3.9.42, Bar to KW 25.6.43, DFC 26.5.45, VM 5th Class 1.6.45
Sergeant Josef Kania	KW 15.8.41
Sergeant Stanislaw Karubin, VM 5th Class, KW	DFM 30.10.41, Two Bars to KW 31.10.47
Sergeant Jan Kowalski	KW 1.2.41, Bar to KW 19.2.42, Second Bar to KW 20.12.43, VM 5th Class 8.3.45, DFC 10.4.46
Sergeant Jan Palak	KW 1.2.41, Bar to KW 10.9.41, Second Bar to KW 20.10.43, VM 5th Class 1.6.45, DFC 10.4.46
Sergeant Edward Paterek	KW 1.2.41, KIA air accident 28.3.41
Sergeant Jan Aleksander Rogowski, KW	Two Bars to KW 20.10.43, VM 5th Class 25.6.45
Sergeant Antoni Siudak	KIA 6.10.40, VM 5th Class 1.2.41
Sergeant Leon Switon	
Sergeant Eugenius Szaposznikow, VM 5th Class, KW	Bar to KW 1.2.41, DFC 30.10.41, Second Bar to KW 30.12.44, Third Bar to KW 31.10.47
Sergeant Miroslaw Wojciechowski	KW and Bar 1.2.41, Second Bar to KW 10.9.41, VM 5th Class 15.11.42

Sergeant Stefan Wojtowicz, VM 5th Class   KIA 11.9.40

Sergeant Kazimierz Wunsche, VM 5th Class   KW 10.9.41, Bar to KW 20.8.42,
Second Bar to KW 20.12.43,
Third Bar to KW 30.12.44

Many of the pilots earned gallantry awards for combat which are not mentioned in the main text. Details, where traced, are included below:

(A) Squadron Leader R.G. Kellett was awarded the DSO, *London Gazette*, 25 October 1940:

> 'Distinguished Service Order.
> 'Squadron Leader Ronald Gustave KELLETT, DFC (90082), Auxiliary Air Force.
> 'Squadron Leader Kellett, as commander of his squadron, has built up and trained his personnel to such a fine fighting pitch that no fewer than 113 enemy aircraft have been destroyed in the space of one month, with very few casualties sustained by his squadron. He has frequently led the wing formation with judgment and success. The gallantry and fine leadership displayed by Squadron Leader Kellett have proved an inspiring example.'

(B) Squadron Leader R.G. Kellett's leadership of the squadron was acknowledged by the Polish Government-in-Exile, when he was awarded the VM 5th Class on 12 December 1940.

(C) Acting Squadron Leader A.S. Forbes, DFC, was awarded a Bar to the DFC, *London Gazette*, 4 November 1941:

> 'Bar to the Distinguished Flying Cross.
> 'Acting Squadron Leader Athol Stanhope FORBES, DFC (37499), Reserve of Air Force Officers, No. 66 Squadron.
> 'This officer has participated in numerous operational sorties during the last five months. In addition to many arduous convoy patrols he has led wing formations as escort to bombers, on missions over France. He has also carried out many attacks on enemy ground targets with a large measure of success. Squadron Leader Forbes has always shown the greatest keenness to engage the enemy and has undoubtedly contributed materially to the high standard of operational efficiency of the squadron. At his own request he has been permitted to make long flights out over the sea, alone, in an endeavour to engage enemy aircraft.'

(D) Flight Lieutenant J.A. Kent was awarded the DFC, *London Gazette,* 25 October 1940:

'Distinguished Flying Cross.
'Flight Lieutenant John Alexander KENT, AFC (37106).
'Early in October 1940, this officer, when entirely alone, attacked forty Messerschmitt 109s and shot down two of them. He has personally destroyed at least four enemy aircraft.

'Flight Lieutenant Kent has been responsible in a large measure for the fighting efficiency of his squadron and has materially contributed to its successes. He has proved himself a born leader.'

(E) Squadron Leader J.A. Kent was awarded a Bar to the DFC, *London Gazette,* 21 October 1941:

'Bar to the Distinguished Flying Cross.
'Acting Wing Commander John Alexander Kent, DFC, AFC (37106).
'This officer has led his wing in an efficient and fearless manner on many operational sorties within the last two months. He has now destroyed a further six enemy aircraft, bringing his total successes to thirteen destroyed and three probably destroyed. Wing Commander Kent has set a grand example.'

While acting as a flight commander with No. 303 Squadron, Flying Officer Witold Lokuciewski (flying BL655) was shot down over France on 13 March 1941. He was injured and made a PoW. Lokuciewski was sent to Stalag Luft III and took part in the Great Escape. He was recaptured and returned to the camp.

There is considerable confusion regarding Flying Officer Ludwik Witold Paszkiewicz's rank. The Squadron ORB and combat reports are inconsistent, referring to his rank as anything from pilot officer to flight lieutenant – even the Squadron ORB for the same day's operations will refer to him as a pilot officer in the 'general report', and as a flying officer in the 'work done' section.

(F) Sergeant Josef František was awarded the DFM, *London Gazette,* 27 September 1940 and was awarded a Bar to the DFM, *London Gazette,* 28 October 1940.

Notes

1. Pilot Officer (77465) Robert Henry Shaw, RAFVR, is remembered on the Runnymede Memorial, Panel 10.
2. Flight Lieutenant (90256) Harry Bryan Lillie Hillcoat, AAF, was the son of Henry and Edith Mary Hillcoat, of Bromsgrove, Worcestershire. Hillcoat was 25-years-old and is remembered on the Runnymede Memorial, Panel 4.
3. Pilot Officer (82157) George Louis Joseph Doutrepont, RAFVR, was reintered at Brussels Town Cemetery, Belgian Airmen's Field of Honour following the cessation of hostilities.
4. Sergeant (787554) Vladimir Horsky, RAFVR, is remembered on the Runnymede Memorial, Panel 15.
5. Flying Officer (P-1293) Ludwik Witold Paszkiewicz, VM, KW, RAF (flying L1696 RF-M), was killed-in-action at 0935 hours. His Hurricane crashed at Crowhurst Farm, Borough Green, Wrotham, Kent. Paszkiewicz was 35-years-old. Flying Officer L.W. Paszkiewicz was awarded the DFC, *London Gazette*, 30 October 1940.
6. Sergeant (P-5125) Tadeusz Andruszkow, RAF, was buried in Northwood Cemetery, Section H, Grave 208. He was 20-years-old and was born in Lwowie, Poland.
7. Flight Lieutenant A.S. Forbes was awarded the DFC, *London Gazette*, 22 October 1940 and was awarded a Bar to the DFC, *London Gazette*, 4 November 1941.
8. Pilot Officer J.E.L. Zumbach, VM 5th Class, KW, was awarded the DFC, *London Gazette*, 30 October 1941, and was awarded a Bar to the DFC, *London Gazette*, 15 November 1942.
9. Flying Officer (C/900) Otto John Peterson, RCAF, was the son of Peter and Magdalene Peterson; husband of Helen Marian Peterson, of Halifax, Nova Scotia, Canada; B.A. (University of Saskatchewan). Peterson was 24-years-old and was buried at Brookwood Military Cemetery, Section 3, Row K, Grave 1A.
10. Pilot Officer (42707) Frederick Cecil Harrold, RAF, was the son of Frederick Charles and Florence Nightingale Harrold, of Cambridge. Harrold was 23-years-old and was buried at Cherry Hinton (St Andrew) Churchyard.
11. Flight Lieutenant J.A. Kent was awarded the AFC, *London Gazette*, 2 January 1939 and was awarded the VM 5th Class, *London Gazette*, 24 December 1940.
12. Flying Officer W. Urbanowicz, VM 5th Class, KW, was awarded the DFC, *London Gazette*, 30 October 1941.
13. Pilot Officer Miroslaw Feric, VM 5th Class, KW was awarded the DFC, *London Gazette*, 30 October 1941.
14. Sergeant M. Belc, VM 5th Class, KW, was awarded the DFC, *London Gazette*, 15 October 1942.
15. Sergeant S. Karubin, VM 5th Class, KW, was awarded the DFC, *London Gazette*, 30 October 1941.
16. Sergeant Eugenius Szaposznikow, VM 5th Class, KW, was awarded the DFM, *London Gazette*, 30 October 1941.
17. Sergeant Josef František, DFM and Bar was the RAF's highest scorer during the battle, with seventeen 'kills'. He had been awarded the Polish Virtuti Militari 5th Class and would later be awarded the Czech Military Cross.

Chapter 3

Sergeant Leonard 'Joey' Jowitt, MiD, No. 85 Squadron

Sergeant Leonard Jowitt was a pre-war 'Halton Brat' who had re-mustered as a sergeant pilot. Flying with No. 85 Squadron he fought throughout the Battle of France and during the first phase of the Battle of Britain.

Leonard 'Joey' Jowitt was born on the 22 July 1911, in Failsworth, Manchester, to Leonard and Emily Jane Jowitt. He had two sisters – Elsie (born on 12 January 1914) and Ethel (born 22 January 1916). Leonard's father had fought in the Royal Field Artillery during the First World War, surviving only to die of tuberculosis over a decade on, as a result of the conditions suffered in the trenches. Of Leonard's six paternal uncles, two, Arthur and Clarence, were killed-in-action.

On 10 January 1928, aged 16-years-old, Leonard Jowitt enlisted into the RAF as an aircraft apprentice (Serial No. 562160), training as an airframe fitter at RAF Halton, working on aero-engines. Leonard served in India with No. 20 Squadron between 23 January 1932 and 30 March 1934, being advanced to leading aircraftman on 1 May 1933. For his service overseas, Jowitt received the India General Service medal, with Mohmand 1933 Clasp, which he later proudly wore for a studio photograph.

Back on a Home Establishment in March 1934, Leonard retrained as an air-gunner, following which he was posted, on 3 September 1937, to No. 502 (Bomber) Squadron, stationed at Aldergrove. With the expansion of the RAF following the rise of Nazi Germany, there was a call for an increase in the number of pilots and Leonard was one of the many former RAF Halton apprentices, known collectively as the 'Halton Brats', to be selected.

Leonard entered No. 6 Flying Training School, Netheravon, on 22 January 1938. He was promoted to corporal on 1 July 1938, in recognition of his efficiency and disciple while attending his course, which he successfully completed on 20 August 1938, passing out as a sergeant pilot.

Sergeant Jowitt was posted to 'B' Flight, No. 85 Squadron, then stationed at RAF Debden, and recently reformed (1 June 1938) from elements of No. 87 Squadron's 'A' Flight, commanded by Flight Lieutenant D.E. Turner. The squadron flew Gloster Gladiators, until re-equipped with Hawker Hurricanes, the first of which arrived on 4 September 1938.

Flight Lieutenant A.C.P. Carver commanded the squadron between 13 August and 1 November 1938, seeing the pilots through their conversion onto the new type, before handing over the reins to Squadron Leader D.F.W. Atcherley.

Having successfully made the leap from biplane to monoplane, Jowitt settled down into squadron life, flying what was then the RAF's top fighter.

Jowitt joined the squadron in air gunnery practice over Salisbury Plains on 6 April 1939, the pilots getting their first experience of firing the Hurricane's guns against ground targets. Then followed a period of intense training as the inevitability of armed conflict became apparent. The squadron largely concentrated on flying 'interceptions', mock combats, while also practicing air-to-air firing against a drogue.

Meanwhile, No. 85 Squadron's Operational Record Book (ORB) recorded that on 27 June the squadron was, 'attached to the Field Force as part of the RAF Component – under the Command of 60 Wing.' For the moment, however, the squadron remained at their RAF Debden station.

With war looming, at 2359 hours on 23 August, No. 85 Squadron received Signal X.213 from the Air Ministry, ordering the 'mobilization of all units of the RAF'. Consequently all leave was cancelled, pilots and ground staff were recalled, while the armourers busied themselves making up ammunition belts ready for immediate action – the squadron was officially placed at a state of Readiness.

No. 85 Squadron's overseas posting began on 9 September 1939, when their Hurricanes took off for Northern France where they formed a part of the Air Component (No. 14 Group) of the British Expeditionary Force (BEF), under Group Captain P.F. Fullard. Nos. 1 and 73 Squadrons (Le Havre – Octeville) and Nos. 85 and 87 Squadron (Rouen-Boos), formed No. 60 (Fighter) Wing under Wing Commander J.A. Boret, MC, DFC.

No. 60 (Fighter) Wing's role was to give air cover to the Bristol Blenheim and Fairey Battle squadrons flying out of air bases around Rheims. The unit's ORB reveals that with the light bombers confined to Allied airspace and reconnaissance sorties, No. 85 Squadron initially flew mainly base and Channel patrols. On 29 September, Jowitt's squadron transferred over to Merville, but the airfield had to be abandoned due to the heavy mud, moving over to Seclin, near Lille, on 12 November, with detachments operating out of Le Touquet and St Inglevert (in order to maintain Channel patrols).

It was during one of these patrols in defence of the Channel Ports, flown on 21 November, that Flight Lieutenant R.H.A. 'Dickie' Lee recorded the squadron's first 'kill' of the war when he destroyed an He 111, which was seen to dive into the waters off Boulogne, exploding on impact.

Lee, who was Lord Trenchard's godson, was later awarded the DFC for the destruction of this aircraft, the Squadron ORB recording on 8 March 1940:

'Notice was received that Flight Lieutenant R.H.A. Lee had been awarded the Distinguished Flying Cross for his outstanding brilliance and efficiency in his capacity of Flight Commander, terminating in the destruction of a Heinkel aircraft.'

The award was promulgated in the *London Gazette* of the same date:

'Air Ministry,
8 March 1940.
ROYAL AIR FORCE.
'The KING has been graciously pleased to approve of the following awards:—
'Awarded the Distinguished Flying Cross.
'Acting Flight Lieutenant Richard Hugh Antony LEE (33208).'

Meanwhile, on 6 December, the squadron was honoured with a visit by His Majesty King George VI, in the company of the Duke of Gloucester and Viscount Lord Gort. No doubt His Majesty, as was the tradition, took time out of his day to meet the pilots and senior ground staff. Leonard and the other sergeant pilots would, at any rate, have seen a fleeting glimpse of the King, perhaps even being offered the royal hand.

There was some 'action' during the royal visit, the Squadron ORB noting that: 'Whilst in the operations room orders were given to a section of aircraft which were at Readiness to take-off and intercept an enemy raid over Calais.' It is not clear if, in this instance, the scramble was staged for the Royal Party, as nothing came from the resulting patrol.

A second VIP tour occurred on 16 December, when The Right Honourable Neville Chamberlain, MP, 'inspected aircraft on the tarmac and officers and airmen of both squadrons in the hangar.' The Prime Minister had worked tirelessly for peace, but when war became inevitable his policies at least allowed time for the rearmament of the RAF, which was still largely equipped with biplanes at the beginning of 1939.

The New Year saw a change of command, with Squadron Leader J.O.W. Oliver taking over from Squadron Leader D.F.W. Atcherley on 8 January 1940. Both men were able commanders, the squadron being most fortunate in this respect.

During this phase of the war Jowitt's name only appeared on the flying roster sparingly, making one, or possibly two, local flights a month during the winter and early spring, with the occasional operation patrol or escort. Essentially, his logbook was ticking over with sufficient hours to keep him considered operational and no more.

For the rest of the squadron, the daily routine of patrols and practice flying continued but, frustratingly, without further combats. No doubt Jowitt and his fellow pilots were keen to put all of their training into action and to test their mettle; but this would have to wait.

In a sobering reminder of the ever-present dangers in flying, the squadron lost Sergeant S.W. Lenton[1] (flying L1978) during an affiliation exercise with Lysanders on 6 March. Lenton's Hurricane suffered engine failure during take-off at about 0945 hours. He attempted to land downwind at Mons-en-Chaussée, but crashed and died in the wreckage.

Meanwhile, Jowitt's name began to appear more frequently on the flying roster, although the majority of the squadron's sorties remained restricted to sector patrols, with the occasional scramble.

No. 85 Squadron was still based at Seclin when Hitler unleashed his war-machine on France and the Low Countries in the early hours of 10 May. The first indication of the new offensive came at 0410 hours when, as No. 85 Squadron's ORB recorded:

'The Blitzkrieg started, and the first intimation the squadron received was the sound of innumerable Hun aircraft roaring overhead.'

The duplicate Squadron ORB, compiled sometime after the event, noted its composition on this momentous day:

Squadron Leader J.O.W. Oliver

'A' Flight
Flight Lieutenant J.R.M. Boothby
Flying Officer K.H. Blair
Pilot Officer J.H. Ashton
Pilot Officer J.W. Lecky
Pilot Officer A.G. Lewis
Pilot Officer D.V.G. Mawhood
Pilot Officer T.G. Pace
Pilot Officer M.G. Rawlinson
Pilot Officer S.P. Stephenson
Sergeant G. Allard
Sergeant L.A. Crozier
Sergeant J. McG. Little

'B' Flight
Flight Lieutenant R.H.A. Lee, DFC
Flying Officer W.N. LePine
Pilot Officer D.H. Allen
Pilot Officer A.B. Angus
Pilot Officer J.A. Hemingway
Pilot Officer D.H. Wissler
Pilot Officer P.P. Woods-Scawen
Sergeant A. Deacon
Sergeant L. Jowitt

Details of the squadron's operations during the Battle of France were largely lost following the destruction of their original ORB due to enemy action. Once back in England a retrospective ORB was compiled. This, however, was based on documents which had already reached Fighter Command's HQ and the memories of the surviving officers, and therefore did not include all air operations, nor a record of who flew on which patrol, or the serial numbers of the aircraft involved.

Sergeant Jowitt was a member of 'B' Flight, but would have flown both as a part of his flight and as and when required, his gallantry later being recognized through a Mention-in-Despatches. With the original paperwork lost, the story of the squadron's battle must be seen as a window into the actions which led to Jowitt's 'Mention'.

Before dawn on that fateful day (10 May), within minutes of sighting the enemy overhead, the squadron was in action – they would remain in the thick of the combat until withdrawn ten days later. Two sections scrambled, and were soon airborne and seeking out the enemy. During this first patrol, 'B' Flight's Flight Lieutenant R.H.A. Lee (flying N2388 VY-R), Flying Officer D.H. Allen and Pilot Officer P.P. Woods-Scawen, each claimed a Henschel Hs 126, with an He 111 also being destroyed.

'A' Flight was also soon in action, when, at about 0500 hours, Squadron Leader J.O.M. Oliver (flying P2821), Pilot Officer J.W. Lecky and Flight Sergeant G. Allard (flying N2319), combined in the destruction of an He 111 north of Lille.

The enemy was initially seen some distance away and there was a danger that the squadron's Hurricanes might not be able to close in to within combat range. Squadron Leader Oliver pulled the boost button to overhaul the enemy bomber. His combat report read:

'Fired two bursts from astern and rear-gunner, who had been firing tracer, ceased fire. [The] E/A started to spiral and slowed right down, descending slowly and steeply. I fired three long bursts, 45 degrees deflection, at pilot. [The] E/A passed into steep dive underneath me'
(signed) Squadron Leader J.O.W. Oliver.

Pilot Officer Lecky got into the action too:

'Took off at 0430 hours. Climbed to 18,000ft, formatting on section leader. Saw E/A [and] overhauled him from astern and opened fire [near Lille]. After second burst [the] rear-gunner of E/A ceased to fire. I closed to 50 yards range, firing a long burst. [I] followed E/A, which was smoking heavily from both engines, down to 2,000ft. Lost E/A in darkness, most likely Do 17.'
(signed) Pilot Officer J.W. Lecky.

Flying Officer Allard's combat report added to the general narrative:

'Patrolling north of Lille [I] saw [an] E/A over Armentieres. [I] closed with E/A, he immediately opened fire with tracer from rear gun. I opened fire at 300 yards range diving down on him. I continued to close until [at 20 yards] a cloud of black smoke covered my own aircraft. [I] saw him go in steep spiral and was about to follow when I saw another fighter engage him. I broke off the engagement.'

Meanwhile, 'A' Flight's Flight Lieutenant J.R.M. Boothby, Flying Officer K.H. Blair and Pilot Officer D.V.G. Mawhood (flying VY-S) came up against a formation of Ju 88s of VIII./LG 1. Boothby was able to claim one destroyed, but Mawhood was wounded by return fire from another, his aircraft's tail and canopy receiving rounds. Despite being blinded in one eye by splinters, he successfully force-landed at Mons-en-Chaussée.

Flight Lieutenant Boothby's combat report read:

'Attacked left-hand machine [at 18,000ft over Lenines] firing long burst. [The] enemy's engine stopped and oil poured over attacker from engines, from both of which smoke came … broke away and delivered second attack – other aircraft [Pilot Officer Mawhood] attacked right-hand machine immediately after, apparently hitting it, but a shot passed through [his] windscreen, shattering [the] Perspex and wounded [the] pilot.'

(signed) Flight Lieutenant J.R.M. Boothby.

In a separate engagement, Flying Officer K.H. Blair destroyed a Ju 88 north of Gand, while flying at 10,000ft. His combat report was timed at 0445-0500 hours:

'[An] enemy aircraft opened fire at about 1,000 yards. I closed to 400 yards and gave E/A three bursts of four seconds. Heavy smoke [was seen coming] from starboard engine of [the] E/A. [The] E/A then dived steeply and I lost sight of it in ground mist.'

The Junkers Ju 88, piloted by Feldwebel Ernst Schade, crashed, but not before its crew were able to bail out to be taken as PoWs.

Within forty minutes of taking off, the Hurricanes had landed and were being rearmed and refuelled.

The squadron was soon back in the air, and, at 0730 hours, 'B' Flight's Flight Lieutenant H.A. Lee, Flight Officer A.B. Angus (flying N2472), and Pilot Officer P.P. Woods-Scawen, were in action against a formation of three He 111s of II./KG 27, which Lee engaged from 500 yards:

'I fired [a] short burst and finished [my] ammunition on closing to 200 yards. No apparent results except black smoke from one engine. My aircraft [was] shot [up] badly.'

Flight Officer Angus then joined in the attack. Despite damage to his own aircraft from return fire, which led to an engine seizure, he was able to claim the bomber's destruction:

'I sighted [the] enemy first and informed F/Lt Lee by wireless, [and] gave chase. Lee fired, then I came in to attack, closed to 50 yards after two bursts and saw [the] rear-gunner disengage. [The] starboard engine of the E/A cut out.'

Flying Officer Angus' Hurricane, N2472, was also hit in the engine by return fire from a Ju 88, which he probably destroyed:[2]

'I returned home. Engine seized and I force-landed at Celles-Edcanaf. The last I saw of [the] E/A [it] was diving to ground near Gand.'

Angus lost oil pressure, but was able to make a safe landing in Belgium, making his own way back to the squadron a few hours later.

During the early afternoon, at 1445 hours, a patrol was returning from Vimy when 'A' Flight's Flight Sergeant Allard sighted an He 111 of III./KG 1, which he destroyed, while Pilot Officer J.H. Ashton got a brace of He 111s.

Flight Sergeant G. Allard reported in his debriefing:

'[I] saw [an] He 111 on [my] left. [I] climbed into sun to 8,000ft and aligned quarter attack. [My] first burst registered so [I] attacked from other quarter. Each time I closed to within 50 yards. [I made a] line astern attack from 300 yards. As I closed, [the] E/A dived into ground in flames one mile from Condescourt.'
(signed) Flight Sergeant G. Allard.

The 'kill' was confirmed by Pilot Officer Martin.

There was no let-up, and the squadron was again in action between 1820 and 1830 hours. Commanding 'A' Flight, Flight Lieutenant J.R.M. Boothby encountered a formation of twenty-five to thirty He 111s of III./KG 54, claiming a share in the destruction of one, damaging a second:

'Leading Red Section on patrol at 15,000ft over base. I sighted a large formation of twin-engine A/C and reported facts to operations. [The] E/A were circling so [I] waited to find places to join in with section. [The] ring broke up on [the] far side and some six other Hurricanes got in first. [I] brought [the] section into action and attacked an already smoking aircraft. This went into a steep dive so I left it, breaking out of the dogfight to the right. I then spotted two aircraft of the leading enemy formation diving for cover. I [selected one and] dived on it and used the rest of my ammunition, leaving it smoking with wheels down.'
(signed) Flight Lieutenant J.R.M. Boothby.

Meanwhile, Pilot Officer J.W. Lecky also engaged the damaged He 111, which he finished off.

'A' Section's Flying Officer T.G. Pace also claimed one He 111 destroyed three miles north of Lille, opening firing at 200 yards and closing to 50 yards:

'[I] followed leader to attack, picked out one escaping [He 111] and delivered a stern attack, one quarter attack and a final stern attack. [The] E/A dived steeply to ground.'
(signed) Flying Officer T.G. Pace.

The pilots of 'B' Flight were also in action against the He 111s at 1820 hours. Pilot Officer J.A. Hemingway (flying L1979 VY-X) reported:

'I was on patrol at area Hallin-Courtrai when I observed AA shell bursts which attracted [my] attention to nine He 111s. I left formation [flying at 11,000ft] and attacked nearest He 111 in stern attack. I opened fire at 250 yards and closed to 50 yards [firing three bursts]. [I] broke away to left and downwards. [I] saw clouds of smoke and flame coming from [the] E/A. I was so close that my engine was covered with enemy oil. [The] E/A fell to earth in [a] slow spiral and then dived: between Desselghem and Waeken. [I] noticed when [the] E/A [was] shot down [I] passed [a] parachutist on his way down.'
(signed) Pilot Officer J. Hemingway.

Meanwhile, Flying Officer N.W. LePine claimed a second He 111 out of the same formation:

'[I] attacked left rear aircraft. By the time I was in range this E/A was ahead of others. I fired burst of 150 rounds [at 250 yards]. [I] had to break away. When I returned to attack, [the] E/A was diving east, emitting smoke [from] both engines. I attacked another E/A and fired a burst of 150 rounds per gun. This E/A had already been engaged by another Hurricane and [its] port engine was out of action.'
(signed) Flying Officer N.W. LePine.

Another He 111 fell to the guns of Flying Officer T.G. Pace, who engaged the enemy at 15,000ft while over the squadron's airfield. His combat report read:

'[I] followed leader to attack, picked one escaping [bomber] and delivered stern attack, quarter attack and final stern attack. [The] E/A dived steeply to ground.'
(signed) Pilot Officer J.W. Lecky

Later that day 'A' Flight's Flying Officer T.G. Pace and Sergeant G. Allard were scrambled and engaged two He 111s flying at 10,000ft south of Cambrai, between 2025 and 2035 hours.

Red 1, Sergeant G. Allard, claimed an He 111 damaged:

'I attacked the right-hand aircraft, and Red 2, the left-hand. We closed the attack [from 300 yards] to 50 yards approx. I found it essential to break away upwards and in front. I then delivered an attack from the quarter, and saw that both aircraft were losing oil, and black smoke came from the engines. I carried on the attack after Red 2 ran out of ammunition, and before breaking away, saw both aircraft losing height. The undercarriage of the port enemy aircraft was hanging down.'
(signed) Sergeant G. Allard.

Red 2, Flying Officer T.G. Pace, also claimed an He 111 damaged. His combat report continues the narrative:

'[I] opened fire at 200 yards and closed to 50 yards. [I] delivered a quarter attack, next developing into a No. 1 [attack] using [my] remaining ammunition as a very good sight was obtained. [When last seen, the] Heinkel had [its] undercarriage down and [its] starboard engine [had] stopped and smoke issued from it. [The] rear-gunner stopped firing after [my] first attack.

'I noticed black smoke coming from the machine Red 1 was attacking.'
(signed) Flying Officer T.G. Pace.

The squadron's day was not yet over and they were called upon to fly further defensive patrols. At about 2040–2100 hours a section of No. 85 Squadron's Hurricanes intercepted stragglers from I./LG 1 or KG 27. Flying Officer K.H. Blair destroyed two He 111s and Pilot Officer M.G. Rawlinson damaged a third. 'A' Flight's Flying Officer Blair's combat took place between Arras and Vitry:

'I attacked two E/A flying in formation at 8,000ft, approx. The first E/A's starboard engine caught fire and black smoke poured out of it. Another friendly fighter attacked the first E/A and I attacked once more when friendly fighter had finished. Black smoke and oil completely obscured the target after my second burst of fire, and [it] began to descend. I then turned my attention to the first [E/A] who had been firing at me. In my second burst, black smoke appeared from the engine and fuselage, and [the E/A] appeared to be gliding to the ground.'
(signed) Flying Officer K.H. Blair.

'A' Flight's Pilot Officer M.G. Rawlinson shared Blair's second He 111. His combat report read:

'Enemy in sight all the time, flying in two sections of three and two. [I] followed section of two. Flying Officer Blair opened fire in front from quarter on No. 1, when he broke away smoke poured from both engines. Rear-gunner was still alive, shooting at him. [I] closed and overshot E/A after ammunition was expended, but [the] rear-gunner was out of action. When last seen [the] E/A was in a shallow dive with oil and smoke pouring from both engines.'
(signed) Pilot Officer M.G. Rawlinson.

Meanwhile, 'B' Flight's Blue Section, Flight Lieutenant R.H.A. Lee, Flying Officer D.H. Allen and Pilot Officer P.P. Woods-Scawen, engaged a Ju 88 at 7,000ft, while flying six miles to the north-west of St Armand:

'Section of three attacked in line astern. After first aircraft attacked, [its] starboard engine caught fire and one member of [the] crew successfully jumped by parachute. [We] attacked second and third aircraft, and set [the]

E/A completely on fire and they crashed in flames. [While attacking the] first aircraft [I] shot off 50 rounds per gun, [and the] second aircraft 100 per gun, third aircraft 30 per gun.'
(signed) Flight Lieutenant R.H.A. Lee, Pilot Officer P.P. Woods–Scawen, Flying Officer D.H. Allen.

Credited with a hand in the destruction of two enemy aircraft, Flight Lieutenant Lee landed with several holes in the fabric of his aircraft, the result of return fire, while a splinter had given him a leg graze.

The Squadron ORB summarized the events of the hectic day:

'Intermittently throughout the day as each section and flight landed, the pilots and aircraft were on the ground only long enough to allow for rearming and refuelling, and so it went on from dawn till dusk; by the end of the day the squadron had a total bag of seventeen enemy aircraft to their credit, with the loss of two more of our aircraft'

These claims may be summarized:

Flight Lieutenant J.R.M. Boothby	one He 111 (shared), one He 111 probable
Flight Lieutenant R.H.A. Lee	one Ju 88 probable (shared), one Ju 88 (shared)
Flying Officer D.H. Allen	one Ju 88 (shared)
Flying Officer A.B. Angus	one Ju 88 probable (shared)
Flying Officer K.H. Blair	one He 111, one He 111 (shared)
Flying Officer W.N. LePine	one He 111
Pilot Officer J.H. Ashton	two He 111
Pilot Officer J.A. Hemingway	one He 111
Pilot Officer T.G. Pace	one He 111, one He 111 probable
Pilot Officer M.G. Rawlinson	one He 111 (shared)
Pilot Officer P.P. Woods–Scawen	one Ju 88
Sergeant G. Allard	one He 111, one He 111 probable

That night the squadron's airfield was attacked, one bomb landing within twenty yards of the pilots' billets, but without leading to any serious injuries.

The squadron's pilots would win a number of gallantry awards for their exploits over France and the Low Countries. The first of these to be earned was the DFC awarded to Flying Officer K.H. Blair for gallantry during 10 May, as confirmed by the citation which accompanied the announcement made in the *London Gazette* of 31 May 1940:

'Distinguished Flying Cross.
'Flying Officer Kenneth Hughes BLAIR (39704).
'This officer has shown exceptional keenness both before and during the present operations. He has engaged, successfully, two enemy bomber aircraft,

viz., at dawn, one day in May, when he succeeded in being the first off the ground in pursuit of a Heinkel, and at dusk on the same day, when he successfully attacked another Heinkel between Arras and Vitry. He had a very narrow escape when a bomb landed within twenty yards of a room in which he was sleeping. He was badly shaken, but insisted in volunteering and taking part in a patrol over Maastricht, when he engaged two Messerschmitt 109s.

The squadron flew a number of offensive patrols out of Seclin during the following day, 11 May, providing cover for the advance of the BEF. These operations included one over the Tongres-Maastricht sector, during which Flight Lieutenant R.H.A. Lee led his section against a formation of Do 17s from I./KG 76. A combined attack by Flight Lieutenant R.H.A. Lee, Flying Officer D. Allen and Pilot Officer P.P. Woods-Scawen saw the destruction of one Dornier, while a second was claimed by Lee.

Flight Lieutenant Lee's Hurricane, N2388 VY-R, was damaged, possibly by flak or return fire from a Do 17 while over Maastricht, and he was forced to take to his parachute. Landing behind enemy lines, Lee donned an old overcoat given to him by a Belgian civilian. He was later captured and locked in a barn by German troops, who took him for a civilian, but escaped to rejoin the squadron. Flight Lieutenant Allen's Hurricane was also hit by flak, but he was able to make it back to base.

Lee returned to the squadron during the following day, 12 May, the Squadron ORB recording that:

'He had been shot down and had to bail out – he was only slightly wounded. He descended by parachute in or near a village in Belgium which was in the process of being reoccupied by the German mechanized forces. He borrowed a peasant's smock and walked through the German lines and reported all he had seen to the first English unit he met; the information proved to be of greatest value.'

As a result of these exploits, and in recognition of his growing tally, Flight Lieutenant R.H.A. Lee, DFC, was awarded the DSO, *London Gazette*, 31 May 1940:

'Distinguished Service Order.
'Flight Lieutenant Richard Hugh Anthony LEE, DFC (33208).
'This officer has displayed great ability as a leader and intense desire to engage the enemy. On one occasion he continued to attack an enemy aircraft after his companion had been shot down and his own machine hit in many places. His section shot down a Dornier 215 in flames one evening in May, and another in the course of an engagement the next day. In his last engagement he was seen at 200ft on the tail of a Junkers 88, being subject to intense fire from the ground over enemy-occupied territory. This officer escaped from behind German lines after being arrested and upheld the highest traditions of the service.'

Lee would receive both awards from the hands of His Majesty the King at a special ceremony held at RAF Debden on 26 June. Among the other pilots receiving gallantry awards was Pilot Officer Gerald 'Zulu' Lewis, the pair having flown over in the squadron's Miles Master.

Meanwhile, Seclin was raided again a little after noon on the eleventh, with a string of bombs detonating close to the officer's quarters, but without causing any casualties.

Airborne again, the squadron was soon in action. Squadron Leader J.O.W. Oliver (flying P2821) and Sergeant G. Allard (flying N2319) both claimed a brace of I. and III./KG 27's He 111s. Oliver returned slightly wounded. Meanwhile, Pilot Officer J.A. Hemingway shared a Do 17 before being shot down by German flak, making his own way back to the airfield. The squadron's medical officer removed shrapnel from his right knee and ankle.

The squadron's Hurricanes had their first taste of combat against Bf 109s when Flying Officer K.H. Blair took on two of the fighters while patrolling near Maastricht. The engagement, however, proved inconclusive. Elsewhere, Flying Officer D.H. Allen led Pilot Officers J.A. Hemingway and P.P. Woods-Scawen in the destruction of a Do 17 of II. (F)/123. Allen's Hurricane was later damaged by flak and limped back to base. Hemingway (flying L1979 VY-X) attacked a Fieseler Storch, which dived to treetop level with the Hurricane in hot pursuit. As a result, Hemingway was hit by flak and crash-landed, but he was able to make his own way back to Seclin airfield.

The day's exploits had earned Flying Officer D.H. Allen the DFC, which was promulgated in the *London Gazette*, 31 May 1940:

'Awarded the Distinguished Flying Cross.
'Flying Officer Derek Hurlstone ALLEN (39840).
'This officer has taken part in all combats with Flight Lieutenant R.H.A. Lee, following his section leader with great loyalty. In May 1940, he took part in shooting down a Junkers [Ju 88], and the next day another enemy aircraft of the same type. On the latter day, after his aircraft had been severely damaged by anti-aircraft fire, he did not hesitate to attack, with vigour and determination, a Junkers 88 over enemy-occupied territory and shot it down.'

The citation refers to his destroying a Ju 88, whereas the squadron records mention Do 17s. Aircraft destroyed after 11 May are not mentioned at all, helping to date the initial recommendation.

Another pilot, whose exploits were recognized, was Sergeant G. Allard, who had already brought his total to three destroyed and one probably destroyed. He was awarded the DFM, *London Gazette*, 31 May 1940, the first of three gallantry medals earned in 1940:

'Awarded the Distinguished Flying Medal.

'Sergeant Geoffrey ALLARD (563859).

'This airman has shown outstanding flying ability, and at all times his coolness and confidence have assisted all pilots who have flown with him. He has been largely responsible for keeping up the high morale and fighting ability of his section. Altogether, in his combats during recent days he has destroyed four enemy aircraft. Without exception he has pressed home his attacks with outstanding courage, which has been a fine example to his section.'

During 12 May, the squadron flew an escort operation to Blenheims of Nos. 15 and 107 Squadrons. At about 0900 hours, with their primary mission completed, the Hurricanes of Nos. 85 and 87 Squadrons broke off to engage the enemy, scoring a mixed bag.

No. 85 Squadron's tally for the day was seven enemy aircraft destroyed, including five He 111s, a Dornier 17 and a Ju 88, and may be summarized:

Squadron Leader A.O.W. Oliver	one He 111 and a Do 17 destroyed
Pilot Officer A.G. Lewis (flying VY-E)	one He 111 and a Bf 109 destroyed
Sergeant G. Allard	two He 111s destroyed
Unknown pilot, possibly Jowitt	one Ju 88 destroyed

No. 87 Squadron's claims included

Squadron Leader J.S. Dewar	one Ju 87 destroyed
Flying Officer R.L. Glyde	one He 111 destroyed
Flying Officer H.T. Mitchell	one Ju 87 destroyed
Pilot Officer W.D. David	one He 111 destroyed

The enemy made a third raid in as many days on the squadron's airfield, again failing to cause any major collateral damage.

No. 85 Squadron was in action again throughout 13 May, beginning early when they took on a formation of He 111s of II./KG 4 and their escort of Bf 110s. Squadron Leader J.O.W. Oliver (flying P2821) claimed two He 111s. Other pilots claiming Heinkels included Flight Lieutenant R.H.A. Lee, and Flying Officers D.H. Allen and K.H. Blair, each bagging a brace, with Flight Lieutenant J.R.M. Boothby and Pilot Officer J.W. Lecky destroying two more between them (although the Luftwaffe records, often found wanting, only acknowledge the loss of three Heinkel 111s). By the end of the day the squadron had accounted for thirteen enemy aircraft.

On a later patrol the squadron was bounced by Bf 109s, when Squadron Leader Oliver (flying P2821) was shot down by Leutnant Winfried Schmidt of VIII./JG 3, south of Diest. Oliver parachuted to safety, making his own way back to the squadron later that day. In reply, Sergeant A. Deacon destroyed the Bf 109 piloted by Obergefreiter Heinz Schlandt.

On 14 May, the airfield was once again bombed by the enemy. While at about 0900 hours, Nos. 85, 87 and 607 Squadrons were scrambled to engage a large formation composed of He 111s and their escort of Bf 109s. No. 85 Squadron destroyed five Heinkel 111s from I. and III./KG 27, two falling to the guns of Flying Lieutenant R.H.A. Lee, with Flying Officer A. Angus destroying an He 111 and sharing a second with No. 87 Squadron's Pilot Officer W.D. David (flying L1630).

Flying Officer (40281) A.B. Angus was awarded the DFC, *London Gazette*, 31 May 1940. The citation takes his score up to the 14 May, as it includes the bomber shared with Pilot Officer David, but not his two subsequent victories claimed on the 15 and 16 May (the day Angus was killed-in-action):

'Distinguished Flying Cross.
'Flying Officer Allan Benjamin ANGUS (40281).
'This officer has shown great determination in taking every opportunity of engaging the enemy and pressing home his attacks. He took part in an inconclusive attack on a Junkers 88 which resulted in serious damage to the enemy aircraft. His own aircraft was hit and as a result he had to force-land in Belgium. Acting on his own initiative he rejoined the squadron in a few hours. In May, while on patrol, he intercepted and shot down in flames a Heinkel 111, and on the same patrol took part in shooting down a second enemy aircraft of the same type with Flying Officer [W.D.] David.'

Pilot Officer David, who claimed a second He 111, was later awarded the DFC (*London Gazette*, 31 May 1940) and Bar (*London Gazette*, 4 June).

Meanwhile, No. 87 Squadron's Pilot Officer P.L. Jarvis (flying L1616) claimed an He 111, but was shot down by a Bf 109 of II./JG 27, west of Maastricht. Pilot Officer G.C. Saunders (flying L1612) was shot down by a Bf 110 of ZG 1; he later died in Lille Hospital (19 May 1940).[3]

Jowitt and his fellow pilots were flying operations from dawn to dusk, getting little sleep in the hours between. Their CO had been unable to rest any of his pilots until the arrival of a batch of reinforcements, which came none too soon:

Seconded from No. 242 Squadron's 'A' Flight were:

Flight Lieutenant D.R. Miller
Pilot Officer M.K. Brown
Pilot Officer L.E. Chambers
Pilot Officer A.H. Deacon
Pilot Officer A.H. Wiens

Meanwhile, as the squadron suffered further losses, additional pilots arrived at various dates during the squadron's battle over France, these included:

Pilot Officer R.W. Burton
Pilot Officer H.D. Clark

Pilot Officer Count M.B. Czernin
Pilot Officer A.V. Gower (from hospital)
Pilot Officer J.E. Marshall
Pilot Officer R.W. Shrewsbury
Sergeant H.H. Allgood
Sergeant L.R. Butler
Sergeant C.H. Hampshire (recalled from leave)
Sergeant H.N. Howes
Sergeant C.A. Rust
Sergeant F.R. Walker-Smith

No. 85 Squadron claimed four He 111s on 15 May, with one shot down by Flight Lieutenant H.A. Lee and two claimed by Flying Officer A.B. Angus. Meanwhile, Sergeant D.H. Allard claimed another, which crashed and burned out within a mile and a half of the airfield. The wreckage of the lone raider was inspected by some of the pilots and ground crew when it was noted that, 'nothing of interest could be found except six unexploded (50 kilo) bombs – the occupants and plane were a smouldering mass of ruins.'

Meanwhile, Sergeant C. Hampshire damaged an He 111 during the same patrol.

During a single patrol between Ath and Namur, made shortly after noon – an escort to a Lysander of No. 13 Squadron – the squadron lost three Hurricanes. Flying Officer D.H. Allen (flying P2828) was forced to bail out at 1315 hours following combat with Bf 110s of V./ZG 26 east of Ath. He made it back to base and was soon back in action. Flying Officer T.C. Pace (flying L1694) was shot down by Bf 110s of the same unit, making a crash-landing, his aircraft burning out. Pace received severe burns and had to be evacuated to England for treatment. Meanwhile, Pilot Officer J.H. Ashton (flying L1775) took to his parachute south of Ath, the third of the Messerschmitts's victims; he returned to the squadron the following day.

Eight enemy aircraft were destroyed on 16 May, including at least one unattributed aircraft, a Bf 110. It is possible that this fighter fell foul of Jowitt, adding to a total which was to earn him a Mention-in-Despatches.

No. 85 Squadron's Sergeant L.A. Crozier was patrolling when he sighted what he believed to be an enemy bomber approaching Glisy airfield. Lining up his target, he fired a burst which silenced its starboard engine. The bomber, a Blenheim, L4852, of No. 53 Squadron, had already been damaged by 'friendly' anti-aircraft fire before receiving further damage. The attack had taken place over Amien and the reconnaissance aircraft made an emergency belly-landing at Glisy, at 1630 hours, crashing during his approach. The aircraft was piloted by Flight Lieutenant B.B. St G. Daly, who was badly burned, as were his navigator, Sergeant W.R.B. Currie, and air-gunner, AC2 P.J. Blandford.

At about 1330 hours, No. 85 Squadron's pilots were sitting in their cockpits at Readiness when they were scrambled to defend their own airfield from attack by He 111s of III./LG 1, escorted by Bf 109s of V./JG 2. Flight Lieutenant R.H.A. Lee and Sergeants S. Allard and C. Hampshire claimed an He 111 destroyed, probably sharing a single aircraft, while Sergeant A. Deacon successfully engaged one of the Bf 109 escort.

Sergeant L.A. Crozier (flying N2389) was shot down and suffered burns before he was able to take to his parachute. Meanwhile, replacement pilot, Sergeant H.H. Allgood (ferrying L1898) was shot down, crash-landing north-west of Lille, wounded. The Hurricanes were claimed by the Bf 109s of Unteroffizier Hans-Joachim Hartwig and Oberleutnant Helmut Bolz, Staffelkapitän of V./JG 2.

During the same engagement, Flying Officer A.B. Angus (flying L1641) and Pilot Officer M.G. Rawlinson (flying P2535) each destroyed two enemy aircraft, before being shot down by Bf 109s of V./JG 2 south-west of Lille. It is believed that Flying Officer Angus[4] fell victim to Leutnant Schetelig, while Pilot Officer Rawlinson[5] was probably shot down by Leutnant Hepe.

Meanwhile, No. 87 Squadron's, Flying Officer R.M.S. Rayner and Pilot Officer W.D. David (flying L1630), shared in the destruction of a Bf 109. Their squadron lost Sergeant A.N. Trice (flying L2000), who was shot down by a Bf 109 of V./JG 2, while west of Mons.[6]

Taking on a wing patrol along the Luxembourg border at 1730 hours, No. 85 Squadron was bounced by Bf 109s, with Flying Officer Count M.B. Czernin (flying L1640) and Pilot Officer H.D. Clark (flying P2824) falling victim to Leutnant Hillecke of II./JG 26 and Hauptmann Knüppel, Gruppenkommander of II./JG 26, while still over Seclin (Clark had arrived on attachment from No. 213 Squadron on 14 May). Both pilots force-landed, but it was three days before Czernin was able to return to his squadron. Meanwhile, five Bf 110s of I./ZG 1 were engaged, with one destroyed by an unknown pilot. While there is no evidence to suggest that Jowitt was responsible for the claim, it remains a possibility, as he was singled out for recognition for bravery during the campaign, despite only having one confirmed 'kill'.

Battle-weary, Flight Lieutenant R.H.A. Lee, Flying Officer K.H. Blair, Pilot Officers J.H. Ashton and J.A. Hemingway, and Sergeant G. Allard, were granted leave and flown in an Ensign back to the UK on 17 May. Flight Lieutenant J.R.M. Boothby and Pilot Officer J.W. Lecky were granted forty-eight hours leave. Lecky would be killed in a car crash the following day, with Boothby injured; they were making their way back to the squadron.

Flight Lieutenant J.R.M. Boothby was still recuperating from injuries when he learned of his awarded of the DFC, which was promulgated in the *London Gazette*, 31 May 1940:

'Distinguished Flying Cross.
'Flight Lieutenant James Robert Maitland BOOTHBY (39023).
'This officer has consistently led his section with skill and efficiency. He himself shot down three enemy aircraft in one day.'

Meanwhile, with the squadron pushed to its limits, Flying Officer J. Jeffries and Pilot Officer G.E. Pittman were posted from No. 17 Squadron as replacements, helping maintain the unit at full strength.

At about 1600 hours the squadron engaged seven Bf 109s from Stab and I./JG 3. Pilot Officer P.P. Woods-Scawen (flying N2319) claimed two enemy fighters, but was forced to bail out following combat. His Hurricane was claimed by Leutnant Helmut Reumschüssel. Pilot Officer R.H. Wiens, on detachment from No. 242 Squadron's 'A' Flight, and Sergeant C. Hampshire, both claimed a Bf 109.

The 18 May began badly for the squadron, with a patrol flown at 0700 hours in the company of No. 87 Squadron, during which they were bounced by a dozen Bf 110s of I./ZG 26 while flying between Le Cateau and Cambrai. Flying Officer D.H. Allen[7] (flying P2701) was shot down and killed, while Flying Officer W.N. LePine (flying N2425) was shot down in the same vicinity. He bailed out, wounded, and became a PoW.

Flying Officer L.E. Chambers (flying L1922), and Pilot Officers R.H. Wiens (flying L1665) and M.K. Brown (flying N2320), were shot down by Bf 110s of I./ZG 26. Wiens walked away from a crash-landing, while Brown was wounded. Chambers was also wounded, but parachuted into captivity. All three were on secondment from No. 242 Squadron's 'A' Flight and had been thrown in at the deep end with less than twelve hours on type.

During the afternoon, Nos. 85 and 87 Squadrons were in action once again, engaging a formation of Bf 110s, gaining a number of victories:

No. 85 Squadron's claims were:

Pilot Officer R.H. Wiens	one Bf 110 destroyed and a Bf 110 probable
Sergeant C.E. Hampshire	one Bf 110 destroyed

No. 87 Squadron claimed:

Flying Officer R.F. Watson	one Bf 110 destroyed
Pilot Officer C.W.W. Darwin	one Bf 110 destroyed

Meanwhile, on 19 May, No. 85 Squadron was ordered to transfer to Merville, but before making the move they accounted for a further sixteen enemy aircraft.

Flying Officer Count M.B. Czernin was detailed to mount a base patrol at 0600 hours, encountering a formation of seven Do 17s of IX./KG 76 high above him. Czernin pursued the enemy as far as Valenciennes, where he caught up with the vic of bombers, destroying two, although Luftwaffe records only acknowledging one aircraft lost:

'I attacked the last one on the starboard side from out of the sun, and immediately he broke away with his port engine on fire. He did not come out of the resulting dive and crashed in flames in a wood by a railway east of Valenciennes. I attacked the formation again, spraying fire from a beam attack

and saw one more Do 17 break away and dive down with smoke coming from both engines. At about 10,000ft he burst into flames and seemed to break up.'
(signed) Flying Officer M.B. Czernin.

Meanwhile, at about 1000 hours, Pilot Officers A.G. Lewis (flying No. 213's AK-A) and P.P. Woods-Scawen (flying P2547), both claimed a brace of Bf 109s, Flying Officer J. Jeffries claiming a fifth as probably destroyed. Woods-Scawen's combat report was timed at 1015 hours and read:

'I saw three Hurricanes engaged in combat with several E/A. I took off and shot down one E/A in flames five miles east of Sedan after [a] burst of two seconds. The puff of smoke when this E/A crashed was seen from the aerodrome. I climbed to 5,000ft and engaged a second Me 109, which dived emitting smoke to the ground after several bursts of three seconds [fired] from 100 yards.'

Having run out of ammunition, and with two Bf 109s making an attacking approach, Woods-Scawen was forced to pull away and didn't see his second victim crash.

At noon, Flying Officer S.P. Stephenson led a section strength patrol of Lille, with orders to land at Merville. Flying alongside Stephenson were Pilot Officers A.H. Deacon and A.G. Lewis, and Sergeants L. Jowitt and J. McG. Little (flying P2562).

Sergeant J. McG. Little destroyed two He 111s of III./KG 28 (witnessed by Pilot Officer Deacon of No. 242 Squadron's detached 'A' Flight) before being shot down in flames near Lille by one of their escort, a Bf 109 of I.(J)/JG 2 or II./JG 2, possibly flown by Leutnant Tismar.

Meanwhile, Pilot Officer A.H. Deacon shot down an He 111, seeing the pilot bail out. On detachment, Flight Lieutenant D. Miller of No. 242 Squadron's 'A' Flight received battle damage to his Hurricane (P2808) following an engagement with Bf 109s of I./JG2, but he made base.

Jowitt destroyed an He 111, part of a formation of nineteen enemy bombers flying at about 7,000ft in the area of Carvin/Seclin. His combat report, timed at 1230 hours, read:

'I took off to intercept bombers which bombed base. One broke away from the formation and I attacked from the rear at a range of 100 to 150 yards. It started smoking and throwing out oil. I fired again and it burst into flames. I followed it down and saw it crash and explode half a mile south of Templeuve, in the fork of the railway junction.'
(signed) Sergeant L. Jowitt.

Firing at close range, Jowitt demonstrated all the skill of an experienced combat pilot, further fuelling the speculation that this was not his only victory during the campaign.

Meanwhile, Pilot Officer A.G. Lewis (flying No. 213's AK-A) had been forced to break formation and was making for Seclin when he was bounced by three Bf 109s. The leader overshot and received a concerted burst and dived straight in. The other two tried to race for home, but with Lewis' use of the booster, they too were caught and destroyed, making his total five confirmed for the day.

The combat occurred within sight of Squadron Leader J.O.W. Oliver, who later informed Lewis that he was being recommended for an immediate award of the DFC.

Pilot Officer A.G. Lewis' DFC was announced in the *London Gazette,* 25 June 1940:

'Distinguished Flying Cross.
'Pilot Officer Albert Gerald LEWIS (41303).
'Pilot Officer Lewis has, by a combination of great personal courage, determination and skill, shot down five enemy aircraft, single-handed, in one day. He has destroyed in all a total of seven enemy aircraft and, by his example, has been an inspiration to his squadron.'

Lewis later recalled the events on 19 May in a letter:

'I was jumped by a patrol of three Me 109s as I was about to return to base, troubled by a loose gun panel; [I only] became aware of [an] attack as tracer streamed by. [I] turned into [the] attack and found the leader coming straight at me. Somehow his cannon shots missed and he rolled into a steep turn almost on his back, and pulled away. Suddenly there was his belly at point-blank range. I rammed the nose of the Hurricane down, my head hitting the top of the cockpit glasshouse, and pressed the gun button; fuel spewed out from the L-shaped tank which the pilot sat on, and, with fuel streaming behind him, the pilot flew straight down into the deck and exploded. By the way he handled his plane, I imagine the pilot to be experienced, possibly an instructor, with two greenies or fledglings, as the other two made half-hearted attacks, formed up together and headed home, towards Brussels.

'The fight had occurred in the Roubaix area on the Franco-Belgian border. My first inclination was to leave well alone, but realizing we had the extra boost in the Hurricane if we needed it for short duration, I pulled out the boost control, and followed the two. I don't think they were aware of me following them, as I was able to position myself slightly below and behind. They were sitting ducks; short bursts into each and they plummeted straight down into the deck at a steep angle. I was able to pinpoint the wreckage and submit my report.'

No. 85 Squadron suffered the loss of Sergeant J. McG. Little[8] who was killed-in-action, no sign of his aircraft, or of Little, was ever found, but it is presumed that he fell to the guns of an enemy fighter during the general melee.

The squadron made a further patrol at 1550 hours, Pilot Officer P.P. Woods-Scawen engaging the Bf 109 of I./JG 3 flown by Leutnant Heinz Schnabel at 5,000ft, which was badly damaged and subsequently crash-landed near Philippeville:

'I was leading Blue Section. I saw a single E/A travelling east. I suspected a trap so I broke away, the remainder of the section to cover me, and delivered a stern attack on the E/A from 100 yards giving one burst of two seconds. The E/A dived steeply emitting smoke and made a crash-landing in a field five miles west of Lourmai.'

Later, during the same patrol, Woods-Scawen sighted a Do 17. Again suspecting a trap, he searched above before attacking a formation of seven Bf 109s head-on at 10,000ft, south-east of Lille. Having sent the leader down smoking, Woods-Scawen turned to make a second attack, at which point his Hurricane was hit in the engine by a cannon shell and he was forced to bail out south-east of Lille, shot down by Unteroffizier Wemhöner of V./JG 26:

'I attacked them head-on, firing continuously from 600 yards till they passed under me, hoping to spray them. I saw the leading A/C pouring smoke as it dived away. I turned as rapidly as possible and engaged the remaining six in the same manner, but what appeared to be a cannon shell hit my engine, which burst into flames. I evacuated my A/C with all speed and landed safely by parachute two miles south-west of Lille. I was shot at twice by French [soldiers] on the way down.'
(signed) Pilot Officer P.P. Woods-Scawen.

Pilot Officer P.P. Woods-Scawen was awarded the DFC, *London Gazette*, 25 June 1940. The citation made particular reference to the combat of 19 May:

'Distinguished Flying Cross.
'Pilot Officer Patrick Philip WOODS-SCAWEN (40452).
'During May 1940, this officer destroyed six enemy aircraft, and assisted in the destruction of others. On one occasion, although heavily outnumbered, he attacked without hesitation a large formation of enemy aircraft, shooting down two of them. His own aircraft was hit by a cannon shell and he was slightly wounded, but succeeded in escaping by parachute and rejoined his unit. He has displayed great courage, endurance and leadership.'

The narrative tactfully omits to mention that his wounds were inflicted by over-eager French soldiers who, not for the first time, took pot-shots at an unarmed RAF pilot descending by parachute. Woods-Scawen returned to operations in time to play a key role in the squadron's Battle of Britain.

Flying Officer Patrick 'Woody' Woods-Scawen (flying P3150) was killed-in-action with No. 85 Squadron on 1 September 1940, following combat with a

Bf 109. He bailed out, but his parachute failed to open and he fell to his death near the grounds of The Ivies, Kenley Lane, near Kenley. Tragically, his brother, Pilot Officer C.A. 'Tony' Woods-Scawen, DFC, who flew with No. 43 Squadron, died in almost identical circumstances on the following day (his DFC being announced only days later in the *London Gazette* of 6 September).

No. 85 Squadron flew further sorties on the 19 May. At 1630 hours the squadron engaged twenty-four He 111s of KG 54. Squadron Leader M.F. Peacock (flying L2141 VY- H) bailed out following combat with an He 111, north-east of Seclin. Flying Officer M.B. Czernin claimed an He 111 and probably shared a second with Peacock, although Luftwaffe records indicate that only the bomber piloted by Unteroffizier Johann Kettner was lost.

Czernin's combat report read:

'[I] was ordered up with whole flight to attack enemy approaching base. [The] E/A split up immediately and I picked out one and stuck to his tail. He took no avoiding action and after a longish burst went down in flames. [I] attacked a second and saw smoke and oil pouring from [its] port [engine] and [the] E/A started to descend.'

At this point Czernin ran out of ammunition and was forced to pull out of the attack.

Despite the valiant efforts of the squadron, some of the bombers got through to bomb Seclin airfield.

Meanwhile, on the general front, the enemy were continuing in their advance and orders were given to evacuate the airfield during the evening of 19 May. The ground crews destroyed the 'lame ducks', as Jowitt and the other pilots flew off, heading for nearby Merville. Pilot Officer A.G. Lewis later recalled their reception on landing:

'We were bombed and attacked and our brand new, variable-pitch propeller Hurricanes were ground strafed and made unserviceable.'

Acting Squadron Leader M.F. Peacock assumed command of No. 85 Squadron on 20 May, with the transfer away of Squadron Leader J.O.W. Oliver to HQ No. 60 Wing. Oliver had been grounded due to the inhalation of glycol when his Hurricane was damaged in combat. Meanwhile, the wounded Pilot Officer P.P. Woods-Scawen and Sergeant A.H. Deacon returned to the UK in an air transport.

At about 0700 hours, while on a morning patrol twelve miles to the south of Arras, Flying Officer M.B. Czernin sighted and destroyed an Hs 126 in a combat, which went from 400ft down to treetop level:

'I did a No. 1 Attack, which seemed to have no effect, but he dived to about 20ft. I followed him and got in a long beam attack, after which he crashed down in a field. The pilot and observer got out, seemingly unhurt, and ran across the field. I turned and got in one burst on them and both went down.'

Patrolling at 0945 hours, Sergeant H. Howes (flying P2555), engaged a formation of twenty Do 17s of I./KG 3 with their escort of Bf 110s from I./ZG 2, while flying to the north-west of Abbeville. Flying close in on the bombers, Howes was able to pick them off almost at will, destroying four aircraft, with a fifth damaged. Howe's Hurricane was damaged by the defending Bf 110s and he was eventually forced to pull out of the attack:

'[An] Me 110 attacked me from the rear. I avoided the attack and observed more Mes above me; during this period eleven of the E/A had broken away from wave and were heading for Abbeville. I had extra height than E/A so made one quarter and rear attack on the port flank, sending one E/A down in flames. I made another attack from almost above the leader of E/A on the port flank, he crashed into the ground and burst into flames. The Mes were making things really hot for me by this time, so I flew into close-range (approx. 150 yards) at the rear E/A, firing at the whole wave as they came into my sights. My A/C was badly hit during this attack and I commenced to dive, I gained combat at 10,000ft and saw three E/A going down, apparently very much out of control, thick smoke coming from two of them.'
(signed) Sergeant H. Howes.

Howes' Hurricane had sustained combat damage and he made a forced-landing near Abbeville, at 1015 hours, hit by a Bf 110 of I./ZG 26, possibly the aircraft claimed by Hauptman Makrocki.

The squadron lost three pilots in what was one of their last operations during the France campaign, when Acting Squadron Leader M.F. Peacock[9] (flying P2551) and Pilot Officer R.W. Shrewsbury[10] (flying P3426) were killed at about 1400 hours during a ground strafing mission along the Cambrais-Arras Road. Meanwhile, Pilot Officer R.W. Burton[11] (flying P2427) died when his Hurricane crashed near Querrieu, north-east of Amiens. Flying Officer M.B. Czernin reported accurate ground fire, while an exploding petrol bowser sent flames high into the air. It is not clear if these caused the loss of their CO and Shrewsbury. Czernin's combat report concluded; 'I banked away and when I looked round, smoke and flames reached to about 150ft. I am under the impression that the two following machines were caught by the explosion as I saw no more of them.' Meanwhile, the Bf 109s of II./JG 3 made claims. Gruppenkommandeur Hauptman Erich von Selle (two 'kills'), Leutnant Franz von Werra of II./JG 3 and Leutnant Rudolf Heymann of IV./ JG 3, were each credited with a Hurricane destroyed. One of Werra's victories may have been Pilot Officer Burton.

Meanwhile, Merville airfield was bombed by eight enemy aircraft at about noon and orders were given, 'to destroy all squadron files, records and ciphers etc. and move by road to Boulogne.' At this point only four of the squadron's Hurricanes remained serviceable. These and the air transport were to fly to RAF Hendon.

Pilot Officer A.G. Lewis recalled that the Hurricanes deemed unserviceable were put out of action by having Bofors guns turned on them. Bf 109s also came down and strafed the aircraft in their pens. Following the latter air strike, only two Hurricanes remained airworthy. These were flown out by Sergeant C. Hampshire and Pilot Officer Lewis. Jowitt and the remaining pilots were airlifted to safety in an RAF transporter.

The remnants of No. 85 Squadron embarked for the UK on 21 May, the ground echelon returned via Boulogne. During their time in France, largely under the command of Squadron Leader J.O.W. 'Doggie' Oliver, the squadron had become the second most successful RAF unit, claiming sixty-four and a half 'kills', with a further twenty-one probables and five damaged. The victories came at a price, with seven pilots killed, one PoW and five wounded. Their tally compares favourably with the highest scoring RAF unit, No. 3 Squadron, which recorded sixty-seven confirmed 'kills'.

Squadron Leader J.O.W. Oliver, was recognized with the double award of the DSO and DFC, both promulgated in the, *London Gazette*, 31 May 1940:

'Appointed a Companion of the Distinguished Service Order.
'Squadron Leader John Oliver William OLIVER, DFC (262808).
'This officer commanded a squadron in France until he was invalided to England on 19 May 1940. The small losses in his squadron were directly due to his leadership and instruction. Over fifty enemy aircraft have been brought down by the squadron, of which Squadron Leader Oliver himself accounted for at least eight. Although ill from the effects of glycol when his engine was damaged, he did not allow his condition to handicap his flying or his administration. He was an incomparable fighter commander and his personal example in the air and on the ground was a very great inspiration to his pilots. It was, in fact, necessary to restrain him from flying again after his aircraft had been shot down and he had landed by parachute.'

'Distinguished Flying Cross.
'Squadron Leader John Oliver William OLIVER (262808).
'This officer commanded his squadron well and has led two escort formations of twenty-four aircraft, each to a distance of 140 miles from their base. During these escorts the formations accounted for more than a dozen enemy aircraft. In addition, in May 1940, he shot down an enemy aircraft which crashed at Hazebrouck and he has led his section magnificently on many occasions. His sangfroid and calm outlook have encouraged his squadron to a remarkable degree and the excellent spirit of the squadron and his gallant leadership is reflected in the successes attained.'

The battle-scared squadron remustered at their pre-war base at Debden on the 22 May. Here they received new aircraft and an influx of replacement pilots, some of whom were fresh from flying school and their conversion course at an OTU.

Meanwhile, Squadron Leader P.W. Townsend, DFC, arrived on the following day to assume command – Oliver's replacement, Peacock, having been posted 'missing, believed killed-in-action'. Townsend had previously served as a flight commander with No. 43 Squadron, with whom he had destroyed two enemy aircraft and shared a third, all during the so-called Phoney War.

Townsend had been awarded the DFC, *London Gazette*, 30 April 1940, and was soon to receive a Mention-in-Despatches on 11 July 1940. Townsend's DFC citation read:

'Distinguished Flying Cross.
'Flight Lieutenant Peter Wooldridge TOWNSEND (33178).
'In April, 1940, whilst on patrol over the North Sea, Flight Lieutenant Townsend intercepted and attacked an enemy aircraft at dusk and, after a running fight, shot it down. This is the third success obtained by this pilot and in each instance he has displayed qualities of leadership, skill and determination of the highest order, with little regard for his own safety.'

The charismatic Peter Townsend quickly set about rebuilding the squadron around Sergeant Jowitt and the five or six remaining combat seasoned pilots, bringing it back up to operational efficiency. The better part of June was spent putting the replacement pilots through their paces, flying battle climbs, formation practice and mock-combats.

Many of these new pilots, including Pilot Officer J.L. Bickerdyke and Sergeant J.H.M. Ellis, learned their art under the careful tuition of Sergeant Jowitt. Leonard's nephew, Doug Bray, later wrote of his uncle; 'He was lively, irrepressible and always at the centre of things.'

This is confirmed by the recollections of his CO and fellow pilots alike, and it is notable in the rare photograph of squadron members taken at about this time in front of one of the squadron's Hurricanes, enjoying a pint. Here, evidence of the morale building high jinks which Jowitt engaged in may be seen in his heavily cropped haircut, which was as a result of a lost bet in the pilot's room.

Recalling Leonard Jowitt, his CO, Peter Townsend, wrote:

'I see him as of medium height, sturdily built, with brown hair and a moustache. He was a good pilot and had already gained combat experience in France. He was popular and something of a joker. With another pilot, Patrick Woods-Scawen, he had an act which made us all laugh; I vaguely recall that it was the presentation of a medal by a French general, accompanied with the usual gesticulations and ending with the accolade (a kiss on each cheek).

'He had a narrow escape a day or two before being shot down [*sic*]. In the pilot's room, a pilot handed his Colt to another, who calmly placed it against his hand and pulled the trigger. The pistol was loaded and the bullet pierced the pilot's hand and hit the fountain pen in Leonard's breast pocket; he was sent spinning by the blow and, seeing the other pilot's blood on the floor, thought it was his own. He was quickly reassured, though his chest was badly bruised; the bullet, if I remember rightly, was recovered from his pocket. Poor Sergeant Jowitt was shot down next day [sic] into the sea off the Suffolk coast while attacking a formation of bombers which were attacking one of our convoys.'

Group Captain Townsend's memory of the incident places it only days before Jowitt's death. A contemporary family account, however, affirms that he received his injuries a little after Peter Townsend took over command, and therefore a few weeks before Jowitt's death. The belief in the family was that Jowitt had handed his own revolver over to the second pilot, who had gained a reputation for always returning early. The same source maintains that the offending pilot was quickly removed from the squadron. Meanwhile, Leonard Jowitt is said to have been given leave and visited his family and his Liverpool sweetheart, Hilda Robinson, while still recovering from his injuries.

The evidence provided by Jowitt's family asserts that Jowitt had apparently been perched on the arm of a chair when the bullet struck him in the chest and sent him spinning. It was believed that this fact and the contents of his breast pocket, including a pen, saved him from further injury.

The family's anecdotal evidence was repeated by Leonard Jowitt's nephew, Doug Bray, who wrote; 'He was thought to be fireproof after a bullet glanced his chest when his pistol went off accidentally in the mess. He was very proud of the scar.' Again, the suggestion is that Leonard's injury occurred some time in late May or early June.

Meanwhile, during these vital few weeks of operational training, the new squadron members picked up invaluable tactical knowledge, and learned how to fly and fight as a part of a team. Under the guidance of the more experienced pilots, they had begun flying convoy escorts by the middle of the month, but continued with the rigorous training element of their flying.

Doug Bray explained; 'Len Jowitt used to try to impart some of his [combat] knowledge and experience to them.' The squadron's record during the Battle of Britain giving testimony to the value of their training.

The squadron had received a further reinforcement on 25 May, when Flight Lieutenant H.R. Hamilton was posted from No. 611 Squadron, as 'A' Flight Commander. Although experienced on type, he was yet to go into combat and would lean heavily on his juniors until combat savvy.

The training had not been without its setbacks. On 31 May the squadron lost two of the new pilots, Sergeant L.R. Butler[12] (flying N2536) and Sergeant P.L. Gossage[13] (flying P3584), as a result of an air accident during mock-fighting, crashing two miles north of Debden. The latter had flying in his blood and would, no doubt, have gone on to be a senior officer in the service, had he survived.

Meanwhile, by the beginning of July, No. 85 Squadron was once again declared fully operational, and was carrying out scrambles, defensive and convoy patrols as a part of its daily duties. The squadron regularly made three or four patrols a day, many of these operations being flown out of their forward base at RAF Martlesham Heath, or RAF Debden's satellite airfield at RAF Castle Camp. The latter, from where the squadron flew the occasional night patrol, had only been established at the outbreak of the war and still had a grass strip and no permanent structures, only a tented encampment.

It was while resting at RAF Castle Camp between sorties that Dickie Lee was asked to put on a bit of a show for visiting dignitaries. Lee was still recovering from a leg wound received while operating over France. Nevertheless, he went on to push his Hurricane to the limits. One WAAF recalled that, 'he was soon airborne and inverted before one would think possible, and gave an exhibition of flying a Hurricane I have never seen surpassed.'

One apocryphal account stated that Lee's inverted antics were so daring that after he landed grass had to be removed from his aircraft's radio antenna – the one on the top of the fuselage, not the one under the wing.

With the replacement pilots now trained up, the squadron saw action again on 8 July, while on a morning patrol over their forward base. Following a vector, Flight Sergeant G. Allard, was able to close to within effective range, firing two, three-second bursts from astern, destroying an He 111 of KG 1. The bomber was seen to crash into the sea off Felixstowe; Allard's eleventh confirmed 'kill'. Flight Sergeant Allard had the opportunity for an even dozen on the following day, but this time the He 111 was able to escape into cloud cover.

Throughout 10 July, the squadron flew standing patrols over a convoy sailing along the east coast, while on the following day, Peter W. Townsend (flying P2716 VY-F) was shot down twenty miles off Harwich during an attack on Do 17s of II./KG 2. He was rescued by HM Trawler *Cape Fenisterre*. Townsend's combat report revealed that during the engagement he had severely damaged the Dornier (which crash-landed at Arras with three wounded), but return fire damaged his vulnerable coolant system, causing the engine to seize up.

No. 85 Squadron was once again at Readiness before dawn on 12 July and flew flight and section strength escort patrols throughout the day in protection of Convoy Booty off Felixstowe. Taking off from RAF Martlesham Heath at 0825 hours, Sergeant Jowitt led a section strength patrol against a large enemy formation of He 111s and Do 17s reported closing on the vessels east of Aldeburgh. A standing patrol made by No. 17 Squadron had been guarding the vessels when they came under attack by anywhere from nine to a dozen He 111s of III./KG 53, which they engaged, but could not prevent from sinking a 2000-ton vessel.

No. 17 Squadron claimed:

Pilot Officer K. Manger (flying P3873)	one He 111 destroyed (shared)
Pilot Officer G.E. Pittman (flying P2552)	one He 111 destroyed (shared)
Sergeant D. Fopp (flying P3760)	one He 111 destroyed (shared)
Sergeant G. Griffiths (flying P3536)	one He 111 destroyed, one He 111 destroyed (shared)

No. 85 Squadron's Hurricanes arrived over the convoy while an He 111 was lining up to drop its bombs, but their presence meant the bomb aimer was successfully

unnerved and missed his target. Flying beyond the limits of their Bf 109 escort, the He 111s were vulnerable to attack and the Hurricanes waded in.

Between 0835 and 0840 hours, 'B' Flight's Pilot Officer John Bickerdyke[14] (flying P3409), shot down a German bomber while at 6,000ft:

'I took off at 0825 hours from Martlesham with two other aircraft of Blue Section [Sergeants Jowitt and Rust], to proceed to point noted above [ten miles east of Aldborough] to intercept enemy raid on convoy. When at 700 yards I observed [eight-ten] E/A in loose formation at approx. 1,000ft below us attacking convoy. I dived from 7,000ft at the nearest enemy aircraft and opened fire at approx. 400 yards, closing to fifty yards and [the] E/A burst into flames and dived into sea.'
(signed) Pilot Officer J.L. Bickerdyke.

Sergeant C.A. Rust (flying P3487) closed in on the formation, firing a total of 1,440 rounds, damaging an He 111, which he considered was unlikely to make base:

'I attacked [the] nearest He 111. My first attack was a dive from 7,000-6000ft on starboard beam and [the] rear-gunner was put out of action. My next attack was from port side and I saw my tracer enter [the] port engine and made it billow smoke. The enemy aircraft disappeared in a deep dive in clouds. I was unable to follow as the enemy was in the vicinity.'
(signed) Sergeant Charles A. Rust.

Sergeant Leonard Jowitt (flying P2557) attacked the same formation of He 111s of II./KG 53, but his Hurricane was fatally damaged by return fire and plunged into the sea off Felixstowe. Sergeant Jowitt is believed to have bailed out, but was lost at sea and drowned.

It is not known if Jowitt added to his tally, although at least four He 111s were destroyed and more damaged during the engagement, the claims listed above only amounting to four 'kills', leaving the possibility that Leonard Jowitt damaged or destroyed some, or all of the unclaimed enemy aircraft during his pursuit.

Sergeant Rust recalled:

'We were about thirty miles out in the North Sea. To my memory I was flying alongside Bickerdyke (a New Zealander). My friend Jowitt went chasing after a Hun and did not return, but there was no Mayday call, so I can only imagine the worst.'

Sergeant Leonard Jowitt was 28-years-old. Having pursued the enemy way over the Channel, his Hurricane went down beyond the range of air-sea rescue. Jowitt's body was never found and he is remembered on the Runnymede Memorial, Panel 16.

Leonard Jowitt was posthumously mentioned in the despatches of Air Marshal Sir Arthur Barratt, KCB, CMG, MC, covering the France Campaign, published on 22 July, notification of which was announced in the *London Gazette*, 1 January 1941.

The following pilots flew with No. 85 Squadron during the Battle of France and up until 12 July 1940:

Squadron Leader John Oliver William Oliver, DSO, DFC	Squadron Commander
Squadron Leader Michael Fitzwilliam Peacock, DFC	Squadron Commander, KIA 20.5.40
Squadron Leader Peter Wooldridge Townsend, DFC	Squadron Commander, Bar to DFC 6.9.40 *(A)*, DSO 13.5.41 *(B)*, CVO 1947
Flight Lieutenant James Robert Maitland Boothby, DFC	
Flight Lieutenant Harry Raymond Hamilton	'A' Flight Commander, KIA 29.8.40
Flight Lieutenant Jerrard Jefferies (later Latimer)	DFC 1.10.40. Czech MC 24.12.40, KIA 5.4.43
Flight Lieutenant Richard Hugh Anthony Lee, DFC, DSO	'B' Flight Commander, KIA 18.8.40
Flight Lieutenant D.R. Miller	(on secondment from 242 Squadron)
Flying Officer Derek Hurlstone Allen, DFC	KIA 18.5.40
Flying Officer Allan Benjamin Angus, DFC	KIA 16.5.40
Flying Officer Kenneth Hughes Blair, DFC	Bar to DFC 19.5.44 *(C)*
Flying Officer J. Jeffries	DFC 1.10.40 *(D)*
Flying Officer W.N. LePine	PoW 18.5.40
Flying Officer Thomas Gilbert Pace	KIA 3.12.41
Flying Officer Stanley Philip Stephenson	
Pilot Officer John Henry Ashton	DFC 14.3.41 *(E)*
Pilot Officer John Laurence Bickerdyke	Died, air accident 22.7.40
Pilot Officer M.K. Brown	(on secondment from No. 242 Squadron)
Pilot Officer Roger William Burton, RAFVR	KIA 20.5.40
Pilot Officer L.E. Chambers	(on secondment from No. 242 Squadron)
Pilot Officer H.D. Clark	
Pilot Officer Count Manfred Beckett Czernin	DFC 1.10.40, MC with SOE 1.12.44, DSO 2.11.45
Pilot Officer A.H. Deacon	(on secondment from No. 242 Squadron)

Pilot Officer Peter Leslie Gossage	KIA 31.5.40
Pilot Officer Arthur Vincent Gower	DFC 1.7.41 *(F)*, KIA 24.10.43 as CO of No. 183 Squadron
Pilot Officer John Allman Hemingway	DFC 1.7.41 *(G)*
Pilot Officer John William Lecky	Died, car accident 18.5.40
Pilot Officer Albert Gerald 'Zulu' Lewis, DFC	Bar to DFC 22.10.40 *(H)*
Pilot Officer James Lockhart	KIA 5.4.42 with No. 258 Squadron
Pilot Officer James Eglington Marshall	DFC 29.4.41 *(I)*, Died, air accident 18.4.42
Pilot Officer David V.G. Mawhood	
Pilot Officer Geoffrey Edward Pittman	
Pilot Officer Michael H.G. Rawlinson	KIA 16.5.40
Pilot Officer Richard William Shrewsbury	KIA 20.5.40
Pilot Officer Stanley Philip Stephenson	
Pilot Officer Russell Henry Wiens	(on secondment from No. 242 Squadron)
Pilot Officer Denis Heathcote Wissler	KIA 11.11.40
Pilot Officer Patrick Philip Woods-Scawen, DFC	KIA 1.9.40
Sergeant Geoffrey Allard, DFM	Bar to DFM 13.9.40 *(J)*, DFC 8.10.40 *(K)*, Died, air accident 13.3.41
Sergeant Harold Henry Allgood	KIA 10.10.40
Sergeant Lionel Roy Butler, RAFVR	KIA 31.5.40
Sergeant Len A. Crozier	KIA 18.5.40
Sergeant Albert Henry Deacon	
Sergeant John Mortimer Ellis, RAFVR	KIA 1.9.40
Sergeant Cyril Edward Hampshire	
Sergeant Harold Norman Howes, DFM	KIA 22.12.40
Sergeant Leonard Jowitt	KIA 12.7.40
Sergeant Stewart W. Lenton	Died, air accident 6.3.40
Sergeant John McGregor Little, RAFVR	KIA 19.5.40
Sergeant Charles Alan Rust	
Sergeant Francis Richard Walker-Smith	Died, air accident 13.3.41
Sergeant Ernest Reginald Webster	

Many of the pilots earned gallantry awards for combat which are not mentioned in the main text. Details, where traced, are included below:

(A) Acting Squadron Leader P.W. Townsend was awarded a Bar to the DFC, *London Gazette*, 6 September 1940:

'Bar to the Distinguished Flying Cross.
'Acting Squadron Leader Peter Wooldridge TOWNSEND, DFC (33178).
'In July, 1940, whilst leading a section of the squadron to protect a convoy, this officer intercepted about twenty or thirty enemy aircraft, destroying one and severely damaging two others. The enemy formation was forced to withdraw. Under his command, the squadron has destroyed eight enemy aircraft while protecting convoys against sporadic enemy attacks. In August 1940, his squadron attacked some 250 enemy aircraft in the Thames Estuary. He himself shot down three enemy aircraft, the squadron as a whole destroying at least ten and damaging many others. The success which has been achieved has been due to Squadron Leader Townsend's unflagging zeal and leadership.'

(B) Squadron Leader Townsend was awarded the DSO, *London Gazette*, 13 May 1941:

'Distinguished Service Order.
'Acting Wing Commander Peter Wooldridge TOWNSEND, DFC (33178), No. 85 Squadron.
'This officer has displayed outstanding powers of leadership and organisation, combined with great determination and skill in air combat. By his untiring efforts he has contributed materially to the many successes obtained by his squadron. Wing Commander Townsend has been engaged on active operations since the war began and has carried out numerous operational flights, both by day and night. He has destroyed at least eleven enemy aircraft.'

(C) Acting Wing Commander K.H. Blair, DFC was awarded a Bar to the DFC, *London Gazette*, 19 May 1944:

'Bar to Distinguished Flying Cross.
'Acting Wing Commander Kenneth Hughes BLAIR, DFC (39704), Reserve of Air Force Officers.'

(D) Flying Officer J. Jeffries was awarded the DFC, *London Gazette*, 1 October 1940:

'Flying Officer Jerrard JEFFRIES (39286).
'This officer has led his flight with skill and gallantry. His determined leadership and skilled training have contributed largely to the success of his squadron. He has destroyed four enemy aircraft and severely damaged another two.'

(E) Pilot Officer J.H. Ashton was awarded the DFC, *London Gazette*, 14 March 1941:

'Distinguished Flying Cross.
'Pilot Officer John Henry ASHTON (77456), Royal Air Force Volunteer Reserve, No. 145 Squadron.
'This officer has displayed great courage in his engagements against the enemy and has destroyed at least five of their aircraft. Four of these he shot down while serving with his squadron in France. His keenness for operations, under any conditions, has been an inspiration to his fellow pilots.

(F) Flying Officer A.V. Gowers was awarded the DFC, *London Gazette*, 1 July 1941:

'Distinguished Flying Cross.
'Flying Officer Arthur Vincent GOWERS (40166), No. 85 Squadron.'

(G) Flying Officer J.A. Hemingway was awarded the DFC, *London Gazette*, 1 July 1941:

'Distinguished Flying Cross.
'Flying Officer John Allman HEMINGWAY (40702), No. 85 Squadron.'

(H) Pilot Officer A.G. Lewis, DFC, was awarded a Bar to the DFC, *London Gazette*, 22 October 1940:

'Awarded a Bar to the Distinguished Flying Cross.
'Pilot Officer Albert Gerald LEWIS, DFC (41303).
'One day in September 1940, this officer destroyed six enemy aircraft; this makes a total of eighteen destroyed by him. His courage and keenness are outstanding.'

(I) Acting Flight Lieutenant J.E. Marshall was awarded the DFC, *London Gazette* 29 April 1941:

'Distinguished Flying Cross.
'Acting Flight Lieutenant James Eglington MARSHALL (70809), No. 85 Squadron.'

(J) Sergeant Sergeant G. Allard was awarded a Bar to the DFM, *London Gazette*, 13 September 1940:

'Awarded a Bar to the Distinguished Flying Medal.
'563859 Sergeant Geoffrey ALLARD, DFM.'

(K) As a pilot officer, G. Allard was later awarded the DFC, *London Gazette*, 8 October 1940:

No. 235 Squadron Bristol Blenheim LA-N, flown by Flying Officer R.J. Peacock DFC. (*Reginald Peacock Archive*)

No. 235 Squadron pilots and aircraft. (*Reginald Peacock Archive*)

Squadron Leader R.J. Peacock's DFC medal group: (left to right) Distinguished Flying Cross, 1939–45 Star with Battle of Britain clasp, Atlantic Star, Africa Star with 1942–43 clasp, War Medal. (*Reginald Peacock Archive*)

Chapter 1

No. 235 Squadron pilots enjoying a pint in the officer's mess. Flying Officer R.J. Peacock centre. (*Reginald Peacock Archive*)

Bristol Blenheim in flight. (*Reginald Peacock Archive*)

Recommendation for
Distinguished Flying Cross

FLYING OFFICER REGINALD JOHN PEACOCK
40257

This Officer has carried out approximately one hundred hours operational flying as a Leader of a Section during the last three months.

He has on all occasions displayed a fine offensive spirit, and has led his Section with great coolness and determination.

On two occasions his Section has been attacked by superior enemy forces, and although on both occasions his two following aircraft have been shot down, he has carried on and completed the patrol on his own.

On 12th May, when attacked by eight M.E. 109's, this Officer succeeded in shooting down one and seriously damaging another.

On the 27th June, whilst one of six carrying out a reconnaissance of the Zuider Zee, the formation was attacked by M.E. 109's.

Flying Officer Peacock did all in his power to keep the offensive on our side, and having beaten off the 109's carried out the reconnaissance of the Zuider Zee on his own. At the end of this patrol he encountered a Heinkel seaplane, which he attacked, and only broke off the engagement when all his ammunition was expended.

BUCKINGHAM PALACE

The Queen and I offer you our heartfelt sympathy in your great sorrow.

We pray that your country's gratitude for a life so nobly given in its service may bring you some measure of consolation.

George R.I.

C. Peacock, Esq.

The gravestone of Squadron Leader R.J. Peacock, DFC, bears the quote, 'Who dies if England lives.' (*Reginald Peacock Archive*)

Copy of the citation for Flying Officer Peacock's award of the DFC. (*Reginald Peacock Archive*)

Condolence slip from the King and Queen. (*Reginald Peacock Archive*)

Chapter 2

No. 303 Squadron's Hurricane RF-J under general maintenance. (*Jan Kowalski Archive*)

Post-war image of Flight Lieutenant Jan Kowalski, DFC, VM, KW**. (*Jan Kowalski Archive*)

Pencil drawing of Jan Kowalski by Anne Kennington. (*Courtesy of Anne Kennington*)

Flight Sergeant Jan Kowalski, 1941. (*Jan Kowalski Archive*)

His Majesty King George VI during his visit to No. 303 Squadron at RAF Northolt. (*Jan Kowalski Archive*)

Chapter 2

Jan Kowalski's medal group (left to right): Distinguished Flying Cross, 1939–45 Star with Battle of Britain clasp, Air Crew Europe Star with France and Germany clasp, Africa Star with 1942-43 clasp, War Medal, Virtuti Militari (5th Class), Polish War Cross with Two Bars. (*Jan Kowalski Archive*)

German bullet recovered from the cockpit of Sergeant Jan Kowalski's Hurricane on 26 September 1940. (*Jan Kowalski Archive*)

C I T A T I O N. D.F.C.

Flight Lieutenant. JAN KOWALSKI. (P.1909).

During the Battle of Britain on the 26.9.40. Enemy Bombers escorted by Fighters raided Southampton. F/L. Kowalski attacked the fighter cover and shot down One M.E. 109.

On the 27.9.40. F/L. Kowalski attacked a strong formation of Enemy Bombers in the vicinity of Gatwick. He kept attacking the formation until he exhausted his ammunition. As a result of this attack he damaged a H.E. 111., putting one of its engines out of action.

From 14.3. - 15.6.43. F/L. Kowalski flew with the Polish Fighter Team during the campaigning in North Africa. He carried out 38 Operational Sorties on Bomber Escorts and Ground Straffing.

On the 17.9.44. F/L. Kowalski led a flight on an Armed Recce. in the vicinity of ERNAY. The flight was attacked by 8 F.W. 190's. During the ensuing dog fights 5 F.W. 190's were damaged without any losses being sustained by the flight.

On the 26.9.44. F/L. Kowalski led a Section of Four Aircraft on an armed Recce, in the vicinity of BREDA, a group of enemy transport was observed. In spite of the intense flak which was encountered after the first attack, F/L. Kowalski continued to attack the column, diving at it several times. Four enemy MET. were left burning and Two damaged.

On the 1st January, 1945, 317 Squadron returned from an operational sortie, Enemy Aircraft were attacking B.60 the Wings home base. In spite of the fact that his cannons had jammed F/L. Kowalski attacked several F.W.190's trying to chase them off.

F/L. Kowalski has taken part in 211 sorties of all descriptions.

Awarded the D.F.C.

The official citation for Jan Kowalski's DFC. (*Jan Kowalski Archive*)

No. 303 Squadron's pilots and ground crew pictured with one of their unit's Spitfires, 1941. Flight Sergeant Jan Kowalski indicated by arrow. (*Jan Kowalski Archive*)

No. 85 Squadron pilots in France in early 1940.
(*Leonard Jowitt Archive*)

Sergeant Leonard Jowitt
following the presentation of
his 'wings'. Jowitt wears the
India General Service Medal,
with clasp for Mohmand, 1933.
(*Leonard Jowitt Archive*)

No. 85 Squadron's
Hurricanes
photographed at
RAF Debden, 1939.
(*Leonard Jowitt
Archive*)

Fitter's course at RAF Sealand. Leonard Jowitt, middle row, fifth from left. (*Leonard Jowitt Archive*)

A member of the ground crew operating a starter trolley. No. 85 Squadron Hurricane, France 1939–40. (*Leonard Jowitt Archive*)

No. 85 Squadron's VY-G during a scramble in France, 1940. (*Leonard Jowitt Archive*)

An informal line-up of No. 85 Squadron pilots in front of one of their Hurricanes. Sergeant Jowitt, third from right (June-July 1940). Full line-up, left to right: Pilot Officer J. L. Bikersdike, Flying Officer P. Woods-Scawen, Pilot Officer J. Lockhart, Flight Lieutenant R.H.A. 'Dickie' Lee, Sergeant L. Jowitt, Flight Lieutenant Bieber (MO), Sergeant E.R. Webster. (*Leonard Jowitt Archive*)

Sergeant Leonard Jowitt sporting a close haircut, which was a forfeit for losing a bet in the mess. (*Leonard Jowitt Archive*)

No. 85 Squadron plaque. (*Leonard Jowitt Archive*)

An 85 Squadron Hurricane on a scramble during the summer of 1940. (*Leonard Jowitt Archive*)

Sergeant Leonard Jowitt's medal group (left to right): Indian General Service Medal with Mohmand 1933 clasp, 1939–45 Star with Battle of Britain clasp, War Medal with MiD Oak Leaf. (*Leonard Jowitt Archive*)

GVI RI

This scroll commemorates
Sergeant L. Jowitt
Royal Air Force
held in honour as one who
served King and Country in
the world war of 1939-1945
and gave his life to save
mankind from tyranny. May
his sacrifice help to bring
the peace and freedom for
which he died.

562160 Sergeant L. Jowitt
Royal Air Force
was mentioned in a Despatch from
Air Marshal Sir Arthur Barratt, K.C.B., C.M.G., M.C.
dated 22nd July 1940
for gallant and distinguished services.
I have it in command from the King to record His Majesty's
high appreciation of the services rendered.

Archibald Sinclair
Secretary of State for Air

Mention-in-Despatches certificate named to
Sergeant Leonard Jowitt. (*Leonard Jowitt Archive*)

Casualty scroll presented to the parents of Sergeant
Leonard Jowitt. (*Leonard Jowitt Archive*)

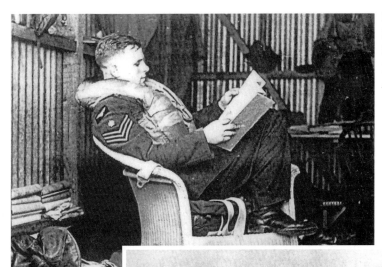

Flight Sergeant E.G. 'Gil' Gilbert at Readiness, Kenley, 1940. (*'Gil' Gilbert Archive*)

'Gil' Gilbert on a mock scramble, Church Fenton, 1940. (*'Gil' Gilbert Archive*)

'Gil' Gilbert at dispersal. (*'Gil' Gilbert Archive*)

Pencil drawing of 'Gil' Gilbert by Anne Kennington. (*Courtesy of Anne Kennington*)

Squadron Leader D. MacDonell. (*'Gil' Gilbert Archive*)

'Gil' Gilbert on a scramble. (*'Gil' Gilbert Archive*)

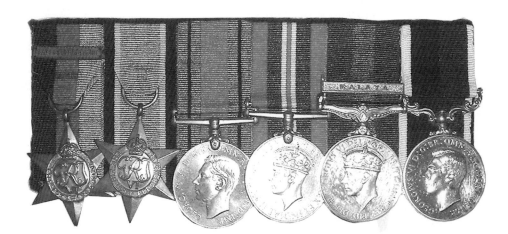

'Gil' Gilbert's medal group (left to right): 1939-45 Star with the Battle of Britain clasp, Air Crew Europe Star, Defence Medal, War Medal, General Service Medal with Malaya bar, RAF Long Service and Good Conduct Medal. (*'Gil' Gilbert Archive*)

'Gil' Gilbert's log book with newspaper-cutting relating to the Heinkel 111 he shared with 'Andy' Laws. (*'Gil' Gilbert Archive*)

'Gil' Gilbert featured in 'Any Time's Fighting Time'. (*'Gil' Gilbert Archive*)

Robert Reid with his red MG sports car. (*Robert Reid Archive, via Simon Reid*)

Robert Reid astride his Hawker Hurricane. (*Robert Reid Archive, via Simon Reid*)

Squadron Leader Robert Reid and navigator, with his personal Mosquito. (*Robert Reid Archive, via Simon Reid*)

Padded 'wings' attributed to Squadron Leader Robert Reid. (*Robert Reid Archive*)

A gun-camera image of the fateful attack in Dalsfjord on 23 March 1945. (*Robert Reid Archive, via Simon Reid*)

Studio photograph of Squadron Leader Robert Reid. (*Robert Reid Archive, via Simon Reid*)

The Steinsvik Memoril, Norway. (*Robert Reid Archive, via Simon Reid*)

Air Efficiency Award of Flight Lieutenant R. Reid, RAFVR. (*Robert Reid Archive, via Simon Reid*)

Winter's Sidcot Suit Squadron badge. (*Douglas Winter Archive*)

Vickers Supermarine Spitfire of No. 72 Squadron, late 1939–early 1940. (*Douglas Winter Archive*)

Vickers Supermarine Spitfire of No. 72 Squadron, late 1939–early 1940. (*Douglas Winter Archive*)

No. 72 Squadron pilots pictured at RAF Acklington, June 1940. Back Row (left to right): Sergeant J. Gilders, Pilot Officer E. Males, Sergeant W. Rolls. Front Row (left to right): Sergeant J. White, Sergeant N. Glew. (*Douglas Winter Archive*)

Winter's cloth Squadron badge. (*Douglas Winter Archive*)

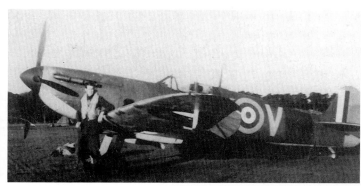

No. 72 Squadron Spitfire. (*Douglas Winter Archive*)

Winter's Spitfire, 1939. (*Douglas Winter Archive*)

Pilot Officer D.C. Winter's medal group (left to right): 1939–45 Star with Battle of Britain clasp, Air Crew Europe Star, War Medal. (*Douglas Winter Archive*)

Bilsley Medal awarded to Douglas Winter. (*Douglas Winter Archive*)

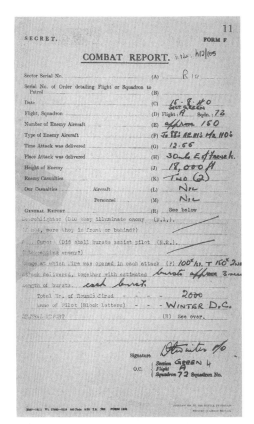

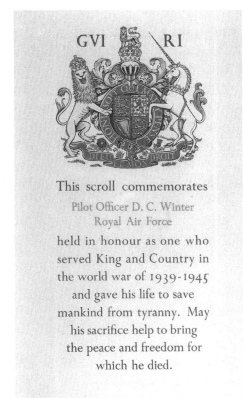

Pilot Officer D.C. Winter's combat report. (*Douglas Winter Archive*)

Commemoration Scroll named to Pilot Officer Douglas Cyril Winter. (*Douglas Winter Archive*)

'Distinguished Flying Cross.

'Pilot Officer Geoffrey ALLARD, DFM. (44551).

'Between 30 August and 1 September 1940, this officer destroyed seven enemy aircraft; previously he had destroyed ten and shared in the destruction of others. He has displayed outstanding skill and courage in combat against the enemy.'

Notes

1. Sergeant (564249) Stewart Worthington Lenton, RAF, was the husband of Lucy I.P. Lenton, of Sutton Bridge, Lincolnshire. Lenton was buried at Peronne Communal Cemetery Extension, Plot 5, Row G, Grave 25.

2. Pilot Officer Angus' victim was probably the Heinkel of Stab II./KG 27 flown by Leutnant Hans-Wilhelm Hover.

3. Pilot Officer (4162) Gordon Cranleigh Saunders, RAF, was the son of Frederick and Claudia Saunders, of Wellington City, New Zealand. Saunders was 23-years-old and was buried at Fenain Communal Cemetery.

4. Flying Officer (40281) Allan Benjamin Angus, RAF, was the son of Benjamin and Daisy Angus; husband of Catherine Joan Angus, of Kennington, Kent. Angus was 22-years-old and was buried at Frentin Communal Cemetery, Grave 3.

5. Pilot Officer (40851) Michael Henry Grayson Rawlinson, RAF, was the son of Lieutenant Colonel Arthur Richard Rawlinson, OBE, and Ailsa Margaret Rawlinson, of Woking, Surrey. Rawlinson was 22-years-old and was buried at Adegem Canadian War Cemetery, Plot XI, Row J, Grave 8.

6. Sergeant (565017) Alan Newton Trice, RAF, is remembered on the Runnymede Memorial, Panel 20.

7. Flying Officer (39840) Derek Hurlstone Allen, DFC, RAF, was the son of Alfred E. and Sylvia S.M.H. Allen, of Leicester. Allen was 22-years-old and was buried at Poix-du-Nord Communal Cemetery (Extension).

8. Sergeant (741292) John McGregor Little, RAFVR, was the son of James and Christina Little, of Dalmuir, Dunbartonshire. Little, who was 22-years-old, is remembered on the Runnymede Memorial, Panel 16.

9. Squadron Leader (90124) Michael Fitzwilliam Peacock, RAF, was the son of T.C.H. Peacock and of Kathleen S. Peacock of Chalvington, Sussex. Peacock was a Double Blue, Oxford, and Captain of Richmond Rugby Football Club, and a Barrister at Law (Middle Temple). He was 28-years-old and was buried at Arras Communal Cemetery, Plot Y, Row 1, Joint Grave 64-65.

10. Pilot Officer (41874) Richard William Shrewsbury, RAF, was the son of Richard William and Dorothy Anna Shrewsbury, of Hall Green, Birmingham. Shrewsbury was 19-years-old and was buried at Arras Communal Cemetery, Plot Y, Row 1, Joint Grave 64-65.

11. Pilot Officer (78440) Roger William Burton, RAFVR, was the son of William and Catherine Alice Burton, of Cockfosters, Hertfordshire. Burton was 22-years-old and was buried at Querrieu British Cemetery, Row E, Grave 15.

12. Sergeant (742521) Lionel Roy Butler, RAFVR, son of Harry and Selina Margaret Butler, of Caversham, Reading, Berkshire. Butler was 19-years-old and is remembered at Cambridge Crematorium, Column 1.

13. Sergeant (74703) Peter Leslie Gossage, RAFVR, was the son of Air Marshal Sir Ernest Leslie Gossage, KCB, CVO, DSO, MC, Inspector General of the RAF (who flew with No. 6

and commanded Nos. 56 and 8 Squadrons, and was the first Air Officer Commanding No. 11 Group), and Lady Gossage (nee O'Brien), of Buxted. Gossage was buried at Buxted (St Margaret the Queen) Churchyard.

14. Pilot Officer Bickerdyke died some ten days later in a flying accident at Castle Camps, performing aerobatics while coming in to land. Pilot Officer (36266) John Laurence Bickerdyke, RAF, was the son of James and Monica Laura Bickerdyke, of Nelson, New Zealand. Bickerdyke was 21-years-old and was buried at Wimbish (All Saints) Churchyard.

Chapter 4

Pilot Officer Ernest George 'Gil' Gilbert

Ernest 'Gil' Gilbert's No. 64 Squadron was late converting onto Spitfires and was still on a steep learning curve when they went into action over the Dunkirk Beaches – Gil recalled how they lost three pilots, including their CO, in a single day's operations. Regrouped, they made the most of the lull before the storm, and were ready to take on the Luftwaffe over Kent and the Channel during the Battle of Britain.

Gil Gilbert was born in Chatham, Kent, on 4 November 1912. Educated at Chatham Junior and Technical schools, he gained a good School's Certificate, which opened the way for a 'blue collar' job. Gil's father worked in the shipyard as a draftsman, designing vessels for the Royal Navy:

'My father was offered promotion and the opportunity of working abroad, but decided to stay at Chatham. I, however, had the "bug" for adventure and wanted to see more of the world.'

And so, Gil enlisted as an apprentice aircraft fitter in the Royal Air Force on 6 September 1928 (serial No. 562706), serving at 2nd Wing, School of Technical Training, RAF Halton. Here he qualified as an engine fitter, before being posted to RAF Eastchurch (1931-34), serving for a short spell at the RAF's Armament Experiment Wing.

In response to the remilitarization of Germany under Hitler's Nazi Party, the RAF began to strengthen Home Defence. Gil was one of many 'other ranks', known as 'Halton Brats', to be trained for aircrew duties.

Having passed through the rigorous selection process, Gil was posted for his *ab initio* flying training to No. 5 Pilot Training School at RAF Sealand, on 1 October 1934.

Gil later recalled: 'We were issued new flying kit on arrival; a thick one-piece flying suit, known as a "Sidcot suit", flying helmet, goggles and boots.'

Much of the rest of the day was spent finding their way around the base and settling into their accommodations. Meanwhile, all thought was on their first taste of flying in one of the machines that many of the trainees had spent the last few years maintaining:

'Naturally we were all nervous; the next few hours might make or break our RAF careers. One was keyed-up and ready to get the first hurdle out of the way.'

Gil and his fellow pilots under training didn't have too long to wait: 'I made my first flight, in the Avro Tutor [K3247] on the following day, under the instruction of Sergeant Brendenkamp.'

As an LAC trainee pilot, Gil made his first solo flight with nine and a half hours flying time on the dual-control Avro Tutor. Then followed the standard pattern of flights:

> 'In those first few weeks we got to grips with some of the essentials of flying, including forced landings, stalls, how to control the Tutor in a spin, and instrument flying.'

When the trainees weren't in the air building up their flying experience, they were in the classroom learning about the workings of the aero-engine, studying meteorology, etc.

Of course, Gil and the other former Halton apprentices had one up on some of their fellow pupils, as they knew their aircraft inside out. Gil explained that; 'As well as regular flying assessments, we had both practical and written tests on all aspects of the pilot's training. One had to achieve an average score of over sixty per cent, otherwise one was off the course, and that was it.'

With his training going well, Gil progressed on to flying the Bristol Bulldog, then the RAF's front-line fighter, which he first flew on 9 April 1935.

Gil was awarded his pilot's brevet on 22 August 1935, having then completed nearly eighty-nine solo flying hours. His next posting, which came on 11 September, was as a sergeant pilot, when he joined No. 6 (Bomber) Squadron, then flying the two-seater Demon, Gordon and Hart in Ismailia. Gil recalled that he arrived in October, when the squadron's Fighter Flight was in the process of being reformed:

> 'We spent the next few weeks practicing air-to-ground and air-to-air firing. Of course, one didn't need to do this on the firing range, as one had the whole of the desert as one's practice ground.'

On 6 January 1936, Gil was transferred away to No. 29 Squadron, based at El Amrya, flying Demons. This period was to prove uneventful, other than for a fuel leak which led to a forced landing: 'Even routine flights had the potential to end badly, as not all of the local tribesmen were happy with our presence. One carried a "chitty" which had various translations of a message which hopefully would gain one safe conduct if one came down.'

When the Air Ministry decided to reform No. 64 Squadron, Gil's 'D' Flight joined elements of No. 6 Squadron at Heliopolis, on 19 March, taking the Egyptian Scarab beetle for their squadron badge. Gil would later recall that his fascination with the culture of Ancient Egypt stemmed from this posting, although he didn't find time to see many of the sights in his youth; 'One had other things on one's mind at the time; including the fairer sex!' Gil chuckled when once pressed on the subject. Gil followed his interest in Egyptology during his post-war years, becoming a member of several Egyptology societies.

Gil recalled; 'The squadron transferred to Ismailia, where we practiced dogfighting and air-to-air firing.'

With the Abyssinian Crisis still a concern, the squadron's duties were largely in a policing role and as a deterrent to further Italian expansionism.

A second squadron was reformed, flying Demons, as a result of the Abyssinian Crisis. No. 74 Squadron was stationed on Malta, and, like No. 64 Squadron, was destined for home defence as soon as the political tension died down.

Meanwhile, on 19 August 1936, not long after being declared operational, No. 64 Squadron returned to the UK and a posting to RAF Martlesham Heath, where they were to form a part of Home Defence.

Gil recalled that while at RAF Martlesham Heath the squadron trained for both the day and night-fighter role, also demonstrating that they could go on the offensive in a ground war:

'As well as practicing dogfighting and air-to-air combat, we also flew ground strafes and practiced bombing.'

Later, on 18 May 1938, the squadron transferred to RAF Church Fenton, where they continued their training, which Gil recalled included dogfights in their Demons, now fitted with air-gunner's turrets: 'We took on the Fairey Battle and Bristol Blenheim, both monoplane bombers.'

Gil noted in his logbook that the Blenheim was far superior to their Demon biplanes. It was not long, however, before the squadron was re-equipped with the fighter version of the aircraft:

'The Bristol Blenheim was a fighter-bomber. Our aircraft were adapted as fighter aircraft by having a box of four Browning machine guns attached between the wheels.'

These guns were operated by Gil as pilot, so in flight he became used to positioning the Blenheim for the best shot, either from astern of his target, or using the more complicated deflection shooting (allowing his target to travel into the path of his bullets).

Gil had consistently demonstrated his abilities as a pilot and his natural leadership both in the air and on the station. Consequently, Gil's name was put forward for promoted to flight sergeant, which came through on 1 March 1939. This meant Gil was responsible for keeping discipline amongst the NCO pilots and air-gunners on the squadron. Naturally commanding respect from his comrades, Gil had no difficulty fitting into the new role.

In the wake of recent events in Europe, and Hitler's policy of expansionism, the country had further stepped up its programme of rearmament. The need for more front-line fighter aircraft was high on the RAF's agenda with the Hawker Hurricane and Vickers Supermarine Spitfire being widely introduced. No. 64 Squadron, however, was still flying the twin-engine Bristol Blenheim when war was declared. The squadron's training intensified, while Gil's logbook revealed the continuation of their dual role; as well as the regular fighter patrols and escorts, protecting the Home Fleet, they also flew dive-bombing and anti-shipping strikes.

It was while on a routine training flight, on 19 December, that Gil had a narrow escape:

'I lost all power from my port engine and I was forced to make a crash-landing. There was no time to make for a landing-strip. I just had to scan the horizon for a suitable piece of ground. Well, the ground was coming up, closing at an alarming rate. I managed to lift the nose sufficiently to avoid trees, putting down on farmland.'

Both Gil and his crew escaped injury, while their Blenheim had to be taken off the squadron strength for repair.

In late March 1940, No. 64 Squadron received its first Spitfire, Gil making his initial flight on the new type at the end of the month:

'We were then to be re-equipped with Spitfire Mark 1s, preparatory to which we had a couple of landings and take-offs in a dual-control Miles Master.'

Despite the superior speed and handling of the Master over anything that Gil had flown before, nothing could fully prepare him for the grace and power of Reginald Mitchell's creation:

'I did my first solo in a Spitfire on 30 March 1940, and found it a most enjoyable experience.
    'Above all it was an exceptional aircraft for all phases of flying, particularly for aerobatics.'

The Spitfire went through many marks, the squadron being initially equipped with the earliest combat version (Mark 1):

'As it was a fixed-pitch airscrew, the variable pitch came in later; it took rather a lengthy run to get airborne. Landing initially was rather a problem, as the nose of the Spitfire stuck out rather a long way ahead. Thus, on landing, when one came to get the tail down into the landing position, the nose came up and the runway disappeared from view.'

Gil explained that to avoid this problem the pilots soon learned to make their approach off to one side and lose height by side-slipping in: 'The Merlin engine was fitted with steel exhaust pipes and landing at night could be difficult [due to the glare of the exhaust].'

This issue was problematic when trying to locate the faint glow of the enemy's exhausts and when the pilot was coming in to land:

'When the engine was throttled back, exhaust flames poured out of the steel exhausts, temporarily blinding one and cutting off the view of the runway lights. A landing pattern came to be set up in which a turning glide would be made to the flow path and landing pattern assumed at the last minute.'

The leap from Blenheim to Spitfire was monumental and needed a whole new mindset. There then followed a period of intense retraining when the squadron worked on attacks and formation flying, as well as getting in some gunnery practice. Meanwhile, the routine patrols and scrambles to investigate possible raiders continued:

'We flew part of our time on Blenheims and the rest on the new Spitfire. Both aircraft only had rudimentary gunsights, and that was what we had to train on – and when we first went into action.'

The modernization process had its downside and led to the break-up of long standing partnerships, with the squadron's observers and air-gunners being posted to other units. The squadron had to 'reform' from the nucleus of officer and NCO pilots that remained.

Although his initial flights went well, on 23 April, Gil had what he described as 'an unpleasant experience' when a tyre burst on take-off:

'I had to fly around and use up some fuel before making a wheels-up landing. I bent the prop and damaged the underside of the fuselage wings and air intake – but walked away from it unscathed.'

Belly-landings were always dangerous affairs, as a single spark could as easily detonate fuel tanks filled with 100 Octane vapour, as much as one filled with fuel. Gil, who was rightly praised for bringing his aircraft back without any serious damage, took the mishap in his stride and was soon back in the air again putting another Spitfire through its paces, flying formation practice and mock dogfights. Meanwhile, on 30 April, Gil flew his first operational patrol in a Spitfire; combat would come only a few weeks later.

With the remainder of the squadron still operating out of RAF Church Fenton, 'B' Flight temporarily transferred over to RAF Catterick, from where they flew routine patrols and escorts between 1 and 11 May.

Following the invasion of France and the Low Counties on 10 May, the RAF saw an escalation in operations of all types. With pressure mounting on the squadrons already operating over the Channel, No. 64 Squadron flew down to RAF Kenley, Surrey, on 16 May. Initially, their role was as Home Defence, replacing the Hurricane squadrons then operating in and over France. Later they were deployed in defence of the retreating BEF. Dowding's refusal to send Spitfire squadrons to operate out of French bases meant that they would fly out from our own shores. Meanwhile, Gil (flying L1052) took off on a sector reconnaissance and patrol, made between 1515 and 1546 hours on 20 May. During the day, a much depleted No. 615 Squadron arrived back from France, regrouping and flying operations out of the station until 29 August.

At 1820 hours on the following day, 21 May, Gil's Green Section took off to make a patrol of the Boulogne area: 'We were followed about ten minutes later by Red and Yellow Sections.'

While over their patrol area, two Ju 88s were sighted, but escaped into cloud. Gil latched onto a third, which he pursued over the Calais-Boulogne area: 'I fired my first shots in anger; two deflection shots, but without making a positive claim.'

Gil's squadron was still using a crude ring and dot sight, which reduced his accuracy, while he may also have fired from long-range. Following their first combat, many pilots re-adjusted the harmonization of their machine guns from the recommended 350 yards to 200 yards.

Meanwhile, 'A' Flight's Pilot Officer J.J. O'Meara (flying K9846), had better luck and damaged a Ju 88 while flying ten miles north of Cap Gris Nez. The combat took place at 1945 hours:

'I was No. 3 in Yellow Section when we saw three Ju 88s and the section leader gave orders for a No. 1 Attack on one aircraft. When I was pulling up into position, an E/A dived beneath me and released a bomb at a ship. I broke away from the section and attacked from astern and got in one burst, but [the] gunner continued to fire and [as I] attacked [the] E/A dived to sea level and began turning steeply in both directions. I attacked again from above and to port of the E/A using a slight deflection and used the remainder of my ammunition in the attack. The port engine of the E/A caught fire, black smoke and flames being visible, [while] shooting from the enemy rear-gunner ceased shortly before this. We were still at sea level and the E/A was turning to port. My guns had ceased firing and I broke away to starboard and on turning back I could see no sign of the E/A. My outer starboard gun jammed with 296 rounds left, due to broken link.'
(signed) Flying Officer J.J. O'Meara.

Further offensive patrols were flown between 22–28 May, but as Gil explained: 'Without the aid of the controller system, one was flying blind. Consequently the squadron was unable to intercept the enemy.'

No. 64 Squadron flew a patrol over Dunkirk between 1650 and 1820 hours on 29 May, when they were bounced by Bf 109s. During the fairly one-sided combat they lost their CO, Squadron Leader E.G. Rogers[1] (flying L1052), along with Flying Officer R.T. George[2] (flying K9832) and Pilot Officer H.B. Hackney[3] (flying K8906). In reply, Flight Lieutenant D.B. Hobson (flying R9869) damaged a Bf 109, while Flight Sergeant C. Flynn (flying K9813) claimed another, but his own aircraft was damaged by return fire. Pilot Officers A.J.A. Laing (flying L1075), H.P.F.

Patten (flying L1035) and M.T. Wainwright (flying L1037), and Flight Sergeant G.H. Hatch (flying N3293), fired their guns with inconclusive results.

Gil, who had missed the previous day's mission, flew on two of the squadron's four patrols made on 30 May. His first sortie came at 1535 hours, when nine Spitfires patrolled Dunkirk, but without engaging the enemy. Landing at 1750 hours, Gil remained at dispersal and was back in the air again at 1930 hours, taking off on a wing patrol over Dunkirk, made in the company of No. 610 Squadron. The operation was repeated the following day between 1555 and 1800 hours when the Spitfires were subjected to heavy flak from the advancing enemy forces. Gil simply noting in his logbook, 'accurate anti-aircraft fire'.

However, during the patrol Bf 109s and Bf 110s were engaged, with Flying Officers D.M. Taylor (flying N3273) and H.J. Woodward (flying L1038), along with Pilot Officer H.P.F. Patten (flying N5280), each destroying a Bf 110, while Pilot Officer J.J. O'Meara (flying N3298) claimed a Bf 109.

The enemy had the advantage of height and approached up-sun with Flight Lieutenant L.F. Henstock (flying L1063), Flying Officer A.J.O. Jeffrey (flying P9421), Flight Sergeant C. Flynn (P9369) and Sergeant A.E. Binham (flying L1087) also engaged, their aircraft sustaining battle damage. The squadron lost Flight Sergeant G.H. Hatch[4] (flying K9813), who was badly wounded and taken prisoner. Hatch later succumbed to his wounds on 26 September.

During a flight strength sweep flown between 1920 and 2115 hours, Flying Officer A.J.O. Jeffrey caught two Ju 88s at their newly captured landing-ground, strafing and destroying both. The patrol otherwise passed off without incident.

On 1 June, as Operation Dynamo, the evacuation of the British Expeditionary Force (BEF) from Dunkirk, was drawing to a conclusion, No. 64 Squadron flew an offensive patrol over Dunkirk between 1550 and 1730 hours. During a brief engagement with enemy fighters the squadron was unable to make any claims, but lost Pilot Officer T.C. Hey[5] to enemy action.

The Dunkirk patrols continued as the remnants of the BEF were evacuated off the beaches, Gil taking part in one of the last of these operations, which was flown during the early hours of 2 June.

With the vast majority of the BEF saved, the squadron was afforded a very brief period of rest, but was back flying operations on 6 June. The squadron made two uneventful offensive patrols, a third following on 8 June. Meanwhile, a brace of scrambles were flown on 10 June and again on 11 June, but without any interceptions being made.

The squadron had better luck on 12 June when the combined efforts of radar and ground observations placed Gil and, later, Sergeant Adrian 'Andy' Laws, in a perfect position to destroy a lone He 111 on the return leg of its mission.

Initially, only Gil (flying N3230) was scrambled, getting off the ground at 0720 hours. However, once airborne, the controller had difficulty in communicating with him and so his pal, Sergeant A.F. Laws (flying L3275), joined the hunt. Both pilots made separate interceptions, Gil taking the lead, making his attack at 0745 hours near Gatwick at 6,000ft:

'I, as Green 1, was ordered to scramble and climb to 15,000ft. Just after leaving ground I tested my contactor and found it was U/S so I was told to patrol Horsham. At approx. 0743 hours, when at 12,000ft, I noticed another aircraft about 500ft below me about one mile to port. I dived underneath and established his identity as a Heinkel 111. I broke away and carried out a No. 1 Attack, getting in a short burst of approx. two seconds at 150 yards range. [The] E/A evasive action was to throttle right back to a very slow speed and then turn quickly, either port or starboard. Enemy fire appeared to come from blister guns and possibly top gun as well, but it was inaccurate. After this attack [the] E/A dived into clouds at 10,000ft. I resumed an easterly course and, after about three minutes, again saw [the] E/A about 6,000 to 4,000ft below and about one mile to port. I carried out a further No. 1 Attack at between 100 and 150 yards using up the remainder of my ammunition. I observed a large amount of black smoke coming from its port engine and [the] E/A finally was lost in cloud at 600ft approx. twelve miles east by south of Chatham. During this attack enemy fire was only observed coming from one position, either upper gun or starboard blister. Fire was not accurate, tracer was observed going well to the port side of my aircraft during both attacks and my machine was not hit. [The] E/A was camouflaged dark brown and green on top and light blue underneath. Crosses underneath main planes were very prominent. One of my guns (Port 4) had a stoppage after forty rounds due to misfire. I landed at Kenley at 0909 hours. Sergeant Laws (Green 2) left Kenley about ten minutes *[sic]* after me, but we were flying independently of each other and he attacked this E/A later.'
(signed) Flight Sergeant E.G. Gilbert.

Green 2, Sergeant A.F. Laws, arrived on the scene to finish the Heinkel off; his combat report was timed at 0807 hours and read:

'As Green 2, I was ordered off alone (after it had been learned that Green 1, which had left ten minutes earlier *[sic]*, had a faulty R/T) at 0735 hours on a course [of] 150 degrees – further orders followed to alter course to 110 degrees at height of 2,500ft. I lost R/T touch until crossing coast approximately west of Herne Bay. Control then ordered [a] course of 030 degrees, later to 040 degrees, and warned me that [the] E/A was flying out to sea at zero altitude. My height when crossing coast had been 5,000ft in order to avoid clouds, but weather was clear over sea and I lost height gradually. I sighted [the] E/A at 0807 hours, heading east at approximately 600ft (my height was then 3,000ft); I flew ahead of [the] enemy towards sun, losing height and turned for a beam attack. I carried out two beam attacks from either side, opening fire at 250 yards. The E/A, when first seen, and during the action, was travelling slowly (about 160mph) as though one engine was damaged. [The] E/A dived to sea level and made gentle turns each way, the tail unit occasionally touching the sea. At this moment two other Spitfires joined in, carrying out attacks

from astern and above. I joined in with similar attacks until remainder of my ammunition was expended. [The] E/A had then settled on water and crew was inflating [a] dinghy. I circled for a short period, being last to leave the scene. During [the] engagement, gunfire was observed from rear top position only and this was inaccurate – my machine was not hit. Camouflage on top of plane was dark brown and green on underside of plane. I believe that this was the E/A attacked earlier by F/S Gilbert (Green 1) who left Kenley about ten minutes *[sic]* before me.'
(signed) Sergeant A.F. Laws.

Gil's logbook recorded: 'Various – Heinkel intercepted. ½ kill to me, ½ to Laws'.

Sergeant Andy Laws and Gil were close friends. Laws had enlisted as an aircraft hand with the RAF in 1931. He applied and was accepted for pilot training, and began flying at No. 4 Flight Training School at RAF Abu Sueir in July 1935. He joined No. 64 Squadron at Ismailia on 20 April 1936, and served alongside Gil as a sergeant pilot, both later being promoted to flight sergeant and commissioned as pilot officer.

The destruction of a Heinkel He 111 by Sergeant Andy Laws and Flight Sergeant Gil Gilbert was recorded in one of the local newspapers, Gil sticking the cutting into his logbook:

'Heinkel shot down on SE Coast

'A Heinkel 111 bomber was shot down by a British fighter off the Kent coast today. This was confirmed by the Air Ministry following reports that anti-aircraft guns had been in action.

'A Spitfire pilot dived more than 11,000 feet to make the first attack on the Heinkel shortly after 8 o'clock.

'After firing all his ammunition he saw the Heinkel dive into cloud with black smoke pouring from its port engine.

'A second Spitfire took up the chase, followed closely by two more. They saw the Heinkel staggering slowly, low over the water with its tail splashing the surface and the pilot trying in vain to continue his flight.

'Finally, the Heinkel came to rest on the sea and two members of the crew climbed out onto their dingy. They were picked up and taken to hospital in a Kent coastal town.

'The pilot had an arm wound and the mechanic, who weighed 18st, a head injury. A local fisherman rescued them.'

The press cutting was annotated by Gil with the words: '3 more dead' (referring to the remainder of the crew).

The squadron flew two more scrambles during the day, but was not able to make contact with the enemy, which turned back. The Luftwaffe was still probing the RAF's command and control system, and such raids, which turned out to be feints, were not uncommon

Two uneventful scrambles were made on 17 June, while three days later, a total of five scrambles were flown by the squadron's Spitfires, without results, Gil taking part in two patrols over the south-east coast.

Gil flew an offensive patrol over Northern France on 21 June, similar patrols being mounted from 23 to 25 June, but without drawing the enemy up to engage.

In partnership with Andy Laws, Gil flew a scramble on 27 June, but the pair were unable to repeat their earlier success. Meanwhile, the squadron's Spitfires made a further incursion over Northern France. The mission was repeated on the following day. These operations were designed to take the fight to the enemy, but were to become unpopular with many of Fighter Command's pilots. The Luftwaffe simply waited until the RAF's fighters were on their return leg – their pilots tired and running short of fuel for combat – and bounced them when they were at their most vulnerable.

In the company of Flight Sergeant A.F. Laws and Sergeant J. Whelen, Gil flew on a scramble between 0645 and 0730 hours on 29 June, but once again the pilots were frustrated as the raid turned back.

A patrol was flown by Sub-Lieutenant F.D. Paul, Flying Officer D.M. Taylor and Pilot Officer D.K. Milne between 1850 and 2000 hours on 1 July. Following the controller's vector, the trio shared in the destruction of a Do 17, while forty-five miles south of Beachy Head. Pilots from No. 145 Squadron fired on the same bomber.

At 1643 hours, on 3 July, a sneak attack was made by a lone Do 17, flying below radar. Approaching RAF Kenley it dropped its bombs in amongst the fighters dispersed around the perimeter. The squadron's Spitfires scrambled to pursue the raider, but were unable to make an interception.

The squadron made a section strength armed reconnaissance over the Pas de Calais between 1955 and 2115 hours on 5 July. Flying at 22,000ft, the Spitfires were bounced by Bf 109s of JG 51 with the loss of Pilot Officer D.K. Milne[6] (flying P9607) who was shot down by Bf 109s over Rouen. During the ensuing combat Sub-Lieutenant F.D. Paul (P9450) destroyed a Bf 109. His own aircraft was damaged by return fire and limped back over the Channel before making a crash-landing at RAF Hawkinge.

No. 64 Squadron made two uneventful patrols during 6 July. Airborne again between 2015 and 2135 hours on 7 July, Gil took part in a patrol over the Channel following reports of a raid heading for an eastward-bound convoy approaching Folkestone. Both Nos. 64 and 65 Squadrons were scrambled too late and arrived over the convoy after the bombers had dropped their payloads. Meanwhile, Bf 109s of JG 27, acting as air cover, bounced No. 65 Squadron's Spitfires over Folkestone, shooting down Green Section's Flying Officer G.V. Proudman[7] (flying R6615), Sergeant P.S. Hayes[8] (flying N3129) and Pilot Officer N.J. Brisbane[9] (flying R6609). The squadron's Flight Sergeant W.H. Franklyn chased two Bf 109s almost as far as France, claiming both destroyed.

No. 64 Squadron encountered a formation of Bf 110s, and while Gil, 'had a squirt at a few', he was unable to make a claim, Sub-Lieutenant F.D. Paul (flying L1035) and Flying Officer A.J.O. Jeffrey (flying P9421) each destroyed a Messerschmitt Bf 110 off Calais to even out the score.

Gil flew on a flight strength scramble between 1250 and 1350 hours on the following day, 8 July, without making contact with the enemy, who had turned back before the squadron could close to engage.

A total of four scrambles were flown at various strengths during 9 July, Gil joining a flight strength interception patrol made between 1625 and 1705 hours:

'One was often scrambled off by the controller and vectored onto this raid or that, but the plots often turned back; the enemy was probing our defence system, you see.'

No. 64 Squadron was scrambled at 1340 hours on 10 July, flying to the aid of Convoy Bread which was under attack off Dover. Also vectored against the same raid, estimated at two dozen Do 17s, twenty Bf 110s and twenty Bf 109s, were Nos. 32, 56, 74 and 111 Squadrons.

The enemy was already under attack; as No. 64 Squadron's Spitfires arrived, the Bf 110s broke from their defensive circle and headed back over the Channel; the Spitfires gave chase. Sub-Lieutenant F.D. Paul (flying N3230) claimed two Bf 110s, probably destroying a third. Flying Officer D.M. Taylor (R6700) claimed a Bf 110, but was only allowed a second as probably destroyed. Pilot Officer H.P.F. Patten (L1075) also filed a combat report, claiming one Bf 110 destroyed.

No. 56 Squadron had attacked the enemy at about the same time, making the following claims:

Flight Lieutenant J.H. Coghlan (flying P3547)	one Bf 110 destroyed, two Bf 109s damaged
Flight Lieutenant E.J. Gracie (flying P3554)	one Bf 110 destroyed (shared)
Sergeant C. Whitehead (flying L3356)	one Bf 110 destroyed (shared)

No. 32 Squadron claimed:

Squadron Leader G.G.R. Bulmer (flying P3679)	one Do 17 destroyed (shared)
Flying Officer J.B.W. Humpherson (flying N2588)	one Do 17 destroyed (shared)
Sergeant L.H.B. Pearce (flying 2755)	one Do 17 destroyed (shared)

No. 74 Squadron claimed:

Flight Lieutenant W.E.G. Measures (flying K9871)	one Bf 110 and one Do 17 damaged
Flying Officer J.C. Mungo-Park (flying K9878)	one Do 17 destroyed
Pilot Officer D.G. Cobden (flying P9399)	one Do 17 damaged
Pilot Officer B.V. Draper (flying P9393)	one Do 17 damaged
Pilot Officer P.C.B. St John (flying L1089)	one Bf 109 damaged
Pilot Officer P.C.F. Stevenson (flying P9206)	two Bf 109s damaged

No. 111 Squadron claimed:

Flying Officer H.M. Ferris (flying P3458)	one Bf 109 destroyed, Do 17 damaged
Flying Officer T.P.K. Higgs (flying P3671)	one Do 17 destroyed

Flying Officer T.P.K. Higgs[10] collided with a Do 17 of III./KG 2 off Folkestone at about 1300 hours, during a head-on attack (an extremely risky tactic, which generally succeeded in breaking up the enemy's formation, and which Keith Park later advocated). Higgs bailed out but drowned, his body being washed ashore.

Meanwhile, No. 64 Squadron's Spitfires flew two uneventful convoy escorts in a bid to ward off further attacks. On the following day, 11 July, the squadron made four patrols, Gil joining a flight strength scramble at 1510 hours.

The Squadron Operational Record Book (ORB) noted three uneventful convoy operations during 12 July, the Spitfires maintaining a standing patrol between 0430 and 0800 hours. Gil explained:

'One approached the convoy on a wide arc, giving them plenty of warning of one's approach – the RN gunners had a reputation for firing upon anything that flew within range.

'One had to maintain standing patrols, you see, with sections taking it in turns to station themselves overhead. There wasn't sufficient time to scramble a squadron once an enemy raid was already on its way to bomb a Channel convoy; they could be overhead in twelve minutes against our fifteen.

'It was a drain on men and resources, but [it was] the only way we could be on hand to defend the merchantmen.'

Ultimately the pressures of maintaining standing patrols over the Channel convoys were too great for Fighter Command's No. 11 Group and they were virtually banned. But as Gil explained:

'We later found out that much of what had been sent through the Channel could have gone across land by rail. So it was something of a hollow victory for the Luftwaffe really.'

Gil made an uneventful flight strength scramble at 1615 hours on 13 July, before being ordered to pancake:

'We remained in our cockpits while our Spitfires were refuelled and were airborne again on an offensive patrol [made between 1720 and 1800 hours], entering into combat with the enemy off Dover.'

Once again Sub-Lieutenant F.D. Paul (flying L1035) was in the thick of the action, claiming a Bf 109, although the aircraft, of JG 51, actually crash-landed in France.

Sergeant A.E. Binham's Spitfire, K9795, was hit by the Dover Barrage while in combat with Bf 109s and force-landed at RAF Hawkinge, Binham was uninjured. The same fate befell Sub-Lieutenant J.H.C. Sykes, who made a wheels-up landing.

The loss of two Spitfires was a salutary lesson, and in future the pilots would skirt around the barrage, or be forced to let the enemy go, rather than risk pilots and aircraft.

The Spitfires, including Gil's N3230, were quickly refuelled and rearmed, and were back in the air again at 1820 hours, when they flew an uneventful mission across the Channel. A section strength offensive patrol followed at 1925 hours, again only twenty minutes after the Spitfires touched down. Gil was, however, rested for what turned out to be the last operation of the day, but remained at Readiness.

An offensive patrol was flown on 14 July, with Gil airborne between 1020 and 1220 hours, but the enemy could not be drawn into a response. The squadron was scrambled on an interception patrol during the afternoon, but the controller was heard to radio, 'Freema Squadron – pancake', which was the order to recall, the threat having gone away. A further uneventful scramble was made at 0625 hours on the following morning.

Action, however, wasn't too far away. Scrambled at 1140 hours on 17 July, Sub-Lieutenant J.H.C. Sykes damaged an enemy aircraft, but a reinforcement patrol was scrambled too late and failed to make contact with the enemy, which had already withdrawn, and the opportunity for more 'kills' was lost.

Gil flew on a squadron strength convoy patrol between 1330 and 1455 hours. Flying Officer D.M. Taylor (flying P9705) was shot down and wounded during a surprise attack by Bf 109s from JG 2, which was delivered at 1400 hours. He force-landed at Hailsham and was admitted to Eastbourne Hospital. No other member of the patrol saw the enemy aircraft's hit and run pass. The squadron flew a further three section strength patrols during a busy day, Gil flying on one of these made between 1800 and 1945 hours:

'We took off and stooged around waiting for a vector from the controller, but after a couple of false alarms we were ordered down.'

One uneventful scramble was flown on 18 July, on what turned out to be a quiet day for the squadron. However, during the second scramble of the following day, which was made between 1550 and 1630 hours, they engaged the enemy off Dover. The controller's vector put the Spitfires right onto the path of the enemy and they were able to position themselves to come down on the Messerschmitt Bf 109s from out of the sun. With the element of surprise on their side, the Spitfires reeked havoc. Flying Officer H.J. Woodward (flying K9991) and Pilot Officer J.J. O'Meara (flying P9369) each destroyed a Bf 109, while Flying Officer A.J.O. Jeffrey (flying P9421) claimed two Bf 109s. In the general melee, Flying Officer H.J. Woodward collided with an enemy aircraft, losing his wingtip. Meanwhile, Pilot Officer J.J. O'Meara's cockpit hood and part of a control surface were damaged by return fire.

During the day, Flying Officer A.J.O. Jeffrey (flying P9421) was scrambled to investigate a plot which turned out to be an He 115 attempting to lay mines in the Thames estuary in broad daylight. Flying without an escort, the Heinkel He 115 was easy prey and was sent down in flames. Jeffrey was later awarded the DFC, *London Gazette*, 13 August 1940, although his latest combat victory was omitted from the citation:

'Awarded the Distinguished Flying Cross.

'Flying Officer Alister John Oswald JEFFREY (39740)—now reported missing.

'This officer has displayed gallantry and skill in engagements against the enemy. He has destroyed three enemy aircraft in air combat, and on two occasions has carried out attacks on enemy bases, destroying at least four aircraft on the ground.'

No. 64 Squadron flew a night-fighter patrol between 0020 and 0145 hours on the morning of 21 July, making four uneventful flight strength scrambles between 0555 and 1015 hours. There was no further trade for the rest of the day, during which only routine flights were made.

Gil flew on a squadron patrol between 1600 and 1630 hours on 22 July, joining a flight strength scramble between 1700 and 1730 hours:

'By this stage I was getting a little over eager to get a shot at the enemy again. Other pilots were starting to build a score, and I wanted to justify myself and my training – the service had invested a lot of time in one, so one needed to bring down a few. Well that was how I felt anyway.'

The Battle of Britain was in its first phase, with the Luftwaffe still only testing out the RAF's defences, continuing to send raids which turned back at the last minute, after the controller had committed his squadrons. In this vein, four uneventful patrols were made between 0930 and 2015 hours on the following day, 23 July. The squadron, meanwhile, flew three uneventful patrols between 0445 and 0920 hours on the following day, as the 'cat and mouse' game continued.

At 1430 hours on 25 July, eight of No. 64 Squadron's Spitfires were scrambled, joining twelve from No. 54 Squadron and a flight of No. 111 Squadron's Hurricanes. Once airborne the fighters were vectored onto thirty Ju 88s of III./KG 4 and fifty-plus Bf 109s targeting a convoy of twenty merchant vessels and their destroyer escort off Folkestone. No. 64 Squadron's CO, Squadron Leader A.R.D. MacDonell (flying L1055), claimed a Ju 88, but was hit by return fire from a second. However, Flying Officer A.J.O. Jeffrey[11] (flying P9421) was shot down in combat by one of the Bf 109 escorts, and crashed into the Channel off Dover at 1455 hours. His body was later washed up on the Dutch coast.

Meanwhile, three more of No. 64 Squadron's Spitfires were scrambled to give support, as was No. 111 Squadron, which was led into the air by Squadron

Leader J. Thompson. The Hurricanes followed their CO into a head-on attack, which broke up the Ju 88's formation and they turned tail for home, the Bf 109s following suit.

During the combat No. 54 Squadron recorded the following claims and losses:

Squadron Leader J.A. Leathart (flying R6708)	one Bf 109 destroyed unconfirmed
Flight Lieutenant B.H. Way (flying R6707)	one Bf 109 destroyed
Pilot Officer C.F. Gray (flying R6893)	one Bf 109 destroyed unconfirmed

Pilot Officer D.R. Turley-George (flying P9387) crash-landed at 1500 hours following combat damage sustained while engaged with Bf 109s over the convoy.

Pilot Officer A. Finnie[12] (flying R6816) was killed-in-action over the convoy when he was attacked by a Bf 109. His Spitfire crashed at Kingsdown at 1810 hours.

Having dispersed the enemy bombers, No. 111 Squadron tackled their fighter escort, making the following claims:

Flight Lieutenant R.P.R. Powell (flying P2888)	one Bf 109 damaged
Pilot Officer R.R. Wilson (flying P3595)	one Bf 109 destroyed, one Bf 109 damaged
Flight Sergeant S.D.P. Connors (flying P3943)	one Bf 109 destroyed (shared)
Sergeant R. Carnall (flying P3922)	one Bf 109 destroyed (shared)
Sergeant J.T. Craig (flying P3046)	one Bf 109 damaged

During a section strength patrol, flown between 1445 and 1545 hours, Sub-Lieutenant F.D. Paul (flying L1035) claimed a Bf 109. A further patrol was made between 1610 and 1710 hours, but no contact was made as the raid appeared to turn back. The Spitfires were quickly refuelled and made ready for the next raid, which wasn't long in appearing on the horizon, with a section strength scramble made at 1730 hours in defence of a convoy which was under attack off Dover. Fifteen minutes into the patrol, and while off Folkestone, the Spitfires were bounced by Bf 109s, with the loss of Sub-Lieutenant F.D. Paul[13] (flying L1035).

Gil explained:

'A parachute was seen, and there was good reason to hope that he'd survived. We understood that a German E-boat picked him up, but he must have been wounded, because he died later [30 July] as a PoW. It was sad, but it was just one of those things.'

In retaliation, Flight Lieutenant F.L. Henstock (flying R6700) badly damaged a Bf 109, while Flying Officer C.J.D. Andreae (flying N3230) saw enough of the enemy to take evasive action and escaped without damage. Meanwhile, ten of No. 54 Squadron's Spitfires were scrambled to reinforce. They engaged the enemy, but no further claims were made.

Four patrols were flown between 0645 and 1655 hours on 26 July, but without contacting the enemy. The pattern was repeated on the following day, the scrambles beginning at 0910 hours, with Gil flying on one patrol made between 1115 and 1215 hours. By this time Gil's name had been put forward for a commission:

'I was one of the senior pilots in the squadron. As a flight sergeant I'd often lead a section, even a flight strength patrol, if none of the more experienced pilots were available. I guess we took it in turns, especially when it came to convoy escorts or the more "routine patrol", whatever they were, because even a base patrol could turn into something bigger.'

The squadron made three patrols on 28 July, with Gil participating in one flown between 1945 and 2115 hours. Again the operations continued the next day, the only contact with the enemy being made during a section strength patrol flown between 0710 and 0750 hours, when the Spitfires intercepted a dozen Bf 109s. During the engagement Squadron Leader A.R.D. MacDonell (flying R6973) shot down a Bf 109, badly damaging a second and shooting down a Ju 87. Flight Sergeant A.F. Laws (flying R9450) set one Bf 109 on fire, while Pilot Officer J.J. O'Meara (flying R6645) was able to use the protection afforded by his CO and Andy Laws to mix it up with the Stuka dive-bombers, destroying two and badly damaging a third. Meanwhile, Sergeant A.E. Binham's Spitfire, R6643, was caught in the sights of one of the Bf 109s and shot up, and force-landed at St Margaret's Bay. Binham escaped without injury.

Three squadron, flight and section strength patrols were flown on 31 July, but on each occasion the enemy turned back.

The squadron wasn't called into action until 2020 hours on 1 August, when a flight strength patrol was flown, but the raid was a feint and the enemy turned away and the Spitfires landed without having fired their guns.

The false alarms proved tiring, with the pilots never knowing when the order to scramble would be given, whether they would face a mass enemy raid, a lone raider or reconnaissance aircraft, or empty skies.

While the next few days were quiet for the squadron, things soon picked up again and at 0815 hours on 5 August, Squadron Leader A.R.D. MacDonell led a flight strength patrol from their advanced landing ground at RAF Hawkinge; relieving No. 615 Squadron, which was on a convoy escort between Beachy Head and Dover. Another section was scrambled off five minutes later to reinforce, once an approaching raid of Bf 109s from JG 54 was identified. The squadron closed with the enemy and Pilot Officer A.G. Donahue (flying K9991) destroyed a Bf 109, claiming a second probably destroyed. Flying Officer H.J. Woodward (flying N3293) claimed a Bf 109, unconfirmed. Sergeant J. Mann (flying R6700) destroyed a Bf 109, while Pilot Officer A.G. Donahue (flying K9991), who had only arrived two days earlier, destroyed a Bf 109, but his own aircraft was damaged by return fire off the French coast. He landed at RAF Hawkinge, uninjured. Flying in the second wave, Sergeant L.R. Isaac[14] (flying L1029) was shot down by a Bf 109 off Folkestone at 0850 hours. None of the squadron witnessed Isaac's fate and his Spitfire plunged into the Channel without a trace. Back at RAF Kenley, when it became clear that his aircraft would have run out of fuel, if it hadn't been lost in action, the young sergeant pilot's name was erased from the duty roster.

Sergeant Isaac would have been well known to Gil, both as a personal friend in the mess and as one of his charge, but there could be no time to dwell on the squadron's losses, no matter how hard they were felt.

An uneventful section strength patrol followed between 1255 and 1330 hours:

'By this time I'd just the one "shared" to my credit; the Heinkel Andy Laws and I shot down between us. So while every sortie on type gave one a better chance of survival, one still wanted to test one's mettle against the 109, which was the best fighter the enemy had at the time.'

While the squadron flew a flight strength scramble at 1130 hours on 7 August, Gil's logbook notes he took part in a mock dogfight as part of an airfield defence exercise; 'six Spitfires attacked five Hurricanes (mock dogfighting). Excellent dogfight. Hurricanes too easy.'

It must have been a reassurance to Gil to know that he could out-turn and out-fight the RAF's Hurricane, but still the Bf 109s remained an illusive beast which he knew he had to conquer if he was to survive the battle.

The squadron's first patrol on 8 August was flown at 0515 hours, with a second made between 1000 and 1100 hours, reinforced five minutes later by a flight strength patrol, during which Sergeant J.W.C. Squier was injured and force-landed at Capel-le-Ferne when he was bounced by Hauptmann J. Troutflot, flying a Bf 109 of III./JG 51, at 1110 hours. Squier was admitted to hospital, his Spitfire, P9369, being written off. The remainder of the squadron landed and was quickly refuelled, with a flight strength scramble made at 1120 hours, patrolling base at 8,000ft, with No. 41 Squadron's Spitfires ordered to patrol RAF Manston. Four German formations approached the coast, one neared Dungeness at 1125 hours, making a sweep as far as Maidstone before heading home. The second crossed the coast near North Foreland, but altered its course and did not cause further concern. The third plot crossed the coast at Pevensey before flying towards Beachy Head. No. 32 Squadron was scrambled, but arrived too late. Meanwhile, a little before noon, radar plotted enemy aircraft in the Straits, heading for the Goodwins and RAF Manston.

No. 64 Squadron made contact with a formation of Bf 109s of III./JG 51 north of Dover. Taking the squadron into the attack, Squadron Leader A.R.D. MacDonell (flying R6995) destroyed a Bf 109, while Sergeant J. Mann (flying R6975) destroyed a Bf 109 and damaged another. Flying Officer H.J. Woodward and Sergeant P.S. Hawke both damaged a Bf 109. The squadron suffered a fatality. Pilot Officer P.F. Kennard-Davis[15] (flying L1039) was shot down in flames while in combat with a

Bf 109. His Spitfire crashed and burned out at West Langdon, Kent, at 1205 hours. Pilot Officer Kennard-Davis bailed out, but had suffered several bullet wounds. Despite initial reports that he was in good spirits and keen to get back to the squadron, Kennard-Davis' wounds proved more serious and he died in the Royal Victoria Hospital, Dover, on 10 August.

Meanwhile, No. 41 Squadron was also scrambled too late to intercept the initial attack, but engaged a second formation of Bf 109s off Manston, making the following claims:

Flight Lieutenant J.T. Webster (flying R6611)	one Bf 109 destroyed, two Bf 109s unconfirmed destroyed, one Bf 109 destroyed (shared)
Pilot Officer R.W. Wallens (flying R6883)	one Bf 109 destroyed, one Bf 109 destroyed (shared)

No. 610 Squadron, also from RAF Hawkinge, joined the same combat, but without making any claims.

On 9 August, Gil took part in a squadron patrol made between 1555 and 1723 hours, leading the combat, when the Spitfires were bounced by Bf 109s. Sergeant J. Mann was shot at by Bf 109s, cannon shell splinters jammed in his control column. Mann somehow managed to reach RAF Kenley, making a heavy landing. He had received burns to the face when the shell exploded and received plastic-surgery at the Victoria Cottage Hospital, East Grinstead, in doing so becoming one of Archibald MacIndoe's Guinea Pigs.

The following day, 10 August, saw a section scramble at 0735 hours, but the Spitfires were quickly ordered down to conserve fuel.

Gil joined a section strength patrol flown between 0730 and 0815 hours on 11 August. Radar had plotted a force of about thirty enemy aircraft seven miles east of the South Foreland, flying at 15,000ft. Once airborne, No. 64 Squadron was vectored to Dover, with No. 32 Squadron scrambled off from RAF Hawkinge at 0742 hours with orders to patrol their home base. Meanwhile, No. 74 Squadron was scrambled from RAF Manston, but were too late to prevent the Bf 109s from making a strafe of the Dover barrage balloons. Both Nos. 32 and 74 Squadrons engaged formations of Bf 109s over the Channel, the latter with some success.

No. 74 Squadron reported the following claims and loss:

Squadron Leader A.G. Malan (flying R6757)	one Bf 109 unconfirmed destroyed
Flying Officer W.H. Nelson (flying R6839)	one Bf 109 unconfirmed destroyed
Pilot Officer D. Hastings (flying R6773)	one Bf 109 damaged
Pilot Officer J.C. Mungo-Park (flying R6772)	one Bf 109 damaged
Pilot Officer D.N.E. Smith (flying R6962)	one Bf 109 unconfirmed destroyed
Pilot Officer H.M. Stephen (flying P9492)	two Bf 109s unconfirmed destroyed, one Bf 109 damaged

Pilot Officer P.C.F. Stevenson (flying P9393)   one Bf 109 unconfirmed destroyed

Pilot Officer Stevenson bailed out near Dover at 0810 hours following combat with Bf 109s. He was picked up by a motorized launch.

No. 32 Squadron's only claim was made by Pilot Officer A.R.H. Barton (flying N2596), who destroyed a Bf 109 over Dover.

Meanwhile, a flight strength scramble was flown at 0932 hours against a force of Bf 109s on another fighter sweep, with Squadron Leader A.R.D. MacDonell (flying X4018) and Pilot Officer L.F.D. King (flying N3293) each destroying a Bf 109, Pilot Officer J.J. O'Meara damaging another. On landing at 1015 hours, the Spitfires were quickly turned around, with the pilots at Readiness awaiting a second scramble.

Nos. 32 and 74 Squadrons were likewise scrambled at 0940 hours and 0950 hours respectively, meeting the enemy off the coast.

During the ensuing combat No. 74 Squadron claimed:

Squadron Leader A.G. Malan	one Bf 109 damaged
Pilot Officer J.C. Freeborn (flying R6840)	one Bf 109 unconfirmed
Warrant Officer E. Mayne (flying K9871)	one Bf 109 unconfirmed and one Bf 109 damaged

No. 32 Squadron's Pilot Officer P.M. Gardner (flying P3679) damaged a Bf 109 over Dungeness.

On what was their third patrol of the day, No. 64 Squadron made a flight strength scramble between 1146 and 1225 hours, when Pilot Officer J.J. O'Meara (flying R6683) and Sergeant J. Mann probably destroyed Bf 109s. Squadron Leader A.R.D. MacDonell (flying X4018) and Sergeant J. Mann (flying R6975) each damaged a Bf 109. During the general dogfight, Pilot Officer C.J.D. Andreae's Spitfire, N3293, was damaged by a cannon shell.

Meanwhile, flying with 'B' Flight, Flight Sergeant A.F. Laws (flying P9447) destroyed a Bf 109 which had been on Gil's tail: 'I still hadn't got a 109 to my credit, but I was thankful to Andy for shooting this one down. He'd bounced me, but Andy saw him and turned the tables.' The combat took place at 1215 hours while four miles north of Folkestone. Flight Sergeant A.F. Laws fired two, three-second bursts at 250 yards:

'Whilst on patrol as Blue 2 with Red and Yellow Sections, several small formations of Me 109s were sighted above and behind at approximately 18,000ft. Squadron Leader manoeuvred to engage and sections broke away during [the] ensuing dogfight. I saw my section leader (Flight Sergeant Gilbert) circling over cloud layer with an Me 109 on his tail. I dived to within range and gave a three-second burst from dead astern. Gave another three-second burst whilst enemy aircraft was turning. [The] E/A flew away on [its] side into cloud, possibly out of control. I followed through cloud myself about

five miles out over Channel. [I] could not see anything of E/A so returned to forward base to rearm.'
(signed) Flight Sergeant A. F. Laws.

The enemy launched a number of raids throughout the day, 12 August, but No. 64 Squadron was not called into action until the late afternoon. Four formations, two of fifty-plus, one of thirty-plus and one of twenty enemy aircraft, were plotted approaching the coast in the squadron's sector. The controller scrambled Nos. 32, 64 and 501 Squadrons to patrol their home bases against attack. Meanwhile, Nos. 54 and 56 Squadrons were ordered to Dover.

The raids crossed the coast near Dover, New Romney and North Foreland at about 1730 hours, the latter being attacked by Nos. 54 and 56 Squadrons, intercepting the bombers. No. 32 Squadron engaged a force of thirty Do 215s and their escort of the same number of Bf 109s between Dover and Whitstable. Meanwhile, No. 501 Squadron attacked a force of bombers that raided its forward base at RAF Hawkinge.

Scrambled at 1645 hours, and reinforced by Gil's Blue Section at 1700, No. 64 Squadron engaged the enemy formation which had earlier crossed the coast near Dover. Flying Officer H.J. Woodward (flying X4067) destroyed a Bf 109. Sergeant J. Mann (flying R6623) destroyed a Bf 109 (unconfirmed), while Pilot Officer J.J. O'Meara (flying R6683) damaged another. Meanwhile, Sergeant P.S. Hawke (flying K9805) claimed a Do 215 probably destroyed. Gil, who had a number of enemy aircraft in his sights, but never long enough to fire a telling burst, recalled that: 'I scared a few, but didn't make a claim.'

Pilot Officer A.G. Donahue (flying X4018) was wounded in the right leg when shot down by a Bf 109 over the south coast. He bailed out, burned, at 1740 hours, his Spitfire crashing at Sellindge.

No. 32 Squadron, meanwhile, reported the following claims, with one loss:

Flight Lieutenant M.N. Crossley (flying 93146)	one Bf 109 destroyed, one Bf 109 damaged
Pilot Officer P.M. Gardner (flying P3147)	two Bf 109s probably destroyed
Pilot Officer D.H. Grice (flying N2425)	one Do 215 damaged
Pilot Officer J.B.W. Humpherson (flying P3112)	one Bf 109 probably destroyed
Pilot Officer K. Pniak (flying R4106)	one Bf 109 probably destroyed
Pilot Officer J.E. Proctor (flying N2458)	one Bf 109 probably destroyed
Pilot Officer R.F. Smythe (flying P3522)	one Do 215 destroyed
Sergeant E.A. Bayley (flying P3481)	one Do 215 damaged
Sergeant W.B. Higgins (flying N2524)	one Bf 109 probably destroyed

Pilot Officer A.R.H. Barton (flying N2596) was shot down over Dover at 1700 hours, crashing at RAF Hawkinge, safe.

No. 54 Squadron claimed:

Flying Officer A.C. Deere (flying X4019)	two Bf 109s probably destroyed
Sergeant W. Klozinsky	two Bf 109s probably destroyed

No. 56 Squadron also got in amongst the bombers and made a number of claims, with one loss:

Flying Officer P.S. Weaver (flying P3554)	one Do 17 destroyed
Flight Sergeant F.W. Higginson (flying US–A)	one Do 17 damaged
Sergeant G. Smythe (flying US–K)	one Bf 109 destroyed

Pilot Officer A.G. Page (flying P2970 US–X) was shot down by return fire from a Do 17 and bailed out badly burned, north of Margate and was rescued by a tender and the Margate Lifeboat at 1750 hours.

No. 501 Squadron's only claim was made by Pilot Officer J.A.A. Gibson (flying P2986), who destroyed a Bf 109.

Pilot Officer A.G. Donahue, who was hospitalised for several weeks as a result of the wounds he received in the combat, rejoined No. 64 Squadron in mid–September and on 29 September was transferred to No. 71 (Eagle) Squadron, before returning to No. 64 Squadron on 23 October.

In the meantime, No. 64 Squadron was in action again on 13 August, '*Adler Tag*', or 'Eagle Day', when Gil joined 'A' Flight on a scramble between 0635 and 0745 hours. Once airborne, the controller vectored the Spitfires onto a formation of Do 215s, which immediately turned south for home, with No. 64 Squadron's Spitfires in hot pursuit. Latching on to the bombers, Pilot Officer R.L. Jones (flying R6623) damaged a Do 215, which was later attacked and destroyed by Flying Officer H.J. Woodward (flying X4067). Pilot Officers R. Roberts (flying L1038) and P.J. Simpson (flying K9805), and Flight Sergeants Gil Gilbert (flying N3230) and A.F. Laws (flying P9447) each damaged a Do 215.

Red 2, Pilot Officer R.L. Jones' combat was timed at 0705 hours, south of Portsmouth, firing six bursts of four seconds at 300 to 250 yards:

'I was Red 2 when E/A [fifteen Do 215s and Bf 110s] were sighted – manoeuvred to attack enemy aircraft flying in loose vic formation. On being sighted they turned south. I followed my leader and did a No. 2 Attack on left-hand side Dornier, all my tracer went into [the] enemy machine. On turning to attack the second time I saw about ten Me 110s above me in a circle. I turned to attack and fired on the leading Me 110. Damage not noticed – no ammunition and I withdrew.'
(signed) Pilot Officer R.L. Jones.

Red 3, Pilot Officer P.J. Simpson engaged a Do 215 at 18,000ft over Chichester, firing a five-second burst at 200 yards, closing to 50 yards. His combat was timed at 0700 hours:

'We were told to scramble and patrol base [at] Angels 7. Soon we were vectored and I, Red 3, heard Yellow 1 Tally-Ho to starboard and I then sighted eight Do 215s. We dived to attack and I delivered an astern attack, giving about a three-second burst, [before I] broke away and found one [Do 215] on my port side. I chased it round in a circle for a time and gave short bursts at very close-range. The Do 215 then straightened out, and the undercarriage dropped down and rear gun was firing. I then broke away as I had no more ammunition and returned to base.'
(signed) Pilot Officer P.J. Simpson.

Yellow 1, Flying Officer H.J. Woodward, engaged the enemy at 12,000ft while over Chichester, firing several bursts at very long range and one long burst at under 250 yards. His combat report was timed at 0700 hours:

'As Yellow 1, I was leading the squadron eastwards at about 16,000ft when I saw enemy bombers approaching from starboard at about 12,000ft in open formation astern. I called the squadron and dived to do a beam attack on one of the rear bombers. I fired a short burst without result. I then turned behind the bomber and carried out a No 2 attack, also without result, though the rear-gunner, who had fired on my first attack, did not fire now. I broke away and held off to port while two more Spitfires attacked the bomber from astern, apparently without result. I then closed dead astern slowly, fired several bursts at rather long opening range and a long burst at under 250 yards. I saw a burst of my tracer entering both of the E/A's wings. The E/A's starboard engine then caught fire and I believe the whole inboard starboard wing was on fire. The E/A broke sharply left from its formation and dived down. I broke away. The E/A was seen by Red 3 (Pilot Officer Simpson) spiralling steeply down on fire. I returned to the coast and did a beam attack on another E/A without result, and was then out of ammunition.

'We intercepted about Chichester and pursued the E/A (about six) southward out to sea, where they were joined by another formation of six or more coming from the west.

'The above E/A was shot down about twenty miles out to sea, south of Tangmere.'
(signed) Flying Officer H.J. Woodward.

The combat officially made Woodward an ace. He was duly awarded the DFC, *London Gazette*, 1 October 1940:

'The Distinguished Flying Cross.
'Flying Officer Herbert John WOODWARD (70833).
'This officer has destroyed five enemy aircraft and has displayed leadership
and courage of a high order.'

Meanwhile, Yellow 3, Flying Officer R. Roberts, engaged a Do 215 at 14,000ft over
Chichester, firing two short bursts at 200 yards. His combat was timed at 0700 hours:

'As Yellow 3, I fell into line astern on receiving "Tally Ho" from Yellow 1. I
attempted an astern attack on E/A, but had to abandon this as I was not gaining
much on the E/A. I broke away and climbed up again between the enemy and
the sun. Several E/A were circling about 1,000ft below me and I dived on these,
but was only able to give two bursts of a second or so each at the E/A, owing to
my excess speed. A thin trail of smoke came from the port engine.'
(signed) Flying Officer R. Roberts.

Blue 1, Gil Gilbert, engaged a Do 215 at 0715 hours, while ten miles south of
Portsmouth, firing three, three-second bursts at 300 to 200 yards:

'Ordered to patrol at 15,000ft and given vector of 240 degrees. I was leading
Blue Section and enemy A/C were observed on starboard about three miles
distance. [The] enemy appeared to be on a northerly course, but immediately
on sighting us made south at high speed. I carried out No. 2 Attack on [the]
port aircraft. [I] observed rear fire which appeared to be inaccurate. After [my]
second attack [the] E/A stopped firing, but no further damage was noticed.'
(signed) Flight Sergeant E.G. Gilbert (Blue Section).

Blue 2, Flight Sergeant A.F. Laws, attacked a Do 215 at 15,000ft, ten miles south
of Portsmouth, firing five, two-second bursts at 350 yards. His combat was timed
at 0700 hours:

'Enemy aircraft seen flying in loose vic formation – heading north-east.
Apparently, on sighting our squadron they immediately turned and scuttled
south. No. 2 Attack was ordered by Yellow Leader and I settled on [the]
starboard flank bomber of the formation. No evasive action [was] taken by
[the] formation – rear-gun fire seemed to pass well above. My enemy aircraft
broke from formation and commenced [a] series of tight diving turns – [I]
found it difficult to get [my] sights on [it] until he straightened up and dived
south for cloud layer. [There was] no rear fire after he broke formation. [I] lost
him in cloud and could not see any other aircraft so returned to base. [The]
enemy appeared to be well armoured – I'm sure my fire was entering [the]
fuselage.'
(signed) Flight Sergeant A.F. Laws.

No. 43 Squadron engaged the same formation in the Littlehampton area, as they retired, making the following claims:

Squadron Leader J.V.C. Badger (flying P3971)	two Ju 88s damaged
Flying Officer C.A. Woods-Scawen	two He 111s probably destroyed
Flight Lieutenant T.F. Dalton-Morgan (flying P3972)	one He 111 destroyed
Flying Officer C.K. Gray	one Do 17 damaged
Pilot Officer F.R. Carey	one Ju 88 probably destroyed, one Ju 88 damaged
Pilot Office R. Lane	one He 111 destroyed
Pilot Officer H.C. Upton (flying V7206)	one Do 17 probably destroyed
Sergeant J.L. Crisp	one Bf 110 damaged
Sergeant A.L.M. Deller (flying L1739)	one Ju 88 probably destroyed
Sergeant J.H.L. Hallowes (flying P3386)	one Ju 88 probably destroyed
Sergeant J.P. Mills	one Bf 109 probably destroyed

No. 64 Squadron made a further flight strength scramble at 1545 hours, but without making contact with the enemy.

Gil joined a squadron strength scramble at 1240 hours during 14 August, but the raid appears to have turned back and the Spitfires were ordered to pancake to await a possible further scramble. Meanwhile, the squadron flew a section scramble between 1315 and 1400 hours on the following day, again without making contact with the enemy.

Around eighty-eight Dornier Do 17s were plotted approaching Deal, escorted by more than 130 Bf 109s. Meanwhile, a force of fifty to sixty Bf 109s was plotted heading towards the Dungeness area, which they approached at 1430 hours. Over the next eight minutes the controller scrambled Nos. 32, 64, 151 and 266 Squadrons with orders to patrol a line between Manston and Hawkinge.

No. 64 Squadron's Spitfires engaged some of the escorting Messerschmitt Bf 109s, which they pursued back over the Channel, recording a number of 'kills', with the combats timed at about 1455 hours.

Red 1, Squadron Leader A.R.D. MacDonell, attacked a formation of four Bf 109s, destroying a Bf 109 and damaging a second, at 22,000ft, ten to fifteen miles south-west of Dover, firing five bursts at 200 yards:

'I was Red 1. No. 64 Squadron was ordered to proceed to a position behind Dover at a height of 20,000ft. On nearing the coast I approached Dover from the west in order to use the sun to the best advantage. At a height of 22,000ft, while patrolling mid-Channel, I saw the Dover defences open fire. I manoeuvred the squadron and approached from the west, at the same time

sighting about twenty Me 109s on the same level crossing the Channel ahead of us from south to north. The squadron, with the exception of the last section, were in close formation with me. The last section was about half a mile astern. I engaged four Me 109s and opened fire on the leader at a range of 250 yards in a climbing turn. The E/A turned sharply towards France and was joined by about five others. A running fight ensued. I opened fire at very close range [of] 100 yards, or even less, at an Me 109 camouflaged in very light colours with yellow painted wing tips. I gave three long bursts from below and astern. The E/A turned quite slowly onto its back and then dropped inverted. A moment later a part of the starboard wing came away from [the] E/A, which developed an extremely high spin and struck the sea. Two Me 109s engaged me at a height of about 8,000ft. I concentrated on one and opened fire from the quarter with four or five short bursts. The E/A appeared to have been hit in the engine and slowed up rapidly, with bursts of black smoke coming from it. I closed again and opened with a short burst from the port quarter. My ammunition was then exhausted. I followed the E/A in a tight spiral towards the sea, but was unable to observe the result of my engagement. A formation of between six to ten Me 109s then attacked me, so I returned to base. These aircraft did not pursue me over our own coast.'
(signed) Squadron Leader A.R.D. MacDonell.

Yellow 1, Flying Officer A.J.A. Laing, damaged a Bf 109 ten to fifteen miles south-west of Dover, firing a five-second burst at 350 to 200 yards:

'The CO manoeuvred the squadron and approached from the west, suddenly sighting twenty Me 109s on same level crossing mid-Channel ahead of us from south to north. Another formation of about twenty or more Me 109s approached and attacked from astern on our starboard quarter. We engaged as soon as possible. Red, Yellow and Blue Sections were close together in section astern, and Green some distance behind. I ordered Yellow Section into line astern and headed straight into the first formation of E/A. A dogfight developed, and suddenly an Me 109 came diving down at my starboard bow out of the sun and disappeared under my port wing. I lost him momentarily and dived after him and saw him still diving steeply. I gave him a five-second burst and noticed a fair amount of black smoke coming out of his exhausts. I suddenly realized that there was another E/A on my tail, for some tracer went past me, and I lost sight of the first [E/A], as I went into a spin. When I recovered I was down to about 12,000ft and noticed another aircraft diving steeply, seemingly out of control with a lot of smoke coming from it. I didn't know whether it was an E/A or not, as I only got an astern view which was difficult to see against the dark blue sea, but managed to take a short camera gun film of same; then I again saw some tracer go past, and I went from my dive into an aileron turn and headed for the Dover coast. I succeeded in

shaking off [the] pursuing aircraft and headed for home base where I was ordered to land.'
(signed) Flying Officer A.J.A. Laing.

Green 1, Flight Sergeant A.F. Laws, engaged a formation of thirty Bf 109s, destroying his second confirmed Bf 109 mid-Channel at 21,000ft, firing two, three-second bursts at 250 yards:

'I was Green 1. Whilst on patrol with squadron, two formations of enemy fighters [were] encountered, one above and ahead, and the other to starboard – squadron leader closed in to attack and usual dogfight developed. [I] caught one Me 109 in beam attack whilst enemy aircraft was at top of climbing turn. [I] followed him in dive and fired two bursts from astern – [I] saw aircraft burst into flames and pieces break away. [I was] attacked by several others – [I] chased one in dive to east and fired remaining ammunition – no results observed.'
(signed) Flight Sergeant A.F. Laws.

Gil (flying N3230) probably destroyed a Bf 109 at 1425 hours, three miles north of Cap Gris Nez at 22,000ft, firing a five-second burst at 100 to 50 yards:

'As Blue 1, I was with the squadron patrolling mid-Channel at 25,000ft, when one formation of Me 109s was sighted above and to starboard. Squadron closed in to attack and a dogfight developed. I noticed an Me 109 chasing a Spitfire and firing at him. I closed in to about 100 yards and fired a five-second [burst] at approx. ten yards. [The] E/A emitted clouds of black smoke and dived towards the sea. At that moment there was a shattering in my cockpit, and my A/C was enveloped in clouds of steam. I turned towards Dover with [the] E/A still firing at me, and I took evasive action by violent turns to port and starboard. Owning to the steam I could not see out of the cockpit, so I undid my straps, raised myself and flew the aircraft by looking over the top of the windscreen.
    'On approaching [the] Dover defences [the] E/A broke away. I noticed at this time that my airspeed indicator and the coolant temperature gauge had been shot away.
    'I lowered my undercarriage and made a normal landing at Hawkinge.'
(signed) Flight Sergeant E. Gilbert (Blue Section, Blue 1).

Flight Sergeant Gilbert's Spitfire had also sustained damage to the glycol system, with the coolant leaking into the cockpit.
    Gil annotated his logbook, giving some additional information on his real plight:

'Squadron attacked approximately 100 Me 109s. I saw Me 109 shooting at Spitfire. Shot it down, but Me 109 behind me fired at me. One bullet removed coolant temp gauge from dashboard and cockpit filled with steam. [I] lost height towards Dover when [the] Me departed. [I] stood up in cockpit to land aircraft at Hawkinge with no air speed indicator. A most unpleasant experience.'

Gil later recounted the events which led to his claiming the Messerschmitt Bf 109:

'The squadron was in formation over the Channel at 25,000ft in the area of Cap Gris Nez. I was in my usual position leading Green Section [flying N3230] with Laws and Whelan. Our job was to fly over the squadron from side to side to look for enemy aircraft that might have been above and behind, and in a position to attack. If there were any aircraft in sight the leader would be warned according to the clock code. The leader would be heading towards twelve o'clock and a typical warning may have been, "Enemy aircraft five o'clock above" and the CO would know what action to take.

'Just before 3pm, two flights of enemy fighters were seen approximately 3000ft below us in a position three miles north of Cap Gris Nez. Our leader, Squadron Leader MacDonell, did his usual trick of diving down through the enemy formations and we fired at the enemy aircraft as they came into our sights. All aircraft became mixed up in individual dogfights. I noticed a Bf 109 firing at a Spitfire and I closed in on him and opened fire at about 100 yards range. He leaked a lot of black smoke, broke away from the Spitfire and dived steeply towards the Channel. I had no time to watch him closely as I was being attacked myself. I was experiencing all sorts of trouble and my cockpit filled with what I thought was smoke. I thought that I was on fire and I knew that the only way out of that sort of trouble was to bail out. It almost immediately came to me that I was not on fire, but that my cockpit was full of steam due to a damaged coolant system. The 109 behind me was still taking potshots at me as I endeavoured to weave my way towards Dover. I could not see very well owing to the steam in the cockpit so I had to [undo my straps and] partially stand up in the cockpit to see where I was going. Eventually, after what seemed to be an eternity, I hove in sight of Dover when the 109 turned away. My engine had long since seized up and, having enough height, I managed to make a dead stick landing at Hawkinge, an airfield quite close to Folkestone.

'Afterwards it transpired that I had suffered a great deal of damage, and my airspeed indicator and my temperature gauge had been shot away.'

Gil's Spitfire had sustained additional damage. The tailplane was hit and the wings holed; the damage could not all be attributed to the Bf 109 cannon and machine-gun fire, but also to the Dover Barrage firing on his Spitfire as it limped home. Meanwhile, the Bf 109's bullets that entered the cockpit caused further issues, as was later discovered:

'When the parachute was sent for examination it was found that a bullet had entered the pack and it had done quite a lot of damage to the silk. I was told that if I had jumped the parachute would probably have shredded.'

Despite taking a toll on the enemy fighters the squadron didn't escape unscathed. During the combat the squadron lost Flying Officer C.J.D. Andreae[16] (flying R6990), who was shot down by Bf 109s over the Channel. His body was never recovered.

No. 64 Squadron flew a flight strength patrol between 1610 and 1630 hours, but without making contact with the enemy. Further uneventful patrols were made at 1640 and 1845 hours, when the Spitfires were vectored onto large enemy formations which somehow evaded them.

The squadron flew a section strength scramble at 1140 hours on 16 August. Radar had picked up formations of enemy aircraft coming across the Channel on three fronts. One wave, which consisted of an estimated 100-plus Do 17s and their Bf 109 escort, was heading for the Thames estuary. A second force was flying between Brighton and Folkestone, while a third flew towards the south coast, possibly targeting either Southampton or Portsmouth. No. 54 Squadron was scrambled from RAF Hornchurch, while No. 56 Squadron took off from North Weald, flying towards the Thames estuary where, joined by No. 64 Squadron, they engaged the enemy. One of No. 64 Squadron's Spitfires was damaged, while No. 56 Squadron's Pilot Officer L.W. Graham (flying V7368) was shot down and forced to bail out, wounded, near Manston at 1205 hours. Despite firing at a few Bf 109s, no claims were made.

Two of No. 64 Squadron's pilots, Pilot Officer P.J. Simpson and Sergeant J. Mann, were soon back in the air again, on a flight strength scramble flown between 1220 hours and 1315 hours. Once airborne the Spitfires were vectored onto an enemy formation. During the combat that followed, Squadron Leader A.R.D. MacDonell (flying P9554) destroyed a Bf 109 (unconfirmed) with another probably destroyed, damaging a third. Meanwhile, Pilot Officer P.J. Simpson (flying L1068) destroyed a Bf 109. Flying Officer A.J.A. Laing (flying R6975) probably destroyed a Bf 109. Sergeant J. Mann (flying L1038) was wounded during the combat and made a forced-landing at RAF Hawkinge.

Squadron Leader A.R.D. MacDonell's combat report recorded that he engaged a force of twenty Bf 109s mid-Channel at 1240 hours, firing a five to ten-second burst at 250 yards, closing to 200 yards:

'I was Red 1 of No. 64 Squadron. Eight aircraft were ordered to patrol base at 15,000 ft. While climbing, one Dornier [was] sighted above base at 30,000ft. Blue Section [was] detached to attempt to engage; [the] remaining five aircraft [were ordered] to proceed to forward base. I led the formation to forward base via Dungeness in order to approach from the sun.

'Nearing forward base at 21,000ft, [our] formation was in two sections line astern. One formation of E/A was sighted north-east of Dover at 24,000ft and another formation of about twenty Me 109s was approaching 1,000ft below our formation on the starboard beam. I ordered sections into line astern and turned south, passing over the enemy. Our formation then half rolled onto the enemy and engaged. I opened fire at one Me 109 which I attacked from quarter deflection astern. Range 250 yards. [The] E/A [was] damaged and seen to be hit by my No. 2 (Pilot Officer Simpson). I engaged [a] second Me 109 over mid-Channel and opened fire astern and above, with two long bursts. [The] E/A shook violently, flicked into a dive and struck the sea directly beneath me. This aircraft had yellow wing tips [which] appeared round, as opposed to square.

'I then saw a Spitfire diving on the tail of an Me 109. [As the] Spitfire opened fire, [the] E/A turned over and dived inverted. [The] Spitfire broke away. I closed with [the] E/A which had recovered and was diving vertically. I fired one long burst into [the] tail of [the] E/A, but it dived into the sea. The aircraft was undoubtedly hit by [the] Spitfire (Pilot Officer Simpson).

'I engaged [an] Me 109 which was circling above me. [The] E/A turned behind me, I stall-turned and found [the] E/A ahead and above me. I opened fire from beneath [the] E/A's tail with two long bursts. [The] E/A went down towards [the] French coast in shallow dive. Several bits came away from the region of [the] cockpit, and [its] dive became very steep. No black smoke [was seen]. I returned to 11,000ft and flew back towards Dover. Over mid-Channel I encountered one Me 109 which got on my tail and fired cannon over me. I manoeuvred for several minutes and got two long bursts from beneath and astern. [The] E/A turned and dived beneath me in [the] direction of Dover. I had exhausted [my] ammunition, but followed at 5,000ft. On approaching Dover I saw a sudden splash in the sea about four miles off Folkestone. On investigating, this appeared to be the wreckage of an E/A. There was a large patch of oil and a piece of the aircraft which appeared to be yellow. I flew round the spot and then over Folkestone, but there was no sign of a survivor. I then returned to base.'

(signed) Squadron Leader A.R.D. MacDonell, CO 64 Squadron.

Red 3, Pilot Officer P.J. Simpson, destroyed a Bf 109 mid-Channel at 1240 hours, firing a three-second burst at 200 yards:

'I was flying Red 3 when Red 1 "Tally-hoed" and I saw about twenty to thirty Bf 109s on starboard and port sides slightly below. Red 1 ordered line astern and we went into attack. As soon as they saw us, the Me 109s split up and I saw Red 1 do a good deflection shot at one Me 109. I then broke away and went after one Me 109 which was heading south-west and diving. I caught [the] E/A up and delivered an astern attack. I gave it a short burst of about three seconds at about 200 yards and broke away to left and climbed. The Me 109 went into a vertical dive and Red 1 saw it go into the Channel.'

(signed) Pilot Officer P.J. Simpson.

Yellow 1, Flying Officer A.J.A. Laing, probably destroyed a Bf 109 mid-Channel at 20,000ft at 1240 hours, firing a five-second burst at 300-200 yards:

'While climbing, one Dornier [was] sighted above base [at] 30,000ft. Blue Section detached to attempt to engage. Remaining five aircraft ordered to proceed to forward base. I led Yellow Section (two aircraft) astern of Red Section (three aircraft). We approached base via Dungeness to approach from [out of the] sun. On nearing forward base at 20,000ft, one formation of E/A was sighted north-east of Dover at 24,000ft. Another formation of about twenty Me 109s was approaching 1,000ft below our formation on starboard beam. Our section went into line stern and turned south, passing over enemy. Our formation half rolled onto [the] enemy and engaged. I found myself diving off the top of a stall turn right on top of an Me 109 and, giving full deflection, opened fire at 300 yards, closing to 200 yards. [The] E/A shuddered and part of the port wing broke off. It fell in a steep side slip out of control. I noticed more Me 109s approaching from the sun and this took my attention off the one I had destroyed. I evaded by diving steeply for Hawkinge as I thought there might be some bombers over there, but found it was all quiet so I contacted [the] controller who ordered me to return to land at home base. Pilot Officer Jones (Yellow 2) confirms seeing the Me 109 shudder and part of the wing tip break off, and the E/A go into a steep uncontrolled side slip. The CO (Squadron Leader MacDonell) also saw me attacking the Me 109 from above and saw it falling away in a steep side slip.'
(signed) Flying Officer A.J.A. Laing.

Gil was involved in the dogfight, but didn't manage to bring anything down, although he did twice succeed in getting on the tail of aircraft, which turned out to be 'friendly'. Even in the thick of battle, Gil remained cool enough to spot the lack of tail struts which would have identified a Bf 109 from the astern view. He annotated his logbook, 'chased two Hurricanes. 'A' Flight got five Me 109s.'

Landing, the Spitfires were checked over for battle damage, refuelled, rearmed and in a matter of minutes were ready for action. As a former fitter, Gil appreciated more than most the skill and devotion to duty of the ground crews, especially his own: 'One got to know one's ground crew very well, and they you – in the air one's life depended on them – it was a relationship of absolute trust.'

A flight strength scramble was flown between 1655 and 1740 hours, intercepting a raid by He 111s of KG 27, escorted by Bf 110s, which crossed the coast near Brighton. Also engaged were the Hurricanes of Nos. 1 and 615 Squadrons.

Once airborne, the controller gave Squadron Leader A.R.D. MacDonell a vector and he put the squadron into a battle climb. Approaching the enemy from above and out of the sun; they were well positioned for the attack. Squadron Leader A.R.D. MacDonell (flying P9554) and Pilot Officer P.J. Simpson (flying L1068) shared in the destruction of an He 111, MacDonell damaging a second before being shot down near Uckfield, at 1715 hours, by one of the Bf 109 escorts. He bailed out, safe.

Simpson's Spitfire, meanwhile, was damaged by friendly anti-aircraft fire. Flying Officer A.J.A. Laing (flying R6975) and Pilot Officer R.L. Jones (flying N3293) shared an He 111, damaged, while Flight Sergeant Gilbert (flying P9596) and Sergeant J. Whelan (flying K9895) damaged another.

The following combat reports were timed at approximately 1720 hours.

Red 1, Squadron Leader A.R.D. MacDonell, wrote:

'The squadron intercepted a large raid of about thirty He 111s, which was flying on a southerly course in four groups, closely packed at a height of 17,000ft. A large mass of escorting fighters, Me 109s, were sighted about 8,000ft above the bombers and six miles astern. The squadron was flying due west at the time of the interception. I chose the second group of bombers, which appeared to be more straggled than the others, and opened the attack from above and astern, singling out one He 111 and firing a burst of five seconds. The port engine of the E/A stopped and burst into flames. As I turned to port to break away I was hit in the starboard aileron by crossfire from another E/A in the formation. This temporarily jammed my aileron and I fell away in a left-handed diving turn before I freed the control by harsh use of the control column. I climbed up to return to attack a second He 111 which was the rearmost aircraft of the fourth group. I opened fire from the port quarter and gave three, five-second bursts from a range of about 150 yards. [The] E/A turned to starboard out of formation and began to spiral slowly down. I received [an] attack from astern and above, and finished my ammunition. [The] E/A continued to spiral down with both engines windmilling. [The] E/A salvoed bombs and disappeared into clouds, leaving a trail of black smoke behind it. I broke away and saw another He 111 some distance ahead going down with both engines on fire. I assumed this to be the one I originally attacked. (This is now confirmed by Pilot Officer Simpson who was flying as my No. 2.)

'I was about to set course for base and was diving shallowly towards clouds at 6,000ft, when I saw an aircraft directly astern of me in my mirror. Before I had time to take evasive action, the aircraft had opened fire from very close range and I was hit in the elevator, cockpit hood, instrument panel and radiator. I dived into clouds and broke into clear air at 15,000ft about fifteen to twenty miles south-west of Tunbridge. My engine then seized and appeared to be on fire. I opened the hood, undid my harness, opened the side panel, took off my helmet and abandoned the aircraft by parachute at 12,000ft. I landed near Heathfield at 1750 hours. My aircraft crashed in flames a mile from my position.'

(signed) Squadron Leader A.R.D. MacDonell, OC No. 64 Squadron.

Red 3, Pilot Officer P.J. Simpson, claimed a shared He 111 over Tunbridge, firing short bursts of three-seconds, closing to 50 yards:

'I was flying Red 3 when we sighted about thirty He 111s and about twenty Bf 109s, 5,000 to 6,000ft above the bombers, who were at 17,000ft. Red 1

ordered line astern and we went in to attack the nearest vic formation. I was about 300 yards behind Red 1; we were slightly above the bombers. He attacked No. 3 of the enemy formation. I saw him fire and the port engine stopped and emitted clouds of black smoke and flames. He broke away and I went into attack, opening fire at 300 yards and firing short bursts of about three seconds dead astern, closing to about fifty yards. I saw the starboard engine stop and catch fire. The enemy aircraft broke away and started to go down out of control. I broke off my attack and was engaged by seven Me 109s and was hit by five shells and had to retire from the battle.'
(signed) Pilot Officer P.J. Simpson.

Flying Officer A.J.A. Laing damaged two He 111s in a strafing attack while over Tunbridge:

'Eight Spitfires of No. 64 Squadron took off from Kenley at 1658 hours to intercept Raid 17. Each section went into aircraft line astern and selected one of the many flank sections of three He 111s in close vic, and did a beam attack. Having ordered Yellow 2 [Pilot Officer Jones] into line astern, I attacked a section of He 111s in close vic heading towards their port beam. I opened fire at about 450 yards, giving full deflection on their leader. Immediately, I was met with terrific crossfire from the three E/A, but pressed home the attack till I was within fifty yards of the leader when I broke away underneath them. I gave two seven-second bursts in quick succession. As I purposely kept the same deflection all the time I saw the guns of the rear He 111 in No. 3 position stop firing, and, as I approached nearer the formation, the bullets from my gun crept forward to the nose of No. 3 He 111 and then started to hit the tail of the leading He 111, and similarly ran the whole length of that machine's fuselage, stopping the gunners crossfire considerably and finally smashing the Perspex which I saw flying off at 50 yards just as I broke away. I consider that No. 2 He 111 must have got a number of rounds in it also, but did not see any damage done to it as No. 3 was in the way. Yellow 2 immediately followed up behind me and did a similar attack.'
(signed) Flying Officer A.J.A. Laing.

Yellow 2, Pilot Officer R.L. Jones, damaged a brace of He 111s while flying at 17,000ft over Tunbridge, firing a three to eight-second burst at 300 yards:

'I was Yellow 2 when we were scrambled up to Angels 20, climbing through clouds at Angels 19. We sighted about forty He 111s and a big formation of Me 109s, 6,000ft above the enemy bombers.
   'We were ordered into line astern. Yellow 1 did [a] beam attack on No. 3 of enemy vic of three going south. I followed up and also did a beam attack, giving a long burst. I closed to 100 yards and then broke off the attack. Yellow 1 then did another beam attack and I followed up with a No. 2 Attack, giving

long bursts of about eight seconds, closing to 150 yards. As I broke away I saw an enemy aircraft emitting black smoke and breaking away from [the] vic.'
(signed) Pilot Officer R.L. Jones.

Gil reported engaging a formation of forty-plus enemy aircraft, composed of He 111s and Bf 109s at 17,000ft. Avoiding the protective screen of Bf 109s, he headed for the bombers, which were the main target. Closing in, Gil fired a two-second burst at 300 to 200 yards, claiming an He 111 damaged:

'I was flying as Blue 1 when [the] squadron attacked approximately forty He 111s at 17,000ft. Blue 3 became lost in cloud, but Blue 2 [Sergeant Whelan] and I carried out No. 4 attacks on near right-hand section of Heinkels. Crossfire [was] experienced on [my] first attack, but on subsequent attacks only [the] pilot of No. 2 Heinkel fired. Explosive ammunition was seen to be hitting [the] enemy aircraft, but no vital part appeared to be damaged.'
(signed) Flight Sergeant E.G. Gilbert (Blue 1).

Gil noted in his logbook: 'Attacked approximately 100 Heinkel III's. Did No. 4 Attack with Sergeant Whelan – damaged rear section of Heinkel. No observed result.'

Meanwhile, No. 1 Squadron's claims and losses included:

Squadron Leader D.A. Pemberton (flying P2751)	one He 111 destroyed
Flying Officer A.V. Clowes (flying P3169)	one He 111 and one Ju 88 destroyed
Flying Officer G.E. Goodman (flying P2686)	one He 111 destroyed
Flying Officer P.G.H. Matthews (flying P3042)	one Bf 110 destroyed
Pilot Officer H.N.E. Salmon (flying P3678)	one Bf 110 destroyed
Pilot Officer C.M. Stavert (flying P3782)	one He 111 destroyed
Flight Sergeant G.F. Berry (flying P3276)	two He 111 probably destroyed

Squadron Leader D.A. Pemberton was hit by return fire from an He 111, but made base.

Flying Officer P.V. Boot (flying P3653) received damage from return fire from an He 111, making a forced-landing at Hog's Back.

Also engaged against the same enemy formation was No. 615 Squadron, whose pilots made the following claims:

Squadron Leader J.R. Kayll (flying P3251)	one He 111 probably destroyed (shared)
Flight Lieutenant J.G. Saunders (flying P3161)	one He 111 damaged
Flying Officer K.T. Lofts (flying P3111)	one He 111 destroyed
Pilot Officer D. Evans (flying L1992)	one Bf 110 damaged
Pilot Officer L.M. Gaunce (flying P2966)	two Bf 110 damaged, one He 111 damaged (shared)
Pilot Officer P.H. Hugo (flying P2953)	one He 111 damaged (shared)
Pilot Officer J.A.P. McClintock (flying R4192)	one He 111 probably destroyed
Pilot Officer C.R. Young (flying L2075)	one He 111 destroyed, one He 111 damaged
Sergeant P.K. Walley (flying P2571)	one He 111 probably destroyed

There was a lighter moment to the day, as Gil was 'ribbed' remorselessly by his pal Andy Laws and the other NCO pilots when copies of that day's *Daily Express* were circulated around at dispersals. Earlier in the month a press photographer had visited the station, taking a number of images of Gil, which were used for a photo piece entitled; '*Any Time's Fighting Time With These RAF Boys.*'

'A morning in the life of a Flight Sergeant in the RAF Fighter Command.
1. An airman who has been sleeping near his machine wakes [and] looks at his watch in the half-light.
2. Nine-thirty am. He tries the chairs to find the most comfortable one, looks hopefully at the books for something new, reads all the newspapers.
3. Ten o'clock. "Half-harness" calls for adjustments. This is a favourite resting position.
4. Ten forty-five. Action. He's had his orders to join a formation at a given height. Putting on the rest of his harness as he runs, he takes off in fifteen seconds.
5. Well, that's over. Back from his patrol, the flight sergeant makes out his report – "How d'you spell that town, Bill?" – and he's then free to sleep in his chair again, reads, do anything but leave the rest building, where he must always be ready while his turn of duty is on, to take off again – in fifteen seconds.'

One of the NCO pilots cut the feature out and pasted it to the wall at dispersals, where it remained until the squadron transferred away, when Gil removed the whole section as a unique keepsake.

During the early afternoon of 18 August, a large force of enemy bombers had been plotted heading for the coast, which it reached a little before 1300 hours, crossing the Weald of Kent unopposed and heading to RAF Kenley.

No. 615 Squadron was scrambled at 1245 hours, with No. 64 Squadron taking off fifteen minutes later. The Spitfires were over their own airfield minutes later when it was bombed.

Gil's No. 64 Squadron engaged a formation of fifty-plus enemy aircraft, including He 111s, Do 17s, Do 215s, Ju 88s and Bf 109s, over RAF Kenley at 1325 hours.

In a rare opportunity to get at the enemy bombers, Squadron Leader A.R.D. MacDonell (flying R6623) claimed a Do 17 (unconfirmed), and damaged a Ju 88. During the same dogfight Flight Lieutenant F.L. Henstock (flying R6990) damaged a Do 215. Sergeant P.S. Hawke (flying P9557) destroyed an He 111 (unconfirmed). Meanwhile, Flight Sergeant A.F. Laws (flying P9430) destroyed a Bf 110 (unconfirmed), shooting it off the tail of an unknown Hurricane. Laws also shared in the destruction of an He 111 with Gil (flying P9596). Pilot Officer J.J. O'Meara (flying X4067) destroyed a Ju 88 (unconfirmed), sharing in the destruction of a second. Pilot Officer J.J. O'Meara was awarded the DFC, *London Gazette*, 24 September 1940, the two 'kills' having added to his growing score:

'Distinguished Flying Cross.
'Pilot Officer James Joseph O'MEARA (40844).
'Pilot Officer O'Meara has displayed a very high degree of skill and devotion to
    duty in all operations against the enemy, and has destroyed at least six enemy
    aircraft. His example and keenness have been outstanding.'

Squadron Leader A.R.D. MacDonell claimed the other half of the shared Junkers Ju 88, firing five-second bursts at 150 yards:

'The squadron was ordered to patrol base at 20,000ft. While directly over base
    at 21,000ft I saw the first bomb explode on the hangars. [The] squadron was
    in sections line astern stepped down. I dived to 7,000ft and saw many Dornier
    215s and He 111s flying in a straggled formation at 12,000ft. [The] squadron
    zoomed and engaged enemy singly. I attacked one Do 215 from astern and
    below, opening fire at 250 yards and rapidly closing to 150 yards. [The] E/A
    was hit in both engines, stalled almost vertically and spun slowly down, finally
    crashing near Biggin Hill. [I] engaged [the] second enemy bomber, [a] Ju 88,
    and exhausted [my] ammunition in two bursts. [The] E/A slowed to port, and
    [its] port engine emitted black smoke. [The] E/A salvoed [its] bombs and [a]
    Hurricane then engaged it. I then saw about twenty Me 109s at a height of
    approximately 20,000ft. These aircraft were circling but made no attempt to
    attack. I dived to 5,000ft and rallied the squadron, landing at Redhill.'
(un-signed) Squadron Leader A.R.D. MacDonell.

Squadron Leader A.R.D. MacDonell's leadership in the air had been largely responsible for many of the squadron's successes. The shared He 111 raised his official tally to nine enemy aircraft destroyed or shared, for which he was awarded the DFC, *London Gazette*, 6 September 1940:

'Distinguished Flying Cross.
'Squadron Leader Aeneas Ranald Donald MACDONELL (33120).
'This officer has shot down nine enemy aircraft and damaged four others. He has been particularly successful as a leader and has displayed the highest courage, setting a splendid example to his squadron.'

Meanwhile, at his debriefing, Sergeant P.S. Hawke reported:

'I was patrolling at 22,000ft when we sighted E/A. I was flying as Green 3. We dived to approximately 7,000ft and then climbed up again to a formation of bombers. I got in a quarter deflection burst of four seconds approximately on an He 111, following it up with an astern attack of several medium bursts. There was no return fire and I attacked again from slightly beneath. This time the E/A dropped its port wing, turned over and went down in flames. Approx. range was 200 yards, closing to 80 yards. [The] E/A went down approximately sixteen miles south-west of base.'
(unsigned) Sergeant Peter S. Hawke.

Engaging a formation of fifty-plus enemy aircraft, composed of Bf 110s, Bf 109s, Ju 88s, He 111s and Do 215s, in the Kenley area at 12,000ft, Flight Sergeant A.F. Laws claimed an He 111 and a Bf 110 destroyed:

'When at 20,000ft over base [I] saw bomb explosion on base. [The] enemy formation [was] sighted and engaged at 12,000ft as Green 2 [I] followed Green 1 [Gil Gilbert] in attack on Heinkels. Green 1 expended ammunition on one He 111 – I followed on same bomber and, after two bursts, [the] enemy burst into flames and crashed near [a] church south of Biggin Hill, [I] climbed again to attack [a] mixed formation of bombers and Me 110s, [I] chased [an] Me 110 [which was] on [the] tail of [a] Hurricane and after several bursts [the] enemy's port engine was on fire and he dived in vertical dive to ground. [I] finished off ammunition on Heinkel 111 – [which was] possibly damaged. [I] returned to base.'
(signed) Flight Sergeant A.F. Laws.

Gil shared in the destruction of the He 111:

'As Green 1 on patrol Kenley, at 22,000ft, [I] saw [the] aerodrome being bombed and dived to 12,000ft and saw formation of bombers heading SE, [I] attacked with Green 2 (F/Sgt Laws), [a] section of three Heinkel 111s and

crippled [the] starboard engine of No. 2 of section. He dropped behind, and Green 2 and myself carried out a number of No. 1 and 2 Attacks. [The] E/A's evasive tactics were stall turns, but from one of these he hit the ground and burst into flames beside a church south of Biggin Hill.'
(signed) Flight Sergeant E.G. Gilbert.

Gil's logbook entry read:

'Kenley bombed. Attacked rear section of three Heinkels. Put starboard engine on No. 2 out of action. Attacked him as he broke formation. He dived straight in from 6,000ft. Missed church just south of Biggin Hill by twenty yards. One Heinkel 111.'

The squadron's home base had taken a pounding during the raid, Gil noting: 'Returned [to] Kenley. Forty-nine unexploded bombs on aerodrome. Do 17 crashed just behind dispersal.'

No. 615 Squadron also engaged the enemy over RAF Kenley, recording the following claims and losses:

Squadron Leader J.R. Kayll (flying R4194)	one Bf 109 damaged
Flight Lieutenant H.S. Giddings (flying R4194)	one Do 215 probably destroyed
Flight Lieutenant J.G. Sanders (flying P3811)	one He 111 destroyed, one Ju 88 destroyed, one Ju 88 (shared)
Pilot Officer C.R. Young (flying P3231)	one Do 215 destroyed, one Do 215 probably destroyed

Flight Lieutenant L.M. Gaunce (flying P2966) was wounded in combat by a Bf 109 near Sevenoaks and forced to bail out.

Pilot Officer P.H. Hugo (flying R4221) was wounded and crash-landed near Orpington following combat with Bf 109s.

Pilot Officer D.J. Looker (flying L1592 KW-Z) was wounded by fire from a Bf 109 over Sevenoakes and by anti-aircraft fire from the airfield defences at RAF Croydon.

Sergeant P.K. Walley (flying P2768) was killed-in-action when his Hurricane crashed at Morden Park following combat with Bf 109s.[17]

No. 64 Squadron's last scramble of the day, 18 August, was made between 1740 and 1830 hours: 'The raid turned back; anyway, we were ordered to pancake.'

On 19 August, No. 64 Squadron flew north to RAF Leconfield, their role at RAF Kenley being taken over by No. 616 Squadron.

The squadron had chalked up a fair score of enemy aircraft, but had paid the price, with four pilots killed-in-action and the same number wounded. Their lack of hours on Spitfires had been telling at the beginning of the battle, while replacement pilots had also become casualties. Gil and his old pal, Andy Laws, must have reflected on the losses when they heard the news that the unit was being rested.

Flying in No. 12 Group, operations were generally more routine with convoy escorts and sector patrols. There were fewer large-scale raids to contend with, although the Luftwaffe was not averse to sending long-range reconnaissance missions and small raids into the squadron's sector. At night the enemy would soon come in larger numbers, targeting the ports and industrial cities.

At 0740 hours on 24 August, the squadron made its first scramble under No. 12 Group, when a brace of Spitfires were vectored onto a suspicious plot, but no contact was made – this was very much a sign of times to come.

In September, while still based at RAF Leconfield, No. 64 Squadron's 'B' Flight was detached to operate out of RAF Ringway. It was during this time that a number of new pilots arrived, being trained up to operational standard:

> 'It became standard practice for pilots fresh from flying school to be sent to a
> squadron with combat experience, one that was being "rested" like 64. Andy
> and I would take them up and show them the ropes; dogfighting and all the
> manoeuvres that they never taught one in flying school.'

While some of the pilots remained to continue the nucleus of the squadron, others, with fewer operational hours under their belt, were not considered in need of a rest and were posted onto squadrons back in No. 11 Group.

Meanwhile, both flights were called upon to fly regular patrols, without encountering the enemy. The training wasn't all plain sailing, however, and on 5 September, Sergeant D.E. Lloyd (flying R9563), who had recently been posted from No. 17 Squadron, crashed, but escaped major injury.

While combat was less frequent in No. 12 Group, there was still the ever-present danger of enemy raiders targeting the industrial Midlands, the steel industry, and the docks in the north. On the following day, 6 September, Sergeant H.D. Charnock (flying K9903) encountered one of these raiders, coming off worst, and was forced to bail out following combat with a Bf 110 at 1930 hours near RAF Ternhill, Shropshire. He was unhurt. The squadron flew patrols in pairs or at section strength on 7 and 17 September, but again there was no sign of the enemy.

Meanwhile, Gil learned of his promotion to the rank of pilot officer with effect from 7 September (seniority 26 August 1940), *London Gazette,* 4 October. Officially he left the service and rejoined as an officer (serial No. 44548):

> 'This necessitated a new uniform. So before one was properly dressed one was
> effectively barred from the sergeant's mess, while one couldn't be seen in the
> officer's mess either; one was in a sort of military limbo.'

Gil flew operational sorties on 14 and 17 September, but without making contact with the enemy. There was, however, still some action to be had, and, on 18

September, while flying out of RAF Ringway on a patrol between 1850 and 2005 hours, Flying Officer D.M. Taylor (flying P9557) probably destroyed a Do 215. Gil, meanwhile, made two uneventful patrols during the day. The pattern continued until the end of the month, Gil flying three sorties on 20 September, completing another six operational flights up until 26 September.

The squadron's battle was over and it must have seemed as though Gil and his friend Andy Laws were going to make it; they had survived combat through the darkest days of the defence of the Dunkirk beaches and the early phases of the Battle of Britain. Gil was delighted at the news that Andy was being commissioned and would soon join him in the mess – the two had been inseparable as NCOs.

Meanwhile, any complacency on the squadron was ended when they suffered a further loss on the 27 September. Operating out of RAF Leconfield, Sergeant L.A. Dyk[18] (flying X4032) took off on a section strength patrol at 0940 hours, but failed to return. His Spitfire was lost over the sea; cause unknown.

Then came, what for Gil was the hardest blow of all, the death of Andy Laws, only recently promoted and the much deserved recipient of the Distinguished Flying Medal. Pilot Officer A.F. Law[19] (flying P9564) was flying mock combats with some of the squadron's newer pilots on 30 September, when he collided with Sergeant F.F. Vinyard's Spitfire, K9805, at 1030 hours. Laws' Spitfire lost its tail; an eyewitness reported seeing it free-falling, tumbling over and over until it crashed, four miles north of RAF Leconfield; there was no chance for Andy to break free, trapped by centrifugal force in the cockpit of his doomed aircraft.

Gil had the sad duty of writing a letter of condolence to Andy's widow. Andy had only recently learned that he was to be a father.

Although commissioned, Laws hadn't yet purchased his officer's uniform and was still messing with the sergeant pilots. He never lived to read the announcement of his DFM, which was promulgated in the *London Gazette,* 1 October:

'Awarded the Distinguished Flying Medal.
'514143 Flight Sergeant Adrian Francis Laws.
'This airman has taken part in numerous operational flights since May 1940.
He has destroyed five enemy aircraft and damaged another two. His initiative, courage and tenacity have been outstanding.'

Sergeant F.F. Vinyard[20] (flying R6683) survived the incident, only to die a few days later, on 6 October, while on patrol off Flamborough Head. At 1420 hours, he entered cloud alongside two other members of the section, but was missing when they emerged. His exact fate remains a mystery and no wreckage was ever found.

Meanwhile, training continued. The squadron had flown only a handful of sorties on 2, 4 and 6 October, making more patrols on 10 and 11 October, but without making contact with the enemy. Gil flew on a scramble between 1550 and 1610 hours on 11 October as the training programme was winding down.

News reached the squadron of a transfer back into the thick of the combat. On 13 October, they flew south to RAF Biggin Hill, transferring to RAF Coltishall, Norfolk, two days later.

Patrol strength scrambles were flown on 19, 20, 24 and 26 October, Gil flying on three of these. Meanwhile, the squadron flew a scramble between 1800 and 1820 hours on 27 October, when Gil (flying P9556) and Sergeant E.R. Limpenny (flying L1030) pursued a Do 17, which Limpenny damaged.

Gil made two scrambles on the following day, 28 October, but was unable to engage the enemy.

No. 64 Squadron flew out of RAF Hornchurch, Essex, from 11 November, when Gil was in combat for the last time.

Taking off alongside No. 603 Squadron, No. 64 Squadron's Spitfires patrolled at 25,000ft, before being vectored to defend a convoy off North Foreland. The squadron engaged a formation of thirty to forty Bf 109s while twelve miles north of Foreland, the enemy was between 25,000 and 4,000ft, covering a small number of Ju 87s which were dive-bombing the convoy.

No. 603 Squadron's Spitfires were the first to dive into the attack, No. 64 Squadron initially remaining above, wary of high-flying Bf 109s ready to bounce the Spitfires once they committed to combat, before being brought down from 25,000ft into the attack. The first pass broke up the enemy formation, while a series of dogfights ensued.

Squadron Leader A.R.D. MacDonell led the squadron. His combat report was timed at 1215 hours:

'No. 64 Squadron was in line astern on No. 603 Squadron at 24,000ft, when about thirty Me 109s were sighted ahead and above at a distance of about eight miles. Both squadrons were then over a convoy, in a position about twelve miles north-east of North Foreland. The high formation of enemy aircraft made no attempt to engage, and, in view of the bomb splashes falling on the convoy, I led the squadron down to 5,000ft, where Me 109s were encountered, either dive-bombing the convoy or escorting dive-bombers which were seen heading south-east. I estimated about twelve to twenty Me 109s in the vicinity of the convoy. I attacked one Me 109 from above and astern, and opened fire at 250 yards. My surplus speed carried me right underneath the enemy's tail and I was unable to see any result. Two Spitfires then joined me and we went into a pair of Me 109s. I attacked one which had broken away south-east and opened fire at about 300 yards from above the quarter. The E/A made a sharp right-hand turn and dived to within about 40ft of the sea. As the E/A levelled up, I attacked again, this time from dead astern. White steam and smoke, as well as black smoke from the engine, was pouring from E/A, but owing to an excessively high radiator temperature, I broke off and returned to base. A Hurricane and another Spitfire were about to attack the Me 109 from above.' (signed) Squadron Leader A.R.D. MacDonell.

The Squadron Intelligence Officer, Flying Officer A.W. Tap recorded:

'Sergeant Chadwick (Yellow 1) exhausted his ammunition on one Me 109, opening fire at 200 yards. He saw his explosive bullets striking the cowling of the E/A, which went down from 6,000 to 1,000ft.

'Sergeant [J.W.] Slade (Yellow 3), following Yellow 1, attacked the same Me 109, when Yellow 1 broke away, firing a short burst at 200 yards and saw white stars bursting under the E/A; he broke away on seeing two Ju 87s which he attacked without visible results. Yellow 3 was fitted with Cinegun.

'Flight Sergeant [H.W.] Charon (Blue 2 – a French subject) exhausted his ammunition in an attack from his starboard quarter and dead astern on one Me 109. He broke away to avoid collision and so was unable to observe the result of his attack.

'Three other pilots [including Gil Gilbert] fired short bursts at Me 109s without visible result.'

The patrols continued, but without further combat victories. On 28 November, Pilot Officer W.N.C. Salmond (flying K9950) bailed out safe near Tunbridge Wells, Kent, when his aircraft caught fire in mid-air. Meanwhile, No. 64 Squadron continued to fly daily patrols and scrambles against large formations of enemy aircraft well into December of 1940. However, Gil had, by this time, completed his tour of operations. He was selected for a pilot instructor's course at the Central Flying School, Upavon, on 1 December 1940. Fortunately, Gil's temperament ideally suited this role and so he was to fly as an instructor from January 1941 until September 1944, being promoted to flying officer as of 7 September 1941 (*London Gazette*, 30 September 1941, with seniority of 26 August), and advanced to flight lieutenant as of 7 September 1942 (*London Gazette*, 18 September 1942, with seniority 26 August). Gil remained in the RAF after the war, serving in various capacities including flying control and air traffic controller. In 1953 he was awarded the General Service Medal with the bar for service in Malaya. He left the RAF on 4 November 1962, retaining the rank of squadron leader.

No. 64 Squadron pilots who flew operationally between 10 July and 30 October 1940:

Squadron Leader Aeneas Ranald Donald MacDonell, DFC	MiD 28.12.45, CB 1.1.64 as Air Commodore
Squadron Leader Norman Cyril Odbert	OBE 13.6.46, later Group Captain
Flight Lieutenant Lawrence Frederick Henstock	
Flight Lieutenant Desmond Bogan Hobson	
Flying Officer Christopher John Drake Andreae	KIA 15.9.40

Flying Officer Alistair John Oswald Jeffrey, DFC   KIA 25.7.40

Flying Officer Alexander James Alan Laing

Flying Officer James Joseph O'Meara, DFC   Bar to DFC 18.3.41 *(A)*,
                                                  DSO 27.10.44 *(B)*

Flying Officer Hubert Paul Frederick Patten

Flying Officer Ralph Roberts

Flying Officer Peter James Simpson   DFC 17.12.40 *(C)*

Flying Officer Donald Murray Taylor

Flying Officer Michael Terry Wainwright   AFC 1.1.51

Flying Officer Herbert John Woodward, DFC   KIA 30.10.40 with No. 23
                                                  Squadron

Sub-Lieutenant Francis Dawson Paul   DoW 30.7.40

Sub-Lieutenant Geoffrey Bruce Pudney   KIA 26.8.41

Sub-Lieutenant John Humphrey Charlesworth
Sykes

Pilot Officer Percival Harold Beake   DFC 5.9.44 *(D)*

Pilot Officer Herbert Robert Case   KIA 12.10.40

Pilot Officer Arthur Gerald Donahue   DFC 27.3.42 *(E)*

Pilot Officer John Knight Down

Pilot Officer Gordon Eric Ellis

Pilot Officer George Ernest 'Gil' Gilbert

Pilot Officer Trevor Gray

Pilot Officer Richard Leoline Jones   AEA

Pilot Officer Peter Frank Kennard-Davis   DoW 10.8.40

Pilot Officer Leonard Frank Douglas King   KIA as CO of No. 105
                                                  Squadron 19.3.45

Pilot Officer Adrian Francis 'Andy' Laws, DFM   KIA 30.9.40

Pilot Officer John Lawson-Brown   KIA 12.5.41

Pilot Officer John Phillip Lloyd   AFC 1.1.43

Pilot Officer John Gilbert Pippett   KIA 22.2.41

Pilot Officer Harry Robert Godfrey Poulton   DFC 25.5.43 *(F)*, POW
                                                  January 1944

Pilot Officer Hugh William Reilley   KIA 17.10.40 with No. 66
                                                  Squadron

Pilot Officer John Hampton Rowden   KIA 9.4.41

Pilot Officer William Noel Compton Salmond

Pilot Officer Donald Arthur Stanley	KIA 25.2.41 with No. 611 Squadron
Pilot Officer Alfred Roberts Tidman	KIA 17.9.41
Pilot Officer Watson	
Sergeant Arthur Edward Binham	AFC 14.6.45
Sergeant Dennis Frederick Chadwick	
Sergeant Harry Walpole Charnock	DFM 7.4.42 *(G)*, DFC 26.2.43 *(H)*, Belgium Order of Leopold 1947, Croix de Guerre with Palm (Belgium) 1947
Sergeant Maurice Philipe Cesar Choran (France)	KIA 10.4.42 with No. 340 Squadron
Sergeant Xavier de Cherade de Montbron	Died air accident 21.4.55
Sergeant Horace Arthur Cordell	
Sergeant Leslie Arthur Dyke	KIA 27.9.40
Sergeant David Fulford	DFC 4.11.41 *(I)*
Sergeant Roy Daniel Goodwin	
Sergeant Peter Sydney Hawke	AFC 1.1.46
Sergeant Charles Leonard Hopgood	KIA 5.12.40
Sergeant Lewis Reginald Isaac	KIA 5.8.40
Sergeant Arthur Charles Leigh	DFM 9.9.41 *(J)*
Sergeant Eric Ronald Limpenny	
Sergeant David Edward Lloyd	KIA 17.3.42
Sergeant Jack Mann	DFM 23.4.41 *(K)*
Sergeant Ian Walter Matthews	KIA 1.9.42 with No. 238 Squadron
Sergeant Trevor Guest Oldfield	KIA 27.9.40 with No. 92 Squadron
Sergeant Kenneth Bruce Parker	KIA 15.10.40 with No. 92 Squadron
Sergeant James Pickering	AFC 1.1.46
Sergeant Thomas Wood Savage	KIA 10.7.41 with No. 92 Squadron
Sergeant George Wardrop Scott	AFC 8.6.44, MBE 1.6.53
Sergeant John William Slade	DFC 22.1.43 *(L)*, KIA as Squadron Leader with No. 337 Wing 19.9.45

Sergeant John William Copous Squier
Sergeant Frederick Fenton Vinyard   KIA 6.10.40
Sergeant John Whelan   AFC 14.6.45, MBE 1.1.59

Many of the pilots earned gallantry awards for combat which are not mentioned in the main text. Details, where traced, are included below:

(A) Flying Officer J.J. O'Meara, DFC, was awarded a Bar to the DFC, *London Gazette*, 18 March 1941:

> 'Bar to the Distinguished Flying Cross.
> 'Flying Officer James Joseph O'MEARA, DFC (40844), No. 91 Squadron.
> 'This officer has performed excellent work as a fighter pilot in the many and varied missions which have been allotted to him. On a recent occasion he led an offensive operation which extended as far as Holland, and in which troops and a gun-post were machine-gunned; an armed ship was also attacked. Flying Officer O'Meara has now destroyed at least eleven enemy aircraft. He has set an excellent example.'

(B) Flying Officer J.J. O'Meara, DFC and Bar, was awarded the DSO, *London Gazette*, 27 October 1944:

> 'Distinguished Service Order.
> 'Squadron Leader James Joseph O'MEARA, DFC (40844), RAFO, No. 131 Squadron.
> 'Squadron Leader O'Meara has completed a notable tour, and throughout has displayed a high degree of skill and gallantry. His genius for leadership has been most evident and has contributed in a large way to the operational efficiency of the squadron he commands. He is a relentless fighter and has destroyed twelve enemy aircraft and damaged many more.'

(C) Flying Officer P.J. Simpson was awarded the DFC, *London Gazette*, 17 December 1940:

> 'Distinguished Flying Cross.
> 'Flying Officer Peter James Simpson (41875), No. 111 Squadron.
> 'This officer has taken part in numerous engagements against the enemy over a long and intensive period of operations, both in France and in England. He has shown exceptional keenness and skill, and has destroyed at least five hostile aircraft.'

(D) Acting Squadron Leader P.H. Beake was awarded the DFC, *London Gazette*, 5 September 1944:

'Distinguished Flying Cross.
'Acting Squadron Leader Percival Harold BEAKE (84923), RAFVR, No. 164 Squadron.
'This officer has commanded the squadron for several months and during the period has led his formation on many sorties against heavily defended targets with good results. He is a first class leader whose great skill, thoroughness and untiring efforts have contributed materially to the successes obtained. Squadron Leader Beake has destroyed two enemy aircraft.'

(E) Flying Officer A.G. Donahue was awarded the DFC, *London Gazette*, 27 March 1942:

'Distinguished Flying Cross.
'Flying Officer Arthur Gerald DONAHUE (81624), Royal Air Force Volunteer Reserve, No. 258 Squadron.
'This officer has carried out many low-level reconnaissance sorties and has successfully attacked enemy shipping and ground objectives. On one occasion, whilst carrying out an attack against enemy troops attempting a landing, Flying Officer Donahue silenced the enemy's fire, thus enabling the rest of the formation to press home their attacks with impunity. He has destroyed several enemy aircraft.'

(F) Flight Lieutenant H.R.G. Poulton was awarded the DFC, *London Gazette*, 25 May 1943:

'Distinguished Flying Cross.
'Flight Lieutenant Harry Robert Godfrey POULTON (84925), Royal Air Force Volunteer Reserve, No. 64 Squadron.'

(G) Warrant Officer H.W. Charnock was awarded the DFM, *London Gazette*, 7 April 1942:

'Distinguished Flying Medal.
'901005 Sergeant Harry Walpole CHARNOCK, No. 19 Squadron.
'This airman has displayed great skill and courage in air combat and has destroyed at least four enemy aircraft. He has, on occasions, led his flight, and his high standard of morale has set an inspiring example.'

(H) Warrant Officer H.W. Charnock, DFM, was awarded the DFC, *London Gazette,* 26 February 1943:

'Distinguished Flying Cross.
'Warrant Officer Harry Walpole CHARNOCK, DFM (901005), No. 72 Squadron.

(I) Pilot Officer D. Fulford was awarded the DFC, *London Gazette*, 4 November, 1941:

'Pilot Officer David FULFORD (63787), Royal Air Force Volunteer Reserve, No. 118 Squadron.
'Distinguished Flying Cross.
'This officer has participated in a number of operational sorties. During these operations he has been responsible for damaging enemy wireless stations and anti-aircraft posts; he has also damaged a number of ships. Pilot Officer Fulford has displayed courage and keenness, and has destroyed two enemy aircraft and assisted in the destruction of a further two.'

(J) Sergeant A.C. Leigh was awarded the DFM, *London Gazette*, 9 September 1941:

'Distinguished Flying Medal.
'748525 Sergeant Arthur Charles LEIGH, Royal Air Force Volunteer Reserve, No. 611 Squadron.
'This airman pilot has displayed great skill and courage in operations, including fifty sweeps over enemy territory. Sergeant Leigh has destroyed two Messerschmitt 109s, probably destroyed another four and assisted in the destruction of a Dornier 17. His judgment and determination, especially in low-flying attacks over Northern France, have set an excellent example.'

(K) Sergeant J. Mann was awarded the DFM, *London Gazette*, 23 April 1941:

'Distinguished Flying Medal.
'741491 Sergeant Jack MANN, Royal Air Force Volunteer Reserve, No. 91 Squadron.
'This airman has displayed great keenness in his many operations against the enemy and has destroyed at least four of their aircraft. His enthusiasm and fighting spirit have been outstanding, and this was particularly displayed on one occasion when, during a patrol, his aircraft was severely damaged through enemy action. With great presence of mind, and despite his aircraft being uncontrollable at the time, he warned his flight commander by radio telephone of the danger from a rear attack by enemy aircraft and almost certainly saved the commander from being shot down.'

Jack 'Jackie' Mann later settled in the Middle East and became headline news when he was held hostage. He faced the many challenges during his imprisonment with great fortitude, winning the admiration and respect of all who knew of his ordeals.

(L) Acting Flight Lieutenant J.W. Slade was awarded the DFC, *London Gazette*, 22 January 1943:

'Distinguished Flying Cross.
'Acting Flight Lieutenant John William SLADE (101518), Royal Air Force Volunteer Reserve, No. 126 Squadron.'

Notes

1. Squadron Leader (37212) Eric George Rogers, RAF, was the son of George and E.G. Rogers, of Teignmouth, Devon. Rogers was 24-years-old and is remembered on the Runnymede Memorial, Panel 4.
2. Flying Officer (40296) Reginald Tyrrell George, RAF, was the son of Reginald Harry and Margaret George, of Newport, Isle of Wight. George was 20-years-old and is remembered on the Runnymede Memorial, Panel 5.
3. Pilot Officer (43167) Herbert Branwell Hackney, RAF, was the son of Flight Lieutenant Herbert Hackney, RAF, and Helena Wilhelmina Hackney; husband of Lillian Selina Hackney. Pilot Officer Hackney was 26-years-old and is remembered on the Runnymede Memorial, Panel 8.
4. Flight Sergeant (510966) George H. Hatch, RAF, was buried at Enghen (Edingen) Communal Cemetery, Grave 7.
5. Pilot Officer (43169) Thomas Charles Hey, RAF, was buried at Sage War Cemetery, Section 8, Row A, Grave 8. Hey was 28-years-old.
6. Pilot Officer (42628) Douglas Keith Milne, RAF, is remembered on the Runnymede Memorial, Panel 9.
7. Flying Officer (39947) George Victor Proudman, RAF, was the son of George and May Proudman, of Woking, Surrey. Proudman was 22-years-old and is remembered on the Runnymede Memorial, Panel 6.
8. Sergeant (740268) Patrick Sherlock Hayes, RAFVR, was the son of Stanley Robert and Agnes Clara Patricia Hayes, of Beckenham, Kent. Hayes was 24-years-old and is remembered on the Runnymede Memorial, Panel 15.
9. Pilot Officer (41897) Norman James Brisbane, RAF, is remembered on the Runnymede Memorial, Panel 7.
10. Flying Officer (36165) Thomas Peter Kingsland Higgs, RAF, was the son of Arthur Hilton Higgs and of Alice Higgs (nee Dunkerley); nephew of Mary K. Higgs, of Shepton Mallet, Somerset. Higgs held a B.A. (Oxon.) Merton College. Higgs was 23-years-old and was buried at Noordwijk General Cemetery, Plot 1, Joint Grave 8.
11. Flying Officer (39740) Alastair John Oswald Jeffrey, DFC, RAF, was the son of John Patrick Jeffrey, and Elizabeth S. Jeffrey, of Edinburgh. Jeffrey was 22-years-old and was buried in Flushing (Vlissingen) Northern Cemetery, Row A, Joint Grave 5.
12. Pilot Officer (79158) Archibald Finnie, RAFVR, was buried at Margate Cemetery, Section 50, Grave 15937.

13. Sub-Lieutenant (A) Frank Dawson Paul, RNVR, was the son of Joseph Dawson Paul and Flavie Leonnie Paul, of Chelsea, London. Paul was 24-years-old and was buried at Hardinghen Churchyard, Military Plot, Grave 1.

14. Sergeant (748158) Lewis Reginald Isaac, RAFVR, was the son of James and Blodwen Matilda Isaac, of Llanelly, Carmarthenshire. Isaac was 24-years-old and is remembered on the Runnymede Memorial, Panel 15.

15. Pilot Officer (42348) Peter Frank Kennard-Davis, RAF, son of Frank Edward and Francis Amellia Kennard-Davis, of Selsey, Sussex. Kennard-Davis was 19-years-old and was buried in Brookwood Cemetery, St Cyprian's Avenue, Grave 202344.

16. Flying Officer (70018) Christopher John Drake Andreae, RAFVR, was the son of Frank George and Georgina Andreae, of Paddington, London. Andreae was 23-years-old and is remembered on the Runnymede Memorial, Panel 5.

17. Sergeant (819018) Peter Kenneth Walley, AAF, was buried at Whyteleafe (St Luke) Churchyard, Row F, Grave 32A.

18. Sergeant (754831) Leslie Arthur Dyke, RAFVR, was the son of Arthur St Clair Dyke and Ada Maud Dyke, of Sutton, Surrey. Dyke was 22-years-old and is remembered on the Runnymede Memorial, Panel 13.

19. Pilot Officer (45092) Adrian Francis 'Andy' Laws, DFM, RAF, was buried in Wells-next-the-Sea Cemetery, Grave 101.

20. Sergeant (748089) Frederick Fenton Vinyard, RAFVR, was the son of Frederick Henry and Annie Lavinia Vinyard, of Erdington, Birmingham. Vinyard was 24-years-old and is remembered on the Runnymede Memorial, Panel 20.

Chapter 5

Squadron Leader Robert 'Robbie' Reid, AEA

Robert 'Robbie' Reid was an early member of the RAFVR. Already in full-time service on the outbreak of the war, Reid was later posted to No. 46 Squadron as a replacement pilot following their losses with the sinking of the carrier *Glorious*. Once regrouped the squadron was quickly declared operational and fought throughout the Battle of Britain. Despite their inexperience, the pilots gave a good account of themselves, but a high casualty rate was almost inevitable.

Robert Reid was born in the market town of Dumfries on 2 September 1908. His parents, Frances (nee Band) and Simon Reid, lived at 22, Castle Street. Robert and his elder sibling, Norman Reid, attended the Dumfries Academy.

Reid completed his education in 1924 and, with a good School's Certificate, found employment in the banking industry; he was to remain with the same branch of the Midland bank until applying for full-time service.

The First World War began a month shy of Robert's sixth birthday and, like many schoolboys, he was no doubt captivated by stories of service life, especially of the antics of the early aviators whose stories were later retold in the Biggles books of First World War ace, W.E. Johns. Robert would almost certainly have been aware of the activities at the little aero-club nearby, established in 1914, at what in 1938 became RAF Dumfries.

As a part of the country's rearmament programme, the government created the Royal Air Force Volunteer Reserve (RAFVR). Robert completed an application form and was invited for an assessment. All went well and he was accepted into the Volunteer Reserve as an AC2, pilot under training, on 3 April 1937, being promoted to the rank of sergeant on the following day. His service number was 740059, notionally making him the fifty-ninth member of the VR.

Between 25 April and 7 May 1937, Reid attended the first annual training at Hanworth (Air Park). The grassed airfield lay in the grounds of Hanworth Park House and was initially established in 1917, and remained operational until 1919. The airfield was reopened on 31 August 1929 by the Duchess of Bedford, and was the venue for the King's Cup Air Race the following year. The *Graf Zeppelin* (D-LZ127) visited two years later, on 2 July 1932. From 1935 the airfield was home to the London Air Park Flying Club (formerly the National Flying Services Ltd., which had gone into receivership in 1933).

From 2 April 1938, Sergeant Reid transferred from the Reserve, moving to No. 29 Squadron on 1 April the following year. Reid attended a course at No. 3 Air Training School between 22 May and 9 June, receiving his wings on 14 July 1939.

Like many pilots of the time, Robert also indulged in his passion for fast cars, owning a PA Sports Car, as well as a more sedate SA Saloon. No doubt he and his fellow aviators were the scourge of the local bobbies, tearing around the country lanes at breakneck speeds.

Despite the rigors of service life, Reid made time to maintain his friendship with his sweetheart, Christina Danby; indeed the relationship blossomed, the two keeping up a regular correspondence. Robert made the journey to see Christina whenever he could and during one of these brief encounters proposed.

On 17 December 1938, the couple were married at St Mary's Church, Lewisham, setting up home in Hornsey, North London; then in Bridlington, East Yorkshire. It was here that they would later raise their two children, Robert and Michael, born in December 1940.

Reid was still with No. 29 Squadron, flying the Bristol Blenheim out of RAF Debden, when war was declared. He remained on the same type when he was transferred to RAF Digby's No. 23 Squadron on 10 November 1939. Meanwhile, on 3 April the following year, Reid was recommended for a commission, which came through on 16 June, when he was released from the service and became a pilot officer on probation.

As a general rule the services preferred to move NCOs to other units once they received their commission. It was considered bad for discipline if newly appointed officers continued to associate with their NCO friends. Consequently, Reid was posted to No. 46 Squadron, also flying out of RAF Digby, using RAF Newton as their rear base. The posting took effect on 20 June. Reid, in the interim, was granted a few days leave to organise his officer's uniform and kit.

No. 46 Squadron's pilots had fought valiantly during the Norway Campaign, before being ordered to evacuate on 7 June. Their CO, Squadron Leader K.B.B. Cross,[1] was ordered to destroy his Hawker Hurricanes, as HMS *Glorious'* deck was considered too short for a landing, and because the Hurricanes had no tail hooks to help them decelerate using the carrier's arrester wires. To a man, the squadron's pilots volunteered to attempt a deck landing, which they achieved by strapping two sandbags to the tails of their aircraft to help reduce their air-speed on touchdown.

At 1545 hours on the afternoon of 8 June, during their return journey, HMS *Glorious* and her escorting destroyers, *Ardent* and *Acasta,* were sighted by the German battlecruisers *Scharnhorst* and *Gneisenau*; all three Royal Navy vessels were sunk.

Remarkably, Squadron Leader Cross and Flight Lieutenant P.G. Jameson[2] survived, while a handful of the squadron's pilots had been forced to return with the Service Echelon owing to a lack of serviceable aircraft.

The squadron was reformed at RAF Digby on 15 June, under the command of Squadron Leader A.D. Murray and sharing the station, until its transfer south on 1 September, with Nos. 29 (Blenheim) and 611 (Spitfire) Squadrons. Reid joined the squadron as a part of an influx of new pilots, many fresh from flying training, who had few hours on type. Reid and his fellow newcomers were put through an intensive training programme and were soon flying the Hawker Hurricane like 'naturals'. Despite the relative inexperience of a number of its pilots, the squadron was nevertheless declared operational towards the end of the month. Their initial operations were fairly mundane, as may be seen from the pages of the Squadron Operational Record Book (ORB).

Solo defensive patrols were flown from 0030 hours until 1900 hours on 26 June, the only excitement being when they were vectored onto a couple of barrage balloons which had slipped their moorings. These were successfully located and brought down, providing valuable practice in following the controller's vectors and in air-to-air gunnery.

Meanwhile, at 1740 hours, Pilot Officer Reid took part in a scramble when a section strength patrol was flown between RAF Manby and RAF North Coates, in anticipation of a German Meteorological flight. After stooging around for over an hour, the controller concluded that the otherwise regular flight had been cancelled and ordered them to pancake. The routine patrols continued over the next few days, with most of the squadron's pilots flying at least one sortie.

Reid, who had not yet flown operationally during July, was at Night Readiness at the squadron's satellite landing ground, code-named 'L1' (otherwise known as Wellingore) on 5 and 6 July, but was not called into action.

During the evening of 9 July, Reid's Blue Section was ordered to patrol Convoy Booty, which was by then lying off Outer Dowsing. The convoy was reported to include twenty-three merchant vessels escorted by two minesweepers, three destroyers and two cruisers. The sortie passed off without incident and would be one of many such operations, which nevertheless drained the pilots both physically and mentally.

The squadron's Battle of Britain began with only occasional patrols, which were flown over the following days, with their first vector not coming until the early afternoon of 20 July, when, frustratingly, the raider turned back while forty miles off the coast at Mablethorpe.

The reformed squadron's first taste of real action came two days later on 22 July, when flight strength standing patrols were flown over Convoy Agent. At 0445 hours, a lone bomber was sighted approaching the convoy and Green Section's Pilot Officer P.R.M. McGregor (flying P3053), along with Sergeants G.H. Edworthy (flying P3064) and E. Bloor (flying P3030), were ordered to make an interception. The Dornier Do 17 was pursued eighty miles off Skegness, with the trio claiming a share in its unconfirmed destruction. The Squadron ORB conceded that: 'Although numerous bursts of fire were obtained and the Dornier badly hit, the result was not conclusive.'

Meanwhile, the squadron suffered its first loss since the Norway Campaign when Pilot Officer A.M. Cooper-Key[3] was killed following an AA co-operation exercise flown on 24 July. Cooper-Key's Hurricane, P2685, experienced an engine failure and crashed into a railway embankment to the west of Peartree Station, Derby, while attempting a forced-landing. There was no time for reflection, the squadron's pilots had a job to carry out – only in later years were the few survivors of the squadron able to take stock of their losses during the summer of 1940.

Convoy escorts were flown in the early hours of 25 July, and again during the afternoon of 7 August, while between 10 and 12 August, No. 46 Squadron flew standing patrols over Convoy Booty. The battle for the convoys continued, despite the mounting losses in terms of shipping and aircraft on other squadrons, and, on 15 August, the squadron's 'B' Flight was ordered to patrol Convoy Arena, which consisted of merchant vessels and eight escorts.

The squadron operated out of RAF Duxford on 18 August, flying patrols over RAF North Weald. Flight Lieutenant A.C. Rabagliati's Red Section intercepted an enemy formation three miles south of Chelmsford. Rabagliati (flying P3597) destroyed a Bf 109, probably destroying a second, while Pilot Officer C.F. Ambrose (flying P3066) damaged three Bf 110s. The combats, which took place at about 1745 hours, were a great fillip to the squadron, which, up until then, had had little to show for its efforts.

The squadron was back on convoy escorts on 19 August, when Reid's Blue Section flew an uneventful patrol over Convoy Arena between 1620 and 1755 hours. These routine patrols continued until the end of the month, when news reached the squadron of an impending transfer out of No. 12 Group.

On 1 September, the squadron moved south to RAF Stapleford Tawney, RAF North Weald's satellite. Here they relieved No. 151 Squadron, which had seen almost continuous combat since 10 May, playing a vital role in the Battle of France, the defence of the Dunkirk Beaches and the early phases of the Battle of Britain. From their new base, No. 46 Squadron would be heavily involved in the defence of London.

Pilot Officer Reid's first operational sortie as part of No. 11 Group came at 1635 hours, when he flew on a routine defensive patrol of RAF Rochford, which turned into a sector familiarization.

Reid made a patrol over Rochford at about noon on the following day, 2 September, rendezvousing with No. 111 Squadron. A formation of over twenty He 111s was intercepted, flying in vics of five at 15,000ft, escorted by Bf 109s and Bf 110s. The raid crossed the coast near Hythe, evidently targeting RAF Eastchurch and RAF Detling.

No. 111 Squadron engaged the enemy, losing Sergeant Dymond[4] (flying P3875), with Flight Lieutenant Giddings' (flying V6538) Hurricane being damaged while leading Red and Yellow Sections in a head-on attack. Pilot Officer Ritchie (flying R4225), meanwhile, made a forced-landing at RAF Rochford, following combat damage sustained during an engagement with a Bf 110. Sergeant Hampshire (flying P3106) probably destroyed a Bf 110 with a seven-second burst, while Sergeant V.H. Ekins (flying P2888) set an He 111 on fire before a Bf 109 intervened and prevented him claiming a 'kill'. Pilot Officer Simpson (flying V7361) also damaged an He 111 before having to return to base with damage resulting from an attack by a Bf 109. Sergeant Brown (flying P3524) damaged an He 111 and a Bf 109.

Meanwhile, at 1730 hours, with raiders targeting RAF Eastchurch and the east Kent coast, No. 46 Squadron was scrambled to patrol over North Weald. Vectored onto the enemy, the squadron made an intercept between Eastchurch and Sheerness, following closely an attack made on the same formation by No. 72 Squadron, during which the latter recorded the following claims and loss:

Pilot Officer E.E. Males	one Bf 109 destroyed
Sergeant B. Douthwaite	one Bf 109 damaged

Squadron Leader A.R. Collins (flying R6806) was wounded in combat, his aircraft being written-off.

During the ensuing combat, Pilot Officer C.F. Ambrose and an unknown pilot shared in the destruction of a Bf 109, which crashed at Tile Lodge Farm, Hoath, the pilot being taken a PoW, while Sergeant E. Bloor destroyed a second Bf 109. The squadron's pilots also claimed two Bf 109s probably destroyed and two damaged. Meanwhile, Flight Sergeant E.E. Williams damaged a Do 215.

The engagement wasn't totally one-sided and Flight Lieutenant Rabagliati forced-landed near Sittingbourne. The squadron also suffered the loss of Pilot Officer J.C.L.D. Bailey[5] (flying P3067), who was shot down over the Thames estuary. Bailey was killed while attempting a forced-landing at RAF Detling.

At 0955 hours on 3 September, No. 46 Squadron was scrambled and vectored onto a formation of thirty Junkers 88s reported as flying west over Southend, at 10,000ft, in six large vics, along with their escort of twenty-five Bf 109 and a similar number of Bf 110s flying high above at 22,000ft.

The enemy made directly for RAF North Weald, carrying out a textbook bombing of the airfield from 15,000ft, hitting the runway, hangars, messes, admin buildings and operations block. Many of the 200-plus bombs were on delayed action fuses. Despite the severe bomb-damage, and thanks to the tenacity of the ground staff and pilots, the airfield remained fully operational.

Scrambled too late to intercept the enemy before they hit the airfield, the Spitfires of Nos. 19 and 603 Squadrons were joined in the attack by the Hurricanes of Nos. 1, 17, 46, 249, 257 and 310 Squadrons.

No. 46 Squadron's Hurricanes dived down into the attack at 1025 hours, with Pilot Officer P.W. Lefevre (flying P2114) destroying a Ju 88, four miles north-west of Southend, while Sub-Lieutenant J.C. Carpenter (flying P3053) destroyed a Bf 110, six miles west of Southend, circling the scene long enough to see two of the crew crawl out of the wreckage. Sergeant Bloor (flying P3024) damaged a Do 215 in the same area. Other claims included Flight Lieutenant A.C. Rabagliati (flying P3756), who damaged two Bf 110s, while Sergeant R.L. Earp (flying P2465) damaged a Ju 88, Sergeant W.A. Peacock (flying P2599) damaged a Do 215 and Sergeant R.E. de C. d' Hamale (flying N2499) damaged a Bf 110; all these combats took place two miles north of Southend.

Sergeant E. Bloor (flying P3024) was shot down in flames while in combat at 1045 hours, but was able to bail out over Canewdon, near Foulness, suffering from slight burns to his face. His Hurricane crashed into the sea wall at Beckney Farm, South Fambridge.

Flying Officer Lefevre, meanwhile, landed at Stapleford with battle damage following combat with a Bf 109.

Another of the squadron's pilots, Flying Officer H. Morgan-Gray (flying P3063), was in combat at 1030 hours when his Hurricane was set alight by return fire from a Do 215 over Rochford and was forced to bail out, wounded. His Hurricane crashed at Apton Hall Farm, Canewdon.

Meanwhile, Flight Sergeant E.E. Williams (flying P3094) landed at RAF Debden with damage sustained in combat off the Essex coast. Williams returned to RAF Stapleford the following morning, suffering from shrapnel wounds to the leg.

During the dogfight the squadron lost Sergeant G.H. Edworthy[6] (flying P3064), who was shot down over the Essex coast at 1035 hours by a Bf 109. His Hurricane crashed in Redwood Creek, River Crouch.

While returning to base the Hurricanes of No. 46 Squadron came across a formation of No. 24 Squadron's Blenheims, which they mistook for enemy aircraft, with disastrous results. Two Blenheims were shot down, with the loss of Pilot Officer D.W. Hogg.[7]

No. 19 Squadron's Spitfires suffered blockages on their machine guns and were only able to claim two enemy aircraft, with another as probably destroyed:

Flying Officer L.A. Haines (flying X4059)	one Bf 110 destroyed
Flight Sergeant G.C. Unwin (flying X6776)	one Bf 110 destroyed
Sub-Lieutenant A.G. Blake (flying R6923)	one Bf 110 probably destroyed

Meanwhile, the other squadrons were able to get in amongst the bombers, which were defended by their escort of Bf 110s.

No. 1 Squadron was also engaged, but made no claims. However, the squadron lost Flight Lieutenant H.B.L. Hillcoat[8] (flying P3044) and Pilot Officer R.H. Shaw[9] (flying P3782).

No. 17 Squadron's claims and losses included:

Flying Officer M.B. Czernin (flying V7408)	one Bf 110 destroyed
Flight Lieutenant A.W.A. Bayne (flying P3027)	one Bf 110 destroyed (shared), one Do 17 destroyed (shared)
Pilot Officer H. Bird-Wilson (flying P3878)	one Do 215 destroyed (shared), one Bf 110 probably destroyed
Pilot Officer D.H.W. Hanson (flying P3539)	one Do 215 destroyed
Pilot Officer D.C. Leary (flying V2741)	one Bf 110 probably destroyed
	one Do 17 destroyed (shared)

Pilot Officer J.K. Ross (flying P3536)	one D 215 destroyed (shared)
Pilot Officer D.H. Wissler (flying P3892)	one Bf 110 destroyed (shared), one Do 17 destroyed (shared)
Sergeant D.A. Sewell (flying P3023)	one Do 215 destroyed (shared)

Sergeant D. Fopp (flying P3673 YB-E) was shot down in flames by a Bf 110 near Brentwood and bailed out with burns.

Squadron Leader A.G. Miller (flying R4224) was hit by a Bf 110 and force-landed.

Flying Officer D.H.W. Hanson[10] bailed out too low after being shot down by return fire from a Do 17.

No. 249 Squadron made no claims, while Sergeant P.A. Rowell's Hurricane (V6633) was damaged by the Dover Barrage.

No. 257 Squadron's claims and losses included:

| Pilot Officer K.C. Gundry (flying P3704) | one Bf 109 damaged |
| Sergeant R.H.B. Fraser (flying V7357) | one Bf 110 probably destroyed |

Pilot Officer C.R. Bon-Seigneur[11] (flying P3578) was shot down by Bf 110s over Ingatestone and bailed out, dead.

Pilot Officer K.C. Gundry landed with combat damage.

Pilot Officer D.W. Hunt (flying L1703) was shot down by a Bf 110 near Chelmsford and was admitted to Billericay Hospital.

Sergeant R.C. Nutter (flying P3706) was slightly wounded in combat with Bf 110s.

No. 310 Squadron's claims included:

Flight Lieutenant J. Jefferies (flying P3142)	one Bf 110 destroyed
Flight Lieutenant G.L. Sinclair (flying P3143)	one Bf 110 and one Do 215 destroyed
Pilot Officer E. Fechtner (flying P3056)	one Bf 110 destroyed
Pilot Officer J.M. Maly (flying V7436)	one Bf 110 destroyed
Sergeant B. Furst (flying V6556)	one Bf 110 destroyed
Sergeant J. Kominek (flying R4085)	one Do 215 probably destroyed
Sergeant F. Koukal (flying P3148)	one Bf 110 destroyed

Sergeant J. Kopriva (flying P8811) was shot down by a Bf 110 and bailed out unhurt.

No. 603 Squadron's claims included:

Pilot Officer J.R. Caister (flying L1057)	one Bf 109 destroyed
Pilot Officer R.H. Hillary (flying X4277)	one Bf 109 destroyed
Pilot Officer A.P. Pease (flying X4263)	one Bf 109 destroyed

Pilot Officer D. Stewart-Clarke (flying X4185) was shot down and wounded by Bf 109s of JG 26 over the Thames estuary. He bailed out and was admitted to Chelmsford General Hospital.

Pilot Officer R. H. Hillary (flying X4277) was shot down in flames, severely burned, following an attack by Bf 109s of JG 26. He was rescued by the Margate Lifeboat.

The squadron was in combat again on the following day, 4 September. While on patrol over RAF Rochford against a raid targeting the oil farm at Thameshaven, at 1315 hours, 'A' Flight was attacked from astern by Bf 109s, which escaped into cloud. Pilot Officer C.F. Ambrose (flying P3066) was shot down during the Bf 109s' pass and bailed out near Southend, unhurt.

Pilot Officer R.H. Barber (flying V7201) was acting in the role of Weaver when the Hurricanes were bounced by a Bf 109. Barber's aircraft was raked with cannon and machine-gun fire, damaging his glycol system, and covering Barber in a mixture of oil and glycol. His Hurricane dived 15,000ft before he was able to regain control, making a belly-landing at Chigborough Farm, Heybridge. Barber was taken to St Margaret's Hospital, Epping, suffering from a broken neck vertebrae and jaw sustained in the heavy landing.

Another victim was Flying Officer R.P. Plummer[12] (flying P3052) who was shot down in flames and forced to bail out, landing at Stambridge, badly burned. Plummer was admitted to Rochester Hospital, later being transferred to Bradford Hospital (when the former was bombed), where he died on 14 September. His Hurricane crashed at Rectory Road, Hawkwell.

Meanwhile, Flying Officer F. Austin (flying P3031) landed at RAF Stapleford on one wheel, as the other oleo leg had bent back, probably due to enemy action. The aircraft overturned, but he was uninjured.

No. 249 Squadron was in action against the same raid over Southend, but was unable to make any claims.

During No. 46 Squadron's second operation, on 5 September, made at 1450 hours, the squadron was ordered to patrol Rochford at 20,000ft. Having formed up with No. 249 Squadron, they were still climbing to make an attack against a large formation of enemy aircraft, 5,000ft above, when they sighted five Bf 109s over the Thames estuary and went in for the attack.

Flight Lieutenant A.C. Rabagliati (flying the four-cannon-armed V7360) destroyed a Bf 109 while five miles south of Sheppey. Pilot Officer A.E. Johnson (flying P3053) destroyed a Bf 109 over Gravesend and Sub-Lieutenant J.C. Carpenter (flying P3201) destroyed a Bf 109, which crashed in flames in the Southsea area. The combats, which took place at about 1520 hours, were not one-sided, as Pilot

Officer C.F. Ambrose (flying P3066) was shot down over Rochford and was forced to take to his parachute.

Flight Lieutenant A.C. Rabagliati's combat report read:

'I sighted one 109 diving towards the ground straight past us; I fired at him, but as he was drawing away only a short burst was delivered from astern (my Nos. 2 and 3 continued the attack right down to sea level). I climbed back to 12,000ft and spotted a 109 on the tail of a Spitfire; I gave this enemy aircraft a three-second burst and he blew up in the air. He took no evasive action.'

Nos. 17, 72, 73, 222, 249, 303 and 501 Squadrons engaged the same raid, with mixed fortunes.

No. 17 Squadron recorded the following victories:

Squadron Leader A.G. Miller (flying P3033)	one He 111 probably destroyed (shared)
Flight Lieutenant A.W.A. Bayne (flying P3894)	one Bf 109 destroyed
Flying Officer M.B. Czernin (flying V7408)	one Bf 109 destroyed, one He 111 destroyed (shared), one He 111 probably destroyed (shared)
Pilot Officer G.E. Pittman (flying V6553)	one He 111 probably destroyed (shared)
Flight Sergeant C.A. Chew (flying P2794)	one He 111 (shared)
Sergeant L.H. Bartlett (flying P2994)	one He 111 probably destroyed (shared)
Sergeant G. Griffiths (flying P2972)	one He 111 probably destroyed (shared)

No. 72 Squadron recorded the following victories:

Pilot Officer D.F. Holland	one Bf 109 destroyed, one Bf 109 damaged

No. 73 Squadron recorded the following victories:

Squadron Leader M.W.S. Robinson (flying TP-B)	one He 111 probably destroyed
Sergeant G.W. Brimble (flying TP-K)	one He 111 damaged

No. 222 Squadron recorded the following victories and loss:

Sergeant D.J. Chipping (flying X4057)	one Bf 109 probably destroyed
Sergeant E. Scott (flying P9364)	two Bf 109 probably destroyed

Sergeant D.J. Chipping bailed out (wounded) when his Spitfire was damaged by the Dover Barrage while in combat with Bf 109s at 1500 hours.

No. 249 Squadron recorded the following victories and loss:

Pilot Officer H.J.S. Beazley (flying V6635)	one Bf 109 probably destroyed
Sergeant H.J. Davidson (flying P3667)	one Bf 109 probably destroyed
Sergeant W.L. Davis (flying V6614)	one Do 17 damaged
Sergeant R. Smithson (flying P2863)	one Do17 probably destroyed, one Do 17 damaged

Flight Lieutenant R.A. Barton (flying V6625) bailed out following combat with a Bf 109 over Shell Haven at 1530 hours.

No. 303 Squadron recorded the following victories:

Squadron Leader R.G. Kellett (flying V7284)	one Bf 109 destroyed, one Bf 109 probably destroyed
Flight Lieutenant A.S. Forbes (flying R4217)	one Ju 88 destroyed
Pilot Officer W. Lapkowski (flying P2985)	one Ju 88 destroyed
Sergeant J. František (flying R4175)	one Bf 109 destroyed, one Ju 88 destroyed
Sergeant S. Karubin (flying P3975)	two Bf 109s destroyed
Sergeant K. Wunsche (flying V7287)	one Bf 109 destroyed

No. 501 Squadron recorded the following victories:

Sergeant R.J.K. Gent (flying P5194)	one Bf 109 probably destroyed
Sergeant J.H. Lacey (flying P8816)	two Bf 109s destroyed

Three patrols were flown over Rochford during 6 September, the latter in the company of No. 249 Squadron, but no enemy aircraft were encountered.

While on patrol over North Weald at about 1700 hours on 7 September, 'A' Flight engaged a formation of eighteen Do 215s in one big open wedge of vics of three, heading north-north-west. The bombers had a large escort of Bf 109s and Bf 110s extending up to 20,000ft. Flight Lieutenant A.C. Rabagliati (flying V7360) led the Hurricanes into the attack, heading for the bombers in formation from the starboard beam and above; as soon as they had done this the Bf 109s dived in, a dogfight taking place over Thameshaven at 1740 hours.

Flight Lieutenant A.C. Rabagliati and Flight Sergeant E. Tyrer (flying V7409) each damaged a Do 215. Meanwhile, engaged by the bomber's fighter escort, Flight Sergeant E. Tyrer damaged a Bf 109; with Pilot Officer P.S. Gunning (flying V6582) probably destroying another.

The Squadron Intelligence Report added:

'Flight Lieutenant Rabagliati (four-cannon Hurricane) aimed for the leader of the second vic of bombers. He opened fire at 300 yards, closing to 100 yards when the cannons ceased firing. No return fire was encountered from the bombers. Total rounds fired 130.'

On 8 September, the squadron was ordered to patrol base at 10,000ft and rendezvous with No. 504 Squadron over North Weald. At about 1215 hours, the wing sighted thirty Do 17s of II./KG 2 and III./KG 2 at 18,000ft in three formations, each in vic-sections forming a large vic, and their escort of a large number of Bf 109s and Bf 110s flying ahead and to port, stepped up from 25,000 to 30,000ft.

The Squadron Intelligence Report read:

'The Hurricanes attacked the bombers from starboard beam above and in front, and several bombers left the formation as a result of the attack. The fighter escort dived down and a dogfight took place over the Isle of Sheppey.'

Sergeant S. Andrew (flying P3525) engaged a Do 17 of II./KG 2 over the London Docks. The bomber exploded shortly after it crash-landed on Rose Farm, Broomfield, at 1240 hours (Oberleutnant Martin Ziems bailed out but was killed. Unteroffizier Heino Flick, Unteroffizier Wilhelm Trost and Unteroffizier Wilhelm Selter were killed). Andrew then attacked a second Dornier, which he damaged, before being forced to break off the attack when his own aircraft was hit by a Bf 109. Andrew was able to make base.

Meanwhile, Pilot Officer P.W. Lefevre (flying V7202) damaged a Do 17 south of the Thames at 1215 hours. Pilot Officer C.F. Ambrose (flying P3756) and Sergeant W.A. Peacock (flying V7232) each probably destroyed a Bf 109, Ambrose also probably destroying a Do 215 and a Bf 110. During the same combat Pilot Officer P.R. McGregor (flying P3053) destroyed a Bf 109 and damaged a Do 17 at 1215 hours, before being hit and making a forced-landing at Happy Valley, Meopham; his Hurricane was written off. Pilot Officer McGowen (flying V7409) force-landed at Biggin Hill with slight damage during the same combat.

Flight Lieutenant N.W. Burnett (flying V6631) was shot down during the engagement and crashed at Hollingbourne. He was sent to Queen Mary's Hospital, Sidcup, suffering from burns.

The squadron lost Sub-Lieutenant J.C. Carpenter[13] (flying P3201), who was shot down while engaging enemy aircraft over Sheppey, and who bailed out, but fell dead. His Hurricane crashed at Bearsted, Maidstone.

While Nos. 253, 504 and 605 Squadrons also made contact with the enemy, although only No. 605 Squadron was able to make any claims, the table includes the loss of one of their own aircraft:

Pilot Officer T.P.M. Cooper-Slipper (flying N2557)	one Bf 109 destroyed, one Do 215 probably destroyed
Pilot Officer C.F. Currant (flying P3580)	one Bf 109 and one Do 215 damaged

Pilot Officer J.S. Humphreys (flying P2765)   one Bf 109 damaged

Pilot Officer A. Ingle (flying P3650)   one Do 215 probably destroyed

Pilot Officer J. Fleming (flying L2061) was shot down in flames by a Bf 109 over Tunbridge Wells. Fleming bailed out suffering from severe burns.

Between 1645-1815 hours on 9 September, Pilot Officer Reid flew on an uneventful squadron patrol over RAF Rochford in the company of No. 249 Squadron. Meanwhile, Reid made several patrols two days later, on 11 September. At 1510 hours, he took off on a squadron strength patrol over North Weald, made in company with No. 504 Squadron. The wing was vectored onto a raid of over eighty enemy aircraft, including a large number of Do 215s flying in tight vics of five and heading north-west. The bombers were closely escorted by Bf 109s at 9,000ft above, with Bf 110s behind and slightly above, ten miles north of Dungeness Point.

Red and Yellow Sections did a beam attack, Reid's Blue Section following on as three of the escorting Bf 110s attempted an interception upon their section.

Pilot Officer A.E. Johnson (flying V6550) damaged a Bf 110, ten miles north of Dungeness, firing a four-second burst from 100 yards. Sergeant R.L. Earp (flying N2497) attacked a Do 215 in the same area, which was seen to drop out of formation with black smoke issuing from the starboard engine. The Dornier was allowed as destroyed.

The bomber's escort was soon in amongst the Hurricanes, and Sergeant d'Hamale (flying V6549) was shot down and received a head wound. Unable to control his crippled Hurricane, d'Hamale was forced to bail out, landing safely at Court Lodge, Bodiam.

During the same engagement Flying Officer P.R. McGregor (flying P3094) was shot down in combat over the Thames estuary and bailed out, injured. He was admitted into hospital. His Hurricane crashed in West Lordine Wood, Staplecross. Sergeant W.A. Peacock[14] (flying V7232) was lost during combat over the Thames estuary and is believed to have crashed into the sea; the combats took place at about 1545 hours.

Nos. 92, 253 and 504 Squadrons took on the same enemy formation:

No. 92 Squadron claims and losses included:

Squadron Leader P.J. Sanders (flying R6634)   one He 111 and one Bf 109 destroyed

Flight Lieutenant C.B.F. Kingcombe (flying R6622)   one He 111 destroyed

Flight Lieutenant J.A. Paterson (flying R6613)   one He 111 destroyed

Flying Officer J.F. Drummond (flying N3248) one Bf 109 probably destroyed

Pilot Officer T.S. Wade (flying P9513)   one He 111 destroyed

Pilot Officer G.H.A. Wellum (flying R6760)   one He 111 destroyed

Pilot Officer D.G. Williams (flying R6616)	one He 111 destroyed
Pilot Officer A.R. Wright (flying X4038)	one He 111 destroyed
Sergeant P.R. Eyles (flying P9828)	one He 111 destroyed

Pilot Officer F.N. Hargreaves[15] (flying K9793) was shot down over Dungeness at 1615 hours and killed.

No. 253 Squadron claimed:

Squadron Leader G.R. Edge (flying P2958)	one Bf 109 destroyed, one He 111 probably destroyed one Do 215 destroyed (shared)
Flight Lieutenant J.H. Wedgwood (flying N2588)	one Do 215 damaged one Do 215 destroyed (shared)
Sergeant W.B. Higgins (flying R2686)	one Bf 109 destroyed, one Bf 110 damaged
Sergeant R.A. Innes (flying P5184)	two He 111s damaged
Nine pilots	one Do 215 destroyed (shared)

No. 504 Squadron made several claims, in return losing one aircraft:

Squadron Leader J. Sample (flying P3415)	one Do 215 probably destroyed (shared)
Flying Officer W. Royce (flying P3388)	one Do 215 probably destroyed (shared)

Pilot Officer A.W. Clarke (flying P3770) was shot down over Romney at 1600 hours.

Pilot Officer Reid was airborne again between 1715 and 1740 hours when 'A' Flight flew an uneventful defensive patrol over their home base at 15,000ft.

The squadron, including Reid, took off at 1050 hours on 11 September, to rendezvous with No. 249 Squadron, but the patrol was cancelled and the squadron pancaked. However, what should have been an uneventful patrol turned to tragedy when suddenly, Hurricane P3525, flown by Sergeant Andrew,[16] broke formation and span down into the ground. There was no word from the pilot and he made no attempt to escape. Under these circumstances it seems most likely that he may have had an oxygen problem and passed out.

On 14 September, the squadron flew a number of uneventful patrols through to the mid-afternoon. Reid's section patrolled RAF North Weald and RAF Hornchurch between noon and 1235 hours. Reid was in the air again at 1545 hours when he took part in a wing patrol of RAF North Weald in the company of No. 249 Squadron. By now Reid was flying his regular Hurricane, V7443.

At 1800 hours, Reid took part in a second wing strength patrol, the squadron making a rendezvous with No. 504 Squadron. Vectored over Maidstone at 15,000ft, the squadron sighted fifty or sixty Bf 109s over Biggin Hill, stepped up from 15,000 to 20,000ft and heading west. The Hurricanes attacked from underneath and a dogfight ensued at about 1850 hours.

Flight Lieutenant Rabagliati (flying V7438) gave a two-second burst at a Bf 109 without effect; firing a longer burst at a second from astern, resulted in the enemy aircraft turning over and going down with smoke and flames issuing from just beneath the cockpit. Rabagliati attacked a third from the quarter but without result. Pilot Officer R. Reid (flying V7443), who was on his third patrol of the day, closed to 250 yards astern and slightly below the rear Bf 109, firing a five-second burst:

'I observed two Bf 109s at [the] end of formation flying close in line astern. I got into position behind and closed to 250 yards, delivering [an attack from] astern [and] from slightly below. The rear Me 109 immediately turned right and dived vertically through the clouds. No flames were seen. I did not follow him down owing to [the] proximity of other enemy fighters. Clouds were almost 10/10 and I did not observe him crash. The machine was obviously badly hit and I claim one damaged.'

(signed) Pilot Officer Robert Reid.

During the same engagement, No. 504 Squadron's Pilot Officer B.E.G. White (flying L1583), destroyed a Bf 109 near Headcorn at 1840 hours.

Pilot Officer Reid was back in the air again on 15 September when he flew on a squadron scramble at 1135 hours. The patrol was made in the company of No. 249 Squadron, led by Flight Lieutenant D.G. Parnall.

Already about to engage were eleven squadrons, which had been scrambled and were making for the enemy. The controller vectored Nos. 72 and 92 Squadron's Spitfires to intercept the raiders between Maidstone and Ashford. Nos. 253 and 501 Squadron's Hurricanes, along with the Spitfires of Nos. 66 and 609 Squadrons were ordered to reinforce.

Soon after the initial interception, Nos. 229 and 303 Squadron's Hurricanes engaged the enemy between Rochester and south London. Meanwhile, Nos. 17 and 73 Squadron's Hurricanes attacked the bombers over Maidstone at about noon.

Radar continued to report incoming raiders, in response to which the controller further reinforced airborne units, scrambled up to thirty minutes earlier, and called upon Nos. 19, 242, 249, 302, 310, and 611 Squadrons, these joined by Reid's No. 46 Squadron. Minutes later, between 1140 and 1142 hours, he scrambled Nos.1 (RCAF), 41, 66 and 605 Squadrons.

Following the controller's vector, Nos. 46 and 249 Squadrons intercepted a formation of twenty Do 17s of I./KG 76 over south-east London at 18,000ft, escorted by a large number of Bf 109s flying 5,000ft above. The 'bandits' were first located with the aid of anti-aircraft fire. The Bf 109s came down to protect their charge and the fighters attacked head-on. With a closing speed of over 500mph, both sides claimed hits, but no 'kills'.

As the squadron closed with the Do 17s, Flight Sergeant E. Tyrer (flying P3066) attacked head-on, firing short bursts with no apparent effect. With the enemy formation breaking up he followed a Dornier down. The remainder of 'A' Flight, which included Pilot Officers P.S. Gunning, Reid (flying V7443) and Seghers, along with Sergeant d'Hamale, followed him in the attack, all firing deflection bursts at the bombers. One Dornier was raked with fire, damaging the starboard engine, while the port engine began to throw out black smoke. Three of the crew bailed out before the aircraft crashed, ten miles south of Biggin Hill, and burst into flames.

Pilot Officer Gunning (flying V7438), having given a short head-on burst at a Do 17 with no effect, then lost height as he headed south to intercept the bombers on their return. Gunning later chased a straggler near Dover which he attacked from astern, but was forced to break off when his windscreen became covered in black oil from the bomber.

Meanwhile, Sergeant G.W. Jefferys (V6550) became separated from the rest of the squadron and observed a Do 17 heading south-east at 15,000ft. Jefferys closed to within effective range, firing a three-second burst from the quarter, but broke off the attack when other friendly aircraft engaged. He then found another Do 17 and fired three, three-second bursts at 200 yards from the beam and quarter. Several other fighters then joined in the attack and the Dornier crashed to the south of London.

Sergeant C.A.L. Hurry (N2599) engaged a Do 17 heading south and carried out a quarter attack until his ammunition was expended. As he peeled off, more fighters engaged and the rear-gunner attempted to bail out, but his parachute streamed over the tailplane. The Dornier was seen to crash and burst into flames. The only damage to Sergeant Hurry's Hurricane was a bullet hole in his mainplane.

Pilot Officer J.D. Crossman (flying V7442) made a stern attack on a Dornier, firing four bursts, resulting in the Do 17's port engine emitting black smoke. The bomber dropped out of formation, losing height. Crossman was credited with the destruction of the enemy aircraft, making the squadron's haul four Do 17s destroyed and probably a fifth.

The presence of the Hurricanes did its job and the Dornier Do 17s broke formation, ditching their payloads, several diving for cover in cloud.

Meanwhile, also flying in the wing, No. 249 Squadron made the following claims:

Pilot Officer R.G.A. Barclay (flying V6683)   one Do 17 probably destroyed
Pilot Officer J.R.B. Meaker   one Do 17 destroyed

The following squadrons also engaged the enemy in an air battle which raged between London and Dover:

No. 19 Squadron claimed:

Squadron Leader W.G. Clouston (flying X4237)	two Bf 110s destroyed
Flying Officer L.A. Haines (flying X4352)	one Bf 109 destroyed
Pilot Officer W. Cunningham (flying X4070)	one Bf 110 destroyed (shared)
Pilot Officer W.J. Lawson (flying X4336)	one Do 17 probably destroyed
Flight Sergeant H. Steere (flying X4351)	one Bf 109 destroyed
Flight Sergeant G.C. Unwin (flying X4179)	one Bf 109 destroyed
Sergeant D.G.S.R. Cox (flying X4353)	one Bf 109 destroyed

No. 41 Squadron claimed:

Flying Officer A.D.J. Lovell (flying X4068)	one Bf 109 destroyed
Pilot Officer G.H. Bennions (flying X4343)	one Bf 109 destroyed
Sergeant E.V. Darling (flying X4338)	one Do 215 damaged

No. 73 Squadron's claims and losses included:

Flying Officer J.D. Smith (flying TP-J)	one Bf 109 destroyed
Pilot Officer C.A. McGaw	one Bf 109 destroyed
Pilot Officer D.H. Scott (flying TP-B)	one Bf 109 destroyed
Sergeant H.G. Webster	one Bf 109 damaged

Pilot Officer R.A. Marchand[17] (flying TP-K) was killed-in-action.

No. 92 Squadron claimed:

Pilot Officer A.C. Bartley (flying X4051)	one Bf 109 and one Do 215 damaged
Pilot Officer H.P. Hill (flying R6616)	one Bf 109 probably destroyed
Pilot Officer R.H. Holland (flying R6606)	one Bf 109 damaged
Flight Sergeant C. Sydney (flying R6767)	one Bf 109 probably destroyed
Sergeant R.H. Fokes (flying R6760)	one Do 17 damaged

No. 242 Squadron claimed:

Sub-Lieutenant R.J. Cork (flying P3515)	one Do 17 destroyed, one damaged
Flying Officer N.K. Stansfeld (flying R4115)	one Do 17 destroyed
Pilot Officer N.N. Campbell (flying V6575)	one Do 17 damaged
Pilot Officer N. Hart (flying P5034)	one Bf 109 destroyed

Pilot Officer H.N. Tamblyn (flying R4115)	one Do 17 destroyed
Pilot Officer P.S. Turner (flying P4385)	one Do 17 destroyed
Flight Sergeant G.S.ff. Powell-Sheddon (flying P2684)	one Do 17 destroyed (shared)

No. 253 Squadron claimed:

Flight Lieutenant R.M.B.D. Duke-Woolley	one Do 215 damaged (shared)
Pilot Officer R.A. Barton	one Do 215 destroyed
Sergeant A.S. Dredge (flying P2865)	one Do 215 damaged (shared)

No. 303 Squadron claimed:

Flight Lieutenant J.A. Kent (flying V6665)	one Bf 109 destroyed
Flying Officer Z. Henneberg (flying P3120)	one Bf 109 and one Do 215 destroyed
Flying Officer J. Zumbach (flying P3577)	one Bf 109 destroyed
Pilot Officer M. Feric (flying R2685)	one Bf 109 destroyed
Pilot Officer W. Lokuciewski (flying P2003)	one Bf 109 destroyed
Pilot Officer L.W. Paszkiewicz (flying V7235)	one Bf 109 destroyed
Pilot Officer M. Pisarek (flying V7465)	one Bf 109 destroyed
Sergeant T. Andruszkow (flying P3939)	one Do 215 destroyed (shared)
Sergeant J. František (flying R3089)	one Bf 109 destroyed
Sergeant S. Wojciechowski (flying V6673)	one Bf 109 destroyed, one Do 215 destroyed (shared)

No. 609 Squadron claimed:

Flight Lieutenant J.H.G. McArthur (flying R6979)	one Do 17 damaged
Flying Officer J.C. Dundas (flying R6922)	one Do 17 damaged
Pilot Officer M.J. Appleby (flying R6631)	one Do 17 damaged (shared), two Do 17 damaged
Pilot Officer J. Curchin (flying R6699)	one Do 17 destroyed (shared) with two Hurricanes
Pilot Officer A.K. Ogilvie (flying X4107)	one Do 17 destroyed

No. 611 Squadron claimed:

Squadron Leader J.E. McComb (flying P7291)	one Bf 110 probably destroyed
Flight Lieutenant W.L. Leather (flying P7302)	one Do 215 destroyed
Pilot Officer S.C. Pollard (flying P7214)	one Do 215 destroyed
Sergeant S.A. Levenson (flying P7823)	one Do 215 destroyed

At 1410 hours No. 46 Squadron was ordered to intercept a raid near RAF Hornchurch. Two pilots broke from formation and encountered the enemy. Pilot Officer W.B. Pattullo (flying N2497) was attacked by six Bf 109s at 15,000ft. He latched onto a Dornier Do 17 over the Thames estuary at about 1515 hours, firing four bursts of three-seconds from 300 to 100 yards:

'On climbing through cloud I was forced to break away from the squadron, so climbed alone to 20,000ft, but came down again to 15,000ft, where I was attacked by six orange-nosed Me 109s. I evaded these and after losing them, sighted a Do 17 on the fringe of cloud at 10,000ft. I attacked and put the rear-gunner out of action and in the same burst set the starboard engine on fire. This A/C promptly lost height and prepared to pancake in the Thames, east of the Isle of Sheppey. While gliding down he released what appeared to be a very heavy caliber bomb at about 100ft, this bomb did not explode. Only the pilot left the aircraft on hitting the water, and the aircraft sank in roughly thirty seconds.

'A Naval pinnace proceeded to the point immediately and presumably took the pilot prisoner.

'I claim this aircraft destroyed.'
(signed) Pilot Officer W.B. Pattullo.

Pilot Officer Johnson (flying V7443) observed a Bf 110, or Ju 88, at 5,000ft, which he attacked from the beam, firing a four-second burst. Three other friendly fighters attacked the enemy which crashed and burst into flames south of the Southend road. The squadron lost the Hurricane flown by Flying Officer R.A. McGowan, who was shot down and bailed out suffering from burns. He later received treatment at the Queen Victoria Hospital, East Grinstead.

No. 11 Group was severely stretched by the raid, Keith Park needing to call upon the Duxford Wing to scramble in order to protect his airfields while his own fighters were in action, and when they were at their most vulnerable, back at their home bases to refuel and rearm. For this brief period it would be down to No. 12 Group to protect London too, should any bombers get through.

No. 46 Squadron flew a third scramble during the day, when at 1725 hours a flight strength patrol was carried out with No. 249 Squadron over North Weald, but no enemy aircraft were seen. And so ended what would later be dubbed Battle of Britain Day.

The squadron flew several routine patrols over their home base on 16 September, Reid flying two similar operations on the following day without encountering the enemy.

No. 46 Squadron flew four patrols in the company of No. 249 Squadron during 18 September. The first of these was made at 1220 hours, when the squadron was scrambled with orders to patrol Gravesend. A formation of fifteen Dornier 215s, with fighter escort, was sighted south of the Thames estuary, flying at 18,000ft.

No. 249 Squadron was leading and made a head-on attack, breaking up the bomber formation. No. 46 Squadron's Flight Lieutenant A.C. Rabagliati (flying P3756) dived on a Do 215 from astern at 12,000ft. The bomber made straight out over Folkestone, with the Hurricane in hot pursuit. Flight Lieutenant Rabagliati closed in, concentrating his fire on the port engine, causing the enemy aircraft to dive steeply towards the sea, with black smoke pouring from the port engine, Rabagliati leaving it skimming the water at 50ft.

Pilot Officer Reid (flying V7443) attacked a Bf 109 from behind and slightly to starboard, allowing deflection. The enemy aircraft dived down in flames east of Maidstone, and was credited as destroyed. Reid fired bursts of three to four-seconds at 200 yards. The combat took place at about 1300 hours:

'Having carried out beam attack on about fifteen Do 215s at 18,000ft, the bombers turned south, and I climbed up and behind them. I suddenly found myself among several Me 109s which I had mistaken for Hurricanes. I got close to one and attacked from behind, slightly to starboard, allowing deflection. The Me immediately put his nose down and I saw him burst into flames. He went straight down east of Maidstone. I did not see him crash as I was myself hit from the rear. However, the Me was burning fiercely and must have crashed.' (signed) Pilot Officer Robert Reid.

During the dogfight No. 46 Squadron lost three Hurricanes – shot down. Sergeant C.A.L. Hurry (flying P3816) bailed out near Chatham at 1255 hours and was detained in Chatham Hospital suffering from burns to the hands and face, as well as a bullet wound to the leg. He was later sent to Queen Victoria Hospital, East Grinstead, where he became one of Archibald McIndoe's Guinea Pigs.

Meanwhile, Pilot Officer P.W. Lefevre (flying V6554) also bailed out in the Chatham district, at 1235 hours, suffering from burns and minor injuries. His Hurricane crashed at Chestnut Avenue, Walderslade. Sergeant G.W. Jefferys[18] (flying V7442) was shot down and killed, at 1230 hours, when his parachute failed to open and he fell dead near Chatham, Kent.

Two further patrols were flown on the 18 September, but these proved to be uneventful, as did those of 20 and 21 September.

During the afternoon of the 22 September, a Junkers 88 flew over the airfield. 'A' Flight was scrambled and made an interception, but the bomber escaped into cloud. The next few days proved uneventful for Pilot Officer Reid. He joined a squadron strength patrol of North Weald, made in the company of No. 249 Squadron at

20,000ft on the following morning, 23 September, also flying on a patrol of RAF Rochford either side of noon on the 24 September.

Reid (flying V7443) made three scrambles during 27 September; the first came at 0850 hours, when the squadron was ordered to patrol North Weald with No. 249 Squadron at 10,000ft. The wing, with Wing Commander V. Beamish shadowing, was vectored onto a formation of twenty Bf 110s of V./LG 1 and II./ZG 76 at 19,000ft, which were sighted flying in a defensive circle south of Maidstone. During the dogfight, Flight Lieutenant Rabagliati (flying P3756) attacked a Bf 110 from below, chased it out to sea, initially badly damaging the port engine, before closing to fifty-five yards and shooting the Messerschmitt down into the sea ten miles south of Rye.

Pilot Officer W.B. Pattullo (flying N2968) attacked another Bf 110 at 19,000ft from beam and astern. One crew member was seen to bail out before the crippled aircraft crashed in flames near Penshurst.

Green 2, Pilot Officer Pattullo, fired six bursts at 250 yards, closing to 50 yards:

'I made an attack on an Me 110 which was flying in a protective formation at 18-19,000ft over Maidstone. In one burst, beam attack, I disabled him, forcing the aircraft away from the formation. I then attacked him from astern, disabling the rear-gunner and putting both engines out of action. The starboard engine had caught fire and began to disintegrate. One man bailed out, the aircraft then dived vertically into the ground near Penshurst, or south-west of Tonbridge.'
(signed) Pilot Officer Pattullo.

Meanwhile, Pilot Officer A.E. Johnson (flying V6758) saw a Bf 110 separated from the main formation and flying 2,000ft below. He dived down, delivering a beam attack, quickly followed by an astern attack. The enemy aircraft was badly damaged, forcing the pilot to crash-land in a field ten to fifteen miles west of Maidstone.

Sergeant R.F. Sellers (flying P3539) delivered an astern attack on another Bf 110, and, in company with three other Hurricanes; it too crash-landed, but south-west of Maidstone.

Flight Sergeant E. Tyrer (flying V6790) fired at another Bf 110 which was making for home across the Channel, seeing debris flying off the aircraft as his rounds struck home. Another Bf 110 was damaged by Pilot Officer E.G.A. Seghers (flying R4074). The combats took place at about 0945 hours.

No. 249 Squadron also engaged the same formation, making the following claims, with the loss of one aircraft:

Flight Lieutenant R.A. Barton (flying V6683)	one Bf 110 (own aircraft damaged)
Flying Officer J.H.S. Beazley (flying V6559)	one Bf 110 damaged
Flying Officer K.T. Lofts (flying V6566)	one Bf 110 destroyed (shared)

Pilot Officer A.G. Lewis (flying V6617)	two Bf 110s destroyed and a third probably destroyed
Pilot Officer J.R.B. Meaker (flying V6635)	one Bf 110 destroyed (shared)
Pilot Officer T.F. Neil (flying V7313)	one Bf 110
Pilot Officer P.A. Worrall (flying V6693)	one Bf 110 damaged
Sergeant E. Davidson (flying V6534)	one Bf 110 destroyed (shared)
Sergeant G.C.C. Palliser (flying V6614)	two Bf 110s damaged

Pilot Officer P.R.F. Burton[19] (flying V6729) was killed-in-action.

The squadron's second scramble took place at 1150 hours when, in conjunction with No. 249 Squadron, they made a patrol over RAF Rochford at 15,000ft. Six Bf 109s were engaged and one of them destroyed. As the Hurricanes dived in for the attack, however, they were bounced from astern by unseen Bf 109s. A dogfight followed, resulting in the destruction of one Bf 109, which crashed in a field four to five miles south-east of Biggin Hill.

Pilot Officer W.B. Pattullo (flying V6790) and Flight Sergeant E. Tyrer (flying V6790) shared the victory, which was timed at 1230 hours and took place south of Maidstone.

Pilot Officer Pattullo fired four bursts of four-seconds at 250 yards, closing to 100 yards:

'As three Me 109s descended upon us from above and behind, I informed Green 3, fell back and followed him, manoeuvring for position. He realized I was there but couldn't shake me off, and I finally got in a quarter attack followed by two more without success; however, after a dive, I followed up and gave him a burst which smashed part of his port wing, and after that he pancaked in a field, in which the aircraft broke its back.

'The general position of the aircraft was south of Detling aerodrome.

'I claim this aircraft destroyed.'

(signed) Pilot Officer Pattullo.

Meanwhile, Pilot Officer K. Mrazek (flying P3816) force-landed at Rochford with his engine damaged due to enemy fire.

No. 249 Squadron's claims included:

Pilot Officer R.G.A. Barclay (flying V6622)	one Bf 109 destroyed
Pilot Officer A.G. Lewis (flying V6617)	one Bf 109 destroyed, damaging a second
Pilot Officer P.A. Worrall	one Bf 109 damaged

Pilot Officer Reid's last scramble of the day came at 1450 hours, when No. 46 Squadron patrolled the Hornchurch line at 20,000ft while in the company of

No. 249 Squadron. The wing was successfully vectored onto a dozen–plus Ju 88s flying in vics of three in line astern, which were intercepted at 17,000ft. The bombers were, however, escorted by a very large force of Bf 109s and Bf 110s flying above, at 25,000ft. The combats took place at about 1530 hours.

Flight Lieutenant A.C. Rabagliati (flying P3066) intercepted a Ju 88 which had broken formation and was flying south at 15,000ft. He delivered an astern attack, which resulted in the starboard engine catching fire. Rabagliati noted that two other Hurricanes had attacked the Ju 88 as the crew bailed out.

Flight Sergeant E. Tyrer (flying V6788) confirmed the destruction of the Ju 88 by Flight Lieutenant Rabagliati. He fired at another Ju 88 which was making for home across the Channel off Maidstone and lumps of the aircraft fell away.

Green 2, Pilot Officer Pattullo (flying V6785), attacked a formation of five Ju 88s, singling out a bomber and opening fire with three bursts of up to five seconds at 250 yards, closing to 50 yards. Pattullo's fire was accurate and devastating, and the port engine blew up. Return fire, however, resulted in several hits on his Hurricane, one of which sent Perspex splinters into the pilot's face so that he was unable to confirm the 'kill':

'I sighted bombers over London and attacked a formation of five Ju 88s above, having been separated from the squadron by fighter attacks. The bomber I was attacking was three in from behind the leader. I opened fire at him and closed in my final attack to 50 yards, firing all the time.

'The front engine of this Ju 88 blew up, but at that moment crossfire hit my aircraft in several places. Splintered glass [sic] hit my face so I was forced to dive away so cannot confirm this loss, but I feel sure it cannot have survived. My aircraft was shot about but not severely. The position of my attack [was] south of Chislehurst.'
(signed) Pilot Officer Pattullo.

No. 249 Squadron, who had one pilot killed, made the following claims:

Pilot Officer R.G.A. Barclay (flying V6622)	one Do 17 destroyed, two Do 17s damaged
Pilot Officer A.G. Lewis (flying V6617)	three Bf 109s destroyed, receiving the DFC for the day's combats
Pilot Officer W.H. Millington (flying V6614)	one Ju 88 (shared)
Pilot Officer T.F. Neil (flying V7313)	one Ju 88 (shared)
Sergeant J.M. Bentley-Beard (flying P3615)	one Do 17 destroyed
Sergeant E. Davidson (flying V6534)	one Ju 88 (shared)
Sergeant J.P. Mills (flying P5206)	one Ju 88 (shared)

Pilot Officer J.R.B. Meaker[20] (flying P3834) bailed out following combat, but did not deploy his parachute.

Pilot Officer Reid flew on a wing strength patrol of Dover and Maidstone at 1000 hours on 28 September, during which No. 249 Squadron lost the Hurricane of Pilot Officer A.G. Lewis, V6617 GN-R, to a high-flying Bf 109. No. 46 Squadron made a similar but uneventful patrol on the following afternoon.

Pilot Officer Reid flew on four squadron patrols on 30 September, largely in the company of No. 249 Squadron. During the first of these, made between 0900 and 1010 hours, Nos. 46 and 249 Squadrons were patrolling over RAF Hornchurch when they were vectored south of the Thames estuary. Here, they sighted about twenty Bf 109s and 110s, but were out of position and unable to make an interception.

A second patrol was flown over the Hornchurch Line for the defence of the capital, between 1315 and 1440 hours. No. 46 Squadron was in the company of No. 249 Squadron, which was leading. Pilot Officer Reid (flying V7443) is not believed to have fired his guns during the sortie, although No. 46 Squadron was engaged by Bf 109s at 1330 hours, when Pilot Officer J.D. Crossman's[21] Hurricane, V6748, crashed in flames at Tablehurst Farm, Forest Row, Sussex.

No. 249 Squadron was also in combat, but made no claims.

No. 46 Squadron was airborne again between 1645 and 1810 hours, with orders to patrol RAF Hornchurch at 17,000ft, with No. 249 Squadron leading. Vapour trails were seen, but the aircraft were too far away to be identified.

Meanwhile, No. 46 Squadron flew numerous uneventful patrols over RAF Rochford, RAF Hornchurch and south of the Thames estuary during 1 and 2 October. Two days later, the Hurricanes operated out of their advanced landing ground at RAF Rochford, maintaining a standing patrol over Convoy Bosom between 0934 and 1155 hours. The vessels were picked up just north of Manston and handed over to other squadrons as they reached Southend.

Two uneventful patrols were flown over the Maidstone area during 5 October, while on the following day Reid's CO, Squadron Leader J.R. MacLachlan, was posted to SHQ RAF North Weald, ineffective sick; Squadron Leader A.R. Collins assuming command. MacLachlan had not been one of those squadron commanders who led from the front. According to the Squadron ORB, he flew only three brief operational sorties during the battle and, on one of these, landed five minutes before the rest of his squadron went into combat and only after the controller had given them a vector onto the enemy.

The squadron made a number of patrols in the Rochford area on 7 October. During one of these, Pilot Officer C.F. Ambrose damaged a Bf 109 over the coast at 1615 hours. Protective patrols and convoy escorts continued to occupy the squadron over the following few days. During one of these patrols, flown with No. 249 Squadron on 10 October, they lost Sergeant E.A. Bayley,[22] whose oxygen failed, and who fell unconscious and nose-dived into the ground.

On 13 October, the squadron flew three patrols over the Hornchurch Line at 20,000ft while in the company of No. 249 Squadron. During the second of these, six Bf 109s bounced Green Section, escaping before a counter-attack could be made. During the brief engagement Sergeant Pearce, who had only joined the squadron two days earlier, was wounded in the arm, making a forced-landing at RAF Biggin Hill.

Two days later, at around 1230 hours, the squadron took off from RAF Stapleford to patrol Sevenoaks. Within minutes of take-off the formation lost three aircraft; Green 3 suffered an engine problem, while Blue 3 and Green 2 both returned early with oxygen issues.

At 1255 hours, and while six to eight miles south-east of Hornchurch, Blue 1, Flight Sergeant Williams, who was leading the squadron, reported sighting twenty to thirty Bf 109s milling 10,000ft above them at 25,000ft. Williams (flying V6550) ordered the squadron into a battle-climb ready to position themselves to attack from astern and out of the sun.

Green 1, Pilot Officer Reid, saw tracers entering the cockpit of Blue 2 and hitting Blue 1 with effect. Reid was unable to assist as a Bf 109 appeared 50ft above him and to the left, hoping to bounce him. Reid had just enough time to react, pulling up the nose of his aircraft and firing a two-second burst into the Messerschmitt's cockpit, and peppering the wing section. The Bf 109 turned over emitting grey smoke and span down out of control. The action took place about eight miles south-east of Hornchurch at 1257 hours.

Reid's combat report read:

'E/A were first sighted in open formation about 5,000ft above us while [the] squadron was gaining height. When at 23,500ft, the ground station gave us a vector of 090 degrees, thus putting E/A between the sun and our tails. I was flying Green 1 in line astern behind Blue Section (which was leading the Squadron). Blue 3 had dropped out earlier, so my position was actually Blue 3. I suddenly saw tracer going into Blue 1 and Blue 2 from above and behind. I saw Blue 2 go down smoking and, at the same time, an Me 109 with yellow nose appeared right above me (about 50ft) and slightly to my left. I swung round, pulled my nose up and fired a two-second burst [firing 400 rounds]. I saw my bullets hitting him right across the wing section and cockpit. The Me turned over to the left and emitted grey smoke. He went down in a spin, obviously out of control. I followed him down for 10,000ft, but did not see him crash as clouds were 9/10 at 2-4,000ft. The Me was a sitting shot and I consider that the pilot must have been killed when I fired.

'I took off at 1230 hours from Stapleford and landed at 1325 hours.'
(signed) Pilot Officer Robert Reid.

Pilot Officer P.W. Lefevre (Red 1) witnessed the action and believed he saw the Bf 109 entering the clouds below him at 2-4,000ft, still out of control. However, without following it down through the clouds, it was not possible to see it hit the ground. The combat had taken place in the vicinity of Rochester and the Medway.

Both Red and Yellow Sections broke up as the attack was delivered and were not in a position to engage the enemy, either individually or in formation. As a result of being bounced, Sergeant A.T. Gooderham (flying V6789) was shot down over the Thames estuary. Gooderham bailed out, suffering slight facial burns, a bruised arm and a damaged knee, but was not detained in hospital. His Hurricane crashed at Gravesend, at about 1300 hours.

Another victim of the attack, Pilot Officer P.S. Gunning[23] (flying N2480) was shot down and killed over the Thames estuary; his Hurricane crashed in a chalk pit at Little Thurrock.

Meanwhile, Flight Sergeant E.E. Williams[24] (flying V6550) was also hit, and with fatal results, his Hurricane crashing into the timber depot of W.R. Barton & Sons Ltd, located in Albion Parade, Gravesend.

The Intelligence Officer's report conceding:

'From the evidence submitted by all, the unfortunate and unhappy experience of No. 46 Squadron on this occasion can be principally attributed to attempting to climb and intercept in full view of high flying enemy fighter aircraft overhead.'

During the hit and run attack, two pilots of JG 26's I Gruppe and two from II Gruppe, each claimed a Hurricane as destroyed. Those making claims were Oberleutnant Henrici and Unteroffizier Scheidt; they got their sixth and third aerial victories respectively. Meanwhile, Hauptmann Adolph and Oberleutnant Grawatsch downed their twelfth and second 'kills', with the Geschwader Kommodore, Adolf Galland, claiming his forty-sixth 'kill'.

On 16 October, a security patrol was carried out over Burnham at 20,000ft by a brace of aircraft drawn from Red Section. Meanwhile, on the following day, Sergeant de Cannaert d'Hamale made a wheels-up landing at Parkers Farm, Woodend, Abbess Roding, following the squadron's second uneventful patrol that day. The cause was put down to poor visibility and fuel shortage.

The squadron joined No. 249 Squadron on a wing patrol on 18 October, while on the following day, 'A' Flight patrolled Convoy Agent, which was twenty-five miles east of Bradwell, with 'B' Flight escorting Convoy Arena, ten miles east of Shoeburyness.

Meanwhile, Nos. 46 and 257 Squadrons made a wing patrol of the North Weald line on 20 October, but without making contact with the enemy.

In company with No. 257 Squadron, the squadron patrolled in the vicinity of Hornchurch at 10,000ft on 22 October, when the squadron lost Sergeant J.P. Morrison[25] (flying R4074), who was shot down and killed while in combat over Dungeness at 1650 hours.

Despite the high rate of attrition, No. 46 Squadron had continued to take on the enemy in the skies over southern England, regardless of the often insurmountable odds. Its role in the Battle of Britain was acknowledged by the first of a number of gallantry medals when Flight Lieutenant A.C. Rabagliati was awarded the DFC, *London Gazette,* 22 October 1940:

'Distinguished Flying Cross.
'Flight Lieutenant Alexander Coultate RABAGLIATI (37209).
'This officer has led his flight and squadron in many engagements against the enemy during which he has destroyed five enemy aircraft and damaged others. He has shown magnificent leadership and courage.'

Patrols were carried out throughout the day on 25 October. During the first of these, it was reported that Blue Leader, whilst flying due south in the vicinity of Maidstone, sighted twenty Bf 109s on his starboard, flying at 25,000ft. Although only 1,000ft below, he was unable to make an interception as the enemy took avoiding action. Later, he saw another group of approximately forty Bf 109s over the Biggin Hill area approaching from a northerly direction, but flying too high to intercept. Pilot Officer W.B. Pattullo (flying V6804), was acting as guard to the squadron at 27,000ft and made a beam attack on the Messerschmitts, damaging one, seeing pieces of the wing and fuselage blasted off.

Pilot Officer Pattullo[26] was again acting as rear-guard on a later patrol, when, without warning, his Hurricane crashed into a house near Rochford. Pattullo was taken to Old Church Hospital, Romford, where he died from his injuries the following day. The cause of the crash was never established.

Two routine operations were made in conjunction with No. 17 Squadron during 26 October, the morning patrol being of the Maidstone Line and the afternoon patrol of the Rochford Line.

Taking off from RAF Stapleford at 0920 hours on 27 October, the squadron patrolled with No. 17 Squadron at 15,000ft over North Weald and Maidstone. The wing was vectored onto a reported Do 17, which evaded them in cloud. 'B' Flight's Pilot Officer C.R. Young later sighted two Bf 109s, which he fired at from long range.

Uneventful patrols were carried out over the Thames estuary, Colchester, RAF North Weald and RAF Hornchurch on the 28 October.

Whilst on patrol with No. 257 Squadron in the vicinity of Maidstone on 29 October, a number of Bf 109s were sighted flying above the squadron at 26,000ft. Five Bf 109s came down to make an attack on the Hurricanes, the remainder forming a defensive circle. One Bf 109 was claimed over the Thames estuary by Flight Lieutenant Rabagliati, with Pilot Officer C.F. Ambrose destroying a Bf 109 off Dungeness, damaging a second.

During the same engagement Pilot Officer Reid probably destroyed a Bf 109 over the Maidstone area; while Sergeant H.E. Black[27] was badly wounded in the leg and received facial burns, his Hurricane crashing in Hothfield Park, near Ashford. The combats took place at about 1645 hours. Black, who had earlier flow with Nos. 32 and 257 Squadrons, was wounded and badly burned. He died at Ashford Hospital on 9 November.

Pilot Officer C.F. Ambrose fired a five-second burst at 150 yards, and a second of the same duration at 100 yards:

'I was Red 1 of 46 Squadron. AA fire was seen off the south coast, east of Dungeness. About eight Me 109s [were seen] in formation and all were flying west, away from gunfire. The squadron [was] vectored south-west to intercept, but before reaching the enemy, more Me 109s appeared 2,000ft above, on our starboard beam on the same course. Angel Leader attacked one, and I closed with the second: after a five-second burst, glycol and oil poured from his radiator. He then stalled and the aircraft, apparently out of control, fell into a vertical dive, crashing into the sea.

'Below I then saw two Me 109s in line astern at about 10,000ft. I attacked the rear machine, giving two, five-second bursts, which apparently had little effect. After I had finished firing, both aircraft turned and dived steeply to sea level.

'I claim one Me 109 destroyed and one damaged.'
(signed) Pilot Officer C.F. Ambrose.

Pilot Officer Reid fired a two-second burst at 150 yards:

'The Me 109 circled above us [at 26,000ft] and dived to attack. I was Green 1, immediately behind 'A' Flight and, when the squadron carried out evasive action, I found myself underneath an Me 109. I was turning violently at the time, but pulled my nose up and fired a two-second burst at about 150 yards range, allowing deflection. I immediately stalled my aircraft and could not observe any result of my fire. However, P/O Ambrose, with whom I subsequently joined formation, confirmed having seen one Hurricane firing at an Me 109 and states that the E/A rolled over several times, going down eventually out of control, as far as he could see, in a wide spiral. I therefore claim one Me 109 as a 'probable'. As this action took place in the vicinity of Maidstone, and if the Me 109 in question finally crashed, it will probably be found in the Maidstone district.'
(signed) Pilot Officer Robert Reid.

Four uneventful patrols were carried out by the squadron over Kent and Essex on 30 October. Meanwhile, on the following day, Flight Lieutenant L.M. Gaunce, DFC, was posted from No. 615 Squadron to command the squadron.

The squadron was engaged in three patrols during 1 November, and on two of these encountered the enemy. Pilot Officer Reid (flying V7617) took part in the squadron's first scramble at 0945 hours, when they formed up in the company of Nos. 249 and 257 Squadrons to patrol the Maidstone Line. The patrol passed off without incident.

No. 46 Squadron's next patrol came at 1225 hours. Once airborne, the Hurricanes were vectored onto an enemy formation. At 1330 hours, and while in the vicinity of Hawkinge, Red Leader, Pilot Officer C.F. Ambrose (flying V6918), sighted nine Bf 109s in loose vics of three flying north-west at 32,000ft. One vic dived to attack. Seeing this, Pilot Officer Ambrose led his section in a very steep evasive turn, as a result of which they lost contact with 'B' Flight.

'A' Flight's Pilot Officer K. Mrazek (flying P3429) damaged a Bf 109 during a quarter beam attack from above, but was forced to break away with another Bf 109 on his tail. Meanwhile, 'B' Flight sighted several Bf 109s returning home in the Dover area. Flying Officer F. Austin (flying V7617) fired at long-range, but without any visible result. Sadly, Sergeant d'Hamale28 (flying V7616) failed to return from this patrol. He was shot down and killed while in combat with Bf 109s over Hawkinge. D'Hamale's Hurricane was seen to fall away from the combat, and crashed at Smersole Farm, Swingfield, near Dover. His oxygen line had been shot away, but it is not known if this was the reason for his loss.

Later, at 1520 hours the squadron was patrolling Maidstone in the company of No. 17 Squadron when they were vectored onto an enemy formation approaching the Deal-Dover area. Five enemy aircraft were sighted by Pilot Officer C.R. Young (flying V6916), acting as rear-guard to the squadron at 20,000ft. Young reported this at about 1630 hours, but was not heard. A minute later he spotted three more enemy aircraft, one of which he chased out to sea off Dover at 12,000ft. This aircraft, a Savoia-Marchetti Z 1007 with three engines, was engaged and one engine put out of action. No return fire was experienced from this aircraft while rear fire from the other two aircraft was very inaccurate. During the same operation, Pilot Officer K. Mrazek (flying P3429) damaged a Bf 109 near Hawkinge, the engagement taking place at 1630 hours.

No. 46 Squadron made a patrol over RAF Hornchurch in the company of No. 41 Squadron during the morning of 2 November. On the following day, Flying Officer P.W. Lefevre and Pilot Officer C.F. Ambrose were scrambled and vectored onto a lone Do 17, which they engaged at 8,000ft over Gravesend. Both pilots made four passes. Flying Officer Lefevre made one attack from 300 yards, before engaging from quarter and beam, recording numerous hits on the engine and fuselage. He experienced return fire only during the first two attacks. Pilot Officer Ambrose reported that he saw the bomber dropping its payload of a dozen bombs while he made attacks from the starboard beam and quarter. During his third attack Ambrose closed to ten yards, observing black smoke coming from the starboard engine, which cut out. The Dornier was last seen at 500ft, while still descending, and was claimed as shared. The attacks were timed at 1240 hours.

The Do 17 of VIII./KG 3, which was also hit by flak, crashed at Bexley and the crew were killed (one survived but died the following day). Ambrose had already destroyed two Bf 109s, with a Bf 109 and Bf 110 probably destroyed, and a Do 17 damaged.

Pilot Officer C.F. Ambrose was awarded the DFC, *London Gazette*, 24 December 1940.

No operations were flown between 4-6 November, while at 0905 hours on 7 November, the squadron made an uneventful patrol over Maidstone in the company of No. 249 Squadron. Numerous other patrols were carried out throughout the day and, on one of these, flown between 1130 and 1215 hours, a Bf 110 was damaged by Pilot Officer Reid (flying V7603).

Blue Section was ordered to patrol Chelmsford at 20,000ft. Pilot Officer Reid was leading the section as Blue 2, sighting the enemy about ten miles inland from Harwich, above and to the front. Reid tried to radio a warning, but the set was U/S. His combat report was timed at 1210 hours:

'P/O Reid, Blue 2. I was leading the pair of aircraft as Blue 1 had no R/T. I was vectored eventually 290 degrees and saw [the] E/A above and in front. I climbed to 31,000ft and as [the] E/A turned south-east, I was in position to deliver a beam attack (slightly head-on and above). I opened fire at 200 yards, closing to 10 yards, firing for 3-4 seconds. I saw my fire entering [the] E/A, but observed no result as I had to break away quickly. I first saw [the] E/A ten miles inland from Harwich and intercepted it over Chiswich.'
(signed) Pilot Officer Robert Reid.

This action was reported in one of the local Scottish newspapers. The article carried part of an interview with Reid in which he gave a vivid account of the attack, including an insight as to how cold it was at such a high altitude; evidently Reid's flying boots had frozen to the rudder bar during the combat.

Reid broke away, losing 10,000ft in the process and was therefore unable to resume the combat. Meanwhile, Blue 1, Flight Lieutenant Burnett (flying V6816), climbed up-sun of the enemy, following up Reid's attack, as related by the Squadron Intelligence Officer, Flying Officer Eric D. Syson, who reported:

'[He] carried out a beam attack which ended astern, with a long continuous burst at 350 – 150 yards. [The] E/A did a flick half-roll and appeared to be out of control, and when it came out of the resultant dive it was about 4,000ft lower. Smoke was coming from both engines. He attacked again from astern and above, giving [the] E/A the rest of his ammunition at about 250 yards range. [The] E/A stalled and when Blue 1 had recovered there was no sign of it.

'Both pilots thought the E/A was an Me 110, but operations reported that [the] E/A was a Dornier and had come down in Richmond Park. Later, operations said the E/A was an Me 110.

'It was only intended to claim a damaged. But naturally the pilots did not object to having a "Destroyed" thrust upon them, and celebrated accordingly. [The] E/A is understood to have been last seen over Ashford at 20,000ft with both engines smoking.'

Pilot Officer Reid (flying V7603) later flew on an uneventful squadron patrol between 1515 and 1625 hours – targets, however, were becoming thinner on the ground as winter drew in.

Several patrols were carried out on 8 November. During one of these, Flight Lieutenant Farley[29] (flying V6932) was bounced by Bf 109s and shot down, but bailed out, breaking his leg on landing. His Hurricane crashed and burned out. Meanwhile, Pilot Officer Reid (flying V7603) flew on an operation between 1150 and 1330 hours, later joining a Hornchurch patrol between 1625 and 1735 hours. This was to be Reid's last operational flight with No. 46 Squadron and saw Flight Lieutenant A.C. Rabagliati (flying V7610) destroy a Bf 109 off Dover at about 1720 hours.

At about the same time No. 46 Squadron bounced a 'mass of aeroplanes', shooting down the leader, which turned out to be No. 19 Squadron's CO. He was uninjured.

This misidentification, by experienced pilots, demonstrates how mistakes happened in the heat of battle. Fortunately on this occasion there were no fatalities

With his tour of operations completed, and with two destroyed Bf 109s, one probable and two damaged under his belt, Reid had given a good account of himself and was due for a 'rest'. He was posted to the Central Flying School, Upavon, on 11 November, where he undertook a Flying Instructor's course, 'qualifying to instruct on intermediate and elementary training type aircraft'. On 15 December, following a day in limbo, Reid was transferred to No. 11 Elementary Flying Training School, Perth.

Established in June 1936 as No. 11 Elementary & Reserve Flying Training School (E&RFTS), the school's courses were run under contract to the Air Ministry by Airwork Limited. On the outbreak of war, however, there was no longer a Reserve and it was renamed Elementary Flying Training School (EFTS), the civilian instructors being mobilized. Pilot Officer Reid's role was to help put the pilots under training through their twenty-hour *ab initio* flying training on Tiger Moths. The work would be tiring and dangerous, as training schools inevitably lost both pilots and instructors due to air accidents.

On 23 June 1941, Reid joined No. 17 Group's No. 2 Operational Training Unit (OTU), Catfoss, Yorkshire, for flying duties. Here, Reid passed on his combat knowledge to would-be fighter pilots, teaching them the tricks he and his comrades had learned during the Battle of Britain. During his time at the unit he attended No. 14 Course at Central Gunnery School between 14 October and 19 November 1942.

Reid was involved in an air accident on or about 3 May 1943, possibly as a result of a training incident. His service record noting that he was granted fourteen days sick leave, suffering from, 'shock, bruises and a doubtful fractured rib'.

Flight Lieutenant Reid transferred to Coastal Command on 25 June 1943, being posted to No. 236 Squadron, flying Beaufighters. The squadron formed a part of No. 16 Group's Strike Wing, flying anti-shipping strikes out of RAF North Coates. The posting was short-lived, however, and Reid joined the staff of the Central Gunnery School, No. 25 Group, on 5 July 1943, acting as Fighter Instructor. The school was at this time commanded by Group Captain Charles Eric St John Beamish.

Reid's next posting came on 25 March 1944, when he was sent as an instructor to No. 132 OTU, East Fortune, East Lothian; the unit largely operating twin-engine Beaufighters and Beauforts.

Reid attended a brief refreshers course before joining No. 1 FU, Melton Mowbray on 19 August 1944; a further aircraft ferrying post commenced on 11 October, only lasting a week, before he was sent to No. 13 OTU, Bicester, this time in preparation for a much awaited return to air operations. On 8 November 1944, Flight Lieutenant Reid was posted to No. 235 Squadron, flying Mosquito Mark IVs.

No. 235 Squadron had been operating out of Banff as a part of No. 19 Group since September 1943, the following year becoming a part of No. 18 Group, Coastal Command, under the leadership of Wing Commander Max Aitken, DSO, DFC. Also flying out of the airfield and operating Mosquito IVs was No. 248 Squadron, along with No. 333 Squadron's 'P' Flight,[30] while No. 144 Squadron flew operations on Beaufighters. Collectively known as the Banff Strike Wing, their role was to fly low-level armed Rover patrols along the southern Norway convoy routes, targeting U-boats and enemy shipping. The missions were highly dangerous, as the targets were heavily defended by flak-ships and Luftwaffe units.

The Banff Strike Wing was in the process of change and, by 13 November, No. 143 Squadron had arrived, replacing No. 144 Squadron in the same role. During the day a mixed Banff Strike Wing formation attacked enemy shipping located in Rekefjord, sinking a German E-boat, an ASR launch and damaging the merchant vessel *Rosenburg*.

The following day, 14 November, saw the wing in Songnefjord, where the trawler *Sardinien* was sunk, while the merchantman *Gula* was also hit.

On 5 December, the Banff Wing saw further successes when they attacked shipping in Nordgulenfjord, damaging the *Ostland*, *Tucuman*, *Magdelena* and *Helene Russ*. During the operation the wing came under heavy fire from flak batteries. No. 143 Squadron's Mosquito 'P' was shot down and forced to ditch, while No. 248 Squadron's Mosquito 'G' was already on fire before it attacked a heavily armed tug. Such was the tenacity of the wing's aircrew that they pressed on regardless. Almost inevitably, the aircraft received further hits and was lost, along with Flight Lieutenant L.N. Collins[31] and Flying Officer R.H. Hurn.[32]

Gossen airfield was targeted by the Banff Strike Wing on 7 December, with the loss of two of No. 248 Squadron's Mosquitoes and their crew of Flying Officer W.N. Cosman,[33] Flying Officer L.M. Freedman,[34] Flying Officer K.C. Wing[35] and Pilot Officer V.R. Shield, DFC.[36] The wing returned to the same target on 12 December, with attacks made on enemy shipping found in Eidfjord, where the merchant vessel *Wartheland* was sunk and the *Molla* damaged.

At 1221 hours, on 13 December, Wing Commander R.A. Atkinson,[37] led a formation of eighteen Mosquitoes from Nos. 143, 235 and 248 Squadrons, escorted by six Mustangs of No. 315 Squadron and an ASR Warwick from No. 279 Squadron. The operation targeted a German convoy in Eidfjord, with the attacks being launched at about 1510 hours.

Wing Commander Atkinson (flying LA – R) made the first pass, flying at mast level as he prepared to fire his rockets at the D/S *Falkenfels*. Both shore batteries and flak-ships opened fire on the lead aircraft, blowing its starboard wing off; the Mosquito spiraled in close to its target. Neither Wing Commander Atkinson nor Flying Officer Upton[38] survived.

With the death of Wing Commander Atkinson in such dramatic circumstances, the wing had lost not only a supreme tactician, but also an exceptionally brave pilot. His loss must have had an effect on every man under his command; but the heat of the battle there was no time to dwell on their loss, and the squadron pressed on with the attack. The remainder of the formation closed in and fired off their rockets, and raked the vessel with cannon and machine-gun fire. The D/S *Falkenfels* was left smoking.

With the death of their CO, former flight commander, Squadron Leader Norman 'Jacko' Jackson-Smith, DFC, was temporarily given command of the squadron, to be replaced by Wing Commander Junior Simmonds.

Taking off at 1222 hours on 16 December, No. 248 Squadron's CO, Wing Commander G.D. 'Bill' Sise, led six of No. 235 Squadron's Mosquitoes in an attack against the *Ferndale* and *Parat,* both of which elements of the wing had damaged earlier that day. The raid had led to the loss of No. 248 Squadron's Flight Lieutenant J. Kennedy[39] and Flying Officer F.W. Rolls.[40] Flying Officer K.C. Beruldsen's[41] Mosquito LA –S was hit and crashed into a neighbouring hill, killing Beruldsen and his navigator, Pilot Officer T.D.S. Rabbitts.[42]

Meanwhile, No. 235 Squadron lost Flying Officer E.J. Fletcher[43] and Flying Officer A.J. Watson[44] (flying LA –G) on 26 December during an attack on the D/S *Tenerife* and *Cygnus.* A dozen Mosquitoes took off at noon, accompanied by an ASR Warwick, targeting the merchantmen sighted in Leirvik harbour. Squadron Leader Jackson-Smith led the attack, during which both vessels were damaged by rockets.

The Mosquito of Flight Lieutenant 'Bill' Clayton-Graham was hit by flak before being attacked by enemy fighters; he used all of his skill to shake off the enemy and brought his aircraft back to base on one engine. Pilot Officer Fletcher's Mosquito was damaged by the Bf 109 flown by Feldwebel Heinz Halstrick during the same operation. Meanwhile, Flying Officer Smith was attacked by a pair of Bf 109s which he successfully fended off. A second attack led to one Bf 109 being destroyed following a ten-minute combat.

In a separate engagement, the Mosquito of 'Wally' Webster was attacked by six Fw 190s, one of which managed to register hits before Webster could escape.

Warrant Officer H.A. Corbin, CGM, encountered heavy flak, resulting in the loss of power in one engine; despite this damage he was able to outpace the enemy fighters. Corbin's observer, Sergeant Maurice Webb, was awarded the DFM. Both men later evaded capture.

In a cruel twist of fate, No. 235 Squadron lost Flying Officer D.B. Douglas[45] and his passenger, LAC G.P. Robbins[46] (flying HR159), on 9 January 1945, as a result of a flying accident. At 1530 hours, they took off on a test flight. Minutes later the Mosquito was seen to enter a slow barrel roll, stalling out while at 1,000ft.

Worse was to come, when, on 15 January, the Banff squadrons suffered further casualties with the loss of five attacking aircraft during an attack on the *Claus Rickmers,* at Leirvik, No. 235 Squadron losing one of only two Mosquitoes engaged. The mission was flown in two waves, a dozen Mosquitoes of No. 143 Squadron led by Wing Commander Maurice, and two each from Nos. 235 and 248 Squadrons led by Wing Commander Junior Simmonds. The formation was joined by an ASR Warwick, with the usual pair of aircraft of No. 333 Squadron acting as spotters on each flank of the formation.

The air battle began at about 1130 hours, when No. 143 Squadron lost their CO, Wing Commander J.M. Guedj, DSO, DFC, along with his navigator, Flight Lieutenant E. Langley,[47] flying Mosquito 'K'. Also killed were the crew of Mosquito 'D', Flight Sergeant G.A.M. Moncrieff[48] and Flight Sergeant C. Cash,[49] along with the crew of Mosquito 'V', Lieutenant F.E. Alexandre, USAAF[50] and Pilot Officer J.A. McMullin.[51]

During the same operation, No. 333 Squadron lost the Mosquito (HP984 KK-R) flown by Kvm. Kåre Oscar Sjølie and C/M [M] Ingvar Sigurd Gausland, the latter was taken as PoW.

The Mosquito piloted by No. 235 Squadron's Flight Sergeant F. 'Frank' Chew[52] (flying LA –A) was hit in one engine by flak. Flight Sergeant Chew wrestled with the controls and tried to make base, shepherded by other Mosquitoes. With the loss of altitude and airspeed, Chew was forced to ditch near Slåtterøy, but was killed, his observer, Flight Sergeant S.W. Couttie, being taken as a PoW.

No. 236 Squadron's second Mosquito Mk XVIII (Tsetses rocket-firing Mosquito), was piloted by Flying Officer R. Peacock, with his navigator, Flying Officer Field. During the air battle that raged over Leirvik, Peacock singled out an Fw 190A-3 which he spotted on the tail of another Mosquito.

Peacock managed to get the enemy fighter into his sights and got off three shells from his 57mm Molins gun, hitting the enemy aircraft's engine, which began emitting smoke. A few seconds later the Focke-Wulf fell out of the sky and crashed near Austevoll. The pilot was pulled from the wreckage, but died in hospital a few days later.

The Banff Strike Wing was in action again on 25 January, when their Mosquitoes attacked shipping in Eidfjord, sinking the *Ilse Fritzen* and damaging the *Bjergfin*. Two of No. 248 Squadron's Mosquitoes were lost while peeling off to land. Flight Lieutenant D.S.L. Crimp[53] and Flying Officer J. Bird[54] were both killed. The squadron's CO, Squadron Leader H.H.K. Gunnis and his navigator, Warrant Officer A. Mudd, were more fortunate and were able to land their damaged aircraft without injury.

In recognition of his tactical awareness, combined with his outstanding courage in executing low-level attacks, Reid was given command of No. 235 Squadron on 1 February 1945, but his time as CO was sadly to be short-lived.

A wing mission was flown on 12 February, attacking the *Sivas*, which had run aground off Askvoid.

Meanwhile, No. 235 Squadron flew a solo operation on 21 February, when five Mosquitoes took off to target shipping in Lervik. The squadron damaged the *Ibis* and *Gula*, sinking the merchant vessel *Austri*. Between operations, Squadron Leader Reid led training exercises with the new wing-mounted rocket projectiles, which were by then fitted to nearly all of the squadron's Mosquitos (this move negated the need for the special Tsetses aircraft.)

On 7 March, forty of the Banff Strike Wing's Mosquitoes took part in a large-scale attack on self-propelled barges in the Kattegat area. The force was escorted by a dozen P51 Mustangs and two of No. 279 (ASR) Squadron's Warwicks. The attack was made with rockets and led to the destruction of four barges, along with the flak-ship *Innsbruck*. The victories were tempered by the loss of two of No. 248 Squadron's Mosquitoes; the aircraft of Flight Lieutenant Young[55] and his observer, Flight Lieutenant Goodes,[56] which collided with the aircraft of Flight Lieutenant Parkinson as they pulled out of their attack. Flight Lieutenant Harry Parkinson and his observer, Flight Lieutenant Ken Jackson, survived the crash.

During the same operation, No. 235 Squadron lost Flying Officer S.C. Hawkins[57] and Flying Officer E. Stubbs[58] (flying LA- O).

On 17 March, an early morning reconnaissance over Aalesund, a major port for German shipping, revealed a large number of merchant vessels in the harbour.

A large strike force was ordered and, in the early afternoon, the heavily-laden Mosquitoes took to the air. The force comprised of eleven aircraft from No. 235 Squadron, commanded by Squadron Leader Robbie Reid, who flew with his regular navigator, Flying Officer Alex Turner, nine aircraft from No. 143 Squadron, eleven from No. 248 Squadron and two outriders from No. 333 Squadron.

The Mosquitoes took off at about 1345 hours, escorted by a dozen Mustangs. The enemy would have been anticipating a further raid and so the Mosquitoes flew at sea level, making their approach from a little to the south of Alesund, nearing Sula at 1552 hours.

With the earlier reconnaissance having put the German defences on alert, No. 248 Squadron's Wing Commander Roy Orrock made landfall south of Aalesund and circled inland, climbing over the mountains behind the port before swinging down for the attack, which began at 1557 hours. Return fire from the German coastal defences was heavy, and almost immediately Wing Commander R. Orrock's Mosquito (DM-K) was hit by flak and forced to ditch. He was taken PoW, along with his navigator, Flying Officer Wilding.

Undaunted, Squadron Leader Reid quickly assessed the situation ' …there were the merchantmen ahead of us, offering more potential targets than we had dared to hope for.' He led his Mosquitoes into the attack away from the worst of the flak units, firing off his rockets to good effect, strafing his target with cannon fire before pulling away.

No. 235 Squadron's 'A' Flight Commander, Squadron Leader Bill Clayton-Graham, DFC, added: 'Two ships were lying in the inner harbour and five more were just outside as we came in over the hills.'

Squadron Leader Reid remarked: 'There was certainly plenty of flak meeting us; but everyone seemed to be scoring hits with rockets.'

The pilot's aim was good and one vessel received thirty-two separate hits with rockets, fourteen below the waterline, then another vessel received thirty-seven rocket strikes, with only six above the waterline.

Attacking at mast height the Mosquitoes had raked the merchant vessels with fire. Five were sent to the bottom of the fjord. Among the vessels destroyed were the *Iris* and the *Remage*, while the *Stanja* and *Erna* were both badly damaged, along with the *Log,* whose flak batteries were silenced.

The enemy flak was intense and accurate. No. 143 Squadron's 'F' for Freddie was lost, along with its crew of Flying Officer W.J. Ceybird[59] and Flight Lieutenant N. Harwood.[60]

Back at Banff the crews took stock of the situation. Although the war in Europe was drawing to an end and the Luftwaffe's resistance was weakening, the raids on heavily defended shipping in the Norwegian Fjords remained vital in disrupting supplies. The operations had to continue if Germany was to be defeated. Meanwhile, Reid continued the squadron's training programme using the new rail-launched rockets on 18 March.

At 1410 hours on 20 March, Squadron Leader Reid and his navigator, Flying Officer Turner (flying LA-D) took off on a Ranger Patrol. However, due to one of their drop tanks not feeding fuel, Reid was forced to hand over command and return early.

The training continued on the 22 March. The squadron was, however, back on operations on 23 March. At 1523 hours, Reid (flying LA-W) took off at the head of a dozen Mosquitoes of No. 235 Squadron, together with aircraft from Nos. 143 and 248 Squadrons. Commanded by Wing Commander Foxley-Norris, a total of forty-six Mosquitos and ten Mustangs took part in the sweep.[61]

At 1650 hours, Reid peeled No. 235 Squadron away from the formation, making an approach on Vaeroya, guided by their Norwegian outrider of No. 333 Squadron.

Commanded by Squadron Leader Smith (flying DM-F), No. 248 squadron approached shipping near Måloy, but their positioning was poor and they were unable to press home an attack.

Meanwhile, at 1730 hours, Foxley-Norris led fifteen of No. 143 Squadron's Mosquitoes against the *Lysaker*, berthed at Sandshamm, recording thirty-two hits, fifteen below the waterline. No. 143 Squadron's Pilot Officer McCall[62] (flying NE-R), was hit by shore batteries, and his aircraft was seen to catch fire before crashing into the sea. He was lost along with his navigator, Warrant Officer Etchells.[63] Another of the squadron's Mosquitoes (NE-W) was hit in the starboard engine, and Flight Lieutenant Lowe and Flying Officer Ray Hannaford ditched, and were taken PoW, while two more aircraft limped back on one engine.

At about 1720 hours, Squadron Leader Robert Reid (flying LA-W) and his navigator, Flying Officer Turner, led twelve of No. 235 Squadron's Mosquitoes against the munitions ship *Rotenfels*, docked at the southern end of Dalsfjord, near Steinsvik. Reid adopted similar tactics to the Aalesund raid of the 17 March, bringing his Mosquitoes in over the mountains behind the fjord, giving the enemy gunners as little time as possible to react. Despite this, the flak was reported as exceptionally heavy, but Squadron Leader Reid had no hesitation in taking his squadron in a shallow dive down to mast height, leading them in for the attack.

As Squadron Leader Reid lined up ready to fire off his rockets, his Mosquito received a direct hit and immediately plunged into the icy sea about fifty yards short of his target. The aircraft disintegrated on impact, leaving only a cloud of smoke and a surface scatter of debris.

The remainder of the attack screamed over the crash site, launching their rockets into the *Rotenfels*, killing or wounding many of the crew, and setting the vessel on fire, badly damaging the bridge. 'A' Flight Commander, Squadron Leader Clayton-Graham, took over command of the remnants of the squadron and brought them home, escorted by two outriders and ten Mustangs.

No trace of Squadron Leader Reid was ever found, although the body of his navigator was pulled from the water and buried near Trondheim.

In 1950, a memorial commemorating the men's sacrifice was dedicated in the small village of Steinsvik, adjacent to where the *Rotenfels* was attacked by Squadron Leader R. Reid[64] and Flying Officer A.D. Turner.[65] An annual ceremony takes place on the Norwegian day of independence (17 May), when the brave Mosquito crew are remembered. Prominent amongst those gathered are representatives of Reid's family.

Pilots serving with No. 46 Squadron during the Battle of Britain:

Squadron Leader James Robert MacLachlan	CO from June to 6 October
Squadron Leader Alan Duncan Murray	DFC 28.3.41 *(A)*
Flight Lieutenant Walter Ronald Farley	DFC 7.3.41 *(B)*, KIA 21.4.42 as wing commander with No. 138 Squadron
Flight Lieutenant L.M. Gaunce, DFC *(C)*	CO from 31 October 1940
Flight Lieutenant Alexander Coultate Ragagliati, DFC	Bar to the DFC 28.10.41 *(D)*, KIA 6.7.43
Flying Officer Frederick Austin	KIA 17.3.41
Flying Officer Norman Whitmore Burnett	KIA 6.6.41 Malta
Flying Officer Peter William Lefevre	DFC 9.12.41 *(E)*, KIA 6.2.44
Flying Officer Roy Andrew McGowan	
Flying Officer Hugh Morgan-Gray	KIA 22.2.41
Flying Officer Richard Pryer Plummer	PoW 14.9.40
Sub-Lieutenant Jack Conway Carpenter, FAA	KIA 8.9.40
Pilot Officer Charles Francis Ambrose, DFC *(F)*	AFC 29.10.48, CBE 8.6.68
Pilot Officer John Cyril Lindsay Dyson Bailey	KIA 2.9.40
Pilot Officer Robert Hugh Barber	AFC 1.1.43
Pilot Officer Aston Maurice Cooper-Key	KIA 24.7.40
Pilot Officer John Dallas Crossman	KIA 30.9.40
Pilot Officer Peter Stackhouse Gunning	KIA 15.10.40
Pilot Officer Hedley	
Pilot Officer Allan Everitt Johnson	reformed and led No. 243 Squadron 1.6.42-February 1943, KIA 4.7.43

Pilot Officer Percival Graham Leggett

Pilot Officer Peter Reginald McGregor, RAFVR

Pilot Officer Karl Mrazek   DFC 23.6.42 *(G)*, DSO
                                                            18.12.42 *(G)*

Pilot Officer William Blair Pattullo   PoW 26.10.40

Pilot Officer Robert Reid   KIA 23.3.45

Pilot Officer Eugene George Achilles Seghers   C de G (Belgium) 27.7.41 *(H)*,
                                                            DFC 13.2.43 *(I)*

Pilot Officer Franciszek Surma, VM   KW and Bar 10.9.41, Second
                                                            Bar to KW 30.10.41, KIA
                                                            8.11.41

Pilot Officer Cecil Reginald Young   KIA 5.12.40

Flight Sergeant Eric Edward Williams   KIA 15.10.40

Sergeant Stanley Andrew   KIA 8.9.40

Sergeant Herbert Ernest Black, RAFVR   KIA 9.11.40

Sergeant Ernest Bloor   Died, air accident 27.8.40
                                                            while on secondment with
                                                            No. 1 Squadron

Sergeant Roger Emile de Cannaert d'Hamale   KIA 1.11.40

Sergeant Richard Llewellyn Earp

Sergeant Gerald Henry Edworthy   KIA 3.9.40

Sergeant Albert Thomas Gooderham   KIA 2.11.42 with No. 615
                                                            Squadron

Sergeant Charles Alexander Lyall Hurry   AFC 1.1.46

Sergeant George William Jefferys, RAFVR   KIA 18.9.40

Sergeant Joseph Pearson Morrison   KIA 22.10.40

Sergeant William Albert Peacock   KIA 8.9.40

Sergeant Raymond Frederick Sellers, RAFVR   AFC 8.6.44

Sergeant Edward Tyrer   Died, 1.4.1946

Many of the pilots earned gallantry awards for combat which are not mentioned in the main text. Details, where traced, are included below:

(A) Squadron Leader A.D. Murray was awarded the DFC, *London Gazette*, 28 March 1941:

'Distinguished Flying Cross.
'Squadron Leader Alan Duncan MURRAY (34168), No. 73 Squadron.'

(B) Flight Lieutenant Walter Ronald Farley was awarded the DFC, *London Gazette*, 7 March 1941:

'Distinguished Flying Cross.
'Squadron Leader Walter Ronald FARLEY (29089), No. 419 Flight.'

(C) Flight Lieutenant L.M. Gaunce was awarded the DFC, *London Gazette*, 23 August 1940:

'Awarded the Distinguished Flying Cross.
'Acting Flight Lieutenant Lionel Manley GAUNCE (37632)
'This flight commander has displayed excellent coolness and leadership since the return of the squadron to England. In July 1940, his flight took part in resisting an enemy attack on Dover, when three of our aircraft were attacked by forty Junkers 87s. At least two of the enemy aircraft were shot down. Flight Lieutenant Gaunce has shot down three enemy aircraft since returning to England.'

(D) Flight Lieutenant Alexander Coultate Rabagliati was awarded a Bar to his DFC, *London Gazette*, 28 October 1942:

'Bar to the Distinguished Flying Cross.
'Squadron Leader Alexander Coultate RABAGLIATI, DFC (37209), Reserve of Air Force Officers, No. 46 Squadron.'

(E) Acting Squadron Leader Peter William Lefevre was awarded the DFC, *London Gazette*, 9 December 1941:

'Acting Squadron Leader Peter William LEFEVRE (40719), No. 126 Squadron.
'This officer has shown the utmost devotion to duty over a long period of operational flying, in which he has destroyed several enemy aircraft. He carried out over 250 hours flying on convoy patrols over the North Sea as well as participating in other operational missions. Squadron Leader Lefevre has

participated in operations in the Middle East and in July 1941 he attacked an Italian E-boat which was forced to surrender.'

(F) Pilot Officer Charles Francis Ambrose was awarded the DFC, *London Gazette*, 28 March 1941:

'Pilot Officer Charles Francis AMBROSE (42583), No. 46 Squadron.
This officer has taken part in 100 operational missions during which he has destroyed at least two enemy aircraft and damaged several others. He has displayed outstanding courage and a fine fighting spirit throughout.'

(G) Wing Commander K. Mrazek was Wing Commander (Flying) Exeter (Czech) Wing, leading them on the Dieppe Raid in August 1942. He was awarded the DFC, *London Gazette*, 23 June 1942, to which was added the DSO, *London Gazette*, 18 December 1942. He later became Group Captain.

(H) Pilot Officer E.G.A. Seghers was awarded Croix de Guerre (Belgium), *London Gazette*, 27 July 1941.

(I) Pilot Officer E.G.A. Seghers was awarded the DFC, *London Gazette*, 13 February 1943, while serving with No. 91 Squadron:

'Distinguished Flying Cross.
'Pilot Officer Eugene George Achilles Seghers (82162), RAF.'

Pilot Officer Franciszek Surma (KW and Bar 10.9.41, Second Bar 30.10.41) served with Nos. 151, 257 and 607 Squadrons during the Battle of Britain. He arrived at No. 46 Squadron on 18 October, but was posted away three days later.

Author's note:
Pilot Officer Hedley arrived on 18 October 'for flying duties'. Although the squadron was still flying operationally in No. 11 Group, Hedley's name does not appear in the ORB's Form 451's (Detail of Work Carried Out). Whether he flew operationally during the battle can only be proven by a study of his original logbook. He is not listed in Men of the Battle of Britain.

Pilots and aircrew flying alongside Robert Reid with No. 235 Squadron included:

Wing Commander the Honourable J.W.M. Aitken, DSO *(C)*, DFC *(A)*, AEA *(D)*, MC (Czech) *(B)*, RAFVR — Wing Leader, Knighted 1965

Wing Commander Richard Ashley Atkinson, DSO *(F)*, DFC *(E)* and Bar *(G)* — KIA 13.12.44

Squadron Leader Barnes

Squadron Leader John R. Barry

Squadron Leader Norman Jackson-Smith, DFC *(H)*

Acting Squadron Leader William Farquhar Clayton-Graham, RAFVR — DFC 29.5.45 *(I)*

Flight Lieutenant T. Armstrong, DFC *(J)*

Flight Lieutenant Donald Douglas, RCAF — KIA 9.1.45

Flight Lieutenant Tom Flowers — KIA 23.3.45

Flight Lieutenant C. Hardy

Flight Lieutenant Ken Jackson

Flight Lieutenant A. Jacques, DFC *(K)* — Bar to DFC 20.3.45 *(L)*

Flight Lieutenant W. Knowles, DFC *(M)* — KIA 30.3.45

Flight Lieutenant Alfie Lloyd

Flight Lieutenant Geoffrey Richard Mayhew, DFC *(N)*

Flight Lieutenant Harry Parkinson

Flight Lieutenant David Pitkeathy

Flight Lieutenant A.J.C. Proctor

Flight Lieutenant Basil H. Quelch, DFC *(O)*

Flight Lieutenant Noell Russell, DFC *(P)* — Bar to the DFC 2.3.45 *(Q)*

Flight Lieutenant James Davies Taylor, DFC *(R)* — KIA with No. 84 Squadron 8.12.45

Flight Lieutenant J.W.D. Thomas

Flight Lieutenant Douglas Keith Thorburn, DFC *(S)* — KIA 4.5.45

Flight Lieutenant Royce Sydney Turner — DFC 29.5.45 *(T)*

Flight Lieutenant Joseph R. Williams — KIA 23.3.45

Flying Officer Burkett Barber

Flying Officer Joe Barnett

Flying Officer Kenneth Cupples Beruldsen, RAAF — KIA 16.12.44

Flying Officer Douglas Banbury Douglas, RCAF — KIA 9.1.45

Flying Officer S.W. Farrow

Flying Officer Ernest James Fletcher, RAFVR ..... KIA 26.12.44
Flying Officer 'Syd' Gordon
Flying Officer R. Harrington
Flying Officer Sydney Charles Hawkins, RAFVR ..... KIA 7.3.45
Flying Officer Harry Hollinson, DFC *(U)*
Flying Officer J.F. Lettington
Flying Officer A. Lloyd
Flying Officer W. Moffatt, DFC *(V)*
Flying Officer 'Pete' Pennie, DFM *(W)* ..... Queen's Commendation 10.7.54

Flying Officer Smith
Flying Officer Eric Stubbs, RAFVR ..... KIA 7.3.45
Flying Officer Alexander Douglas Turner, RAFVR ..... KIA 23.3.45
Flying Officer Valentine Charles Upton, RAFVR ..... KIA 13.12.44
Flying Officer Alfred James Watson, RAFVR ..... KIA 26.12.44
Flying Officer Ken 'Ginger' Webster
Pilot Officer Ray Harrington
Pilot Officer Harry Hosier
Pilot Officer Tom Damas Sellers Rabbitts, RAFVR ..... KIA 16.12.44
Pilot Officer Eugene George Achilles Seghers, DFC, C de G (Belgium)
Warrant Officer C.A. Cogswell
Warrant Officer Harold Arthur Corbin, CGM *(X)*
Warrant Officer L.W.R. Crocker
Warrant Officer N.M.M. Martin ..... KIA 19.10.44
Warrant Officer Ian Ramsey ..... PoW 19.10.44
Warrant Officer Alfred Fuggett Shimmin, DFC *(Y)*
Warrant Officer E.H. Wilkinson
Flight Sergeant E.C. Brown
Flight Sergeant F. 'Frank' Chew ..... KIA 15.1.45
Flight Sergeant S.W. 'Jock' Couttie ..... PoW 15.1.45
Flight Sergeant Griffith Hodgson
Flight Sergeant Lawrence Thomas ..... KIA 30.3.45
Flight Sergeant W. 'Bert' Winwood
Sergeant Maurice Webb, DFM *(Z)*
Unknown rank Geoff Hinde
Unknown rank 'Wally' Webster

Many of the pilots and aircrew earned gallantry awards for combat which are not mentioned in the main text. Details, where traced, are included below:

(A) Wing Commander John William Maxwell 'Max' Aitken (later Sir John William Maxwell Aitken, 2nd Baronet, DSO, DFC, and formerly 2nd Baron Beaverbrook) was, as a squadron leader, awarded the DFC, *London Gazette*, 9 July 1940:

> 'Air Ministry,
> 9 July 1940.
> ROYAL AIR FORCE.
> 'The KING has been graciously pleased to approve the undermentioned awards in recognition of gallantry displayed in flying operations against the enemy:
> 'Awarded the Distinguished Flying Cross.
> 'Squadron Leader The Honourable Maxwell AITKEN (90128), Auxiliary Air Force.
> 'In May 1940, whilst leading a section of aircraft on patrol over Brussels, this officer attacked one of twelve Heinkel 111s which was finally seen to be losing height with one of its wings on fire, with black smoke pouring from the other. The next day, when leading his section on another patrol, a large number of Heinkel 111 and Junkers 87 aircraft, escorted by Messerschmitt 109s, were sighted. Squadron Leader Aitken attacked, and succeeded in destroying one Heinkel and one Junkers aircraft. During a night in June 1940, in difficult circumstances, he destroyed yet another enemy aircraft. He has displayed great dash and gallantry.'

(B) Wing Commander J.W.M. 'Max' Aitken was awarded the Czech Military Cross, *London Gazette*, 11 August 1942.

(C) Wing Commander J.W.M. 'Max' Aitken was subsequently awarded the DSO, *London Gazette*, 14 August 1942:

> 'The Distinguished Service Order.
> 'Acting Wing Commander The Honourable Maxwell AITKEN, DFC (90128), Auxiliary Air Force, No. 68 Squadron.
> 'A brilliant pilot and a gallant leader, this officer has set a most inspiring example. By his exceptional skill and unswerving devotion to duty, he has contributed largely to the high standard of operational efficiency of his squadron and to the successes it has achieved. One night in July 1942, the squadron destroyed five hostile aircraft, two of which were destroyed by Wing Commander Aitken himself. His total victories number twelve.'

(D) Wing Commander J.W.M. 'Max' Aitken was awarded the Air Efficiency Award on 1 January 1943.

(E) As a flight lieutenant, Atkinson had been awarded the DFC, *London Gazette*, 24 March 1943:

'Flight Lieutenant Richard Ashley ATKINSON (70030), Reserve of Air Force Officers, No. 205 Squadron.

'This officer has carried out many long-distance reconnaissance sorties and, on several occasions, he has successfully beaten off attacking enemy aircraft. One morning in December 1941, Flight Lieutenant Atkinson's flying boat was attacked by enemy aircraft when 300 miles NE of Singapore. The enemy were immediately engaged, but after a fifteen minute combat the flying boat's petrol tank was hit and exploded; the aircraft caught fire and was forced to alight on the sea. The crew, of which two were wounded, were all suffering from burns. They were unable to launch the dinghy and had to remain in the sea for six and a half hours before being rescued by a Dutch submarine. Throughout, Flight Lieutenant Atkinson set an excellent example by his great steadiness and courage.'

(F) Squadron Leader R.A. Atkinson was awarded the DSO, *London Gazette*, 20 April 1943:

'Air Ministry 23 April 1943.

'The KING has been graciously pleased to approve the following awards in recognition of gallantry displayed in flying operations against the Japanese:

'Distinguished Service Order.

'Squadron Leader Richard Ashley ATKINSON, DFC (70030), Royal Air Force.'

(G) Wing Commander R.A. Atkinson was awarded a Bar to the DFC, *London Gazette*, 16 January 1945:

'Bar to Distinguished Flying Cross.

'Acting Wing Commander Richard Ashley ATKINSON, DSO, DFC (70030), RAFO, No. 235 Squadron.

'Since being awarded the Distinguished Service Order, Wing Commander Atkinson has participated in a very large number of sorties. In September 1944, this officer led an attack on two merchant ships, both of which were sunk. In October 1944, Wing Commander Atkinson led a formation of aircraft in an attack on a large barge, a tug and two escort vessels. In spite of intense anti-aircraft fire, the attack was pressed home with great determination. The two escort vessels were set on fire and the tug was seriously damaged. On yet another occasion this officer led a formation of aircraft in an attack on two small ships, both of which were sunk. By his gallant leadership and great tactical ability, Wing Commander Atkinson played a prominent part in the successes obtained.'

(H) Flying Officer N.H.J. Smith was awarded the DFC, *London Gazette*, 27 May 1941:

'Distinguished Flying Cross.
'Flying Officer Norman Henry Jackson SMITH (42270), No. 235 Squadron.'

(I) Flight Lieutenant W.F. Clayton-Graham was awarded the DFC, *London Gazette*, 29 May 1945:

'Distinguished Flying Cross.
'Acting Squadron Leader William Farquhar CLAYTON-GRAHAM (64895), RAFVR, No. 235 Squadron.
'This officer, now engaged on his third tour of operational duty, has participated in numerous attacks against enemy shipping. He has invariably pressed home his attacks from low-level and with great skill and determination, often in the face of heavy enemy opposition. One of his recent missions was in March 1945, when he led a section of aircraft in an attack on shipping in the harbour of Aalesund. The photograph which he obtained was a good proof of the effectiveness of the attack. His devotion to duty has been unfailing.'

(J) Flight Lieutenant T. Armstrong was awarded the DFC, *London Gazette*, 19 January 1945:

'Distinguished Flying Cross.
'Flight Lieutenant Thomas ARMSTRONG (134035), RAFVR, No. 235 Squadron.
'As navigator, Flight Lieutenant Armstrong has participated in many sorties, involving attacks on a variety of targets such as enemy airfields, road communications and shipping. On one occasion, early in his operational career, Flight Lieutenant Armstrong was wounded when his aircraft was attacked by enemy aircraft. Upon his recovery he soon resumed operational flying and participated in many successful missions. More recently, Flight Lieutenant Armstrong has taken part in several determined attacks on shipping, and has set a fine example of skill, courage and devotion to duty.'

(K) Flight Lieutenant A. Jacques was awarded the DFC, *London Gazette*, 10 October 1944:

'Distinguished Flying Cross.
'Flight Lieutenant Arthur JACQUES (128978), RAFVR, No. 235 Squadron.'

(L) Flight Lieutenant A. Jacques was awarded a Bar to the DFC, *London Gazette*, 20 March 1945:

'Bar to the Distinguished Flying Cross.
'Flight Lieutenant Arthur JACQUES, DFC (128978), RAFVR, No. 235 Squadron.'

(M) Flight Lieutenant W. Knowles was awarded the DFC, *London Gazette*, 9 July 1943:

'Distinguished Flying Cross.
'Flight Lieutenant William KNOWLES (102061), Royal Air Force Volunteer Reserve, No. 220 Squadron.'

(N) Flying Officer G.R. Mayhew was awarded the DFC, *London Gazette*, 25 May 1943:

'Distinguished Flying Cross.
'Flying Officer Geoffrey Richard MAYHEW (119339), Royal Air Force Volunteer Reserve, No. 48 Squadron.

(O) Flight Lieutenant B.H. Quelch was awarded the DFC, *London Gazette*, 6 February 1945:

'Distinguished Flying Cross.
'Basil Herbert QUELCH (115130), RAFVR, No. 235 Squadron.'

(P) Flight Lieutenant N. Russell was awarded the DFC, *London Gazette*, 3 October 1944:

'Distinguished Flying Cross.
'Flying Officer Noel RUSSELL (134004), RAFVR, No. 235 Squadron.
'This officer has completed much operational flying during which he has attacked a wide range of targets and inflicted much loss on the enemy. His successes in the air include the destruction of at least three enemy aircraft. Since joining his present squadron, Flying Officer Russell has participated in several attacks on enemy shipping, and his resolute and skillful efforts have contributed materially to the good results obtained.'

(Q) Flight Lieutenant N. Russell, DFC, was awarded a Bar to the DFC, *London Gazette*, 2 March 1945:

'Bar to the Distinguished Flying Cross.
'Flight Lieutenant Noel RUSSELL, DFC (134004), RAFVR, No. 235 Squadron.

'Since being awarded the Distinguished Flying Cross, this officer has participated in numerous sorties, and has displayed a high degree of skill and gallantry throughout. In January 1945, Flight Lieutenant Russell took part in an engagement against a large force of enemy aircraft, four of which were shot down, two of them by Flight Lieutenant Russell himself. This officer has displayed the greatest keenness for operations and has set a splendid example to all.'

(R) Flying Officer Officer J.D. Taylor was awarded the DFC, *London Gazette*, 15 September 1944:

'Distinguished Flying Cross.
'James Davies TAYLOR (141717), RAFVR, No. 236 Squadron.'

(S) Acting Flight Lieutenant D.K. Thornburn was awarded the DFC, *London Gazette*, 28 September 1943:

'Distinguished Flying Cross.
'Acting Flight Lieutenant Douglas Keith THORBURN (121408), Royal Air Force Volunteer Reserve, No. 13 Squadron.'

(T) Flight Lieutenant R.S. Turner was awarded the DFC, *London Gazette*, 29 May 1945:

'Distinguished Flying Cross.
'Flight Lieutenant Royce Sydney TURNER (60125), RAFVR, No. 235 Squadron.
'This officer has completed numerous sorties on his second tour of operational duty. Since forming the squadron he has taken part in a number of attacks on enemy shipping. He has displayed a high degree of skill and his determination to bring his sorties to a successful conclusion has won high praise. In March 1945, Flight Lieutenant Turner participated in an attack against shipping in Aalesaud harbour. Pressing home his attack with great skill, Flight Lieutenant Turner obtained hits on a medium-sized merchantman.'

(U) Flying Officer H. Hollinson was awarded the DFC, *London Gazette*, 10 October 1944:

'Distinguished Flying Cross.
'Flying Officer Harry HOLLINSON (168952), RAFVR, No. 235 Squadron.'

(V) Flying Officer W. Moffatt was awarded the DFC, *London Gazette*, 11 August 1944:

'Distinguished Flying Cross.
'Flying Officer William MOFFATT (161731), RAFVR, No. 140 Squadron.'

(W) Flying Officer 'Pete' Pennie, DFM.
Although given as 'Flying Officer "Pete" Pennie, DFC', in a number of sources, the author believes this to be Flying Officer Ernest Frederick 'Peter' Pennie, DFM, RAFVR, who served in Nos. 603 and 235 Squadrons.
Flight Sergeant E.F. Pennie was awarded the DFM, *London Gazette*, 30 October 1944:

'Distinguished Flying Medal.
'1350204 Flight Sergeant Ernest Frederick Pennie, RAFVR, No. 603 Squadron.
'Flight Sergeant Pennie has displayed commendable skill and courage in air operations. In July 1944, he took part in an attack on an enemy convoy. In the flight, considerable anti-aircraft fire was faced. Flight Sergeant Pennie was wounded and his aircraft was hit repeatedly. Nevertheless, this gallant pilot pressed home his attack, obtaining hits on a ship.'

As a flight lieutenant, Pennie was awarded a Queen's Commendation for valuable service in the air in the Queen's Birthday honours of 1 June 1954, announced in the *London Gazette*, 10 June 1954.

(X) Warrant Officer (1295151) Harold Arthur Corbin was awarded the CGM for service with No. 248 Squadron, *London Gazette*, 17 October 1944. The Recommendation, dated 24 August, read:

'Warrant Officer Corbin has carried out twenty-five operational sorties since joining this squadron, including six shipping strikes against enemy shipping. On 29 June 1944, hc took part in a shipping strike near Ille de Groix and although his aircraft was hit in the port wing, he brought it safely back to base. On 30 June 1944, he took part in a shipping strike at Concarneau and damaged an "M" Class Minesweeper. His aircraft was severely damaged and it became necessary to feather one engine. He brought the aircraft safely back to base and made an excellent landing. On 27 July 1944, Warrant Officer Corbin was flying one of eight aircraft detailed to carry out a shipping reconnaissance of the French coast. A convoy of eight escort vessels was sighted off the mouth of the Loire, and the order was given to attack. During the attack his aircraft was hit in the starboard engine and nacelle, the starboard side of the cockpit, and starboard radiator, the starboard wheel, the petrol cooler and all starboard tanks. Warrant Officer Corbin immediately feathered the starboard airscrew and flew the aircraft back to base, where he made a landing on one engine and with one wheel punctured. Again, on 14 August 1944, he took part in a shipping strike in the Gironde. In spite of heavy anti-aircraft fire from both ships and land batteries, he attacked and damaged a Seetier Class Destroyer. His aircraft was hit in both outer tanks by heavy flak. The port inner tank was pierced and all the fuel lost. One shell entered through the floor of the fuselage, and wrecked the IFF and Gee. The port engine was severely damaged and the starboard engine also hit. The port engine had to be feathered immediately. Warrant Officer Corbin set course for Vannes airfield with fuel streaming from his tanks, without any means of "homing", and with the port engine completely useless and the starboard engine damaged. To add to his many difficulties, the batteries at Ille de Re opened fire with heavy and accurate flak. When he crossed the coast near Vannes it was too dark for him to be able to locate the airfield, which in any case had no flying facilities. He then flew overland and climbed slowly to 4,000 feet. He gave the order to abandon aircraft by parachute at this height and jumped after his observer was clear. Warrant Officer Corbin has not only acted with determination and courage, but he has also shown amazing skill in flying such badly damaged aircraft on three different occasions. I cannot too strongly recommend this warrant officer for the immediate award of the Conspicuous Gallantry Medal.'

(Y) Warrant Officer A.F. Shimmin was awarded the DFC, *London Gazette*, 7 December 1943:

'Distinguished Flying Cross.
'Warrant Officer Alfred Fuggett SHIMMIN (1256389), Royal Air Force Volunteer Reserve, No. 236 Squadron.'

(Z) Sergeant M. Webb was awarded the DFM, *London Gazette*, 19 January 1945:

'Distinguished Flying Medal.
'Flight Sergeant Maurice James WEBB (1578121), RAFVR, No. 248 Squadron.
'Flight Sergeant Webb has participated in very many sorties, including a number of armed reconnaissances and several attacks on enemy shipping. Throughout he has displayed commendable courage and determination, and his undoubted ability as navigator has been an important factor in the success of many missions.'

Notes

1. Later, Air Commodore Kenneth Brian Boyd 'Bing' Cross, KCB (*London Gazette*, 13 July 1959), CB (*London Gazette*, 10 June 1954), CBE (*London Gazette*, 8 June 1944), DSO (*London Gazette*, 13 February 1942), DFC (*London Gazette*, 13 September 1940), MiD (*London Gazette*, 1 January 1942), Norwegian War Cross (*London Gazette*, 6 June 1942), Legion of Merit (US) (*London Gazette*, 11 April 1944), Legion d'Honour (*London Gazette*, 1944), Croix de Guerre (France) (*London Gazette*, 1944), Order of Nassau (*London Gazette*, 18 November 1947).

2. Later, Air Commodore P.G. Jameson, CB, (*London Gazette*, 13 June 1959), DSO (*London Gazette*, 9 March 1943), DFC (*London Gazette*, 23 July 1940), Bar to DFC (*London Gazette*, 7 October 1940), MiD (*London Gazette*, 1 January 1946), Norwegian War Cross (*London Gazette*, 1 October 1943).

3. Pilot Officer (40802) Aston Maurice Cooper-Key, RAF, was the son of Major Astleigh Langrishe Cooper-Key and Kathleen Juliette Cooper-Key, of Hythe, Kent. Cooper-Key was 21-years-old and was buried at Scopwick Church Burial Ground, Row 2, Grave 32.

4. Sergeant (580059) William Lawrence Dymond, DFM, RAF, was the son of Thomas Dymond and Kathleen Dymond (nee Lawrence); husband of Joan Millicent Dymond, of Ruislip, Middlesex. Dymond was 23-years-old and is remembered on the Runnymede Memorial, Panel 13.

   Sergeant W.L. Dymond was awarded the DFM, *London Gazette*, 6 September 1940:
   '580059 Sergeant William Lawrence DYMOND.
   'Since May 1940, this airman pilot has accompanied his squadron on nearly all offensive patrols over France and its engagements over this country. During this period he has shot down eight enemy aircraft, and probably destroyed a further three. Sergeant Dymond has displayed a fine fighting spirit.'

5. Pilot Officer (74660) John Cyril Lindsay Dyson Bailey, RAFVR, was the son of Air Commodore G.C. Bailey, CB, DSO, Bsc, AMICE, RAF, and Mrs Bailey, of Stockland, Devon. Bailey was 20-years-old and was buried at Maidstone Cemetery, Plot C.C.1., Grave 90.

6. Sergeant (564606) Gerald Henry Edworthy, RAF, was the son of Harry and Edith Mary Edworthy, of Teignmouth, Devon. Edworthy was 25-years-old and is remembered on the Runnymede Memorial, Panel 13.

7. Pilot Officer (77977) Douglas William Hogg, RAFVR, was the son of Thomas and Helen Hogg, of Thornliebank, Glasgow. Hogg was 23-years-old and was buried at Glasgow (Eastwood) Old and New Cemetery, Section H (New Part), Grave 278.

8. Flight Lieutenant (90256) Harry Bryan Lillie Hillcoat, AAF, was the son of Henry and Edith Mary Hillcoat, of Bromsgrove, Worcestershire. Hillcoat was 25-years-old and is remembered on the Runnymede Memorial, Panel 9.

9. Pilot Officer (77465) Robert Henry Shaw, RAFVR, is remembered on the Runnymede Memorial, Panel 10.

10. Flying Officer (33363) David Harry Wellstead Hanson, RAF, was the son of Colonel Harry Ernest Hanson, DSO, TD, and of Ivy Alice Hanson (nee Webster), of Rolston, Hornsea. Hanson was 22-years-old and was buried at Mappleton (All Saints) Churchyard.

11. Pilot Officer (42719) Camille Robespierre Bon-Seigneur, RAF, was the son of Camille Robespierre Bon Seigneur, and of Irene Bon Seigneur, of Regina, Saskatchewan, Canada. Bon-Seigneur was 22-years-old and was buried at Saffron Walden Cemetery, Compartment 40, Grave 2.

12. Flying Officer (39753) Richard Pryer Plummer, RAF, was the son of George and Beatrice Ellen Plummer, of Haywards Heath. Plummer was 28-years-old and was buried at Haywards Heath (Western Road) Cemetery, Plot A.C., Grave 164.

13. Sub-Lieutenant (A) Jack Conway Carpenter, FAA, HMS *Daedalus* & No. 46 Squadron, RAF, was the son of Major Frederick Noel Carpenter and Ida May Carpenter, of Llanfaethlu, Anglesey. Carpenter was 21-years-old and is remembered on the Lee-on-Solent Memorial, Hampshire, Bay 1, Panel 3.

14. Sergeant (808268) William Albert Peacock, AAF, was the son of Albert and Catherine Rebecca Peacock, of South Bank, Middlesbrough, Yorkshire. Peacock was 20-years-old and is remembered on the Runnymede Memorial, Panel 18.

15. Pilot Officer (41502) Frederic Norman Hargreaves, RAF, was the son of James Frederick Raymond Hargreaves and Annie Hargreaves, of Manchester. Hargreaves was 21-years-old and is remembered on the Runnymede Memorial, Panel 8.

16. Sergeant (740169) Stanley Andrew, RAFVR, was the son of John William and Amelia Andrew, of Swanland. Andrew was 21-years-old and was buried at North Ferriby (All Saints) Churchyard, Grave 141.

17. Pilot Officer (42070) Roy Archille Marchand, RAF, was buried at Bromley Hill Cemetery, Block 1, Grave 230.

18. Sergeant (754867) George William Jefferys, RAFVR, was the son of Samuel William and Henrietta Jefferys, of Winterbourne. Jefferys was 20-years-old and was buried at Winterbourne Earls (St Michael) Churchyard, North of Church.

19. Pilot Officer (74248) Percival Ross Frances Burton, RAFVR, was buried at Tangmere (St Andrew) Churchyard, Plot E, Row 1, Grave 8. His Commonwealth War Graves listing gives his rank as flying officer.

20. Pilot Officer (42514) James Reginald Bryan Meaker, DFC, RAF, was the son of Edgar Reginald and Lucy Adelaide Kathleen Meaker, of West Dean. Meaker was 21-years-old and was buried at West Dean Cemetery, Grave 243.

21. Pilot Officer (43283) John Dallas Crossman, RAF, was the son of George Edward and Gladys Allyne Crossman, of New Lambton, New South Wales, Australia. Crossman was buried at Chalfont St Giles Churchyard, Grave 13.

22. Sergeant (741004) Edward Alan Bayley, RAFVR, was 29-years-old and was buried at Bromley (St Luke) Cemetery, Section K, Grave 198.

23. Pilot Officer (43474) Peter Stackhouse Gunning, RAF, was 29-years-old and was buried at North Weald Bassett (St Andrew) Churchyard, Row 2, Grave 9.

24. Flight Sergeant (562960) Eric Edward Williams, RAF, was the son of William and Amelia Williams; husband of Joan Margaret Williams. Flight Sergeant Williams was 28-years-old and is remembered on the Runnymede Memorial, Panel 11.

25. Sergeant (754728) Joseph Pearson Morrison, RAFVR, was buried at Newcastle-upon-Tyne (St Andrews and Jesmond) Cemetery, Section O, Unconsecrated, Grave 277.

26. Pilot Officer (43379) William Blair Pattullo, RAF, was the son of Patrick William and Jessie Hood Blair Pattullo, of Eaglescliffe, Co. Durham. Pattullo was 21-years-old and was buried at North Weald Basset (St Andrew) Cemetery, Row 2, Grave 8.

27. Sergeant (740749) Herbert Ernest Black, RAFVR, was the son of Herbert Ernest and Mary Elizabeth Black; husband of Gwendoline Annie Black, of Ibstock. Black was 26-years-old and was buried at Ibstock (St Denys) Churchyard, Grave 1242.

28. Sergeant (129998) de Cannaert d'Hamale, RAFVR. Following the war, d'Hamale's body was repatriated and he was buried at Brussel's Town Cemetery, Belgium Siemens Field of Honour.

29. Flight Lieutenant W.R. Farley had been recalled at the outbreak of the war. He was stationed at North Weald, and flew with Nos. 46 and 151 Squadrons, but not a member of either unit.

Farley later flew special operations, dropping and picking up agents in occupied Europe. He was killed-in-action on 21 April 1942. Wing Commander (29089) Walter Ronald Farley, RAF, was the son of Thomas Alfred and Sarah Ann Farley; husband of Massie Selina Peta Farley, of Knightsbridge, London. Farley was 32-years-old and was buried at Durnbach War Cemetery, Section 9.H., Collective Grave 20-24.

30. No. 333 Squadron's 'P' Flight generally supplied two Norwegian crews, whose role was to fly as outriders and assist with navigation, their knowledge of the fjords being vital to the success of the wing's operations.

31. Flight Lieutenant (129254) Leslie Norman Collins, RAFVR, was the son of Harold Norman and May Collins; husband of Joan Dorothy Collins, of Southampton. Collins was 27-years-old and is remembered on the Runnymede Memorial, Panel 201.

32. Flying Officer (153223) Robert Henry Hurn, RAFVR, was the son of Robert Charles and Lizzie Hurn, of Friern Barnet, Middlesex. Hurn was 24-years-old and is remembered on the Runnymede Memorial, Panel 207.

33. Flying Officer (J/23397) William Nathan Cosman, DFC, RCAF, is remembered on the Runnymede Memorial, Panel 245.

34. Flying Officer (152972) Leslie Morris Freedman, RAFVR, is remembered on the Runnymede Memorial, Panel 206.

35. Flying Officer (J/23429) Kenneth Cecil Wing RCAF, was the son of Marquis and Valia Wing, of Battleford, Saskatchchewan, Canada. Wing was 23-years-old and is remembered on the Runnymede Memorial, Panel 248.

36. Pilot Officer (428055) Veron Rippon Shield, RAAF, was the son of Raymond John and Grace Lillian Shield; husband of Lynne Boyd Shield, of Newtown, Tasmania, Australia. Shield was 28-years-old and is remembered on the Runnymede Memorial, Panel 259

37. Wing Commander (70030) Richard Ashley Atkinson, DSO, DFC and Bar, RAF, was the son of Jack and Emily Henrietta Atkinson; husband of Joan Patricia Atkinson, of Laidley, Queensland, Australia. Atkinson was 30-years-old and is remembered on the Runnymede Memorial, Panel 200.

38. Flying Officer (152680) Valentine Charles Upton, RAFVR, was the son of Charles and Grace Upton, of Holloway, London. Upton was 20-years-old and is remembered on the Runnymede Memorial, Panel 209.

39. Flight Lieutenant (131030) John Kennedy, RAFVR, was the son of Colonel Charles Fraser Kennedy and Constance Francis Kennedy, of Wombleton, Yorkshire. Kennedy was 21-years-old and is remembered on the Runnymede Memorial, Panel 202.

40. Flying Officer (153491) Francis Walter Rolls, RAFVR, was the son of Francis Albert Edward and Margaret Rolls, of Reading, Berkshire. Rolls was 22-years-old and is remembered on the Runnymede Memorial, Panel 209.

41. Flying Officer (410034) Kenneth Cupples Beruldsen, RAAF, was the son of Einar Bjorn and Helen Yeats Beruldsen, of Traralgon, Victoria, Australia. Beruldsen was 22-years-old and was buried at Sola Churchyard, British Plot, B. 9.

42. Pilot Officer (185410) Tom Damas Sellers Rabbitts, RAFVR, was the son of Mr and Mrs D.F.W. Rabbitts, of Farlington, Hampshire. Rabbitts was 21-years-old and was buried at Sola Churchyard, British Plot, B. 1.

43. Flying Officer (151041) Ernest James Fletcher, RAFVR, was the son of James Frederick Fletcher, and of Dora Ethel Fletcher, of Bradford, Yorkshire. Fletcher was 28-years-old and is remembered on the Runnymede Memorial, Panel 206.

44. Flying Officer (151835) Alfred James Watson, RAFVR, was the son of Alfred Francis and Rose Watson, of Tottenham, North London. Watson was 22-years-old and is remembered on the Runnymede Memorial, Panel 209.

45. Flying Officer (J/14533) Douglas Banbury Douglas, RCAF, was the son of Walter and Lela Douglas, of Belleville, Ontario, Canada. Douglas was 23-years-old and was buried at Banff Cemetery, Banffshire, 3rd Compartment, Section D, Grave 20.

46. LAC (978982) Gerrard Patrick Robbins, RAFVR, was the son of Patrick and Isabella Robbins, of Dundee; husband of Pauline Robbins, of Aberdeen. Robbins was 32-years-old and was buried at Dundee (Balgay) Cemetery, Section. G.G., Grave 144.

47. Flight Lieutenant (123938) John Edwin Langley, RAFVR, was the son of Mr and Mrs Charles Langley, of Croydon, Surrey; husband of Doreen Langley. Langley was 31-years-old and is remembered on the Runnymede Memorial, Panel 265.

48. Flight Sergeant (1315277) George Archie Morton-Moncrieff, RAFVR, was the son of Mr and Mrs A.O. Morton-Moncrieff; husband of Olga Grace Morton-Moncrieff, of Wilmington, Devon. Morton-Moncrieff was 21-years-old and is remembered on the Runnymede Memorial, Panel 269.

49. Flight Sergeant (1318226) Christopher Cash, RAFVR, was the son of Albert E. and Lily Cash, of Seven Kings, Ilford, Essex; husband of Margaret H. Cash. Cash was 22-years-old and was buried at Bergen (Mollendall) Church Cemetery, A. 11.

50. The graves of Wing Commander J.M. Guedj, DSO, DFC, and Lieutenant F.E. Alexandre, USAAF, do not come under the jurisdiction of the Commonwealth War Graves Commission.

51. Pilot Officer (189506) John Alexander McMullin, RAFVR, is remembered on the Runnymede Memorial, Panel 268.

52. Flight Sergeant (810195) Frank Chew, RAFVR, was the son of Ernest and Ann Chew, of Ellesmere Port, Cheshire. Chew was 24-years-old and was buried at Bergen (Mollendal) Church Cemetery, Section C, Grave 2.

53. Flight Lieutenant (103006) Darel Spofford Lydston Crimp, RAFVR, was the son of Dr. George Lydston Crimp and Maud Mary Crimp. He was 23-years-old and was buried at Banff Cemetery Banffshire, 3rd Compt, Section D, Grave 22.

54. Flying Officer (152566) John Bird, RAFVR, was the son of Henry and Margaret Annie Bird, of Barnsley. Bird was 22-years-old and was buried at Barnsley Cemetery, Section C, Grave 169.

55. Flight Lieutenant (149866) Richard Graeme Young, RAF, was the son of William and Williamina Young, of Dundee. Young was 28-years-old and is remembered on the Runnymede Memorial, Panel 266.

56. Flight Lieutenant (159094) Geoffrey Vernon 'Jeff' Goodes, DFM, RAF, is remembered on the Runnymede Memorial, Panel 267.

   As a sergeant, Geoffrey Goodes had won the DFM while flying with No. 252 Squadron. The award was announced in the *London Gazette*, 28 September 1943, when Goodes is referred to in his pilot's DFC citation:

> 'Flight Lieutenant Faulkner and Sergeant G.V. Goodes were pilot and observer, respectively, of the leading aircraft of a formation which attacked a medium-sized ship near Preveza harbour in August 1943. The attack was pressed home with great vigour and the vessel was hit repeatedly. Afterwards, Flight Lieutenant Faulkner attacked a tug leaving the harbour. On the return flight, this pilot attacked a heavily armed vessel. Although his aircraft was hit, Flight Lieutenant Faulkner pressed home a determined attack. Throughout the operations, Sergeant Goodes accomplished much good work and obtained excellent photographs. These members of aircraft crew displayed great courage and resolution.'

Faulkner was later awarded a Bar to the DFC, *London Gazette*, 14 December 1943.

57. Flying Officer (152558) Sydney Charles Hawkins, RAFVR, was the son of Frederick and Florence Hawkins, of Chard, Somerset; husband of Grace Winifred Hawkins. Hawkins was 32-years-old and is remembered on the Runnymede Memorial, Panel 267.

58. Flying Officer (153224) Eric Stubbs, RAFVR, was 23-years-old and is remembered on the Runnymede Memorial, Panel 268.

59. Flying Officer (155474) Wilson John Ceybird, DFM, RAFVR, was the son of John W. and Lilian E. J. Ceybird, of Northampton; husband of Joan Emily Ceybird. He was 24-years-old and is remembered on the Runnymede Memorial, Panel 266.
    Flight Sergeant W.J. Ceybird was awarded the DFM, *London Gazette*, 14 May 1943:

    'Awarded the Distinguished Flying Medal.
    '1195282 Flight Sergeant Wilson John CEYBIRD, No. 143 Squadron.
    'In May 1943, Flight Sergeant Ceybird piloted an aircraft engaged on escort duties during a reconnaissance flight off the Norwegian coast. Enemy fighters attempted to intercept and, in the ensuing engagement, Flight Sergeant Ceybird fought off two enemy aircraft with great daring. His observer was killed during the action but Flight Sergeant Ceybird, although deprived of navigational assistance, flew his aircraft more than 300 miles over the sea to reach an airfield in this country. He displayed courage and determination of a high order.'

60. Flight Lieutenant (14442) Norman Harwood, RAFVR, was the son of John Thomas Samuel and Annie Harwood; husband of Marion Harwood, of Audenshaw, Lancashire. Harwood was 28-years-old and is remembered on the Runnymede Memorial, Panel 265.

61. Wing Commander C.N. Foxley-Norris had earlier flown in the Battle of Britain. He was awarded the DSO, *London Gazette*, 29 May 1945:

    'Distinguished Service Order.
    'Acting Wing Commander Christopher Neil FOXLEY-NORRIS (70225), RAFVR, No. 43 Squadron.
    'This officer has a long and distinguished record of operational flying. He has completed numerous sorties on his third tour of duty, during which period he has operated against a wide range of enemy targets. For several months this officer has commanded the squadron. During the period numerous attacks have been made against enemy targets. By his brilliant leadership, exceptional skill and determination, Wing Commander Foxley-Norris has contributed in good measure to the successes obtained.'

62. Pilot Officer (190406) Keith McCall, RAFVR, is remembered on the Runnymede Memorial, Panel 268.

63. Warrant Officer (1620614) James Ashton Etchells, RAFVR, was the son of Alfred and Nellie Etchells, of Stretford, Lancashire. Etchells was 23-years-old and is remembered on the Runnymede Memorial, Panel 269.

64. Squadron Leader (80836) Robert Reid, AEA, RAFVR, is remembered on the Runnymede Memorial, Panel 265.

65. Flying Officer (157949) Alexander Douglas Turner, RAFVR, was the son of Revd Thomas Lindsay and Greta Roughead Turner, of Birkenhead, Cheshire. Turner was 24-years-old and was buried at Trondheim (Stavne) Cemetery, Section A.IV, British, H.7.

Chapter 6

Pilot Officer Douglas Cyril 'Snowy' Winter (43372)

Pilot Officer Winter was a pre-war pilot with No. 72 Squadron, flying Vickers Supermarine Spitfires. During the so-called 'Phoney War', the squadron spent much of the time in No. 12 Group's sector, only later moving south briefly during the final day of the Dunkirk evacuations. It was during these operations that Winter claimed his first victory.

Back in No. 12 Group, Winter added to his tally before the squadron was posted to RAF Biggin Hill at the end of August. With the airfield badly hit by the Luftwaffe, they were immediately transferred to RAF Croydon, from where they flew in defence of the capital, Winter adding more 'kills' to his tally. It was during a dogfight with a Messerschmitt Bf 109 over Elham, on 5 September 1940, that Winter was killed-in-action.

Despite achieving aces status, Winter's gallantry went unrewarded and his name has become largely forgotten.

Douglas Cyril Winter was born in South Shields, the son of Douglas Curle Winter and his wife, Margaret. He joined the RAF in September 1929, then 16-years-old, training initially as an aircraft apprentice as a part of RAF Halton's twenty-first intake.

One of the best ways to get on in the service was to 'get noticed' as a sportsman. Winter was a member of the RAF's athletic team and competed for the King's Cup in 1932. He also excelled as a marksman, twice being awarded a medal at Bisley. However, Winter's aspirations to become a pilot had to go on hold as, having qualified as an engine fitter in 1932, he was sent overseas to service aircraft with the RAF in Egypt and later in Palestine. Winter did not waste his time overseas and quickly came to the attention of his CO, who recommended him for pilot training.

On his return to the UK, Winter re-mustered and undertook an *ab initio* flying course, before being sent to Pilot Training School, passing out as a sergeant pilot and then being posted to No. 72 (Basutoland) Squadron. The squadron had reformed at Tangmere on 22 February 1937, around the nucleus of what had been No. 1 Squadron's 'B' Flight, which was increased to squadron strength.

On 8 December 1937, the newly-promoted Squadron Leader Ronald Beresford Lees assumed command. The squadron flew Gladiators out of RAF Church Fenton, Yorkshire. Now Leeds East Airport, the airfield is located approximately four and a half miles south-east of Tadcaster, North Yorkshire. During the Second World War it formed a part of No. 12 Group, and provided air cover for the heavily industrialized areas around Bradford, Humberside, Leeds and Sheffield. It was here that the squadron received their first Spitfires in April 1939.

Douglas Winter was still serving as a sergeant pilot with No. 72 Squadron when war was declared, the squadron transferring to nearby RAF Leconfield, in the East Riding of Yorkshire, on 17 October. RAF Leconfield was located near Beverley. Originally a part of Bomber Command, the station came under Fighter Command's No. 12 Group from October 1939, the changeover being marked by No. 72 Squadron's arrival.

Flying out of RAF Leconfield their duties mainly included convoy escorts and sector patrols, while at the same time building on their training with mock interceptions, formation flying and battle climbs. The pilots practiced combats too, perfecting the art of attacking from above and out of the sun, flying both against 'friendly' bombers and their own Spitfires.

As an experienced sergeant pilot, Winter would most likely have found himself flying at the edge of one of the RAF's famous, but outdated, vic formations, scouring the skies for the enemy, while his leader navigated. The pilots regularly flew in these tight formations, following their leader's orders, making practice attacks according to Fighter Command's manual. These included the Nos. 1-6 Standard Fighter Attacks for engaging formations of enemy bombers. Very simplified these were:

Fighter Attack No. 1:   A Section of three fighters attack a single enemy bomber from above cloud.

Fighter Attack No. 2:   A Section of three fighters attack a single enemy bomber from below.

Fighter Attack No. 3:   Approaching pursuit or turning. Attack launched from dead astern.

Fighter Attack No. 4:   Attacking a formation of enemy bombers from directly below.

Fighter Attack No. 5:   Attacking a large enemy formation from dead astern.

Fighter Attack No. 6:   Entire squadron making an attack on an enemy bomber formation from dead astern.

These manoeuvres were fine against an unescorted enemy which flew in straight and level flight. Tactics had, however, moved on and the Luftwaffe's bombers regularly flew with a close escort, or with fighters sitting a few thousand feet above and to the rear, ready to catch attackers in a deadly crossfire. Often the enemy fighters were high in the sun, above the bombers, waiting to bounce the RAF's fighters as they came in for an attack.

The Messerschmitt pilots adopted a different approach to the RAF's vic, operating in pairs (rotte) flying wing tip to wing tip, or two pairs, known as the Finger Four or schwarm. This meant that the pilots didn't spend all of their time checking they were in tight formation and could scour the skies for the RAF.

At least for the time being, while serving in No. 12 Group and out of the range of the Messerschmitt Bf 109, No. 72 Squadron's pilots would not have to contend with heavily escorted raids. Unescorted bombers could still pack a punch, especially if they flew in tight formation when their gunners could concentrate their crossfire to devastating effect.

It was while operating out of RAF Leconfield, on 21 October 1939, that the squadron recorded its first victory of the war. Scrambled to investigate a radar plot approaching shipping, No. 72 Squadron intercepted a formation of fourteen enemy aircraft off the north-east coast. Flying Officer D.F.B. Sheen (flying K9959) damaged an He 115 while fifteen miles south-east of Spurn Head at about 1455 hours. A second Heinkel was damaged by Flying Officer T.A.F. Elsdon (flying K9940) in the same area.

Flying Officer D.F.B. Sheen's combat report read:

'Fourteen enemy aircraft intercepted over convoy and attacked whilst flying north and five miles east of convoy [which was] fifteen miles south-east of Spurn Head. [The] E/A formation – leading five in vic and three sections of three, very loose and spread out [with the] rearmost three attempted to provide covering fire, and went up and astern for attack. Section [of aircraft] attacked these three, whereupon they split up and employed individual evasive tactics of steep turns, diving, climbing and throttling back.

'One E/A abandoned evasive tactics and dived steeply, apparently in trouble, and attack broke off.

'[A] second E/A [was] severely damaged and petrol tanks leaking badly. [The] observer [was] obviously killed or badly injured. Proceeded east losing height and skidding after attack broke off through lack of ammunition. Thought not to reach home base.

'[The] main formation left convoy when attacked and made for home, and [was] seen later to be attacked by six fighters,'
(signed) Flying Officer D.F. Sheen.

The attack, although only partially successful, demonstrated the vulnerability of bombers once separated from the main formation and lacking that protective crossfire of the other air-gunners.

Winter's first operation under wartime conditions was made on 27 October, when he flew Spitfire K9958 with Yellow Section on a brief routine operational patrol made at 1100 hours; the first of many that would come in the following weeks and months. Meanwhile, the squadron returned to RAF Church Fenton, Yorkshire, on 1 November 1939, from where they settled into a pattern of regular patrols and escorts, along with the occasional scramble to investigate an unidentified radar plot – these usually turned out to be 'friendly' aircraft flying off-course.

News of a posting reached No. 72 Squadron. But it was not the transfer into No. 11 Group that everyone was hoping for. Instead the squadron moved north to RAF Drem, East Lothian, on 1 December 1939. Here, they operated as part of No. 13 Group, where their duties remained confined to sector patrols, shipping escorts and maintaining a vigil over the Royal Navy's Home Fleet. The squadron also flew

Home Defence for the area around Edinburgh, protecting shipping in the Firth of Forth. The station's original wartime occupants, Nos. 602 and 603 Squadrons, were responsible for bringing down the first enemy aircraft destroyed over British airspace on 16 October 1939, when they destroyed a Ju 88 of I./KG 30 targeting British warships in the Firth of Forth. This at least meant there was the possibility of action between the long hours of routine flying.

On 7 December 1939, No. 72 Squadron's Green and Blue Sections were scrambled at 1018 hours, with orders to patrol Montrose at 2,000ft. Seven He 111s were intercepted while flying down the coast near Arbroath. A number of orchestrated attacks were carried out and all our aircraft returned to base except Flying Officer D.F.B. Sheen (flying K9959), who forced-landed at Leuchars, wounded.

Green Section's, Flying Officers T.A.F. Elsdon (flying K9940) and Henstock (flying K9935), along with Sergeant N.R. Norfolk (flying K9938), damaged an He 111 south-east of Montrose at about 1225 hours. Meanwhile, Blue Section's, Flying Officer D.F. Sheen, Pilot Officer E.J. Wilcox (flying K9936), and Flight Sergeant J. Steere (flying L1078), destroyed an He 111 south-east of Montrose at about 1230 hours. Sheen was wounded in the leg twice when his Spitfire was hit by return fire. A third bullet penetrated the sliding canopy and smashed his earphone before exiting through another section of the canopy.

Flying Officer Henstock attacked a formation of seven He 111s, flying in formations of four and three, firing three bursts of five seconds at 400 to 300 yards:

'[I] attacked three leading aircraft flying [in] tight vic at very low height. [I] did No. 1 attack on No. 2 E/A [and] opened fire [at] 400 yards closing to 300 yards. [The] E/A gradually lost height. I turned east. [The] attack developed into individual attack. One E/A appeared from behind and attempted to join up with vic. This aircraft had undercarriage down, and [was] emitting blue smoke and trace of whitish vapour. Three bursts fired of about five seconds each. [The] E/A's speed [was] approximately 200/240mph. Camouflage all blue on top – very effective.'
(signed) Flying Officer Henstock.

Green 2, Flying Officer T.A.F. Elsdon, attacked the same He 111 at 100ft, firing a burst of 350 rounds from 300 to 100 yards:

'When first sighted, [the] enemy aircraft were dead ahead flying south losing height. Came down finally to 50ft. I made five attacks on No. 2 of enemy formation. On first attack, I attacked from the stern and bluish smoke came from about two points in each mainplane. On second and subsequent attacks I fired deflection [bursts] from the side using the sea as indicating point for my fire. Thus I could ascertain definitely that my bullets were going into [the] E/A during the second, third and fourth attacks. After second attack, greyish white stream came from starboard wing from around the engine. This continued

for ten minutes until I broke away finally and I think it was definitely petrol coming out.'
(signed) Flying Officer T.A.F. Elsdon.

The patrols and escorts continued in the New Year, however, Sergeant Winter's name only occasionally appeared in the Squadron Operational Record Book (ORB). Meanwhile, the squadron flew down to RAF Leconfield on 12 January 1940, transferring back to their former base at RAF Church Fenton the next day. Over the following weeks the harsh winter conditions restricted flying, as for much of the time the airfield remained under a blanket of snow.

When the weather was more favourable, the pattern of humdrum patrols continued, interspaced only by scrambles that turned out to be false alarms. There was some uplifting news, however, towards the end of February, when the following notice appeared in the supplement to the *London Gazette*, dated 20 February 1940:

'His Majesty has been graciously pleased to give orders for the publication of the names of the following officer who has been Mentioned-in-Despatches by the Air Officer Commander-in-Chief.'
Flying Officer T.A.F. Elsdon.

The 'mention' was an acknowledgement of Elsdon's role in damaging an He 111 on 7 December, and was the first of many awards made to the squadron over the following months.

In a further development, No. 72 Squadron arrived at RAF Acklington on 2 March. Meanwhile, Sergeant Winter's name began to feature with more frequency on the flying roster, making a number of patrols and convoy escorts. These sorties helped the pilots further develop their operational flying, but were nonetheless both stressful and tiring to all concerned – any one of the sorties could have lead to combat.

Winter had come to the attention of his CO as a highly dependable NCO, both on the ground and in the air. The Squadron ORB noted on 1 April, 'Sergeant Winter granted Commission as Pilot Officer.'

Despite receiving his commission, Winter continued flying with No. 72 Squadron.

More patrols and scrambles followed, but without contact being made with the enemy. A further boost to the station came towards the end of April when unofficial news came through of the award of the DFC to Flying Officer D.F.B. Sheen. The award, which was a signal honour, reflecting an early success against the Luftwaffe, was promulgated in the *London Gazette*, 7 May 1940:

'The King has been graciously pleased to approve the following award.
'Awarded the Distinguished Flying Cross.
'Flying Officer Desmond Frederick Burt SHEEN (39470).'

Although announced without a citation, the Squadron ORB noted:

'This award was made for attacks on enemy aircraft on 21 October 1939, and 7 December 1939, details of which are in the operations book for those periods, and during which time Pilot Officer D.F.B Sheen was a member of No. 72 Squadron.'

The Squadron ORB added on the following day:

'This is the second award to No. 72 Squadron, the first being when F/O T.A.F. Elsdon was Mentioned-in-Despatches for the same attacks.'

Two days later a shockwave emanated across the whole of Free Europe as the war entered a new, more threatening phase, with the invasion of France and the Low Countries. The Blitzkrieg swept all before it, and, on 26 May, the British Expeditionary Force's retreat to Dunkirk began in earnest. No. 72 Squadron flew down to RAF Gravesend, Kent, on 1 June, making sector reconnaissances before flying operations during what turned out to be the last day of the evacuation.

No. 72 Squadron was ordered to patrol over Dunkirk during the late afternoon of 2 June. They couldn't have wished for better luck, arriving on the scene in time to engage a formation of six Ju 87s. Squadron Leader R.B. Lees (flying P9458), Flying Officer O. StJ. Pigg (flying K9924), Pilot Officer D.C. Winter (flying K9929) and Sergeant B. Douthwaite (flying L1092), each destroyed a Ju 87 Stuka dive-bomber. Flying Officer E.J. Wilcox (flying P9439) destroyed two Ju 87s unconfirmed, while Flying Officer T.A.F. Elsdon (flying K9940) destroyed a Ju 87 unconfirmed. The combats were timed at about 2005 hours.

Red 2, Flying Officer O. StJ. Pigg, fired a four to five-second burst at 300 yards, using 960 rounds:

'At 2000 hours I sighted six Ju 87s in initial dive at 8,000ft in two sections of three over Dunkerque. I informed Red Leader, who immediately turned in a dive to the attack. I sighted one Ju 87 in a dive and positioned myself on its tail. When I was just about to open fire I saw Red Leader was already attacking at close-range. I saw the E/A burst into flames and crash, exploding as it did so. I broke away to port and saw another E/A in my sights taking no evasive action. I opened fire at approximately 300 yards, closing to 50 yards. The E/A continued in its dive with white smoke issuing from it and crashed, bursting into flames as it did so. I noted this on my breaking away and climbed up. Another Ju 87 attacked me from head-on and, as I broke away upwards, received a burst of machine-gun fire through my starboard wing. This damaged my left aileron control and burst my air pressure system.

'I returned to Gravesend and landed with my wheels up as I had no brakes and flaps or aileron controls.'
(signed) Flying Officer O. StJ. Pigg.

Red 3, Pilot Officer D.C. Winter, got in amongst the Ju 87s, firing a five-second burst at close range:

'Whilst on patrol over Dunkirk [the] E/A were observed on our port. Red 1 ordered attack and Red Section dived to attack doing evasive turns to avoid heavy AA fire. Red 1 attacked [the] E/A and, as I was getting into range of another Ju 87, I saw [the] E/A attacked by Red 1 burst into flames, turn over on its back and dive steeply, and break up on hitting the ground. I was then in range of my own target, but it did a very steep slow turn and I could not get him in my sights. I overshot and broke away and Red 4 followed up on [the] E/A. I then attacked another E/A at about 500ft three miles east of Dunkirk, heading east. I opened fire at about 200 yards and closed in to 50 yards. I had quite a lot of return fire from rear of Ju 87 and it stopped when I was about 100 yards from E/A. I noticed no slipstream effect at all. As I was about to break away white smoke poured from [the] E/A, which was also noticed by Red 4. The E/A then turned over on its back and dived vertically. We were then about 200ft and I think it was impossible for him to pull out, as I watched him going down for quite a while and then I turned 180 degrees and couldn't see any more E/A. My burst was for about five seconds.
    'Total rounds fired 1,040.'
(signed) Pilot Officer D.C. Winter.

Red 4, Sergeant B. Douthwaite, fired a five-second burst at 200 yards and seven-second burst at 400 yards, firing 2,800 rounds:

'On receiving the order to attack in line astern, I formed up behind Red 3. Red 2 was behind me. I followed down in formation, doing evasive tactics to avoid heavy AA fire, but lost the section on the last turn. When I found them again, Red 3 was attacking an E/A; I formed behind him and attacked when he broke away at 200 yards range. I broke away, and Red 3 again attacked and I noticed smoke coming from the rear cockpit. I then pursued another Ju 87 which was heading south and diving. I opened fire at 400 yards and gave a burst as the range decreased. I ran out of ammunition at 200 yards. The Ju 87 was still flying, although it appeared to be hit. I then turned round as I was about twenty miles inland and returned home.'
(signed) Sergeant B. Douthwaite.

Blue 2, Pilot Officer E.J. Wilcox, fired a total of 2,240 rounds:

'I observed two bombs explode near a ship off Dunkirk harbour. I dived down from 8,000ft and turned on the tail of [the] E/A. Immediately I opened fire [and] white smoke appeared and after about two seconds fire [at 200 yards] the E/A burst into flames. I saw one parachute open beneath the aircraft. By this time the E/A had crossed the coast. I then saw another Ju 87, which I opened

fire at from astern [four-second burst at 75 yards]. My overtaking speed was too great and after about three-seconds burst, during which time white smoke appeared from [the] E/A, I had to pull up to avoid collision. By the time I had turned [the] E/A had disappeared in the smoke over Dunkirk.'
(signed) Pilot Officer E.J. Wilcox.

'B' Flight's Yellow 4, Flying Officer T.A.F. Elsdon, was five miles south-east of Dunkirk when he made his attack, firing a three to four-second burst at 250 yards:

'When the section [was] detailed to attack the Ju 87s [I] dived down [and] I saw [a] single Ju 87 diving down at about thirty degrees and [at] 200–230mph. I attacked from its port quarter, opening fire at about 250 yards and thirty degrees to the direction of the enemy aircraft. I used full deflection on the sight, which is approximately half normal full deflection at 200 yards. After firing a burst of three or four seconds [firing 700 rounds], the enemy aircraft suddenly bucked to the left and went into a spiral. I followed it down and it was still spiraling down when I had to pull up sharply to avoid hitting the ground. It would be practically impossible for it to pull out from the spiral dive after I lost sight of it and I could not see it in the air after I pulled out of my dive.
    'Tracer fire from the ground nearby was getting very accurate on my machine and I decided I could serve no further purpose by staying to make absolutely certain that it did crash.'
(signed) Flying Officer T.A.F. Elsdon.

With the evacuation concluded and the greater part of the BEF lifted off the Dunkirk beaches, No. 72 Squadron's time at RAF Gravesend was short-lived. There followed a few brief days of sector patrols, before the Spitfires flew north again, back to RAF Acklington, on 5 June.
    The squadron soon settled back into the routine of convoy patrols and the occasional scramble. Meanwhile, a night patrol flown by Pilot Officer R.A. Thompson (flying P9439), on 25 June, led to the destruction of a Ju 88 near Blyth, Northumberland, at 2359 hours. The victory was all the more impressive as the Spitfire had no means of detecting the enemy once in the air, other than the pilot peering into the gloom looking for a glimmer of light from the enemy's exhaust outlets, while contending with the glare of their own aircraft's exhaust.
    Meanwhile, during the mid-morning of 29 June, the squadron was scrambled onto a positive plot which was approaching May Island, off the Firth of Forth.
    Airborne at 0805 hours, Yellow Section's Flight Lieutenant F.M. Smith (flying P9438), Pilot Officer D.C. Winter (flying L1092) and Sergeant M. Gray (flying P9460) shared in the destruction of a Do 17 while 100 miles east of May Island, at 0848 hours. During the same engagement Flying Officer E.J. Wilcox (flying P9457) destroyed an He 111.

Yellow 1, Flight Lieutenant F.M. Smith, fired bursts at 300, 100 and 50 yards, totaling 2160 rounds:

'Yellow Section was ordered to patrol base at 18,000ft. Upon taking off, control vectored the section and ordered [us] to [use] buster when at 9,000ft. [An] unidentified aircraft [was] reported flying east about ten miles east of Holy Island. When about twenty miles east of Holy Island the aircraft was sighted flying east-north-east [at] 12,000ft above the section. I chased the E/A for about twenty minutes until the section overhauled the aircraft at 22,000ft. Yellow 1 flew alongside, about 500 yards to starboard, and challenged the aircraft. No reply was received, so the section approached the aircraft in line astern. He was then recognized to be a Do 17. Yellow 1 attacked from dead astern. As the enemy aircraft stall-turned, a burst of about 100 rounds was fired and white smoke issued from the port engine. I then broke away while Nos. 2 and 3 attacked. After they had attacked I then attacked again and fired a burst from astern. The aircraft stalled-turned, and I closed to about fifty yards and attacked on the port quarter. The bullets were seen to enter the fuselage by the trailing edge of the port wing and smoke and fire could be seen in the fuselage. The aircraft then spiraled steeply to the right and, at about 2,000ft, dived straight into the sea and exploded.'
(signed) Flight Lieutenant F.M. Smith.

Yellow 2, Pilot Officer D.C. Winter, placed the destruction of the Do 17 he claimed at 100 miles east of May Island and at 0846 hours:

'Whilst on patrol (interception) at 0830 hours, on 29 June 1940, a Do 17 was sighted 12,000ft above us. I was Yellow 2 in line astern on Yellow 1. After a long stern chase we caught up with [the] E/A at 23,000ft at approximately 0843 hours.
  'Yellow 1 did an astern attack on [the] E/A and I saw white and black smoke pouring from port engine. Yellow 1 then broke away. I closed in to 200 yards and just as I was about to open fire the port engine burst into flames. I then opened fire [at 150 yards] and smoke immediately poured out of the starboard engine and then [it] burst into flames whilst I was still firing [a five-second burst]. I broke away at approximately fifty yards. The E/A then did a very steep climb and seemed to stall. Yellow 3 then fired an upward shot and then the E/A fell away to starboard.
  'I followed [the] E/A down and with full deflection opened fire at 150 yards. I saw the front cockpit crumple, pieces flying off, and I observed my bullets entering the gunner's and pilot's cabins [firing the last of a total of 2,635 rounds]. The E/A by then was spiraling steeply downwards. I followed him down and at about 2,000ft he dived vertically into the sea and I observed no life in the fuselage. No return fire was observed.'
(signed) Pilot Officer D.C. Winter.

Yellow 3, Sergeant M. Gray, fired 738 rounds in three, two-second bursts. His combat report adds to the narrative:

'...an aircraft was sighted flying at 10,000ft by Yellow 1, the section then proceeded to overhaul this aircraft.

'The aircraft had now climbed to 22,000ft at 0845 hours. Yellow 1 flew on the starboard side of aircraft and challenged it, upon receiving no reply proceeded to make the attack on this machine, which was identified as a Dornier 17.

'After Yellow 1 dived to attack, smoke was seen to pour from the port engine, Yellow 2 closed up and smoke began pouring from both engines.

'Meanwhile, I was flying at 600 yards below Yellow 2 and [observed] returned gunfire from top turret of enemy.

'Then Yellow 2 finished his attacks and [I] proceeded to do an astern attack in the manner of Yellow 1 and 2, but when I opened fire at 200 yards, the aircraft climbed rapidly and assumed a vertical position 100 yards ahead of us.

'I then fired two more short bursts into the fuselage and cockpit, upon which [the] enemy aircraft turned over and went into a spiral dive. Yellow 2 then dived on enemy again and the aircraft crashed into the sea leaving a large pool of burning petrol and oil, but no survivors were seen. Yellow 1 and myself then flew back until land was reached. Yellow 2 became detached and returned alone. Speed of enemy aircraft approximately 260mph when attacked.'
(signed) Sergeant M. Gray.

The squadron was in action again at 0612 hours, on 1 July, when Blue Section's Flight Lieutenant E. Graham (flying P9457), Flying Officer E.J. Wilcox (flying K9959) and Flight Sergeant J. Steere (flying K9935), shared in the destruction of an He 59. The German float biplane was bearing Red Cross markings, but was flying close to a convoy sailing eight miles east of Hartlepool and was therefore considered to be acting in a reconnaissance role.

Blue 1, Flight Lieutenant E. Graham, fired a four-second burst at 200 yards:

'I spotted a twin-engined biplane with floats, coloured white and with large red crosses on upper surface of upper plane, flying at 500ft in south-easterly direction. I circled floatplane two or three times close, flashing the challenge. There was no reply and, on my last circuit, I got a good view of the black Swastika with red background on the fin and rudder. I ordered No. 1 Attack at 0612 hours and went in, overtaking very rapidly from above and behind. Fire was opened about 200 yards range and continued until about 30 yards. My incendiary bullets appeared to hit [the] E/A and I saw faint greyish smoke coming from fuselage. Immediately the water below [the] E/A was covered with splashes and this I took to be petrol. As I broke away to port [the] E/A turned slowly starboard and lost height slowly. I then saw No. 2 and 3 deliver their attack, [the] E/A settling on water during No. 3's attack. No return fire was encountered, though [the] E/A appeared to have both upper and lower gun emplacements.

'Leaving my [Nos.] 2 and 3 circling [the] E/A, I flew off to leading cruiser of nearby convoy. I then flew to [the] coast and found that position of [the] E/A was four miles east of Hartlepool. On my return to [the] E/A I saw that he was going down fairly slowly by the stern. A rubber dinghy was launched as [the] cruiser drew alongside. Three survivors were in [the] dinghy which was rowed towards [the] cruiser. [The] cruiser's longboat was behind [the] sinking E/A, which by this time was standing straight up on tail with trailing edge of planes submerged.

'Blue Section then returned to base.

'A long trail of oil lay on [the] surface of [the] sea along [the] track flown by [the] E/A after attack was delivered.'
(signed) Flight Lieutenant E. Graham.

Blue 2, Flying Officer E.J. Wilcox (flying P9457), engaged the enemy at 18,000ft, firing three, two and seven-second bursts at 300 yards, closing to 100 yards:

'I delivered one attack and fired a burst of four seconds from dead astern. I observed incendiary bullets going into enemy aircraft. After breaking away I saw [the] E/A jettison some small objects which I thought were small bombs. I then delivered a second attack and was just opening fire when [the] E/A touched down on water; after one-second burst I ceased fire. At this time Blue 3 was just ahead and above me. I continued circling [the] E/A as it settled on water and started to sink. [A] rubber dinghy was launched with three occupants. A British light cruiser then appeared and I joined up with my section leader. I clearly saw red crosses on the upper surface of top planes and the letters D-A SAM. A black swastika on a red background was on the rudder.'
(signed) Flying Officer E.J. Wilcox.

Blue 3, Flight Sergeant J. Steere's, combat report read:

'Blue 1 ordered No. 1 Attack. I closed to 250 yards. The [enemy] machine turned right [and] I had a simple deflection shot. The [enemy] machine touched the water and I broke off my attack'
(signed) Flight Sergeant J. Steere.

The crew; Unteroffizier Ernst Ielsen, Unteroffizier Stuckmann (badly wounded), Leutnant Hans-Joachim Fehske, and Obergefreiter Erich Philipp, were picked up by an escorting cruiser. It was claimed that a number of cameras were discovered in the wreckage (which presumably did not sink completely due to the aircraft's floats), confirming suspicions that the aircraft had been on a reconnaissance sortie.

Meanwhile, there were changes on the squadron when, on 24 July, a farewell party was given for Squadron Leader R.B. Lees on his posting to No. 13 Group (Squadron Leader R.B. Lees was attached to the squadron again on 31 August, the posting being curtailed when he was wounded in action on 2 September). On the following day, 25 July, Squadron Leader A.R. Collins assumed command.

The only event of note over the next few days came on 6 August, when Sergeant R.C.J. Staples (flying L1078) crash-landed at Acklington on return from a patrol. Staples, who had served with the squadron since 4 September 1937, and would have been well known to Douglas Winter, was uninjured, but his Spitfire was written off.

On 15 August, No. 12 Group faced its greatest threat during the battle, when at 1208 hours, radar plotted a major raid approaching the coast, a second plot being reported twenty minutes later. Over the following fifty minutes the controller scrambled Nos. 41, 72, 79, 605 and 607 Squadrons.

No. 72 Squadron was scrambled at 1210 hours with orders to intercept a raid heading for Farne Island, and was the first to engage the enemy, originally estimated at thirty-plus. As they approached the coast, the size of the enemy formation was reassessed as between 100 and 150 enemy aircraft, composed of Ju 88s, He 111s of KG 26, with their escort of Bf 110s of I./ZG 76 flying 500 yards astern. The enemy was engaged while flying thirty miles east to the east of the island at 18,000ft. The combats were timed between 1245–1255 hours.

The Squadron ORB recorded: 'Enemy attacks – eleven claimed destroyed, three probable and one damaged.'

The attack was led by 'A' Flight Commander (Red 1), Flight Lieutenant F.M. Smith (flying P9438), who destroyed two Ju 88s and probably destroyed another, firing at 250 yards, closing to 30 yards:

'Upon sighting [the] E/A, Leader ordered attack. Red Section formed echelon starboard and attacked rear section of six Ju 88s.

'Red 1 opened fire at about 250 yards and closed to 100 yards. [The] port engine [was] observed to smoke and bits fell away from fuselage. [I] broke away and fired [a] burst at another aircraft which caused several bits to fall from [the] E/A. The aircraft dived steeply, apparently seriously damaged and Red 1 broke away.

'Red 1 then attacked rear aircraft of six Ju 88s flying in [a] circle. Upon closing to approx. fifty yards [the] E/A exploded. [The] attack broke off and [the] Me 110 [was] sighted attacking leader. [A] short burst [was] fired at [the] E/A with no visible result. Red 1 then attacked rear aircraft of circle of six Me 110s, firing remainder of rounds with no visible effect. [My] rounds [were] then expended so [I] returned to base.'
(signed) Flight Lieutenant F.M. Smith.

Red 3, Pilot Officer D.F. Holland (flying P9238), destroyed a Ju 88 at 18,000ft, firing an initial burst of one second at 400 yards with a second of about four seconds:

'I was flying Red 3 when we sighted [the] E/A. I ordered No. 4 attack. I then took up my position for this attack when I was about 500 yards away from the nearest E/A. I noticed in my mirror a fighter diving down on my tail. I immediately went into a steep left-hand turn and got on his tail. I then identified him as a friendly fighter. Catching up with the main formation I sighted an E/A (Ju 88) diving down towards me and I met him head-on. I opened fire at 450-500 yards, ceasing my fire when we almost collided. I found I was still firing as I broke away. On pulling away to miss the E/A my vision was obscured by my mainplanes, so that I could not see what happened to [the] E/A I had attacked. I then circled to investigate, but could not see any result of my investigations.

'I then found there were no E/A in sight, so I returned to base to refuel and rearm.'
(signed) Pilot Officer D.F. Holland.

Yellow 1, Flying Officer O. StJ. Pigg (flying P9458), destroyed a Bf 110 at 18,000ft, firing two bursts of two seconds at 300-200 yards:

'When enemy aircraft was sighted I was Yellow Leader and was flying No. 2 on Red Leader. He ordered a No. 4 Attack, and I went into the attack on the near formation of Ju 88s. I fired short bursts at two of them at a range of about 400 yards. I then became aware that approximately six Me 110s were converging on me from behind. I immediately broke away from this attack, becoming engaged by the Me 110s. I took short bursts at about two of them, again breaking away to avoid converging attacks from the others. As I broke away I noticed that one of them was diving away steeply below me. I followed him down to the cloud layer at 9,000ft, where I temporarily lost him. I continued on through the clouds and was just in time to see the E/A dive almost vertically into the sea on my port side. I immediately dived onto splash mark and exposed my cine-camera in order to confirm enemy loss. I climbed up again through the clouds, but as I had not contacted any further E/A I returned to base and landed.'
(signed) Flying Officer O. StJ. Pigg.

Meanwhile, 'B' Flight Commander (Blue 1), Flight Lieutenant G. Graham (flying X4034), led his flight into action, personally destroying an He 111 at 18,000ft, firing four bursts of two seconds at 250 yards:

'The squadron, with a leading section of three aircraft, another of four aircraft, and a rearguard of four aircraft protecting the rear and flanks, encountered over 100 E/A of He 111, Ju 88 and Me 110 type, thirty miles east of Farne Isles. The squadron was flying at 22,000ft on course 020 degrees, with the enemy well below flying west in many vic formations, line abreast and line astern. I decided to attack the enemy on his right flank, which was approx.

three miles northward. Circling the flank I warned the rearguard of escort fighters, and then ordered the squadron to attack, leading my Blue Section in a No. 3 stern chase onto three He 111s which were flying behind and slightly above the enemy preceding vics. I opened fire at 250 yards, closing to about 30 yards, and saw smoke burst from the fuselage and port engine. Intense return fire was encountered, but this was inaccurate. On diving away from He 111, I spotted an Me 110 circling above me, so [I] dived straight for the clouds 9,000ft below.'

(signed) Flight Lieutenant G. Graham.

Green 2, Flying Officer T.A.F. Elsdon (P9448), probably destroyed a Bf 110, firing bursts of one to two, and two to three-seconds at 200 yards:

'When I received the order from Green 1 to attack the escorting Messerschmitt 110s, they formed a series of circles of six or seven aircraft each. I went into attack one of three circles, but found considerable difficulty in getting a good sight owing to the fact that they continually attempted to enclose me in the circle. This they once succeeded in doing, but I managed to get away before they fired a shot at me. After extricating myself I found the circle had broken up completely and I was in a position to attack individually. I attacked one with thirty degrees deflection from the starboard quarter and one above with two short bursts. Smoke came from the starboard engine and the machine spiralled into the clouds. I could not confirm his destruction as I did not see him crash into the sea because I saw another Me 110 diving for the cloud in an easterly direction. He disappeared before I could get within range. He did not appear again above or below the cloud, although I waited for a short time in the hope of finding another target.'

Flying Officer Elsdon added a note:

'Not once during the engagement did I observe an Me 110 put itself in a position for its rear-gunner to fire, nor was any return fire experienced from them. I consider, therefore, that the rear-gunner had been sacrificed for an overload of petrol (carried in the bulbous tanks underneath the fuselage) to obtain the necessary range. Once engaged, the Me 110 left the bombers to their own devices.'

(signed) Flying Officer T.A.F. Elsdon.

Green 3, Pilot Officer N.C.H. Robson (flying K9929), destroyed an He 111, firing a two-second burst at 300 yards followed by a five-second burst, closing to point-blank range with a further six-second burst:

'I was flying as Green 3, covering the port rear of the squadron formation when the enemy was sighted in an enormous formation on our starboard side.

Blue and Red Leaders ordered their sections to attack and I remained with the remnants of Green Section above and below the enemy until it was evident there were no escort fighters above us.

'I then watched the formation and saw an He 111 on the port flank of the enemy formation further out than the rest. I opened fire at 300 yards with a short burst and then closing to point-blank range with a six-second burst, [and] saw the starboard engine catch fire. I broke away underneath the enemy and saw him dive into the sea after climbing up. I did not remain to see if there were any survivors, but attempted to find the rest of the enemy formation without success.'
(signed) Pilot Officer N.C.H. Robson.

Green 4, Pilot Officer D.C. Winter (flying K9922), destroyed two Bf 110s while at 18,000ft:

'I was Green 4, acting as rearguard in the squadron's formation. As [the] enemy aircraft were sighted, Blue and Lead Sections prepared to attack. They attacked in turn, and Green 1 and 2 were then on the port side of the E/A. They then attacked, and I was left on my own – Green 3 having attacked himself by then. Still acting as rearguard I flew back and forth over the combats which were then taking place, looking for more fighters, which did not appear.

'Then I decided to attack myself. At the same time seeing an He 111 with its wheels down [and] gliding seawards. I followed it for a while until I saw it hit the sea and disappear. Climbing up again I saw, about 2,000ft below me, at 16,000ft, a circle of Me 110s with a Spitfire in the circle. I waited until one Me 110 was detached a little from the circle on the Spitfire's tail and dived to attack. I waited until I was about 100 yards from it and opened fire [with a three-second burst]. I saw the bullets entering [the] pilot's cockpit. The E/A turned on its back and dived seawards, eventually crashing in the sea. I observed no return fire.

'Climbing up again I found another ring of six Me 110s with three Spitfires in the circle; one of the Me 110s flew to one side and I again dived to attack. In the first burst I opened fire at about 150 yards [with a three-second burst] and the port engine started to smoke. I fired two more bursts which entered the pilot's cockpit. The E/A dived vertically for the sea. I followed it through the cloud and saw it crash in the sea. No return fire was observed, and no markings on the second E/A, on the upper surfaces, under surfaces – pale blue.'
(signed) Pilot Officer D.C. Winter.

Winter's actions probably saved the life of one of his comrades, but certainly led to the destruction of two Messerschmidt Bf 110s.

Also making claims were Flying Officer D.F.B. Sheen (flying X4109), who destroyed a Ju 88 and a Bf 110, also destroying an He 111; his combat timed at 1245 hours. Pilot Officer R.D. Elliot witnessed the destruction of the Bf 110 claimed by

Sheen, who, 'fired at it and it just blew up.' Sheen had hit the Messerschmitt's long-range fuel tank which erupted in a massive fireball.

Pilot Officers R.D. Elliot (flying P9460) claimed a Bf 110, while Blue 3, Pilot Officer E.E. Males (flying N3221), claimed a Bf 110 damaged.

Elliot recalled his victim: 'a 110 came straight dead, head-on at me and I shot at it head-on climbing up, and its port engine went up in flames and it went over my head about ten feet away.'

Pilot Officer R.D. Elliot later recalled that as the squadron went in for the attack, heading for a gap between the He 111s and their escort, the bomber crews released their payloads en masse: 'You could see them falling away from the aircraft and dropping into the sea, literally by the hundreds. The formation became a shambles.'

Having jettisoned their bombs and dived for cloud cover, some of the enemy bombers trailed vapour or smoke, but not all were damaged, thus the squadron evidently over-claimed, with Luftwaffe records stating that only three of its 'kills' actually failed to make base.

Meanwhile, Nos. 41, 79, 605 and 607 Squadrons also engaged the enemy.

No. 41 Squadron, scrambled at 1235 hours, made the following claims:

Flight Lieutenant E.N. Ryder (flying P9430)	one Ju 88 probably destroyed
Flying Officer A.D.J. Lovell (flying X4201)	one Bf 110 destroyed, another probably destroyed
Pilot Officer G.H. Bennions (flying R6604)	one Bf 110 destroyed, Ju 88 destroyed, He 111 damaged
Pilot Officer R.J. Boret (flying R6605)	one Ju 88 probably destroyed
Pilot Officer E.S. Lock (flying R6885)	one Bf 110 destroyed
Pilot Officer J.N. Mackenzie (flying R6756)	one Ju 88 probably destroyed
Pilot Officer O.B. Morrogh-Ryan (flying P9430)	one Ju 88 destroyed
Pilot Officer E.A. Shipman (flying N3126)	one Bf 110 destroyed
Pilot Officer R.W. Wallens (flying N3266)	one Bf 110 destroyed
Sergeant F. Usmar (flying N3162)	one He 111 destroyed

No. 79 Squadron, scrambled at 1242 hours, claimed:

Squadron Leader J.H. Heyworth	one Bf 110 (shared), one Do 17 (shared)
Flight Lieutenant R.W. Clarke	one Bf 110 (shared), one Do 17 (shared)
Flying Officer G.D.L. Haysom	one Bf 110 destroyed
Pilot Officer D.G. Clift	one Bf 110 destroyed
Pilot Officer W.H. Millington	two He 111s destroyed, one He 111 damaged

Pilot Officer B.R. Noble	one Bf 110 (shared), one Do 17 (shared)
Pilot Officer G.H. Nelson-Edwards	one Bf 110 (shared), one Do 17 (shared)
Pilot Officer T.C. Parker	one Bf 110 (shared), one Do 17 (shared)
Pilot Officer G.C.B. Peters	one Bf 110 destroyed

No. 605 Squadron's 'B' Flight attacked the bombers about five minutes after No. 72 Squadron. Its claims and losses included:

Flight Lieutenant A.A. McKellar (flying P3924)	three He 111s destroyed, one He 111 probably destroyed
Flying Officer C.F. Currant (flying P2994)	two He 111s destroyed, one He 111 damaged
Flying Officer I.J. Muirhead (flying L2118)	one He 111 destroyed
Pilot Officer R.E. Jones (N2537)	one He 111 destroyed, two He 111s probably destroyed
Pilot Officer C.W. Passy (flying P3827)	one He 111 destroyed
Unknown pilot	one He 111 damaged

Pilot Officer C.W. Passy crash-landed one mile from Usworth following combat with He 111s of KG 26 off Newcastle.

Pilot Officer K. Schadtler-Law (flying P2717) was hit by return fire from an He 111 of KG 26, making a forced-landing on Hartlepool Golf Course.

No. 607 Squadron was scrambled at 1307 hours and attacked the same formation, making the following claims:

Flight Lieutenant J.M. Bazin (Blue 1)	one He 111 probably destroyed
Flying Officer C.E. Bowen (White 1)	one He 111 destroyed, one He 111 probably destroyed
Flying Officer G.D. Craig (Green 1)	one He 111 and one Bf 110 probably destroyed
Flying Officer W.E. Gore (Yellow 1)	one He 111 damaged
Flying Officer W.H.R. Whitty (Green 2)	two Bf 110s damaged
Pilot Officer J.D. Lenahan (Green 3)	one He 111 destroyed, one He 111 damaged
Pilot Officer S.B. Parnall (Blue 2)	one Bf 110 probably destroyed
Pilot Officer J.E. Sulman (White 2)	one He 111 damaged
Pilot Officer G.H.E. Welford (Red 1)	one He 111 destroyed
Sergeant P. Burnell-Phillips (Yellow 2)	one He 111 (shared), one He 111 destroyed

Sergeant W.G. Cunningham (Red 3)   one He 111 (shared)

Sergeant G.A. Hewett (Blue 3)   one He 111 damaged

Fighter Command's decimation of the raid, scotched the Luftwaffe's idea that they had depleted their reserves to prop up No. 11 Group, and that the North of England remained largely undefended. This would be the only raid of its type on the North during the Battle of Britain.

Following a quiet period of uneventful patrols and escorts, No. 72 Squadron flew down from RAF Acklington to join the fight as a part of No.11 Group on 31 August. It was intended that they should be posted to RAF Biggin Hill. Their arrival, however, was heralded by one of the most devastating raids on the 'Bump'.

During the late afternoon the enemy had mounted further raids in the Maidstone area, also targeting East London, RAF Biggin Hill, and aiming to strike at RAF Hornchurch.

No. 72 Squadron was scrambled at 1750 hours with orders to patrol ten miles south of Maidstone, while No. 79 Squadron took off from Biggin Hill with orders to protect their home base. The squadron was unable to prevent the enemy from dropping 100-plus bombs on the airfield and causing considerable damage to the infrastructure, including the operations room, which had to be transferred off the base.

Once airborne, No. 72 Squadron was vectored onto an enemy formation of thirty Do 17s and the same number of Do 215s, and their escort of 100 Bf 109s, which was engaged at about 1820 hours, with Flight Lieutenant E. Graham (flying X4034) damaging two Do 215s in the Dungeness area. Flight Sergeant J. Steere damaged a Do 215, ten miles south of Rochester – five miles north of Dungeness, while Sergeant M.H. Pocock (flying L1056) damaged a Do 215 in the Dungeness area.

Tenis Leader, Flight Lieutenant E. Graham, reported during his debriefing:

'We were ordered to patrol base at Angels 10. Squadron took off with leading section of four aircraft (Blue), another of four aircraft (Red) and a rearguard of four aircraft in two pairs. About thirty Do 17s, protected by many 109s, were encountered ten miles south of Maidstone at 15,000ft. A head-on attack was attempted on the Do 17s, but I was compelled to break off the attack on account of swarms of Me 109s coming down on our tails. A dogfight ensued, from which I broke away with Blue 3.

'Blue 3 and myself (Blue 1) then encountered about thirty Do 215s, protected by many Me 109s, over Dungeness. I made a beam attack on the Do 215s, raking the leading aeroplanes – my bullets entering the fuselage of at least two E/A. I was then attacked by many Me 109s and, after a dogfight, broke away and returned to base.'

(signed) Flight Lieutenant E. Graham.

'NB: Return fire from Do 215s very concentrated indeed.'

Blue 4, Sergeant M.H. Pocock, engaged a straggler:

'I saw one Dornier 215 away from the rest of the formation, with [its] starboard engine smoking, losing height slowly. I carried out a No. 1 Attack from behind. I dived to 10,000ft, then climbed back to the scene of the engagement and searched round for [the] enemy aircraft. I could not see any after a five minute search and returned to Biggin Hill.'
(signed) Sergeant M.H. Pocock.

Flight Lieutenant F.M. Smith (flying P9438) was wounded and bailed out over Dungeness following combat with an enemy aircraft, at 1835 hours. The squadron's first real action in No. 11 Group left a bitter taste, with the loss of Flying Officer E.J. Wilcox[1], who was shot down and killed in his Spitfire (P9457) over Dungeness at 1910 hours.

Meanwhile, No. 79 Squadron's claims and losses included:

Pilot Officer W.H. Millington (flying P3050)	one Do 215 damaged
Pilot Officer D.W.A. Stones	one Do 215 destroyed, one Do 215 probably destroyed
Pilot Officer O.V. Tracey	one Do 215 destroyed

Pilot Officer W.H. Millington was wounded during combat with a Bf 109 over Romney and crash-landed at 1800 hours.

Pilot Officer E.J. Morris (flying P3877) crash-landed at 1850 hours, damaged by return fire from a Do 17.

With RAF Biggin Hill badly damaged, No. 72 Squadron was redeployed to RAF Croydon, from where they would operate for the remainder of the battle.

At 1045 hours, on 1 September, No. 72 Squadron was scrambled, following hot on the heels of Nos. 1 and 54 Squadrons, to investigate an enemy formation over Tunbridge Wells. No. 222 Squadron, meanwhile, was already closing in on the raiders as they approached their target, the Harland and Wolff works at Tilbury, a detachment also aiming for RAF Hornchurch. The squadron's Spitfires made inconclusive attacks against the bombers before being fended off by their fighter escort, without loss.

No. 72 Squadron was bounced by Bf 109s, with the loss of Flying Officer O. StJ. Pigg[2] (flying P9458), who was shot down by a Messerschmitt Bf 109 over Pluckley, near Ashford, Kent, at 1115 hours. Fighting back, the squadron had a number of successes as testified by their combat reports.

'A' Flight's Blue 2, Flying Officer J.W. Villa (flying P9338), engaged a formation of 100-plus enemy aircraft at 1105 hours, including Do 17s and their escort of Bf 109s while at 15,000ft over Gatwick. Villa damaged a Bf 109:

'I was flying Blue 2 on Tenis Leader, when the squadron [was] ordered to patrol Tenterden. I remained in section with Tenis Leader until I noticed an Me 109 diving down on my tail. I did a tight turn to the right and warned Tenis Leader by R/T. The Me 109 carried straight on and climbed vertically. I continued to turn as I had lost Tenis Leader. I then sighted an Me 109 about 800ft below me doing a medium turn to the left. I dived down and did a quarter attack on it. I gave it one burst of two seconds and saw it going away with black smoke coming from it. I was then attacked by three Me 109s which dived down on my tail. I put my aircraft into a spin with engine on and pulled out about 7,000ft. I was then unable to find any further enemy aircraft, so I returned to base and landed.'
(signed) Flying Officer J.W. Villa.

Meanwhile, Pilot Officer D.C. Winter (flying K9958) claimed an He 113 [actually a Bf 109] near Beachy Head at 1120 hours. His combat report notes the formation consisted of thirty to fifty Do 17, Do 215s and He 111s, escorted by fifty to one hundred Bf 109s and He 113s *[sic]*:

'I was Red 2 in squadron interception when we were vectored onto [an] enemy bomber formation about 200ft above us at approximately 15,000ft, to the north-west of Maidstone. They then wheeled south and Red Section went into attack. Just as I was about to open fire on a Do 17, an Me 109 dived down on my tail, I turned sharply to the right and the E/A shot past me. Then six more Me 109s came down on me and, as I turned to port, an He 113 *[sic]* pulled up in front of me and I had a good bead for about two seconds, during which time I was firing. The He 113 *[sic]* turned over and dived seawards. Then I saw a Do 17, which was attacked by Red 3, covered in black smoke and then it dived vertically to the sea. By then I was being attacked by six more Me 109s and, by doing steep spiral turns, I managed to avoid their fire. After a while I saw the He 113 *[sic]* I had shot at, plane down into the water and sink about two or three miles off Beachy Head. This was confirmed by Red 3. Meanwhile, I was still spiraling steeply and the Me 109s followed me down to about 1,000ft, and then I got down to about 50ft and they left me. It was impossible to get a bead on them owing to their numbers.

'The He 113 *[sic]* was white, or pale blue underneath, and jet black on top with white wing tips. I observed cannon fire from all the Me 109s. I did not get another chance to get at the bombers.'
(signed) Pilot Officer D.C. Winter.

'A' Flight's Red 3, Sergeant M. Gray (flying P9460), claimed one Do 17 probably destroyed out of a formation of thirty spotted at 18,000ft, while two miles west of Rye (Red 1 and 2 fired at the same enemy aircraft, but without result):

'At 1140 hours on 1 September 1940, No. 72 Squadron were searching for an unknown number of bandits over Tunbridge Wells. The bandits were approaching from the north-west of London at a height of 20,000ft when they were first seen by Blue 1 (leading section). Red Section, then being on the right flank of Blue Section, made an attack at the bombers, Red 1 taking the last machine on the port side of bomber formation.

'Red 2 then attacked the outside bomber on the port side of the formation. Myself (Red 3) attacked the bombers [which] Red 1 had appeared to attack.

'I opened fire at 300 yards, closing to 150 yards when I saw the whole [undercarriage] of the machine I had attacked drop down and the machine was enveloped in black smoke.

'It then turned over on its back and dived vertically towards myself, following down in an aileron turn.

'At approximately 4,000ft this aircraft was still diving vertically, completely enveloped in smoke. I then decided to pancake at Croydon as the aircraft was out to sea and I thought my aircraft might be damaged.

'This I did at 1215 hours being the third aircraft to land. My aircraft had two bullet holes in the rear of the rudder.'
(signed) Sergeant M. Gray.

'A' Flight's Red 4, Sergeant B. Douthwaite (flying L1092), encountered a formation of thirty Do 215s, plus their escort of Bf 109s, near Maidstone at between 15,000 and 13,000ft. He destroyed a Bf 109 at 1100 hours:

'I took off from Croydon as Red 4 and weaved up to 13,000ft. AA fire attracted [our] attention [and a formation of] fifteen E/A [was sighted] on port side, and we turned towards it. The E/A apparently turned back at the time and Red 1 led us to the up-sun side of [the] E/A. I paired off with Red 3 and we prepared to attack the enemy bombers on the starboard beam. While approaching to [make the] attack, an Me 109 passed close to me and shot at Red 3. I opened fire at 250 yards and saw my tracer hitting [the] E/A. After approximately three seconds [the] E/A burst into flames. At this moment my aircraft was hit from behind and I half-rolled away to starboard. My glycol system had been hit, and I glided down and force-landed without engine at West Malling. My aircraft was hit sixteen times by bullets and twice by cannon or explosive bullets. Sergeant Pocock landed there about ten minutes later without undercarriage, and was taken off to hospital with wounds in left leg and left wrist.'
(signed) Sergeant B. Douthwaite.

Despite their victories, the squadron had taken a mauling. As Pilot Officer A.L. Winskill, later observed, they, 'still hadn't got out of this rather archaic business of flying in tight formations of three, which was ridiculous. It meant keeping in formation and watching your leader, rather than flying in the loose two formation which the Germans did, which left you completely free to roam the skies.'

It was true that Fighter Command was learning the hard way that speed, flexibility and agility were paramount to survival in the air, along with getting numbers of aircraft into the air as quickly as possible in order to give the pilots the height advantage and position in order to attack the enemy from above and out of the sun.

Fighter Command's largely redundant tactics may have contributed to the death of Flying Officer O. StJ. Pigg and to the loss of Spitfire P9448, flown by Flying Officer R.A. Thompson, who was wounded and bailed out over Hythe following combat with a Bf 110 at 1130 hours. Another of the squadron's casualties was Sergeant M.H. Pocock (flying L1056), who was wounded in the leg and arm when his Spitfire was badly damaged during combat with a Bf 109 over Beachy Head, at 1140 hours. Pocock made a successful belly-landing at West Malling, as mentioned in Douthwaite's combat report. Meanwhile, 'B' Flight's Flying Officer D.F.B. Sheen (flying X4109) was reported safe, having bailed out following combat with enemy fighters at Ham Street, Kent, at 1150 hours.

Of the other squadrons which engaged the same enemy formation, No. 54 Squadron encountered a formation of half a dozen He 111s and their fighter escort over Maidstone, Pilot Officer C.F. Gray (flying X4238) claiming an He 111 destroyed over the town.

No. 1 Squadron intercepted the bombers on their return leg, but could not penetrate the enemy's fighter cover. During the encounter they claimed four Bf 109s, with one fatality:

Flight Lieutenant H.B.L. Hillcoat (flying P3044)	one Bf 109 destroyed
Pilot Officer C.N. Birch (flying V7376)	one Bf 109 destroyed
Pilot Officer P.V. Boot (flying P3169)	one Bf 109 destroyed
Pilot Officer C.A.G. Chetham (flying P2548)	one Bf 109 destroyed

Flight Sergeant F.G. Berry[3] (flying P3276) was shot down and killed by a Bf 109 over Tunbridge at 1130 hours.

Flight Sergeant F.G. Berry was awarded the DFM, *London Gazette*, 20 August 1940:

'Awarded the Distinguished Flying Medal.
'563426 Flight Sergeant Frederick George BERRY.
'On 17 June 1940, whilst leading a section on patrol over Saint Nazaire, to cover the embarkation of the British Expeditionary Force, Sergeant Berry attacked and shot down an enemy bomber about to make an attack on one of the troopships. Sergeant Berry has on many occasions led his section, and often his flight, in combat against the enemy with success. He has displayed exceptional qualities as a leader.'

Meanwhile, No. 85 Squadron appeared to have missed the main raid completely, but entered into inconclusive combats with a gaggle of Bf 109s targeting the barrage balloons protecting Dover Harbour.

A further raid was launched against RAF Biggin Hill, the Luftwaffe also targeting RAF Kenley. Nos. 72 and 222 Squadrons were scrambled to make an interception, followed by Nos. 54 and 253 Squadrons.

No. 72 Squadron was airborne at 1300 hours, initially with orders to mount a patrol of Hawkinge. The Spitfires were vectored onto the enemy over Dungeness and were in combat with a force estimated at forty Do 17s and He 111s, and fifty-plus Bf 109s and Bf 110s. The air battle raged over Dungeness, Tunbridge and Ashford, between 1330 and 1345 hours.

'B' Flight's Blue 1, Flight Lieutenant G. Graham (flying as Tenis Leader), engaged the formation of 100-plus Do 17s, Bf 109s and Bf 110s at 20,000ft, damaging two Bf 109s:

> 'At 1315 hours, the squadron, consisting of a Blue Leading Section of three aircraft and Red Section of three aircraft, and a rearguard of four aircraft, encountered about thirty or forty Do 17s (presumed) approaching the coast at 15,000ft. I decided to attack from head-on, but had to break off the attack before it had been delivered on account of forty to fifty Me 109s diving down from about 20,000ft onto our tails. These Me 109s had been flying ahead of the Do 17s and it was a simple matter for them to foil our initial head-on attack. I was forced to fight the Me 109s and, in the ensuing dogfight, damaged two Me 109s. In a very short space of time I was out of ammunition and was fortunate in losing them in cloud at 14,000ft. I managed to return to base, and on landing my aircraft was found to have three bullets in the oil tank.'
> (signed) Flight Lieutenant G. Graham.

'B' Flight's Green 1, Flying Officer T.A.F. Elsdon, attacked a formation of twenty Bf 110s, destroying two Bf 109s at 20,000ft, ten miles south-east of Croydon, firing four, three to four-second bursts at between 400 and 200 yards:

> 'When I first saw the formation of about twenty Me Jaguars, or 110s, they were flying in two vics north-east. At the same time I saw two Me 109s in my rear-view mirror. While evading them I became separated from my section and the Me 109s dived away. As I approached the Me Jaguars, they formed a circle in tight line astern. I attacked from slightly above and towards [the] centre of the circle, gradually decreasing the deflection to about thirty degrees. Range about 400-200 yards. This produced no results except that the aircraft closed up in line astern.
>
> 'In my second attack I decided to keep a steady burst into the circle and let them fly through. I finished my rounds in this manner, and during one burst, two of them just dropped out of formation and went down. My witness (Sergeant Rolls) on the ground saw the machines falling and crash into the

ground, and confirmed that they were from a circle of aircraft very high up and to the south-east of Croydon.

'Apart from the two Me 109s in the first instance, no other fighters were encountered.

'No other pilot reported seeing bombers form a circle as an evasive tactic.'
(signed) Flying Officer T.A.F. Elsdon.

Pilot Officer R.D. Elliott (flying P9460) probably destroyed a Bf 109, while Flying Officer J.W. Villa (flying P9338) damaged a Bf 109; both combats took place over the Ashford-Dungeness area.

Flight Sergeant J. Steere (flying K9935) probably destroyed a Bf 109 while five miles south of Dungeness at 11,000ft:

'On patrol over Hawkinge, at 14,000ft, we saw a formation of bombers escorted by a large number of Me 109s and 110s, [100-plus enemy aircraft] coming in from the French Coast towards Dungeness. I went into line astern on Blue 2 and flew to meet them. Eight Me 109s flew up to meet me [and] there was a general melee. I found an Me 109 in my sights [and] I gave him quite a long burst [of] three seconds approx. He pulled up, stalled, and black smoke came from him. I could not follow him as I was engaged with another one on my tail. I turned to attack him and he shot off and disappeared. I turned towards Dover and, at 10,000ft, I attacked another Me 109. I gave him a burst and he disappeared into a layer of cloud. I could not follow as there was another Me 109 on my tail, as I turned to get onto him he disappeared. I returned and landed at Croydon.'
(signed) Flight Sergeant J. Steere.

The Squadron ORB also credited Sergeant N.R. Norfolk (flying K9938) as having damaged a Bf 109, but his own aircraft was hit in the tail by return fire and landed at Croydon with battle damage.

Although timed at 1755 hours, the following appears to be a combat report for the same engagement: Red 4, Sergeant B. Douthwaite, encountered a raid composed of three waves of twenty bombers and fighters, including Do 17s, Me 110s and Me 109s. Douthwaite claimed a Do 17 damaged while flying over Maidstone at 15,000ft, firing 2,300 rounds:

'I took off from Croydon as Red 4 and weaved behind the section up to 15,000ft over base. We then proceeded eastwards and sighted enemy formation proceeding south-east on our left. We turned towards them and attacked in line astern from underneath and on his starboard rear. I attacked a formation of three Do 17s in vics and picked on the starboard aircraft. I saw pieces break off it, but the result was not decisive owing to the proximity of other enemy formations, and their heavy crossfire. I could not attack again with my limited ammunition.'
(signed) Sergeant B. Douthwaite.

Also engaged were Nos. 54, 222 and 253 Squadrons:

No. 54 Squadron made the following claims:

Pilot Officer S. Baker (flying R6709)	one Bf 109 probably destroyed
Pilot Officer C.F. Gray (flying X4238)	one Bf 109 destroyed

No. 222 Squadron made no claims.

No. 253 Squadron reported the following claims:

Flight Lieutenant W.P. Cambridge (flying P3032)	two Bf 110s damaged
Pilot Officer J.D.B. Greenwood (flying P5184)	one Do 215 probably destroyed
Pilot Officer J.H. Wedgewood (flying P5179)	one enemy aircraft damaged

Meanwhile, it was reported that as No. 72 Squadron's Spitfires were coming in to land, their places were taken by Nos. 1 (RCAF), 79, 303 and 501 Squadrons, which combined force successfully took on the next wave of enemy bombers and their fighter escort.

A squadron patrol, composed of nine aircraft drawn from Red, Green and Blue Sections, was flown between 0750 and 0845 hours on 2 September. While patrolling at 15,000ft, the squadron was vectored 100 degrees onto thirty Do 17s of III./ KG 3 and their fighter escort of about 100 Bf 109s and Bf 110s. Ten squadrons were scrambled, but only Nos. 72 and 249 Squadrons engaged the enemy, the remaining fighters were ordered to patrol Fighter Command's airfields, which were the enemy's intended targets.

No. 72 Squadron intercepted the enemy over Maidstone at 0800 hours. During the ensuing combat Sergeant W.T.E. Rolls (flying P9338) destroyed a Bf 110 and a Do 17. Sergeant J. White (flying K9940) destroyed a Do 17, Flight Sergeant H. Steere (flying K9935) damaged a Bf 110, while three miles south of Chatham. Meanwhile, Sergeant M. Gray (flying N3093) probably destroyed a Do 17 at 0815 hours, and Sergeant J.S. Gilders damaged a Do 17. One further enemy aircraft was destroyed (unknown type), but was not attributed.

Flying as Tenis Leader, Flight Sergeant J. Steere engaged the enemy at 12,000ft while three miles south of Chatham:

'I was ordered to scramble at 0740 hours. I took off with nine aircraft and circled base, gaining height. I received an order to vector 100. I turned on to this course. Nearing Chatham I saw several enemy aircraft indicated by AA fire. I was slightly below these aircraft so I turned slightly right still climbing. The squadron went

into line astern on me. I turned left to attack, and, as I went in, an Me 110 flew across in front of me, firing from his rear gun. I fired at him [and] he turned left into a spiral – smoke came from his port engine. I followed him down firing, until I saw tracer coming over my port plane. I turned very sharply and "blacked out." When I recovered there was nothing in sight and, as I had expended all my ammunition, I returned and landed at Croydon.'
(signed) Flight Sergeant J. Steere.

Green 1, Sergeant W.T.E. Rolls' combat report read:

'I followed Blue Section in wide formation and was instructed to climb to 15,000ft. We saw the enemy approaching from the east-south-east, and Blue Section led the attack on the bombers while I followed above them. I saw Blue Section break away and the enemy was then turning to [the] south as I approached. I saw one Me 110 leave the formation and dive onto the tail of a Spitfire, and, as no other Spitfire was near enough, I dived after it and came in at the Me 110 from fifteen degrees above and astern, from port. I dived at the Me 110's port engine and put about 640 rounds into it. It caught fire and appeared to fall away [along] with part of the wing, and the machine went over on its back and then went down with flames from the port wing. I had opened fire at 200 yards but did not see any return fire.

'I dived down to the starboard side of it and saw seventeen Do 17s below me at about 12,000ft. I had one in my sights and I fired all my other rounds at it. The fuselage blew to pieces and the engine (port) caught fire. I closed my fire at about 175 yards to 50 yards and then dived again to starboard, and went into a spin to avoid the Me 109 behind. I found myself flying at 4,000ft when I pulled out of the spin.

'Above me, rather separated, I saw three parachutes drifting down, and to my starboard I saw the Do 17 coming down in flames and it crashed into the wood north-east of Maidstone. I went up to investigate the parachutes, being as I could not see the enemy again. I saw one was empty, another appeared to be a sergeant pilot with [a] Mae West and the other had no Mae West, and I circled around him and he landed near a factory at Chatham. I climbed up again to 3,000ft and made for base as we were ordered to return.'
(signed) Sergeant W.T.E. Rolls.

Red Section's Sergeant M. Gray probably destroyed a Do 17 at 0815 hours, firing five bursts of three to four-seconds at 600 to 200 yards (expending 2,800 rounds):

'Upon sighting us the bomber turned away from London in [a] south-easterly direction, losing height gradually.

'The formation leader then carried out an astern attack on these bombers. As I was a little behind the main body of the formation and a little higher, I did not attack at the same time.

'After the attack by the rest of the formation the bombers turned slightly and came towards myself, flying at a height of 13,000ft, in a south-easterly direction.

'I then dived below the leader of the bomber formation and attacked the Dornier 17, No. 5 position in the first vic formation.

'A Messerschmitt 109 then attacked me from astern and dived away.

'The Dornier 17 was then losing height very slowly in a south-easterly direction and I followed it halfway across the Channel until it was about 1,000ft over the sea and eight to ten miles from the coast, and still losing height.

'As all Tenis aircraft had been ordered to land I left the Dornier and landed at Croydon at 0825 hours to refuel and rearm.'
(signed) Sergeant M. Gray.

'A' Flight's Sergeant J.S. Gilders damaged a Do 17, firing several four-second bursts at 500-200 yards (expending 1,400 rounds):

'As I was acting as rearguard above the leading section, I did not attack until the enemy bombers had been turned back by the rest of the squadron. I then attacked a Dornier 17 on left of its formation, which was away from the rest of the bomber formation with another one. I attacked from dead astern and about 1,000ft above. I gave a preliminary burst at about 500 yards, closing in to about 350 yards. This was going around enemy aircraft and appeared to hit it. I then gave another burst at about 250 yards range, but could not continue closing in as I sighted an Me 109 attacking me from astern.

'I then broke away and returned to base. The Dornier 17 had lots of smoke coming from his starboard engine, and left his partner crossing over and going down below the larger formation on his right. I had not time to see whether he continued down.'
(signed) Sergeant J.S. Gilders.

Meanwhile, No. 249 Squadron engaged the enemy over Rochester, making the following claims:

Squadron Leader J. Grandy (flying N4229)	one Do 17 damaged
Flight Lieutenant R.A. Barton (flying P6625)	one Do 17 (shared)
Flight Lieutenant D.G. Parnall (flying V6539)	one Bf 110 damaged
Pilot Officer H.J.S. Beazley (flying P2986)	one Bf 110 probably destroyed
Pilot Officer P.R.F. Burton (flying V3386)	one Do 17 probably destroyed
Pilot Officer J.R.B. Meaker (flying P5206)	one Do 17 (shared), one Do 17 damaged

No. 72 Squadron's Spitfires were in action again the same day, when they were scrambled from Croydon at 1206 hours. The Spitfires were led off by Squadron Leader A.R. Collins. Once airborne, they were vectored onto a formation of Do 17s,

Bf 110s and Bf 109s, returning from a raid on Eastchurch, which was intercepted at 20,000ft over Herne Bay. The bombers were flying in tight vic formations, approximately nine to a vic, line astern with the Bf 109s on their port flank, and the Bf 110s astern and to their left flank.

Squadron Leader Collins ordered Red and Blue Sections into line astern and delivered a No. 3 astern quarter attack in a steep dive. The Spitfires opened fire at 400 yards, closing to 50 yards, in bursts of from two-seconds upwards. Green Section, acting as rearguard, then came into the attack. Green 1 attacked one of about two dozen Bf 110s which had formed two defensive circles. Green 2 followed, and stated that one Bf 110 opened fire long before he was in range. The enemy formation then broke up, and individual attacks followed.

As a result of the squadron's attack they were able to claim a Bf 110 destroyed, with two Do 17s and one Bf 110s probably destroyed, and four Bf 110s damaged.

Squadron Leader A.R. Collins (flying R6806) probably destroyed a Bf 110 and a Do 17 over Herne Bay:

'I was ordered to patrol behind Dover at 15,000ft, but it was not until 1240 hours, when I was at 24,000ft, that I saw the enemy formation flying west over Herne Bay at 20,000ft. The bombers were flying in tight vic, approximately nine to a vic, and the vics were in line astern. The 109s were on their right flank. I ordered Red and Blue Sections into line astern, and delivered a No. 3 [Attack] astern quarter in a steep dive and opened fire at approximately 400 yards, closing to 50 yards at the leading aircraft of the second vic of bombers, but although I saw bullets going into his cockpit, there was no apparent effect. I broke away in my dive and pulled up behind the outside aircraft in the leader's vic of bombers, giving him short bursts into the engines. One engine caught on fire and the other started smoking, and he dived down towards the sea and [I] did not see him hit as I was attacked by four Me 110s, receiving cannon shells in each mainplane. I turned towards one of them and attacked from head-on giving him the rest of my rounds. Smoke came from both engines and he dived down vertically. I did not see him crash as I was busy disengaging myself from the other three Me 110s. I finally landed at Hawkinge, which was our forward base.'

(signed) Squadron Leader A.R. Collins.

Red 1, Sergeant B. Douthwaite, claimed a Do 17 probably destroyed, during his second pass:

'I lost the leader and pulled up and attacked another enemy formation leader, who pulled up and climbed head-on towards me. I continued my fire and saw his port motor start to blaze. He passed about 15ft underneath me. I then turned to port and attacked an Me 109 who was turning steeply to port. I could easily out-turn him and fired until he broke away in a steep left-hand dive; as I had expended my ammunition I did not follow him but returned to

Hawkinge. I was hit seven times and my starboard tyre was punctured, and my starboard flap and gun pipes severed. Also, fabric was torn off my port elevator.'
(signed) Sergeant B. Douthwaite.

Blue 1, Flight Lieutenant E. Graham (flying No. 610 Squadron's DW-S), wrote:

'We encountered two waves of Do 17s protected by many Me 110s at about 19,000ft. Red Section attacked from above and quarter, and I tried to follow but was intercepted by the Me 110s. One Me 110 overshot me and, in taking evasive action, he turned his belly right into my sights.

'I gave him two bursts and he seemed to go away and down in spiral turn. After a dogfight with twenty or thirty Me 110s, during which I was unable to draw a bead, I dived out of the battle and below me saw an E/A twin-engined aircraft spinning down. It crashed and burst into little pieces ten miles north of Dover. When I landed to rearm, Flight Sergeant Steere informed me that he had shot this aircraft down. I confirm this aircraft crashing north of Dover.'
(signed) Flight Lieutenant E. Graham.

Green 1, Squadron Leader R.B. Lees, former CO of No. 72 Squadron, was only visiting the squadron, but took part in the day's scrambles. He had joined the dogfight over Herne Bay and returned with a damaged Spitfire, making a crash-landing at Hawkinge. He practically had to be cut out of the wreckage.

'A' Flight's Green 2, Flying Officer J.W. Villa, probably destroyed a Bf 110, damaging two more:

'I was rearguard. Green 1 turned and attacked one of twenty-four Me 110s which had gone into two defensive circles. I followed Green 1 and attacked another Me 110 head-on and gave him one long burst at about 150 yards just before he broke away from me. He straightened up and fired at me long before I was in range. I saw my bullets hitting him and he stopped firing almost as soon as I opened fire and broke. I lost him going down fairly steeply with smoke pouring out of one engine and the other stopped. I dived down and climbed, and as I came up I attacked another 110 from abeam and underneath. I fired a short burst which I saw hitting him and half-rolled away just before stalling. After pulling out of ensuing dive, I climbed up to one side and attacked another Me 110 head-on the port quarter. This machine was already smoking from an attack by S/L Lees, Green 1. I then saw Green 1 (Squadron Leader Lees) going away with an Me 110 on his tail, and I did a quarter attack on it and fired a long burst. The Me 110 half-rolled.'
(signed) Flying Officer J.W. Villa.

Also flying as rearguard was 'B' Flight's Flight Sergeant J. Steere (flying K9935), who claimed a Bf 110 destroyed as the air battle continued over Canterbury:

'Tenis Leader attacked and I saw approximately fifty Me 110 on the left flank. They turned in towards Tenis Leader and started to form circles. I dived and attacked one; he broke away to the left. I followed him down, firing and I saw him crash and blow up between Dover and Canterbury, near Knowton Station [witnessed by Flight Lieutenant E. Graham].'
(signed) Flight Sergeant J. Steere.

Pilot Officer N.R. Norfolk (flying K9938) damaged a Bf 110, but was shot down by return fire. His Spitfire crashed and burned out at Garrington Farm, near the emergency landing ground at Bekesbourne, at 1300 hours.

Meanwhile, No. 603 Squadron engaged the same raid near Chatham, claiming one bomber and two of the fighter escort. The remainder of the formation continued towards its target.

No. 603 Squadron's claims included:

Squadron Leader G.L. Denholm (flying X4260)   one Bf 109 damaged

Flight Lieutenant F.W. Rushmer (flying X4263)   one Do 17 destroyed

Pilot Officer R.H. Hillary (flying X4277)   one Bf 109 destroyed,
one Bf 109 damaged

Pilot Officer J.S. Morton (flying N3056)   one Bf 109 destroyed

Also engaging the same enemy formation, No. 111 Squadron made contact with twenty He 111s and their Bf 109 and Bf 110 escort at 15,000ft, flying westwards up the Thames estuary. One section made a head-on attack against the bombers, with one crashing into the sea. The remaining action was against the fighter escort. The operational entries in No. 111 Squadron's ORB were made by flight. There are no entries recorded for 'A' Flight for 2 September, and so the aircraft flown by individual pilots in some cases remains uncertain. The squadron claimed the following enemy aircraft damaged or destroyed, also losing one of its pilots:

Flight Lieutenant D.C. Bruce (flying R4172)   one He 111 destroyed (shared),
one Bf 110 damaged

Flying Officer B.H. Bowing   one Bf 110 damaged, one He 111
probably destroyed

Pilot Officer R.J. Ritchie   one He 111 probably destroyed
(shared)

Pilot Officer P.J. Simpson (flying V6539)   one He 111 damaged

Sergeant R.J.W. Brown (flying V7400)   one Bf 109 damaged, one He 111
destroyed (shared)

Sergeant V.H. Ekins   one Do 17 damaged

Sergeant C.W. Hampshire (flying V7222)   one Bf 110 probably destroyed

Sergeant W.L. Dymond[5] (flying P3875) was shot down and killed by a Bf 109 over the Thames estuary at 1250 hours.

The enemy's next big raids were made between 1545 and 1700 hours, when they targeted RAF Eastchurch, RAF Hornchurch and locations along the Thames estuary.

Nos. 72 and 249 Squadrons were scrambled a little before 1600 hours with orders to patrol Dungeness and Rochford respectively.

No. 72 Squadron entered into combat at 1625 hours, when they were vectored over Dungeness at Angels 10, before being ordered to Angels 20. The squadron consisted of Red Section leading with four aircraft and a rearguard of four aircraft (Blue Section) both in box formation.

The squadron intercepted a formation of Do 17s, and their escort of Bf 110s and Bf 109s, five miles south of Dungeness and flying in a north-westerly direction. As on previous occasions, the Bf 110s formed a defensive circle, and No. 72 Squadron was ordered into line astern and an attack was delivered from the rear and above. The enemy turned to starboard and headed back for France, and this element of the main attack may not have returned to our shores, although the remainder of the raid proceeded.

Pilot Officers E.E. Males (flying R6971) and N.C.H. Robson delivered a beam attack, each damaged a Bf 110, while Sergeant B. Douthwaite (flying R6710) claimed two Bf 110s damaged.

Red 2, Sergeant B. Douthwaite, engaged the enemy as they crossed the coast at 20,000ft, claiming two Bf 110s damaged, firing 1,600 rounds:

'When they were about to cross the coast, Leader put us in line astern and [we] were prepared to attack them from the rear and above. The enemy aircraft must have seen us, for they turned starboard and headed back to France. As they were completing this turn we attacked them on the beam from above. The Me 110 which I picked out continued turning to starboard and I saw pieces flying off as I fired. Other Me 110s were forming rings, so I did not follow this one, but attacked another and my bullets appeared to be entering him. I then saw six Me 110s diving on me from behind so I left hurriedly and returned to Hawkinge.'

(signed) Sergeant B. Douthwaite.

The tables would be turned on Sergeant B. Douthwaite a few days later when (flying R6710) he was wounded in combat over Gravesend at 1600 hours on the 11 September. He had to force-land due to battle damage.

Meanwhile, Red 4, Pilot Officer N.C.H. Robson, wrote:

'The section was ordered to attack and I picked out two Me 110s in line astern, and dived on them from about 2,000ft above, firing three bursts of two-seconds. I received return fire at first, but this ceased after my second burst. The starboard engine of the lower of the two Me 110s then seized, but [I] then saw a further Me 110 in my mirror attacking me from astern and broke away my attack.'
(signed) Pilot Officer N. Robson

Flying with Blue Section, Pilot Officer E.E. Males damaged an He 111 at 15,000ft over Herne Bay (at 1615 hours):

'I was flying rearguard on two sections of three when we attacked fifty Me 110s in an anti-clockwise defensive circle. I opened fire at 200 yards and expended all my ammunition.
    'White smoke came from the port engine, but I had to break away because I was attacked from behind by another 110. I then returned to forward base.'
(signed) Pilot Officer E.E. Males.

Squadron Leader R.B. Lees (flying K9840) was slightly wounded when his Spitfire was damaged while in combat over Lympne at 1615 hours. Lees managed to maintain control of the damaged fighter and crash-landed at Hawkinge for the second time that day.
    Attacking the same enemy formation, Flight Lieutenant E. 'Ted' Graham (flying No. 610 Squadron's DW-S) was shot down while in combat over Lympne, at 1610 hours. He escaped without injury. The squadron flew in the company of No. 249 Squadron, which engaged the enemy over the Thames estuary, making the following claims:

Flight Lieutenant D.G. Parnall (flying V5639)	one Bf 110 destroyed, one Bf 110 damaged
Pilot Officer R.G.A. Barclay (flying V6610)	one Bf 110 damaged
Pilot Officer J.R.B. Meaker (flying V6534)	one Bf 110 destroyed

RAF Eastchurch was again the enemy's main target when they returned in force at 1700 hours.
    No. 72 Squadron made a flight strength scramble from RAF Hawkinge at 1709 hours (landing at 1825 hours) with orders to patrol at 15,000ft. Meanwhile, No. 46 Squadron was patrolling between North Weald and the River Thames. The controller scrambled Nos. 85, 257 and 303 Squadrons to reinforce.
    Having already flown a number of operational sorties during the day and with aircraft returning with battle damage, No. 72 Squadron could only muster a flight strength patrol, with four aircraft (Blue Section) leading and a rearguard of two aircraft. Following the controller's vector, the formation headed for Chatham,

where AA fire indicated the enemy's presence; estimated at twenty Do 215s and fifty Bf 109s and Bf 110s.

Closing in on the enemy, the leader ordered a line astern attack, and approached from above and astern and out of the sun. On being attacked, the bombers broke formation, while the Bf 109s dived down to their defence. Individual battles then developed between the Chatham and Herne Bay area.

Pilot Officer E.E. Males claimed one Bf 109 destroyed, while Sergeant B. Douthwaite damaged a second, reporting that he was shot at by a Bf 109 firing rearwards.

Blue 2, Pilot Officer E.E. Males (flying K9940) wrote:

'I was flying Blue 2 in the leading section, with three aircraft weaving behind, when about forty Me 109s were sighted to the east. We were slightly below them, and, after climbing up to their level, during which time they had broken formation and were going round in a circle anti-clockwise, Blue 1 led us in echelon starboard, but I could not get a bead on any enemy aircraft. I broke away and climbed into the sun, and came down on a 109 from 2,000ft above. He dived away for the coast and I had difficulty in keeping up with him from 15,000ft to sea level. I fired several bursts and used all my ammunition while [we] were flying south at 50ft over the sea. White smoke came from underneath the engine and three large pieces fell off, and, after about five minutes, he dived into the sea about three miles from the French coast. There was no sign of the pilot or wreckage. The aircraft was travelling at about 280mph when he went in.'
(signed) Pilot Officer E.E. Males.

Blue 3, Sergeant B. Douthwaite's combat report read:

'We approached the bombers from above and astern. As we dived I saw at least five Me 109s in my mirror preparing to attack us. We carried out evasive tactics on approaching the bombers. I saw an Me 109 chasing a Spitfire. I attacked him while turning from port and starboard, and saw black smoke pour from the region of his port radiator. He immediately turned south. I followed and attacked him from dead astern at 300 yards. I saw red flashes from the starboard side of his fuselage. I had very few rounds left and, on expending these, I broke off the attack [having fired 2,800 rounds] and returned to Hawkinge. One bullet had entered the leading edge of my tail fin from in front and my canopy hood was shattered, these bullets presumably were fired backwards from the Me 109 as I was not attacked by any other aircraft.'
(signed) Sergeant B. Douthwaite.

Squadron Leader A.R. Collins' Spitfire (R6806), was damaged during combat over the Thames estuary at 1730 hours.

Also engaging the enemy were Nos. 85, 257 and 303 Squadrons.

No. 85 Squadron was unable to make any claims.

No. 257 Squadron claimed the following:

Sergeant R.C. Nutter (flying P3706)	one Bf 109 probably destroyed

No. 303 Squadron was more successful, making the following claims:

Flying Officer Z. Henneberg (flying V7246)	one Bf 109 damaged
Pilot Officer M. Feric (flying R4178)	one Bf 109 probably destroyed
Sergeant J. František (flying P3975)	one Bf 109 destroyed
Sergeant J. Rogowski (flying R4217)	one Bf 109 destroyed

It is believed that No. 72 Squadron's Sergeant J. White claimed a Do 17 during the day's combats, but due to the Squadron ORB lacking an accurate record of operations during the first three days of September; it is unclear as to when this occurred. Meanwhile, No. 72 Squadron's ORB is completely silent for 3 September, although Spitfire X4262 is known to have been lost when its pilot bailed out over Marden at 1425 hours. There are no further details surrounding the incident, although the pilot was uninjured.

At around 1230 hours on 4 September, radar plotted a raid massing ready to cross the Channel, heading for Beachy Head and Folkestone; the enemy's targets were RAF Eastchurch and the Kent area.

No. 72 Squadron was scrambled at 1255 hours, with orders to patrol Hawkinge at 25,000ft. Following the controller's vector, the enemy was engaged at 1320 hours. The intelligence officer's report provides the narrative:

'The squadron, consisting of nine Spitfires, took off from Croydon at 1235 hours on 4 September 1940, in formation of two vics of three aircraft (Red and Yellow Section), with a rearguard of three aircraft. The weather was clear, with no appreciable cloud. At approximately 1320 hours, the enemy was sighted in the Tenterden-Tunbridge Wells area in vic and echelon formation, flying at 15,000ft. The enemy consisted of Me 110s and Ju 86s; about thirty in all. On approaching the enemy, the leader ordered Red and Yellow Sections into individual line astern. The Me 110s then attempted to form a defensive circle, but six of our aircraft attacked the leading six and a dogfight followed. Our aircraft employed quarter attack from port, firing bursts of two to three-seconds each, from 200 yards to point blank range. In all, five Me 110s and three Ju 86s are claimed destroyed, and two Me 110s probable. One of our airmen was unable to pull out of a dive and bailed out. Flying Officer J.W. Villa [flying P9338] claims one Me 110 destroyed and one Me 110 probable, Flying Officer T.A.F. Elsdon claims two Me 110s destroyed and one Ju 86 probable, Pilot Officer D.F. Holland [probably flying X3229] claims one Me 110 destroyed and one Me 110 damaged, Flying Officer D.F.B. Sheen claims one Me 110 probable, Sergeant W.T.E. Rolls [probably flying K9841], two Ju 86 destroyed, and Sergeant J.S. Gilders one Me 110 destroyed.'

Flying Officer T.A.F. Elsdon's positioning of the squadron was largely responsible for their successes, something which was acknowledged in his DFC citation. However, the combat was not one-sided. Pilot Officers E.E. Males (flying R6971) and R.D. Elliott (flying N3020) bailed out safe following combat with Bf 110s over Hartfield at 1305 and 1320 hours respectively.

Pilot Officer E.E. Males (flying K9841) made a forced landing following combat at 1730 hours on 10 September. On 27 September he was forced to bail out of his Spitfire (X4340) at 0940 hours following combat with a Bf 109 over Sevenoaks. Males was killed.[6]

Flying as Tenis Leader, Flying Officer T.A.F. Elsdon fired all of his ammunition in two to three-second bursts at 200 to 100 yards:

'No. 72 Squadron was ordered on patrol and took off with nine aircraft, six in main formation and three in rearguard. We were vectored onto [the] enemy and we intercepted between Tenterden and Tunbridge Wells when we were at 18,000ft, and they were preceding north-west. I ordered Red and Yellow Sections into individual line astern for attack. As we did this the enemy broke up their vic and echelon formation, and went into line astern also and prepared to form a circle. I led the six of my main formation into the first six of the enemy before they could join up in a circle.

'In this attack I shot down the leader, [which was] confirmed by Sergeant Rolls, and two others were shot down in this first attack. Subsequently, a dogfight ensued and the Ju 86s joined in, although the pilots who engaged them did not consider they helped the Me 110s.

'During this dogfight no further enemy appeared and the rear guard came in to assist my main formation. Three Ju 86s were shot down confirmed and a further four Me 110s confirmed shot down from the fight. One Me 110 was probably destroyed, but has not yet been confirmed.

'We then saw Me 110s breaking away from the fight and flying 'flat out' for France. Two of us followed and one (Flying Officer Villa) caused him to smoke, but it continued to fly on, and was afterwards engaged by Hurricanes.

'I followed one which went very low over Bexhill. I attacked from dead astern and it started smoking from the starboard engine, but continued to fly about 100ft over the sea. I followed, giving short bursts from 200-150 yards and, as I expended my ammunition, it lost height and dropped into the sea about twenty miles south-south-east of Bexhill.

'This makes a total of nine enemy shot down confirmed, and two probables from this engagement. One pilot (Pilot Officer Males) was shot down but bailed out and has returned uninjured. One other aircraft was damaged by cannon fire but is repairable at unit.'
(signed) Flying Officer T.A.F. Elsdon.

Red 2, Pilot Officer D.F. Holland, engaged a Bf 110 south-west of Ashford, firing 1,200 rounds:

'E/A sighted on port side below [and so] line astern [was] ordered by Red 1 for [an] attack. The E/A went into line astern. I started to attack the rear E/A when I noticed that they were going into a circle. I then turned to port and attacked the leader of the formation of Me 110s head-on. I continued firing until I almost collided with [the] E/A, I then broke away to port. Return fire severely damaged my aircraft.

'As I was closing with E/A, pieces of the aircraft began to fall away.

'On landing, Sergeant M. Gray confirmed [the] E/A diving steeply with white smoke streaming from it.'
(signed) Pilot Officer D.F. Holland.

Blue 3, Sergeant W.T.E. Rolls, entered into combat between Ashford and Tunbridge Wells at 15,000ft:

'I turned steeply to port and did a quarter attack on one of the end Ju 86s [firing 800 to 1,000 rounds]. The port engine started to fire and two of the crew bailed out as I went beneath. I turned steeply again to port and came up from the quarter on another Ju 86 which was in a steep bank.

'I gave a ring and a half deflection shot, and my bullets hit the fuselage at about 200 yards range [using the remainder of his ammunition], and I saw the port engine smoke and the machine fall in. I followed it down and it was burning before it hit a wood south-east of Tunbridge Wells. As I was about to climb up I saw another one crash not far away and it was followed down by Sergeant Gray, who joined up on me. We then went to investigate three parachutes, and saw that two were German and one was an officer from our own squadron [Pilot Officer Males].'
(signed) Sergeant W.T.E. Rolls.

Sergeant Rolls added a footnote to his combat report:

'Firing cannon from back and what appeared to be cannon from the side window. Also tracer and incendiary bullets.'

Flying rearguard, Pilot Officer R.D. Elliot reported:

'The enemy immediately formed protective circles. I climbed to 2,000ft above [the] E/A and made a quarter attack on an Me 110 who was circling with about eight others. I fired from approximately 400 yards. [I] saw a large piece of his starboard wing fall away and his starboard engine set on fire.

'Another E/A appeared to be on the tail of [a] Spitfire – the latter attempting to get free. The pilot of this machine (Spitfire) was Sergeant Rolls (confirmed later) who saw [the] E/A break up and the starboard engine catch on fire. I was too involved to follow [the] E/A to earth.'
(signed) Pilot Officer R. D. Elliott.

Pilot Officer R.D. Elliott was less fortunate two days later, on 6 September, when he was wounded in combat over the Thames estuary at 0920 hours.

Meanwhile, Sergeant J.S. Gilders, flying No. 3 in the rearguard, engaged a Bf 110:

'I attacked an Me 110 that was in the circle. I attacked from almost astern and eventually was right astern. I fired three short bursts and saw bullets hitting his fuselage and wings. His starboard wing and engine were both on fire, and the machine was diving hard and doing little to avoid me. I had a final burst as he dived and had the satisfaction of seeing the machine completely on fire with brownish-black smoke coming back from it. It went down near Ashford and nobody left the machine. I had only a small hole in my port mainplane. Two Germans were seen descending in parachutes near Ashford from another aircraft.'
(signed) Sergeant J.S. Gilders.

Yellow 1, Flying Officer J.W. Villa, engaged two Bf 110s:

'On sighting enemy aircraft, Tenis Leader ordered Red and Yellow Sections into individual line astern. I went into line astern on Red 3 with Yellow 2 and 3 in line astern on me. We dived to the attack. In trying to attack an Me 110 I was attacked by another. I half-rolled and dived out. I climbed up and attacked an Me 110 trying to get on a Spitfire's tail. I fired a short burst and he broke away. I then saw an Me 110 which had got detached from the defensive circle. I dived to within 100 yards of the tail of the Me 110 and fired three long bursts. The Me 110 caught fire and started to dive. The Me 110 took no evasive action except to continue to turn to the left. I broke away down and climbed up again. I then saw four Me 110s endeavouring to reach the coast. I dived down on the rear one and fired a long burst. [The] enemy aircraft started diving with white smoke coming from one engine. I followed it down, doing quarter attacks with short bursts until my ammunition was expended; [the] enemy aircraft was then at 500ft heading for the coast. I broke away and last saw [the] enemy aircraft being attacked by three Hurricanes.'
(signed) Flying Officer J.W. Villa.

Villa later wrote of his innermost feelings during these weeks of high tension. His words provide an insight into the effects of the stress that Fighter Command's pilots were under:

'I was so tired and annoyed at being shot at, I was feeling sick. By then, I really didn't care when I went up whether I'd be coming back or not. And I wasn't alone in those feelings. It wasn't only the interceptions and patrols. It was also the perpetual sitting at Readiness, ready to go off in a flash.'

Elsewhere, No. 222 Squadron engaged the enemy over the Ashford to Maidstone area, claiming two Bf 109s, probably destroying three more and damaging one.

Meanwhile, No. 66 Squadron was in action near Folkestone, claiming one Bf 109 destroyed and five probably destroyed, with Pilot Officer C.A. Cooke (flying R6689) being forced to bail out wounded when he was shot down by a Bf 109. In combat over RAF Tangmere, No. 234 Squadron claimed no less than fourteen Bf 110s and a Do 17 destroyed, and half a dozen Bf 110s damaged, all without loss.

A number of raids developed at about 1000 hours on 5 September, including one on RAF Lympne. No. 72 Squadron was scrambled and intercepted Bf 109s at 27,000ft. Enemy fighters were shot down by Hurricanes and Spitfires from Nos. 43, 111, 234 and 501 Squadrons.

The Spitfires of No. 72 Squadron were scrambled at 1310 hours, with Flying Officers T.A.F. Elsdon (flying K9935), D.B.F. Sheen (flying X4034) and D.C. Winter (flying X4013), joined by Pilot Officer D.F. Holland (flying P9460), and Sergeants J.S. Gilders (flying R6777) and W.T.E. Rolls (flying K9841). The Spitfires took off from Croydon with orders to patrol Hawkinge at 25,000ft. Once in position the squadron was vectored onto a formation of fifty-plus Ju 88s and He 111s escorted by about 100 Bf 109s. Their main targets were the oil storage tanks at Thameshaven.

Meanwhile, at about 1430 hours, a roving staffel of Bf 109s headed for Dover, before flying to the north-east and towards Maidstone, engaging No. 72 Squadron.

Pilot Officer D.F. Holland (flying P9460) engaged a formation of nine Messerschmitts, destroying a Bf 109 and damaging a second. The combat took place at 28,000ft near RAF Hawkinge, at 1425 hours:

'I was flying as rearguard for the squadron when I saw about nine or more Me 109s starting to attack us from above. I shouted, "Me 109s coming down on us," over the R/T and turned to attack the center E/A head-on as they were diving down. I fired a short burst of two-seconds at him. I could see my tracer going into him when he broke away. After my attack the formation of E/A split up. I then attacked one of the E/A as they were trying to form up again. I did a quarter attack on [an] E/A devolving into astern. I gave [the] E/A about [a] twelve-second burst. I saw white smoke pouring from him [and] he then dived slowly down, and seemed to be out of control. I think that I hit the pilot of [the] E/A. I followed him down to about 8,000ft when I was attacked myself by an Me 109. I turned over on my back and dived down, he did not follow me. The last I saw of the E/A I attacked, the machine was smoking furiously. I am convinced that this machine was destroyed.'
(signed) Pilot Officer D.F. Holland.

Wounded during the same combat was Flying Officer D.F.B. Sheen, he bailed out of his Spitfire, X4034, near RAF Hawkinge at 1425 hours. Meanwhile, Sergeant J. White probably destroyed an He 111.

The squadron lost Sergeant M. Gray[7] (flying N3093) who was shot down in combat with Bf 109s over Kent at 1425 hours. His Spitfire fell at Elham Park.

A second fatality was Pilot Officer D.C. Winter (flying X4013), who was shot down in combat with a Bf 109. He bailed out too low and was killed when his parachute failed to deploy. His Spitfire crashed at Covert Wood, Elham, at 1425 hours.

Dowding had said that to win the battle, 'the RAF must bring down four of their [the enemy's] aircraft for every one of ours' – in those few hectic days during the Dunkirk operations, and again in defence of No. 11 Group and over Kent, Winter achieved Dowding's goal. Sadly, like over 500 other heroes of the Battle of Britain, Winter never lived to see the victory he had helped win.

Douglas Cyril Winter was buried with full military honours at Harton Cemetery, Section O, Grave 11795, in his home town of South Shields. He was 26-years-old and left a widow, Marjorie.

The following pilots flew with No. 72 Squadron between 10 July and 5 September 1940:

Squadron Leader Anthony Roland Collins	
Squadron Leader Ronald Beresford Lees	DFC 22.10.40 *(A)*, Bar 26.12.41 *(B)*, CBE 2.6.43, CB 1.1.46, KCB 10.6.61
Flight Lieutenant Edward Graham	
Flight Lieutenant Forgrave Marshall Smith	DFC 30.10.45 *(C)*
Flying Officer Thomas Arthur Francis Elsdon	DFC 8.10.40 *(D)*
Flying Officer Oswald St John Pigg	KIA 1.9.40
Flying Officer Desmond Frederick Burt Sheen, DFC	Bar to DFC 17.10.41 *(E)*
Flying Officer Ronald Alexander Thompson	
Flying Officer Robert James Walker	DSO 12.6.45 *(F)*
Flying Officer Edgar John Wilcox	KIA 31.8.40
Pilot Officer Robert Deacon Elliott, RAFVR	DFC 17.10.41 *(G)* (later Air Commodore)
Pilot Officer Dennis Frederick Holland, RAFVR	
Pilot Officer Ernest Edward Males	KIA 27.9.40
Pilot Officer Norman Robert Norfolk	DFC 7.1.41 *(H)*
Pilot Officer Norman Charles Harold Robson	
Pilot Officer John Wolferstan Villa	DFC 8.10.40 *(I)*, Bar to DFC 26.11.40 *(J)*
Pilot Officer Douglas Cyril Winter	KIA 5.9.40
Flight Sergeant Jack Steere	AFC 13.6.46
Sergeant Basil Douthwaite	

Sergeant John Stanley Gilders	KIA 21.2.41
Sergeant Norman Glew	KIA 17.5.44 as CO of No. 1435 Squadron
Sergeant Malcolm Gray	KIA 5.9.40
Sergeant Ronald Eric Plant	KIA 21.11.40
Sergeant Maurice Henry Pocock	MiD 8.6.44
Sergeant William Thomas Edward Rolls, RAFVR	DFM 8.11.40 *(K)*, DFC 4.12.42 *(L)*
Sergeant Robert Charles John Staples	
Sergeant John White	DFM 24.12.40 *(M)*, KIA 14.6.41

Many of the pilots earned gallantry awards for combat which are not mentioned in the main text. Details, where traced, are included below:

(A) Acting Wing Commander R.B. Lees was awarded the DFC, *London Gazette,* 22 October 1940:

'Distinguished Flying Cross.
'Acting Wing Commander Ronald Beresford LEES (29257).

(B) Acting Group Captain R.B. Lees was later awarded a Bar to the DFC, *London Gazette,* 26 December 1941:

'Bar to the Distinguished Flying Cross.
'Acting Group Captain Ronald Beresford LEES, DFC.'

Lees later commanded No. 324 Wing in North Africa and was SASO HQ No. 242 Group. He was ADC to both King George VI and Queen Elizabeth II, and attained the rank of Air Marshal. Lees was knighted in 1961.

(C) Acting Wing Commander F.M. Smith was awarded the DFC, *London Gazette,* 30 October 1945:

'Distinguished Flying Cross.
'Acting Wing Commander Forgrave Marshall SMITH (37613), RAFO.'

On 7 September, Flying Officer T.A.F. Elsdon (flying X4254) was shot down while in combat with a Bf 109 at 1820 hours, two days after Winter's death. Despite being wounded, Elsdon nursed his Spitfire to Biggin Hill, where he crash-landed.

(D) Flying Officer T.A.F. Elsdon was awarded the DFC, *London Gazette*, 8 October 1940:

'Flying Officer Thomas Arthur Francis ELSDON (33308).

'Since 31 August 1940, this officer has destroyed six enemy aircraft, bringing his total to eight. On 4 September 1940, when leading his squadron, his method of attack was successful in destroying nine enemy aircraft and probably three more. A few days later he brought down the leading aircraft of a bomber formation. His record is outstanding and he has led his section and flight with distinction, showing complete disregard of danger and personal injury.'

(E) Acting Squadron Leader D.F.B. Sheen was awarded a Bar to the DFC, *London Gazette*, 17 October 1940:

'Bar to the Distinguished Flying Cross.

'Acting Squadron Leader Desmond Frederick Burt SHEEN, DFC (39474), No. 72 Squadron.

'Since July 1941, Squadron Leader Sheen has led the squadron, and on occasions the wing, in forty-three offensive operations over Northern France. He has carried out these missions with consistent skill and courage, and under his leadership the squadron has attained a high standard of efficiency. On one occasion the squadron was menaced by a superior number of enemy fighters but, by his coolness and clever tactics, Squadron Leader Sheen saved his unit from suffering heavy casualties and succeeded in destroying at least three of the fighters. Squadron Leader Sheen has personally destroyed a number of enemy aircraft, including one at night.'

(F) Acting Wing Commander R.J. Walker was awarded the DSO, *London Gazette*, 12 June 1945:

'Distinguished Service Order.

'Acting Wing Commander Robert James WALKER (39915), RAFO, No. 45 Squadron.'

(G) Acting Flight Lieutenant R.D. Elliott was awarded the DFC, *London Gazette*, 17 October 1941:

'Distinguished Flying Cross.

'Acting Flight Lieutenant Robert Deacon ELLIOTT (76311), Royal Air Force Volunteer Reserve, No. 72 Squadron.

'This officer has been engaged on operational flying since December 1939. He fought in the Battle of Britain during which he destroyed four enemy aircraft. In addition to participating in many night patrols Flight Lieutenant Elliott has been largely responsible for the training of new members of his squadron. Throughout, he has shown exceptional skill and courage.'

At 1020 hours, on 20 September, Pilot Officer D.F. Holland[8] (flying X4410) was badly wounded in combat over Canterbury and was forced to take to his parachute. He died of his wounds that day.

(H) Pilot Officer N.R. Norfolk was awarded the DFC, *London Gazette*, 7 January 1941:

'Distinguished Flying Cross.
'Pilot Officer Norman Robert NORFOLK (44929), No. 72 Squadron.
'Throughout a long period of operations Pilot Officer Norfolk has shown himself to be a most determined fighter pilot, pressing home his attacks on every occasion. He has displayed great courage and has destroyed at least four enemy aircraft.'

(I) Flying Officer John Wolferstan 'Pancho' Villa had served as flight commander on the squadron since his arrival in early July 1940. He transferred to No. 92 Squadron on 13 October and, by the end of the Battle of Britain, had shot down ten enemy aircraft. Villa was awarded the DFC, *London Gazette*, 8 October 1940:

'Distinguished Flying Cross.
'Acting Flight Lieutenant John Wolferstan VILLA (39768).
'Since 31 August 1940, this officer has destroyed at least six enemy aircraft. One day in September 1940, he was successful in destroying three enemy aircraft unaided and assisted in the destruction of a fourth. Flight Lieutenant Villa has consistently led his flight, and frequently the squadron, with great dash and eagerness, and has proved a keen fighter and a good leader.'

(J) He was awarded a Bar to the DFC, *London Gazette*, 26 November 1940:

'Awarded a Bar to the Distinguished Flying Cross.
'Acting Flight Lieutenant John Wolferstan VILLA, DFC (39768), No. 92 Squadron.
'In October 1940, this officer led his squadron in an attack against an enemy bombing formation attempting a raid on London, and immediately caused the enemy to jettison their bombs and form a defensive circle. He pressed home his attack with great determination and assisted in the destruction of two Messerschmitt 109s, and possibly a further two. He has shown outstanding powers of leadership, skill and courage, and has destroyed a total of thirteen hostile aircraft.'

Villa took over command of No. 65 Squadron in the August of 1941 and was promoted to squadron leader on 1 December. His later commands included No. 504 Squadron (June – December 1942) and No. 198 Squadron (December 1942 – May 1943).

(K) Sergeant W.T.E. Rolls was awarded the DFM, *London Gazette*, 8 November 1940:

'Awarded the Distinguished Flying Medal.

'Sergeant William Thomas Edward ROLLS (745542), Royal Air Force Volunteer Reserve, No. 72 Squadron.

'This airman, after very short experience of operational flying, has taken his place with the best war pilots in the squadron. In each of his first two engagements he shot down two enemy aircraft and has in all destroyed at least six.'

(L) Acting Flight Lieutenant W.T.E. Rolls, DFM, was awarded the DFC, *London Gazette*, 4 December 1942:

'Distinguished Flying Cross.

'Acting Flight Lieutenant William Thomas Edward ROLLS, DFM (116492), Royal Air Force Volunteer Reserve, No. 126 Squadron.'

(M) Sergeant J. White was awarded the DFM, *London Gazette*, 24 December 1940:

'Distinguished Flying Medal.

'Sergeant John WHITE (741363), Royal Air Force Volunteer Reserve, No. 72 Squadron.

'Within a period of eight days in September 1940, this airman destroyed two enemy aircraft and assisted in the destruction of three more. His courage and efficiency over a long period have set a splendid example to his fellow pilots. He has personally destroyed four enemy aircraft and possibly four more.'

Notes

1. Flying Officer (70830) Edgar John Wilcox, RAF, was the son of Ernest John and Grace Alice Wilcox, of Mitcham, Surrey. Wilcox was 23-years-old and was buried at Staplehurst (All Saints) Churchyard.
2. Flying Officer (39678) Oswald St John Pigg, RAF, was the son of the Revd John James Pigg and Mabel Tyson Pigg, of Chatton Vicarage, Northumberland. Pigg was 22-years-old and was buried at Durham (St Oswald's) Burial Ground, Row 1, Grave 90.
3. Flight Sergeant (563426) Frederick George Berry, DFM, RAF, was buried at Pinnery Cemetery, Section G.5., Grave 92.
4. Pilot Officer (41902) John Kenneth Grahame Clifton, RAF, was the son of John Henry and Susie Dorothy Anderson Clifton, of Taunton. Clifton was 21-years-old and was buried at Staplegrove (St John) Churchyard, Row Q, Grave 9.
5. Sergeant (580059) William Lawrence Dymond, RAF, was the son of Thomas Dymond and of Kathleen Dymond (nee Lawrence); husband of Joan Millicent Dymond, of Ruislip. Dymond was 23-years-old and is remembered on the Runnymede Memorial, Panel 13.
6. Pilot Officer (82661) Ernest Edward Males, RAFVR, was the son of Charles Arthur and Rose Edith Males, of Southgate, Middlesex. Males was 20-years-old and was buried at New Southgate Cemetery, Section K, Grave 1383.

7. Sergeant (741816) Malcolm Gray, RAFVR, was the son of George William and Emily Gray, of Heworth, Yorkshire. Gray was 20-years-old and was buried at Fulford Cemetery, Plot 13, Row W, Grave 7.
8. Pilot Officer (77269) Dennis Frederick Holland, RAFVR, was buried at Chaddlewoth Churchyard, North Part.

Bibliography

Bingham, Victor, *Blitzed: The Battle of France May–June 1940*, Air Research Publications, 1990

Bird, Andrew D., *A Separate Little War: The Banff Coastal Command Strike Wing Versus the Kriegsmarine and Luftwaffe in Norway 1944–1945*, Grub Street, 2008

Bird, Andrew D., *Coastal Command: Blenheims in Action from the Phoney War through the Battle of Britain*, Grub Street Press, 2012

Bishop, P., *Fighter Boys: Saving Britain 1940*, Harper Perennial, 2003

Cooksley, Peter G., *1940: The Story of No. 11 Group, Fighter Command*, Robert Hale, London, 1983

Cull, Brian, *249 Squadron at War*, Grub Street Press, 1997

Cull, Brian and Lander, Bruce, with Weiss, Heinrich, *Twelve Days in May: the Air Battle for Northern France and the Low Countries, 10–21 May 1940, as seen Through the eyes of the Fighter Pilots Involved*, Grub Street Press, 1995

Foreman, John, *RAF Fighter Command Victory Claims of World War Two, Part One 1939–40*, Red Kite, 2003

Franks, Norman, *Air Battle Dunkirk 26 May–3 June*, Grub Street, 2000

Franks, Norman L.R., *Royal Air Force Fighter Command Losses of the Second World War, Volume 1, Operational Losses: Aircraft and Crew 1939–1941*, Midland, 2008

James, T.C.G., *The Battle of Britain*, Frank Cass, London, 2000

Mason, Francis K., *Battle Over Britain*, Doubleday & Company, Inc, Garden City, New York, 1969

Mason, Francis K., *The Hawker Hurricane*, Crecy Publishing Ltd., 1990

Ramsey, Winston (Editor), *The Battle of Britain Then and Now*, An After the Battle Publication, 1980

Robinson, A., *RAF Fighter Squadrons in the Battle of Britain*, Brochampton Press, 1999

Shores, Christopher, *Those Other Eagles: A Tribute to the British Commonwealth and Free European Fighter Pilots who Claimed Between Two and Four Victories in Aerial Combat, 1939–1982. A Companion Volume to Aces High*, Grubb Street Press, 2004

Shores, Christopher, and Williams, Clive, *Aces High: A Tribute to the Most Notable Fighter Pilots of the British and Commonwealth Forces in WWII*, Grub Street Press, 1994

Wynn, Kenneth, *Men of the Battle of Britain*, Gliddon Books, 1989

Combat Reports and Squadron Operation Books for the following:

Nos. 1, 1 (RCAF), 32, 41, 43, 46, 54, 64, 65, 66, 72, 73, 79, 85, 87, 92, 111, 213, 222, 227, 229, 234, 235, 236, 238, 242, 249, 253, 257, 303, 310, 333, 501, 504, 603, 605, 607 and 610 Squadrons

Index